Runners on RUNNING

The Best Nonfiction of Distance Running

Rich Elliott

EDITOR

Human Kinetics

Library of Congress Cataloging-in-Publication Data

Runners on running : the best nonfiction of distance running / Rich Elliott, editor.

   p. cm.

  ISBN-13: 978-0-7360-9570-9 (soft cover)

  ISBN-10: 0-7360-9570-5 (soft cover)

  1. Running--Anecdotes. 2. Runners (Sports)--Anecdotes. I. Elliott, Richard, 1950-

  GV1061.R8325 2011

  796.42--dc22

2010033169

ISBN-10: 0-7360-9570-5 (print)

ISBN-13: 978-0-7360-9570-9 (print)

Acquisitions Editor: Laurel Plotzke Garcia; **Managing Editor:** Julie Marx Goodreau; **Assistant Editors:** Elizabeth Evans and Tyler Wolpert; **Permission Manager:** Martha Gullo; **Graphic Designer:** Nancy Rasmus; **Graphic Artist:** Tara Welsch; **Cover Designer:** Keith Blomberg; **Photographer (cover):** Corey Rich/Aurora Photos; **Printer:** Versa Press

Human Kinetics books are available at special discounts for bulk purchase. Special editions or book excerpts can also be created to specification. For details, contact the Special Sales Manager at Human Kinetics.

Printed in the United States of America   10   9   8   7   6   5   4   3   2   1

The paper in this book is certified under a sustainable forestry program.

Human Kinetics

Web site: www.HumanKinetics.com

United States: Human Kinetics
P.O. Box 5076
Champaign, IL 61825-5076
800-747-4457
e-mail: humank@hkusa.com

Canada: Human Kinetics
475 Devonshire Road Unit 100
Windsor, ON N8Y 2L5
800-465-7301 (in Canada only)
e-mail: info@hkcanada.com

Europe: Human Kinetics
107 Bradford Road
Stanningley
Leeds LS28 6AT, United Kingdom
+44 (0) 113 255 5665
e-mail: hk@hkeurope.com

Australia: Human Kinetics
57A Price Avenue
Lower Mitcham, South Australia 5062
08 8372 0999
e-mail: info@hkaustralia.com

New Zealand: Human Kinetics
P.O. Box 80
Torrens Park, South Australia 5062
0800 222 062
e-mail: info@hknewzealand.com

E5191

For Aileen

contents

race 117

bonds 197

heart 231

acknowledgments

I'd like to express my gratitude to the supporting cast who helped make this book a reality.

I'm indebted to three authors whose guides to the literature of running were indispensable resources during the course of my project. Their books pointed me in the right direction and helped me find pearls in an ocean of literature. These books were Bob Wischnia and Marty Post's *Running: A Guide to the Literature* (Garland, 1983) and Roger Robinson's *Running in Literature: A Guide for Scholars, Readers, Runners, and Dreamers* (Breakaway Books, 2003).

Two fine anthologies also led me to several great pieces: *Running: The Power and the Glory,* edited by Norman Harris (Partridge Press, 1986), and Houghton Mifflin's annual collection *The Best American Sports Writing.*

Additionally, I'd like to thank the librarians at the Winnetka Public Library who handled my many book requests with unfailing professionalism.

During this project I pestered old friends and new acquaintances to read my table of contents. They generously offered me their time and their thoughts, drawing on their wisdom about writing and running. My appreciation goes to Jonathan Beverly, Rich Bohn, Bob Carlson, Hal Higdon, Peter Kaye, Don Kopriva, Bob McCray, Dennis Ryan, Dagny Scott, and Rachel Toor.

I'm especially grateful to have a friend who has always been willing to interrupt what he's doing to read what I've written, to give it a critical eye, and to offer the advice of a real pro. Steve Pokin has been that kind of friend.

I also must give a shout-out to a group that has had a big influence—those with whom I've shared many a mile and many a race, my former teammates, coaches, and runners. This fraternity of kindred spirits is a big part of what makes this sport great.

And finally, no words can truly express my thanks to my wife, Aileen, and my children, Matt, Abby, and Anna. No book gets created without the sacrifices of the author's loved ones. My family's unwavering support and love sustained me through many an hour away from them. To you, I can only say, I love you.

introduction

I trace the real origins of this book to a small country many miles from my home where, in my boyhood imagination, a determined group of running buddies, dressed in black singlets, push themselves up the hills of the Waiatarua, their infamous training ground, and turn themselves into world-beaters.

My imaginings came from a book I was reading. I had gone out for high school cross country, the only sport worthy of my scrawniness. Early in the season, after some particularly long and painful run, my coach handed me a book.

"Required reading," he said.

The book was titled *A Clean Pair of Heels*. It was the autobiography of Murray Halberg, one of New Zealand's greatest distance runners. Halberg was an unlikely champion, his left arm severely disabled as the result of a rugby injury. Yet he rose to the highest pinnacle of his sport, winning the 5,000 meters in the Rome Olympics. Halberg's heroic story was irresistible.

So I eagerly tore into the next book from my coach, which was *No Bugles, No Drums*, the autobiography of Peter Snell, Halberg's teammate. Snell had the power of a linebacker and the ability to destroy a field with his kick. Snell won both the 800- and 1,500-meter races in the Tokyo Olympics; he remains the only runner ever to pull off this double.

Fifty years ago the runners from Down Under ruled the distance world. Their autobiographies were nourishment for a young runner's soul. I was swept up in the New Zealand running world. I learned the exotic names of their legendary training runs. I could quote their personal records. I studied their workouts for secrets. I soaked up the ideas of their guru Arthur Lydiard. I searched in vain for a black singlet with a fern leaf on it.

My teammates read those books, too. We pictured ourselves as smaller, skinnier versions of the great Kiwi runners. The word *geek* hadn't been invented yet. To the rest of our schoolmates, we were simply weirdos, and we reveled in our weirdness. We relished the fact that others couldn't see what we all knew: That we had the coolest sport, the most equal-opportunity sport, the one that most directly rewarded hard work and tenacity.

Later my reading interests turned to American literature with the publication of *The Jim Ryun Story*. Another great book! Here is Ryun, a gawky high school freshman, initially an average runner on his team. Then an amazing metamorphosis—two years go by, and in his junior year he breaks the four-minute mile and makes the Olympic team. And the next year he beats the world-record holder, the great Snell! It was unbelievable, and it was true.

And if *he* could do it—that gawky, skinny high-schooler—*why not me*?

Well, why not? I logged my miles. I ran up sand dunes. I did my speed work. And I imagined.

The spring of my senior year found me, the scrawny daydreamer, toeing the line in a 5,000-meter international race in the Los Angeles Coliseum. The race promoter liked to include an up-and-coming high school runner, and that year it was me. The field was loaded. Way down the starting line in lane 1 stood one of my greatest heroes, Ron Clarke, the holder of 17 world records.

On a perfect California evening, the gun went off, and Clarke, adhering to his code, set a brutal pace and never looked back. All the rest of us were splayed around the track, racing for second. I hung on for dear life, ended up beating a few people, and accomplished my goal of not getting lapped by Clarke. I ran my heart out.

I had my 15 minutes of fame. I didn't dream it, it really happened. And I came to understand a truth about running.

What makes a distance runner tick? Sure, hard work is necessary. Mileage, interval work, hills, good nutrition—they're each important. But there's one thing that trumps them all. It is *imagination* that fuels the distance runner.

———————————•———————————

True stories are powerful things for athletes. That's the impetus for this book. My aim was to bring together the best true stories about running, the best writing about runners and races. My hope is that the pieces in this collection will entertain you, provoke you, fire your imagination, and inspire your running, as they have for me.

I envisioned a collection that showcases the poets and philosophers of our sport as well as the legendary battles and heroes. I envisioned a collection that would reflect on the timeless aspects of our sport, stories that would encompass the running experience and would go below the surface to offer insights.

Recently, I went to an art exhibit that featured many of the famous impressionist paintings. Seeing the Monets and Manets and Renoirs all together in one place, seeing the various subjects and styles, I came away with a richer understanding of impressionism. My hope is that *Runners on Running* will have a similar effect: that you'll come away feeling that *this* is what distance running is all about.

To that end, I searched for feature articles, book excerpts, and essays that explore the spirit and heart of the runner and the racer. I favored those that got at the perennial questions. What is it about running that elicits so much joy? What anxieties prey on the racer? What role do mentors play in creating miracles? What bonds are forged by running mates and by competitors? Which heroes belong in our pantheon?

But there's an ocean of good nonfiction about distance running, so how does one begin to choose? I began by setting a few boundaries. The boundaries were arbitrary in a way but necessary to keeping me, as the editor, afloat in a wide sea. Here is what this collection does *not* include:

- There are no instructional articles, although I have fond memories of the first running book I ever owned, Fred Wilt's *Run Run Run*, a collection of articles about training. Since that 1964 book, the how-to of running has been a very well-traveled road, and you can easily find bookshelves of good advice.

- There are no columns. While column writing is an important part of running literature, I chose the longer form for this collection. It makes for a more satisfying meal.
- I steered away from news reports. I like reading race results as much as anyone, but my aim here is writing that has more endurance.
- Finally, I should confess to a preference for the competitive runner. We all start as joggers and we all finish as joggers, but to me, the drama and the loveliness of running are greatest when we are competitors.

———————●———————

Running is blessed with some truly world-class writers. What is it about our sport that produces such wonderful writing? It's no coincidence that most of these writers are runners themselves. If their descriptions are amazingly right on, if their stories nail certain verities about running, it is for this reason: These writers have been there. They've experienced the loneliness of a long run when there are miles to go and the rain has started. They know what it feels like to sprint at the end of a tough race. They understand the injured runner's dark night of the soul. For these writers, their subject is personal.

If their writing epitomizes clear thinking, perhaps it is due in no small measure to all those solitary miles on the road. What else is there to do but think? The runner's body gets honed, and so does his thinking.

If their writing shows a mastery of the craft, perhaps it's because the requirements for great writing are the same as those for great running—discipline, patience, hard work, devotion. Therefore, this anthology celebrates the writers as well as the literature of running. Kenny Moore, Amby Burfoot, Kathrine Switzer, Bernd Heinrich, and the rest of my field—these are writers who know what they are talking about. And as a wonderful bonus, they can really write.

———————●———————

When searching for the best of the best, the anthologist may, as a goal, seek to be objective in his choosing, to adhere to a certain logic and balance, and to disallow personal bias. But ultimately, that is impossible. Every reader, the anthologist included, responds to and judges a reading based on his own experiences.

As I look over the selections that made my finals, I can easily see my biases reflected in the subjects. Stories about two of my old heroes, Murray Halberg and Ron Clarke, made the list, their courage still irresistible to me. In another story, my Kansas teammate Jim Ryun battles his nemesis Marty Liquori in the "Dream Mile," a race I've never forgotten. A story about Pre, my contemporary, also made the finals—he's still exerting his presence after all these years, standing there glaring, cocky as ever. And yes, one of my own stories is in this collection, waiting self-consciously among the other entrants, hoping not to be too outclassed.

So in other words, this is a personal collection. I hope you will like it.

For a simple sport, distance running is rich and deeply layered. If you linger for awhile with these storytellers, you will see running's exquisite strands, and you will come to understand its DNA.

And as you read, I encourage you to imagine. Imagine yourself as the runner you dream to be. See yourself racing through your own Waiatarua loop, drafting along with the greats. Then put this book down and go out for a good hard run.

spirit

So each day I take to the roads as a
beginner, a child, a poet. . . .

There is the theater where we can
write and act out our own dreams.

~George Sheehan, masters runner and author

Running

George Sheehan, 1978

Runner, doctor, philosopher, poet—this unique combination of talents gave rise to the phenomenon of George Sheehan. No one has been better at giving voice to the ineffable joys and personal discoveries of runners. His essays helped make it OK to go nuts over distance running. "Success rests," Sheehan said, "in having the courage and endurance and, above all, the will, to become the person you are, however peculiar that may be."

Every mile I run is my first. Every hour on the roads a new beginning. Every day I put on my running clothes, I am born again. Seeing things as if for the first time, seeing the familiar as unfamiliar, the common as uncommon. Doing what Goethe said was the hardest thing of all, seeing with my own eyes that which is spread before me. Bringing to that running, that play, the attitude of the child, the perception of a poet. Being a beginner with a beginner's mind, a beginner's heart, a beginner's body.

There is no other way to run, no other way to live. Otherwise my runs become dull, uninspired interludes. The running becomes routine, becomes part of the humdrum apathy and indifference which the poet John Hall Wheelock called a shield between us and reality. It becomes a chore, becomes habit. And habit kills awareness and separates us from ourselves.

My awareness begins with my body, my beginner's body. Each day I discover how to breathe. Taste the air. Feel it move through my lungs. I learn to exhale totally and groan and grunt, marking my passage through the fields and trees like some animal.

Each day I search out how to run. Feeling the thrust of the hamstrings. Letting the foot drop below the knee. Arriving at the form the child adopts naturally. The body, a little stronger perhaps, certainly more durable, must come upon these ideas as fresh as if newly thought. And then concentrate on this beginning and bring to it the beginner's joy in doing this tremendously simple yet tremendously complex thing so well.

From then on it becomes more and more difficult. It is relatively easy to return to basics with the body. But to have a beginner's heart and mind is a different matter. To take sight and smell, hearing and touch and become a new Adam in a new Eden is tough going even for a poet. Even for those who live more and participate more in their own existence. And yet like them I must listen and discover forgotten knowledge. Must respond to everything around me and inside me as well.

From George Sheehan, 1978, *Running and Being: The Total Experience* (New York: Simon & Schuster). Reprinted by permission of the George Sheehan Trust.

Poets do this naturally. A really good poet, wrote James Dickey, is like an engine with the governor off. And it's no good for people to say that life should not mean that much to a poet. The really good poet, said Dickey, has no choice; that's the way he is.

The best most of us can do is to be a poet an hour a day. Take the hour when we run or tennis or golf or garden; take that hour away from being a serious adult and become serious beginners. Take an hour away from what Shelley called a life of error, ignorance and strife, and introduce love and beauty and delight.

Those good things began in my beginning. When I was not afraid to respond to my feeling. Before I was taught not to cry. Before I learned that humor had a time and a place and deep emotions had best be concealed, that passion be left unfelt.

When I run I go back to those better days. Now no emotion is foreign to me. I express myself totally. My body and heart and mind interact and open me to the infinite possibilities only a beginner can envision. And I relive that moment in the beginning of things when, as Yeats said, we understand more perfectly than we understand until all is finished.

And what of that finish? "It is development, improvement and completion that means the deterioration of the creativeness," wrote Berdyaev, the Russian theologian, "the cooling down of the creative fire, decay, old age."

I will have none of that. So each day I take to the roads as a beginner, a child, a poet. Seeking the innocence of the beginner, the wonder of the child and the vision of the poet. Hoping for a new appreciation of the landscape, a new perspective of my inner world, some new insights on life, a new response to existence and myself.

There are times, more often than the good times, when I fail. I never do pierce the shield. I return with a shopping list of things to do tomorrow. The miraculous has gone unseen. The message has gone unheard. I have had one of those loveless days on a lovely day for love.

Still, there is always the chance I'll have beginner's luck. And this run, this hour, this day, may begin in delight and end in wisdom.

————————●————————

I am a noonday runner. In the past, and still from time to time, I have run in the morning or evening. But almost always these days, I run in the early afternoon.

You might think this choice of when to run simply a matter of convenience. Of fitting it in when time becomes available. Most people believe that running is running, regardless of when it is done. But I know this is not so. There is a time, as Ecclesiastes wrote, for every purpose under heaven. There is a time for running. Mine is midday. I run at midday because I must. I run at midday because my body and soul tell me to.

My body is at its best in early afternoon. My circulation rhythms at their crest. Like the sun, my energy is at its zenith, my fields of force at maximum. Whatever I do, I do best at this time of day.

But midday has more than physiological importance. When I run at noon, I run at the sixth hour. I run at an hour that has significance that goes back through the history of the race. An hour that reminds me I am participating in an ever-recurring mystery, seeking and making a self I will never fully know. An hour that brings me back to myth and ritual and a feeling for the holy.

In the sixth hour, I am in a time that is recurrent and symbolic. A time that Eliade wrote of as circular, reversible and recoverable. A time that tells me I am a child of the universe born for more than is visible in this world.

Daybreak and sunset have similar implications. The morning run speaks for rebirth and the new life. Just as morning prayers praise the Lord, sing the earth, tell of renewed purpose. And the evening run is for those who have fought the good fight and now desire only the peace an hour's run at a slow, steady pace will give them. When I run in these closing stages of the day, I am a philosopher. I accept life, death, the self, what I have done. I am content.

From this perspective, the morning run is my youth. Running in the morning is to wear the bright morning face. It is for health and fitness and making the team. It is accepting discipline, obeying duty and acquiring self-control.

Midday is adult. The run is in pursuit of goals, the making of the self, the looking for something to leave behind. You must say it is in the Catholic tradition, linking goodness to beauty and proportion and achievement.

If so, the evening run is toward the East, toward that ancient acceptance of things as they are. That mature wisdom with which we see a world that has order and sense. And we know, as Erikson said, that our one and only life cycle was something that had to be and, by necessity, permitted of no substitutions.

One thing we runners know. There is no substitute for running. No matter what age we are. No matter what time we do it.

———————————●———————————

My fight is not with age. Running has won that battle for me. Running is my fountain of youth, my elixir of life. It will keep me young forever. When I run, I know there is no need to grow old. I know that my running, my play, will conquer time.

And there on the roads, I can pursue my perfection for the rest of my days, and finally, as his wife said of Kazantzakis dead at seventy-four, be mowed down in the first flower of my youth.

The fight, then, is never with age; it is with boredom, with routine, with the danger of not living at all. Then life will stop, growth will cease, learning will come to an end. You no longer become who you are. You begin to kill time or live it without thought or purpose. Everything that is happiness, all that is excitement, whatever you know of joy and delight, will evaporate. Life will be reduced to a slow progression of days and weeks and months. Time will become an enemy instead of an ally.

When I run, I avoid all this. I enter a world where time stops, where now is a fair sample of eternity. Where I am filled with excitement and joy and delight, even with the intensity and inner fire and never-ending search for self of a Kazantzakis. I enter a state that will be man's most congenial environment.

"Play, games, jests, culture, we affirm," wrote Plato, "are the most serious things in life." And for the most serious of all reasons, what Kierkegaard called "choosing one's self." Or, to use Plato's thought again, to recapture our original state of perfection.

But isn't that perfection, or at least the bodily part of it, only resident in youth? Not if you persist in your sport, persevere in your play. True, we delight in our bodies in our youth and envy the young as we grow old. But this need not be.

We can continue to keep our bodies in beauty and competence until death claims us. We should know that the fit die young in body as well as in mind and heart. That, like Kazantzakis, whatever their age they will be mowed down in the first flower of their youth.

Running has made me young again. I run now as I did at twenty. I have the same health, the same vigor, the same sensations of power and grace. And I have the strength and speed and endurance of those years younger than me. Not because I am exceptional, but because I do what I do with my whole self. My running is an incitement to energy. It is an outpouring from the very center of my being. It is a vital force that takes me to the peak of my powers and there opens me to myself and to the world and to others.

Running gives me a body and mind and heart willing to follow my own vision, to break the mold, to choose a new course, even perhaps to become the hero that Ortega said we all carry within us. This is a lifelong task. A lifelong of saying, as did Ortega, "That's not it, that's not it." And therefore a life that must be very young and eager and full of enthusiasm, full of sport and play, full of running.

If you would not age, you must make everything you do touched with play, play of the body, of thought, of emotions. If you do, you will belong to that special class of people who find joy and happiness in every act, in every moment. Those to whom leisure is the one thing valuable. Those whom Ruskin called "the proudly idle."

My running and your play may be idleness to those of another mind. But it is the self-awareness, the consciousness, the intensity, that is important, however inconsequential the activity. "Come into the kitchen," said Heraclitus. "The gods are there, too." And out on the roads, and whenever you play, there is fitness and self-discovery and the persons we were destined to be. There is the theater where we can write and act out our own dreams. Having first, of course, gotten down to bone and muscle, and then come to some understanding of the unique once-in-an-eternity person each one of us is.

Running reminds me that any age man is still the marvel of creation. With the passage of time, there is little deterioration of our physical or psychic powers, little worth thinking that is lost. The only important issue, as Rollo May tells us, is not whether a person is twenty or forty or sixty, but whether he fulfills his own capacity of self-conscious choice at his own particular level.

That's a game the playful person almost always wins.

———————————●———————————

Is running an art and the runner an artist? The best answer is that of Picasso. When asked, "What is art?" he replied, "What is not?"

So running is an art along with everything else we do. When I run, I know this to be true. Running is my art and I am an artist however ordinary my performance. Running is for me what the dance is to others. The oldest and highest of the arts. My ancestors ran before they danced. And it is running, not dance, that gives me a perfect conformity of form and matter.

Running also fulfills Herbert Read's definition. Art, he stated, is an escape from chaos; movement ordained in numbers; mass confined by measure; matter seeking the rhythm of life. You could almost believe Read was watching runners while he wrote.

Where better to escape chaos and find order? Where more is movement numbered, in steps, in breaths, in minutes, in miles? Where more sharply is space and mass defined; the runner lean, the road unending? Where else, for me at least, to seek the rhythms of life, to listen to the body, to hear it speak of my soul?

And because body becomes soul, soul becomes body, running is a total experience. It is art and more than art. In itself it provides the thinking and abstractions that precede other arts. "I need hours to read and think about what I've read, to synthesize and be alone," one painter said. "The time spent at the canvas is minor compared with that."

The runner, on the other hand, is always at his canvas. He is always observing, feeling, analyzing, meditating. Always in the process of raiding the preconscious that stores past preconceptions. The preconscious that stubbornly refuses to illuminate the present with what we experienced in the past. And beyond and before it the runner explores his instincts and emotions and even dips into what can only be called mystical states.

Where the runner fails is as an artist. He may be able to express these feelings, these insights, and perhaps does, but no one sees them. He fails in the prime function of the artist, to transmit the understanding of the emotions he has experienced. The spectator sees little of this inner life. Even the poet, tuned to see life at various levels, sees the runner in almost one plane.

"Alone he emerges / Emerges and passes / alone, sufficient." Loneness, motion, sufficiency is the runner. The world knows no more about him.

In time this will change. Running is an old art but only newly resurrected. We are still learning how to develop a total response. In traffic I may be as expressionless as Buster Keaton, but on lonely roads and in empty woods the inner man is becoming visible. There I respond to grass and dirt and fallen leaves.

My running is part of sun and shadow, wind at my face, wind at my back. If you saw me, you would see elation, mastery, struggle, defeat and despair. There I reveal sorrow and anger, resentment and fear; fear of dogs and men and high places, fear of the dark and of being lost and alone.

But what matters whether we can be understood by someone else? By someone who is not a runner? Not certainly to induce them to try it themselves. But rather to encourage them to seek their own art, to become their own artists. To listen for that inner voice calling them to their own way of being in this world. To what they must be.

The runner knows this necessity. I know that although I am free to be anything I choose, I must be a runner. Ortega put it this way: "You are able to be whatever you want to be; but only if you choose this or that specific pattern you will be what you have to be."

When I run, all that Ortega says falls into place. I have found my specific pattern, heard the voice that calls me, found my art, my medium to experience and interpret life. Nor do I worry that running will be inadequate to the task. I know the truth of what William James once said of a young man learning about himself and his instincts and emotions: "Sport came to the rescue and completed his education where real things were lacking."

———————•———————

The distance runner is the least of all athletes. His sport the least of all sports. That he does it at all, either well or ill, implies that he can do nothing else. He has by the process of elimination come to the level of his competence, which is little more than survival.

Nor does he survive in ways we might admire. By challenging his environment, for instance, for conquering his enemies. He performs no feats of skill or strength or agility. He is no Crusoe who would build a new house, a new town, a new city, even a new civilization. He does nothing more than this: bring his body to the performance of a minor art, and attain an inconsequential type of perfection.

And being the least of all athletes, he appears to be the least of all men. A lonely figure on a lonely road, he seems to have no past, no future, and to be living in a present that has no rational meaning.

He performs with perverse intensity an action which has no marketable value. And is completely engaged in what is not only impractical, but even unintelligible to his fellows.

Still, this apparently witless and homeless creature, this most ordinary, most commonplace, this least of all men, has a message. A message we all carry, but sometimes fail to hear.

The distance runner is a prophet. Like the poet, he is the antenna of the race. Like the poet, he does what he does with his whole being. And like the poet, he gives thanks for his "fabulous possessions, his body and fiery soul." Like the poet, he sees himself as a question to himself. And seeks the answer by seeking to be, by creating himself. And again like the poet, he suggests that each one of us has this revelation, this Truth; and that we must find it through our bodies, through experience, and always in the present.

Most of us think of religion as something out of the past that promises something about the future. We ignore the primacy of the present. We forget that the opposite of the present is not past or future; it is absence.

The distance runner who accepts the past in the person he is, and sees the future as promise rather than threat, is completely and utterly in the present. He is absorbed in his encounter with the everyday world. He is mysteriously reconciling the separations of body and mind, of pain and pleasure, of the conscious and the unconscious. He is repairing the rent, and healing the wound in his divided self. He has found a way to make the ordinary extraordinary; the commonplace, unique; the everyday, eternal.

What he does begins in play, moves through suffering and ends in delight. And tells us that we must do the same. That we who began in play as children and move toward a heaven where we will have nothing to do but play will find our revelation and ourselves only in play.

The distance runner has found his play. And with it, he purifies his body. He does not, as the early Fathers suggested, kill his body because it kills him. He accepts it and perfects it and then seeks out suffering, and finds beyond the suffering the whole man. Not at first, of course. At first he explores the possibilities of letting the suffering pass. Of trying every diversion to remove the pain. But in the end, he grasps it and holds it and welcomes it.

This may be an odd way to find the meaning of life. And the distance runner is certainly an odd person to be demonstrating it. But the meaning of life is beyond reason. Genius upon genius has told us so.

The meaning of life is found in revelation, a revelation that is present in each one of us. To be found where our blood and flesh whisper to our unconscious. The distance runner, the least of all athletes, the least of all men, is continually taking his daily encounter with his universe on that inward journey.

Consider your body, he tells us. Not in the memory of past pleasure. Or in anticipation of a glorious future. But for this present moment when you might indeed be in Paradise.

Runners

Roger Hart, 2003

Writer Roger Hart reflects on the many miles he has shared with his two running buddies on the roads of Ashtabula County, Ohio, and of things observed and things learned.

We ran through blizzards, thunderstorms, freezing rain, covered bridges, creeks, campgrounds, cemeteries, parks, a nuclear power plant, county fairs, and, once, a church service. We were chased by goats, geese, a crazed groundhog, guards (the nuclear power plant), a motorcycle gang, an armed man in a pickup, a sheriff's deputy, and dogs, both fierce and friendly. We ran when 2 feet of snow covered the roads, and when the windchill was 30 below. We ran when it was 80 degrees at seven in the morning. We ran on streets, sidewalks, highways, cinder tracks, dirt roads, golf courses, Lake Erie beaches, bike trails, across yards, and along old railroad beds. Seven days a week, 12 months a year, year after year.

During the hot days of July and August, Ed ran without a shirt or socks; I always wore both. Norm ran with a screw in his ankle and joked that it was coming loose. Ed was faster going downhill; I was better going up. The three of us met at a race and became training partners, competitors, best friends. We ran together on Saturday mornings, usually a 20-miler along the shore of Lake Erie or a 22-mile route over hilly country roads through Ashtabula County [Ohio]. We ran thousands of miles and more than a dozen marathons together, but most of the time we ran alone.

We gave directions to lost drivers, pushed cars out of snow banks, called the electric company about downed lines and the police about drunks. We saved a burlap bag full of kittens about to be tossed off a bridge, carried turtles from the middle of the road, returned lost wallets, and were the first on the scene of a flipped pickup truck.

We ran the Boston Marathon before women were allowed to enter and way before the Kenyans won. We were runners before Frank Shorter took the Olympic gold at Munich, before the running boom, nylon shorts, sports drinks, Gore-Tex suits, heart monitors, running watches, and Nikes.

We ate constantly, or so it seemed. My favorite midnight snack was cookie dough or cold pizza. Ed enjoyed cinnamon bread, which he sometimes ate a loaf at a time. Norm downed buttered popcorn by the bucketful and Finnish cookies by the dozen. We all loved ice cream, and drank large vanilla shakes two at a time.

From *Runner's World*, April 2003. Reprinted by permission of Rodale, Inc.

Still, friends said we were too thin. They thought we looked sick and worried something was wrong.

We measured our lives in miles down to the nearest tenth, more than 100 miles a week, 400 a month, 5,000 a year.

The smells! From passing cars: pipe tobacco, exhaust fumes, and sometimes the sweet hint of perfume. From the places we passed: French fries, bacon, skunk, pine trees, dead leaves, cut hay, mowed grass, ripe grapes, hot asphalt, rotten apples, stagnant water, wood smoke, charcoal grills, mosquito spray, road kill. And from ourselves: sunscreen and sweat.

Some people smiled and waved. A few whistled. Once or twice women from passing cars yelled we had nice legs. Others, usually teenage boys in sleek, black cars, yelled obscenities, called us names, gave us the finger, and mooned us. They threw firecrackers, lit cigarettes, soda cans, half-eaten ice cream cones, beer bottles (both full and empty), squirted us with water, drove through puddles to spray us, swerved their cars to force us off the road, swung jumper cables out the window to make us duck, and honked their horns to make us jump.

We saw shooting stars, a family of weasels, a barn fire, a covered wagon heading west, and a couple making love in a pickup. We ran with deer on a golf course, jumped a slow-moving train to get across the tracks, hid in ditches during lightning storms, slid across an intersection during a freezing rain, and dived into Lake Erie to cool off in the middle of a hot run. We drank from garden hoses, gas station water fountains, soda machines, lawn sprinklers, and lemonade stands. We carried toilet paper, two quarters, sometimes a dog biscuit.

We were offered rides by "The Chosen Few" motorcycle gang, old ladies, drunks, teenagers, truckers, a topless dancer (not topless at the time but close, real close), and a farmer baling hay, but we never accepted a single one. We argued about the dancer.

We were nervous before races and said we'd quit running them when we weren't. We won trophies, medals, baskets of apples, bottles of wine, windbreakers, T-shirts, pizza, pewter mugs, running suits, shoes, baseball caps, watches, a railroad spike, and, once, $500. Often we didn't win anything, although we never looked at it that way.

Ed liked to race from the front and dare other runners to catch him. I preferred to start a little slower, stalk those who went out too fast, and sneak up on them around 20 miles when they began to look over their shoulders. I felt like a wolf, and they were the prey. When I passed, I pretended not to be tired, and never looked back.

Our goal was to qualify for the Olympic Trials Marathon, to run faster and farther, to beat other runners.

Did we ever have runner's high? Didn't it get boring? What did we think about? Why did we always look so serious?

Sometimes. Sometimes. Running. We didn't know we did.

One spring day it rained so hard the road was one giant ankle-deep puddle, and Ed was huffing, and our feet were splashing, and it struck us funny. We laughed until we collapsed, tears and rain running down our faces. We joked about the time Ed had to pee and caught himself showering a snake, the time we got lost during a winter storm and refused to turn around, and the time we ran by Don King's ranch and were mistaken for two boxers. (We never understood how anyone could mistake us for boxers, but we loved it.)

We felt guilty about the time we ran into a church service being held in the middle of a covered bridge, and were too tired, too inconsiderate, too stubborn to turn around, so we sprinted down the center aisle, dodging the two men with collection plates, and ran out the other end of the bridge while the congregation sang "Praise God from whom all blessings flow . . ."

And the dogs! The ones that tried to follow us home and the ones that attacked us. The time that Ed, Norm, and I yelled at a growling Doberman, and told it to go home. The owner jumped in his pickup, chased us down the dirt road, swearing he'd shoot us for bothering his dog. We ran through a field and across a four-lane highway, circled back through the woods, hid beneath the underpass, and then jogged into a gas station where we celebrated our escape with ice-cold Cokes.

Or the time a sheriff's deputy stopped his cruiser to protect us from a German shepherd as large as a Poland China hog in a nearby field. The dog jumped through the open window and landed on the deputy's lap, and, while they wrestled in the front seat, we ran, afraid of what might happen if either ever caught up with us.

We found pliers, purses, golf balls, bolt cutters, billfolds, money (once, over $200—returned to an 18-year-old boy—no reward, no thanks), tape cassettes, CDs, sunglasses, school books, porn magazines, a Navajo ring, car jacks, a fishing pole, a pair of handcuffs (no key), an eight ball, and a black bra (36C).

We ran farther and faster. We sprinted up long steep hills by the Grand River until all we could do was stagger. We ran intervals on a dirt track: 20 quarter-miles in under 70 seconds, the last lap in 56 flat. We got light-headed, our hands tingled, and sometimes blood vessels in our eyes ruptured from the effort.

We ran because it beat collecting stamps, because we were running toward something, because we were running away, because we were all legs, lungs, and heart, because we were afraid of who or what might catch us if we stopped.

One winter, while running twice a day, I was on my way home from a 7-mile run, and I couldn't remember if it was morning or night, if when I finished I would shower and go to work or shower and go to bed. I looked at the horizon and the stars, the passing cars, and the lighted barns for a clue, but couldn't figure it out. Ed said one time he went out for a run and bumped into himself coming back from the previous one.

We lost toenails and we pulled muscles. We suffered frostbite, hypothermia, heat exhaustion, sunburn, blisters, dehydration, and tendinitis. We were stung by bees, bitten by black flies, and attacked by red-winged blackbirds. Sometimes, after a long run, speed workout, or a marathon, our legs would be so sore, our Achilles so inflamed, that we could barely walk, and we'd limp or shuffle painfully when going from the couch to the refrigerator or from the front door to the mailbox.

We treated aches with ice and heating pads, or soaked our legs in DMSO, sometimes in Epsom salts and hot water. We tried medical doctors, surgeons, chiropractors, acupuncturists, podiatrists, massage therapists, trainers, and quacks. We were given shots of novocaine and cortisone, told to take ibuprofen, Tylenol, and aspirin. We were warned that we were ruining our knees, our hips, damaging our feet, breaking down too much blood, that we would suffer arthritis and degenerative joints.

But sometimes it was like floating, as if you were sitting on top of a pair of legs that you didn't think would ever get tired or slow down. It was as if the legs were yours but they weren't.

It was as if we were part animal: a running, flying animal. A horse, a bird. It was like feet kissing the pavement and effortless strides, the body along for the ride. It was like sitting in Ed's '67 Corvette, that monster engine gulping high-octane fuel and turning 6,000 rpms, your foot ready to pop the clutch. Like freedom and invincibility. When we ran around corners, we were jets sweeping in formation.

We each had a resting pulse in the low 40s and body fat of 7 percent or less. I was 6' 2", raced at 148 pounds, and went through a pair of running shoes every 6 weeks.

Once, I experienced chest pains, a sharp stab beneath the ribs. A Saturday morning, 22-mile run. Seven steep hills. We raced up the first hill to find out if it was my heart or not, and when I did not drop, we raced up the second and third. After 6 miles the pain eased off, and Ed said if it had been a heart attack, it must have been a mild one. Thousands of miles later, a doctor unfamiliar with a runner's heart sent Ed to the emergency room where he was poked, prodded, hooked up, and given oxygen. Finally, Ed said enough was enough, pulled the IV, and ran home. Two weeks later, he set an age-50 record for the mile in a local meet.

Although we ran faster and faster, it was never quite fast enough. We failed to qualify for the Olympic Trials. Still, four times we drove for hours and slept in our cars to watch others compete for the three Olympic spots.

Then, just as we once stalked other runners, time stalked us. We began looking over our shoulders and thinking about the marathons we had run instead of thinking about the next race. We slowed down. Our bodies balked at 100-mile weeks, and it took longer to recover from a hard run. Sometimes when the weather was bad—very hot was always worse than very cold—we took a day off. Sometimes we would skip a day because we were sore or tired. We stopped giving the finger to those who ran us off the roads. We gained 5, 7, 10 pounds. More.

Now, Ed has a granddaughter; Norm has "screw pains," and I have a retirement clock and deformed toes. We've turned gray, lost hair, and joined AARP. We run 25, 30 miles a week. From time to time, we race, no marathons but shorter races, 3, 4 miles, maybe a 10-K. We measure our lives in days, months, and years, not miles.

Ed and Norm still live in Ohio; I moved to North Carolina, then to Minnesota. We no longer run together, but we keep in touch and reminisce about the time the newspaper ran a front-page story about a group of snowmobilers who had ridden nearly 10 miles on a day when the temperature was 5 below. We had passed them during a 20-mile run. We argue about who threw the rock at the house, whose fault it was we got lost, and which one of us the topless dancer really wanted to take for a ride.

We complain that we're running slower than we once did, and make jokes about timing ourselves with calendars and sundials.

Sometimes when we're running we'll spot other runners ahead of us and the urge to race comes back, and we'll do our best to catch them. Last fall while I was running in a park, I overheard a high school coach urge his runners to pass "the old, gray-haired guy." I held them off for a mile although it almost killed me, and, when I had completed circling the park, I ran by the coach and said, "Old guy, my ass."

But my ass is getting old along with my other body parts. When I sometimes fantasize about one more marathon, the fantasy seldom lasts more than a day. Fast marathons and 100-mile weeks are things of the past.

And what did we learn from running 70,000 miles and hundreds of races, being the first to cross the finish line and once or twice not crossing it at all, those runs on icy roads in winter storms and those cool fall mornings when the air was ripe with the smell of grapes, our feet softly ticking against the pavement?

We learned we were alive, and it felt good. God, it felt so good.

One Runner's Beginnings

Rachel Toor, 2008

When did you first become a runner? Can you remember your feelings as a beginner in the sport, your first sensations, misgivings, discoveries? Rachel Toor, a senior writer for *Running Times*, shares her memories of her first runs with her boyfriend and her dog in the following excerpt from the eloquent *Personal Record: A Love Affair with Running.*

Andrew and I were introduced. We dated. Every week or so I'd threaten to break up with him. We moved in together. There were struggles over the toilet seat *(down*—it belongs down) and the kitchen cabinets *(closed*—they should be closed) and the dishes in the sink *(piled up*—they should *not* be piled up in the sink). But we never argued about Hannah, my dog.

Andrew started taking Hannah along on his runs. She would greet him at the end of the day with yelps and circle dances, and then wait, coiled for action, while he put on his compression shorts and pulled up his white basketball socks to just under his knees. Finally, they'd tear out the door. Some portion of an hour later, they would return home spent and content.

I grew jealous of their time together, and began to feel left out. First, because I was me, I made snarky comments. Then, after being encouraged by Andrew— he was always encouraging, always positive—to join them, I said, with a sneer, "Okay." We went to the trail that loops around Duke's golf course, 3 miles, all hills, woody and lush.

I said, "Okay, let's go," and took off, leaving Andrew in my wake. When he caught up, he suggested that the first mistake many new runners make is to start out too fast. You hurt early and decide that running isn't fun and never do it again.

"I'll set the pace," he said. "Just stay with me."

I complained that the pace he set was too slow.

"I can run faster than this, you know," I said, feeling that this was true, though not knowing it to be so.

"That's okay," he said. "Let's just start out slow."

Not five minutes later I was complaining that I was getting tired.

I did not notice the way the light came through the tall pines or hear the scuttering of birds on the ground. I did not smell the snakes.

"Slow down," he said. "Take it easy."

Hannah ran like a dog—she'd bolt ahead, and then charge back to us.

Reprinted from PERSONAL RECORD: A LOVE AFFAIR WITH RUNNING by Rachel Toor by permission of the University of Nebraska Press. © 2008 by Rachel Toor.

I told Andrew that he didn't have to wait for me, feeling guilty for holding him back. I knew this couldn't be much fun for him, knew that he wasn't getting any needed exercise. Plus, I was angry with him because I wasn't good at this. I hated doing things I wasn't good at. It is easier not to try new things. And it is unpleasant to have someone witness your struggle. Especially if you're an overachieving, high-strung, complaining whiner type.

"Just take it easy," he said.

He told me to walk up the steepest hills, and I argued—that wasn't running. He told me to relax on the downhills, not to try to make up speed or time. I wanted to blast down them.

I argued for the whole 3 miles, but when we stopped running, I apologized, astonished. I'd made it all the way around the loop.

For our next run we went to a more remote part of the Duke Forest where Andrew sometimes ran after work. He often had cuts and bruises from falling.

"How can you fall?" I wanted to know. "Grownups don't fall down."

Andrew did. A lot.

He worked late and ran at night, in the dark, on rocks and roots.

"How can you run at night? How do you see? How can you fall? Don't you get hurt?" I questioned the reasonableness of this whole endeavor.

But then there we were, among loblolly pines and rhododendron, and we were running on a trail along a creek and it was beautiful and we saw deer and snakes and heard birds and the sound of our breathing and our footfalls. And then it began to rain. And I began to complain. We were approaching a hill, a big one. I was at once miserable.

"Tell me about schizophrenia," I barked out. Andrew did. He engaged my mind and I forgot about my body and before I knew it we had crested the hill and were almost back to the car.

———————•———————

It's elemental, running. It's not like doing classical philology or nonlinear dynamics. You don't need to learn two dead languages and read the corpus of ancient literature before you can start to engage; you don't have to have calculus and physics under your belt and be able to think in seventeen dimensions. You just start with one foot and the other follows, because if it doesn't, you will fall. Little kids and animals know this.

I wanted Andrew to advise me on technique, to coach me, but he was a good teacher and knew that first you have to get someone started, and then you refine.

I was impatient and wouldn't stand for good teaching. "Tell me what I'm doing wrong," I'd demand, breathless. He would relent and give me bits and pieces:

Don't clench your fists. If you want to increase your speed, shorten your stride. Going up a hill, take little steps. Going downhill, don't brace against it—just flow. He ran slightly behind me, making me feel that I was leading, that I was the stronger runner. He made me believe I could do it.

"Take it easy," he said.

"Breathe. Don't run so fast you can't talk."

We talked a lot, Andrew and I. He always had stories about family and friends, collections of antics from college and medical school, and explanations of the work of neurotransmitters or the various types of edible fungi. Once, we set out for a run, and I was cold. I'd underdressed and spent the first few minutes chanting, "I'm cold I'm cold I'm cold." That launched Andrew into a rhapsody on thermal equilibration—the physiology of the body's response to external temperatures. Andrew had been a lackluster high school student (though good enough to get into one of the nation's top colleges), but he had a restless curiosity and learned without forgetting anything that captured his attention.

Because we were human, and because we were in a relationship, we also had to have Talks, those terrible relationship talks with long silences and squinty eyes. Whenever we needed one of those sessions, we'd go out for a run. I learned that you can run a whole lot faster if you're pissed off or frustrated. We'd come home talked out, sweaty, having worked through whatever it was that needed working. I'd be exhausted. Andrew and Hannah never even seemed tired.

I began to look forward to running, going more frequently, and longer, just me and Hannah. In the heat of the North Carolina summer, she learned to stop to drink at streams. I asked her to lie down in them—to get her chest wet, to cool herself. She always did as I asked. She loved this new part of daily life. When she saw me get out my running shoes, she'd circle and wag, run to the door, to me, to the door. Her enthusiasm buoyed me.

One day I saw a sign on Duke's campus advertising a 5K race.

"How long is 5K?" I asked Andrew. He told me it was a smidge over 3 miles, just about the distance of the golf course loop, which I was now able to run twice and no longer had to walk the hills. I signed up for the race.

I wasn't used to pushing myself, hadn't ever tried to run faster. I did that day, caught up in the pack of runners. What I wanted was the shirt. I got the shirt just for entering, before the race even started, but I also got something else: Among the thirty- to thirty-four-year-old women, I was the third-place finisher. I got a medal, heavy, silly, on a red, white, and blue ribbon. A medal and a shirt. I liked the idea of a material marker of where I've been and what I've done. Even now, years later, I still do.

Seasons

Hal Higdon, 1971

Few writers can evoke the poetry of running like Hal Higdon. In this essay from his book *On the Run from Dogs and People,* Higdon describes the four seasons of his training in and around his home near Michigan City, Indiana, on Lake Michigan.

There is a certain majesty to the weather of the Middle West. Running outdoors as I do, I get to know it. No television weatherman can tell more than I learn during daily training runs. I look up, while running the beach, at puffs of clouds floating over the horizon and know soon it will rain. I touch the northwest wind after it has crossed 60 miles of open lake, and understand that winter will soon come.

In early winter after the first few inches of fallen snow, I bounce over the golf course. The ground beneath retains its summer springiness. I am rabbit. I run the length of a fairway, then look over my shoulder to see the long dotted line behind. Once, near my mother-in-law's house on the south side of Chicago, I trod a nearby track in inch-deep snow and circled round and round, each time moving a half-lane wide of the previous lap's tracks. At the end the entire track was covered with my presence. Footprints in the snow: a visible mark in space of my effort, more so than mere numbers on the dial of some coach's stopwatch.

As winter continues the snow grows deep, drifts; the ground beneath it becomes hard, rutted. The woods fill up. One cold day on the beach a ridge of ice forms at the water's edge. Two days later the ridge has grown five feet high, a God-made barrier that continues to grow as the northwest winds drive the waves against it to break, splash, freeze. I no longer can run on the beach. Winter has narrowed my vista.

There is the road. Always the road. Near Michigan City the snow plows leap quickly to the fray when the first flakes appear in the air. The sound of their blades scraping the asphalt echoes through the night. Sometimes the plows lose. The passing cars already have beaten the snow flat. I don spikes to grip the packed snow as though it were a rubberized track, the kind that costs hundreds of thousands of dollars to lay down in Olympic stadiums.

Days later the packed snow turns to ice. I change to rubber-bottomed shoes with ridges for traction. Cotton socks. I wear sweat pants, sometimes two pair. A turtleneck sweater. A sweatshirt. Sometimes another. A double pair of mittens: the inside wool, the outside leather. My hands never get cold. A knit cap, red, which on windy days can be turned and pulled down below my chin to form a hideous frost-covered mask. The kind the Green Bay Packers wear while preparing for December games.

A hooded parka, the final barrier against the worst winter can throw at me. Thus clad, I run in sub-zero cold (25 below being my record), and as curious neighbors in warm houses gaze out through glazed windows at my passing, they shake their heads. But I am warmer than they. I finish my run soaked with sweat. I relish in my victory over nature. Peter Snell once said: "I enjoy bad weather because I know that while I'm outside suffering, all of the rivals I'll race next summer are indoors doing nothing." Believe Peter Snell.

Should the weather warm too early, I feel cheated. It happened that way late one January. After a week of snow and crackling cold, the temperatures soared into the thirties. I cursed, because winter had been defeated too easily. I wanted to struggle against it for at least one more month to prove my mettle. It is like a miler who, having anticipated a hard blow against his number one rival, sees that rival stop lame before the final straight. Victory will be his, but with a hollow ring.

More often, winter only seems to flee, then when you have relaxed, it tightens its grip. It is dark late in the morning and dark early at night. I run at noon so I can see the sun. I wonder, will winter last until June? Then one day, it is gone.

The snow releases its hold on the golf course, but leaves mud, a more fearsome enemy. I stay away. On the beaches, the massive ice barrier remains, resisting the rays of the sun, melting reluctantly. There is a surreal quality to the beach now, rough, pitted like the face of the moon, lingering patches of ice, driftwood, stones. I run there anyway. In the low spots on the road, melting snow forms puddles. I dodge onto lawns to avoid wetting my shoes, but the lawns are soggy. I splash through the puddles seeking the high spot in the pavement, watchful always for the approach of a car that may shower me with spray. One day pounding waves rip the last of the ice barrier from the shore and roll across the beach flattening it to highway smoothness. I know now it is spring.

The woods come alive. I run along my old paths again, see the buds emerging on the branches of the trees. It is like time-lapse photography. Each new day we have moved one notch closer to summer. I realize that the grass, brown last week, has turned emerald green. Birds. I run into a wooded area I call Moon Valley, around a series of looping trails, up and down hill. I follow the bridle path that winds through Michiana Shores, a thin trail, bushes on one side, sometimes the backs of houses, meandering along the bank of a creek that soon finds the lake. I head toward New Buffalo on a course that takes me over streets, path, gravel road, golf course, wooded trail, beach, and highway. I can run now in almost as many directions as the compass, and one day I return to a path I have not visited in a week and find myself striding past a blanket of purple flowers, stretching to the next ridge. God is with me in the woods.

The layers of winter clothes vanish now, one by one, until I am running unencumbered, shorts, a shirt, sometimes not even that, barefoot along the soft surface of sand by the water's edge. I splash lightly through the shallow water. It is cold. As it warms, my domain is invaded by bathers, sand castles, outboard motors, bikinis, and soon I leave the beach to them and seek solitude elsewhere. The golfers have reoccupied their fairways, which I cede to them willingly, no more wanting to intrude on their world, than have them intrude on mine. My vista once more narrows.

But I still have the road. Always the road. One day I cross the highway to explore a new route, down country roads, past farmhouses, trailers, billboards, broken-down shacks, garbage piles. Each yard has its dog that comes snapping and snarling to the edge of the road daring me to take one false step toward him. I run on.

Sometimes I drive to the rough cinder track that sits atop the hill next to the junior high. I move in circles of precisely 440 yards, round and round, run, jog, run, jog, my spikes biting into the surface, tearing holes, kicking up dust, run, jog, as the hand on the stopwatch spins, defining my accomplishments, linking me to a more orderly world. At another time, another place, another age of life, I ran frequently into this orderly world, accepting its discipline as one means of fulfilling youthful ambitions. I touch this world only occasionally now. I walk from the track, sit on the curb, throw off my spikes, and run barefoot through the long grass on the infield, dodging through the sprinklers that make the grass grow so that in the fall football players can grind it beneath their cleats.

One day the sky turns black over the lake. Lightning flashes on the horizon. Thunder rumbles. I see the storm moving toward me. It rains. A warm, summer rain. Welcome. The heat that had hung like a damp blanket over my running trails for nearly a week vanishes. I sniff fresh ozone in the air. I splash through a puddle, uncaring. My feet slosh in my shoes. I carry my splattered glasses in one hand. The other brushes the water from my forehead. Sweat stings my eyes. I push the pace harder, harder, harder. I am in no hurry to get home. Rain helps me run faster.

When the children return to school, they abandon the beach to me. I claim it greedily and run toward the harbor, following the crooked line of the shore. Tomorrow when I run there again, the line will have twisted into a new pattern. Above, white trails trace the routes of jet planes, unheard, thousands of feet overhead, heading for eventual touchdowns at O'Hare Field. Two white jet trails move toward each other. I watch, hoping they are at different altitudes. They cross. Each day the sun will set a little further south, casting its glow orange in the surf at the water's edge. I turn at the harbor to return home and the sky changes suddenly to dark blue.

At the end of the run I wade into the water. I swim more in September and October than I do in July and August. One day the sky will turn gray. I will wear a sweatshirt and not wade at the end of the workout. The sand will feel cold under my bare feet. Soon I must go back to wearing shoes. I know now it is fall.

The golfers too have gone, leaving me their spongy carpet. I accept the gift. Sometimes I drive south to the national park, sneaking in around the fence to run among gold, red, yellow leaves. Soon there will be more leaves below me on the trail than above me on the trees. Then I will go for an early run on the beach and find a thin sheet of ice just above the waterline.

One day I test the wind and note that it comes from the northwest more frequently now. I know the sign because I live in the outdoors. A few crystals of white float down as I run along the road. They melt touching the still warm pavement. My vista is narrowing again, and it is time for my double sweatsuit, my gloves, and that knit cap like the Green Bay Packers wear. Another year of seasons has passed.

body

There is nothing quite so gentle, deep, and irrational as our running—and nothing quite so savage, and so wild.

~Bernd Heinrich, ultramarathon champion and biologist

My Old Buick

Don Kardong, 1983

Writer Don Kardong brings welcome humor to a sport that is sometimes taken much too seriously. In this essay he lightens up the runner's age-old obsession—our attempts to fix our ailments and injuries.

I had gone through ten miles of the Twin Cities Marathon in fifty-two minutes. Nothing spectacular, but nothing to be ashamed of. A final time in the 2:16 range seemed likely.

A minute later, I was hunched over at the side of the road, hands on my knees, stomach churning, and speaking to Ralph, as we used to say. I was thinking about my old Buick.

The Buick, a powder-blue Skylark that carried me through high school and college in admirable fashion, was zipping through Northern California one day in 1971 on its way back to Washington, with myself and fellow runner Duncan Macdonald inside, when it began lurching in syncopated fashion. We pulled off the highway, opened the hood, and looked at an engine that had suffered some sort of losing bout with the heat. Water from the radiator had sprayed the underside of the hood and was dripping from the water pump.

We waited for things to cool down a little, then took the next freeway exit to a service station.

"I'm sure it's the thermostat," said the attendant. "Those things clog up in the winter and get stuck when they're supposed to open."

He replaced it, we drove happily down the highway, and twenty minutes later the engine overheated again. We found another station.

"I'd guess it's the thermostat," the attendant said.

"We just replaced it," I told him.

"Well, sometimes even the new ones stick. I can replace it if you want."

He did, and we headed off again. We overheated, found another service station, and heard a familiar story.

"Probably the thermostat," the man said.

"We've replaced the thermostat twice," I said.

"Well," he replied, "maybe you should just take it out. That way the coolant will be sure to circulate."

We left, drove, overheated, found another station.

"Probably the thermostat," the man said.

"I've replaced it twice and finally took it out altogether," I said, overheating myself. "There isn't even one in there."

From Don Kardong, 1985, *Thirty Phone Booths to Boston: Tales of a Wayward Runner* (New York: Macmillan). Reprinted by permission of Don Kardong.

"Not one in there?" he said, surprised. "No wonder you're having trouble. You've got to have a thermostat." He put one in.

Twenty-four hours and a few futile, costly repairs later, we deserted the car and caught a bus to Washington.

And now, a dozen years later in Minneapolis, with my hands on my knees and my stomach in revolt, I was remembering the feelings of frustration I had faced in trying to get that old car going again. Sometimes, it seems, no matter who you consult or what you do, the same old problem keeps rising to the surface, bobbing and weaving in an elusive attempt to avoid getting fixed. And in running the marathon, whatever slight maladjustment might be in one's system is bound to become a major obstacle to success. The old Buick had finally succumbed to a flaw, not unlike the one that hit me at the ten-mile mark in Minneapolis. The Buick's flaw was in the gurgling innards of its system. So was my own.

The first time I remember experiencing midrace nausea was during the 1976 Baltimore Marathon. At the prerace pasta feed, local runner Marge Rosasco asked whether I had ever had trouble with my stomach during a race.

"I used to have trouble with a side stitch," I told her. "Two-thirds of the way into a five- or ten-K race I'd get a really sharp pain in my side. One of the reasons I switched to running marathons was because I don't have the problem in the longer race."

"How about nausea, though?" she asked. "I keep running marathons where I get to about twenty miles feeling fine, right on the pace I want, when all of a sudden I get sick to my stomach. I've tried all sorts of things to cure it, but nothing seems to work. Have you ever had anything like that?"

I was no help to her. The problem with the side stitch had been a recurrent one in college, especially on cross-country courses. I had altered my diet, adjusted my breathing, strengthened my stomach muscles, and tried taking medication to prevent spasm of the colon. Nothing really helped much, though, except moving on to another event.

But throwing up during a race?

"I haven't had that problem since high school, Marge, when I was totally out of shape."

The next day I spent ten minutes next to the road at the nineteen mile mark, stomach heaving uncontrollably, eyes bulging, knees shaking.

"There must be something in the water in this part of the country," I told Marge later.

An old car may perform beautifully for years, dutifully chauffeuring its owner from place to place, never showing great signs of distress, only to suffer a major breakdown when asked to push to the limit on the open road. Runners are not much different, which is why the marathon tends to bring out the worst in us.

Not everyone suffers from midmarathon nausea, but it does seem that most of us have some sort of frailty that peeks its problematic head up during the excessive stresses of the marathon race, or at least during marathon training. At the Twin Cities Marathon the second-fastest American of all time, Dick Beardsley, was suffering through a prolonged absence from his specialty and was working on TV coverage of the race instead. Beardsley's achilles heel has been his achilles tendon, and an operation to correct the problem had sidelined him for months.

"The doctor told me I could be running up to ten miles a day by November," he said.

I didn't tell him about the thermostats.

In fact, injuries incurred during training and racing are much more common than sensitive stomachs in interfering with people's marathon attempts. Many runners find that the amount of training necessary to allow them to feel comfortable running the marathon is well beyond the amount they can handle without sustaining an injury. Usually it's a knee, a hip, an arch, or, as in Beardsley's case, a bad tendon or two that become wrenches in the marathon machinery. And the exact cure is often elusive.

For years I suffered from a sharp pain in my left knee, which was especially acute during downhill running. After five or six years of flirting with ice, aspirin, and cortisone treatments, the pain finally subsided with the development of better running shoes. Apparently the problem was bursitis, but knowing that didn't seem to help much. And though doctors in recent years have gotten better at treating the well-hidden glitches in human athletic machinery, they're not always sympathetic to the excesses of long-distance runners.

A college teammate of mine who had injured his knee complained to his doctor that the joint would tighten up when he tried to run more than five miles a day.

The doctor was incredulous. "Well then, don't *run* more than five miles a day," he said.

It made sense, of course, unless one was tempted by longer distances. And when we pursue faster times at the marathon distance, we generally end up asking doctors to cure things that most people have sense enough to treat by avoiding the cause. Fatal athletic flaws tend to lie outside the realm of ordinary medicine, and as a result we runners often end up speculating about the root of the problem ourselves.

After my first bout with nausea at Baltimore, I was convinced that the only problem had been in the city's water supply. The next year I decided to run in Hawaii. By then, I had forgotten about the nausea.

On the night before the race, Duncan Macdonald and I went out for Mexican food. The next day, I wound up with my hands on my knees at nineteen miles, and Duncan won the race. I suspected foul play.

It seemed reasonable, though, given my own penchant for enjoying an outrageous diet, and given the delicious complexity of our meal the night before, that something in the Mexican dinner was at fault. If not, perhaps the aid stations were to blame.

Thus began the dietary phase of my problem solving, when I adjusted everything on the menu to avoid stomach complications during the race. I passed up electrolyte fluids at the aid stations, then stopped drinking anything at all. I avoided excessive carbohydrate loading the night before the race and stayed away from spicy foods. The next year I won the Honolulu Marathon. My problem, it seemed, had been solved.

Remember the Buick, though? We had deserted it in Northern California, frustrated to the hilt with trying to fix it. But after a week or two, I had it loaded on a truck and shipped home. A local mechanic installed a new engine, and everything seemed to work fine.

"It still runs a little hot," he confided. "But I don't think you'll have a problem with it."

I had my doubts. After repeated service-station stops along the highway in California, my confidence in fixing flaws was not high. I drove slowly in the cool of the night when I headed back to California in the fall. In spite of my caution, the car showed signs of overheating. Before long, I was aware that it wasn't truly fixed and that I would have to avoid long, hot drives if I didn't want a recurrence of the problem.

My marathon "solution," careful attention to prerace and midrace diet, worked out better for a while. I ran several races without hearing much from my stomach. In its place, other problems, mostly muscular, cropped up.

During my two successive Boston Marathons, I developed severe tightness in my calves from the early downhill running, and I realized that a tall runner was destined to have trouble on the Boston course. The second year I proved it to myself by cramping acutely and dropping out at the sixteen-mile point.

It may be that muscular quirks are the fatal flaws of marathon runners more than all other weaknesses put together. Could there be more convincing evidence of the impropriety of human beings racing the marathon distance than the fact that our muscles tend to run out of glycogen at twenty miles? Even I wouldn't expect my Buick to continue down the highway without stopping to fill up every now and then. But I do seem to expect my body to continue running indefinitely on empty.

I'm not sure how many marathons I've run where I've "hit the wall," the phrase we all use to describe muscular despair during the latter stages of the race. But I remember two in a row that, in retrospect, seem typical. The first was in the fall of 1980, when I dodged traffic in the tunnels of Rio de Janeiro for thirty kilometers before slowing precipitously for the final 5K along the beach. With blisters ("the size of Buicks," Woody Allen would say) on both feet, I was told by a spectator that all I had to do was keep moving and I'd get third. I kept moving and finished sixth.

The second, a few months later in Japan, saw me standing at an aid station just past twenty miles, pouring down one cup of juice after another, desperately trying to restore my blood sugar level. After my third cup, the spectators began to chuckle. Embarrassed, I hobbled off toward the finish line.

A friend of mine was once in a similar wasted condition in the last few miles of a marathon, and he convinced himself that he was making progress down the road by sighting objects up ahead, then monitoring his progress toward them. At one point he spotted a pedestrian several hundred yards ahead and made that person his immediate goal.

Staring down at his feet, he ran for a while, then looked up. Not much progress. He looked down at his feet again, ran some more, looked up again. Unbelievably, he still didn't seem to have gotten much closer. Was it possible someone was walking faster than he was running? Finally, after concentrating on his feet and running as long as he could before looking up, he recognized some progress toward his goal. And as he got closer, he suddenly realized that the pedestrian had been walking *toward* him the whole time.

Muscular fatigue, cramping, and depletion, though, no matter how drastic, are just part of the game. Proper training and adjustments in the diet can help alleviate these flaws in our makeup, but can the same be said of regurgitation?

To correct my problems with muscular exhaustion, I went into my next marathon after a full program of carbohydrate depletion and loading. I felt confident of having stored plenty of glycogen for the final miles of the race, convinced that I wouldn't be frustrated by a lack of energy. I was right. Instead, I threw up again.

This time, a woman runner and physiologist I talked to suggested that the nausea was actually a symptom of heatstroke. I had suffered from the heat in Rio de Janeiro, she said, and when you've been knocked down by the heat, it can throw the system off for months and months. The body's ability to regulate its temperature is thrown off, sort of like having a problem with . . . a thermostat.

Well, why not? The cure, then, was to avoid marathons for a while, let the body reestablish its ability to control its own internal heat. This was fine with me. I was planning to give up the event altogether.

For a year and a half I passed up all opportunities to run the twenty-six-miler. The rest did me good, I'm sure; but the attractions of the marathon are many, and by the fall of 1982 I was back in serious training. After months of preparation, I jumped back into the fray at Honolulu. I suffered some nausea at the twenty-one-mile aid station, but the results weren't drastic. I finished ninth, and vowed to try another. In January, I ran 2:16:41 at Houston. Some nausea again, but only briefly. My confidence was returning. For my third marathon attempt after the layoff, I had hopes of something below 2:15. Instead, I stopped at thirteen miles, hands on my knees, stomach rebelling.

I was discouraged by the relapse, but by now I thought I had narrowed the problem down to two main things. First, stomach acid seemed to be present as an irritant. Second, an accumulation of phlegm at the back of the throat seemed to act as a trigger. For my next marathon attempt, at the Twin Cities, I took medication to inhibit the production of stomach acid.

But by ten miles I was thinking about my Buick.

By the time I abandoned that old car in California after repeated attempts at repair, I had learned an awful lot about how a car works. I had eliminated a few suspected causes in its flawed cooling system. (The thermostat, for example, was fine.) And after having learned so much about the problem, I was more determined than ever to find a solution. A new water pump didn't do the job. A new head gasket proved useless. Even a new engine didn't seem to help the car stay cool.

And similarly, after ten minutes of vomiting in Minneapolis, I was more angry than frustrated. I had thought the problem was solved. My stomach disagreed. But I knew I had to be closing in on the culprit. Stomach acid didn't seem to be the real problem. Diet and liquid aid were important, but not central. Heat and humidity were important issues, but was my thermostat really defective?

If you've ever agonized like this, searching for the key to an injury, a quirk, or some other flaw that upsets your running plans, you know how obsessive the quest becomes. After years of struggling with unsuccessful remedies, though, you begin to think that maybe there is no solution, only an inability of the body to perform the task at hand.

My newborn daughter, for example, has been unable to keep food down much of the time. Where most parents would say, "She has your eyes," or "She's got your nose," my wife says, "She's got your digestive system." After trying several things to help her keep the food down, we've finally discovered why she throws up so much. She has "gastroesophageal reflux." This means, of course, that she throws up a lot.

Is the solution, then, as easy as finding the right name? Do I have gastro-esophageal reflux? Hearing a name for my daughter's malady put my mind at ease. Perhaps the solution for running problems could be as easy. Let's call those otherwise unnamed flaws in our human anatomy "zekes," "geeks," "weasels," or whatever. That way, instead of telling someone, "I feel sick to my stomach after running halfway through a marathon, and the feeling often leads to vomiting," I can just say, "I have a stomach zeke," or "I suffered from an intestinal geek at twenty miles." A friend of mine who has had groin pain that's kept him from running for two years can finally stop consulting doctors and offering multiple possibilities for what's wrong. From now on, he can just complain of having a severe groin weasel. Giving the problem a name may put him on the road to recovery.

Once again, though, I have my doubts. My daughter still throws up and, so far, so do I. Finding the name hasn't yet suggested a solution for either of us. Does the final episode of the Buick story offer guidance?

After virtually giving up on fixing the old car, I had resigned myself to driving only in cool weather for short periods of time. Within bounds, then, the car worked fine. Having accepted its fate as a short-distance vehicle, I stopped worrying about it.

As I got in the driver's seat one day, though, I felt a rush of inspiration. Had I ever really checked the radiator? I disconnected it and took it to a radiator specialist.

The most obvious solution of all turned out to be the right one. The lousy thing was so rusted inside that water could hardly circulate. That had been the root of the problem all along. But why hadn't I thought of it earlier?

I'm not sure I appreciated the full extent of the Buick's lesson as I stood on the side of the road in Minneapolis. I only remember the frustration of having another supposed solution prove ineffective. Back to the drawing board.

Now, though, I think the old car's message is clearer. It may be true that some problems, no matter who you consult or how hard you try, keep surfacing like whales, gigantic and immovable. And it may be that our flaws are irreparable. But sometimes, just when we've accepted them, a solution appears, simple and obvious. I hope so.

After the radiator was fixed, the car ran beautifully for years. May we all be so fortunate.

Machine

Leslie Heywood, 1998

Leslie Heywood, a former University of Arizona track and cross country runner, is the author of the memoir *Pretty Good for a Girl: An Athlete's Story*. It is a harrowing tale, a brutally honest look at the pressures faced by a talented woman runner. In the following excerpt we glimpse a day in her life, a troubled young athlete in a chilling spiral, as she compulsively trains, obsessed and tormented by her body.

It's morning, very early, and the air isn't cold or warm but a little flat. I look at the luminous red numbers telling me it's a bit past four. I nod and press my lips together with satisfaction because I've done it again, woken myself up by the discipline of my internal clock. I don't need any machines, I'm one myself. I sit up and look at one of my roommates, also on the team, sleeping deeply in her bed across the room.

Janine won't get up and she won't be out there this early. This is what makes me different, what sets me apart from her. I'm willing to go to great lengths, and she, well, she, if I could talk about it but out of politeness I don't, is a little lazy, not like me, who survives on six hours of sleep to leave enough time for training and Latin at eight, the time you're always sure to be able to get the class you want because most people are too lazy to get out of bed. My mother keeps asking why I can't be more like Janine, who smiles at my mother and seems happy, talks to her in a pleasant way. "She's balanced, Leslie," my mother says. "You could learn something from her. You're too extreme. Winning isn't everything." I suppress the urge to hit her when she says this.

Why can't my mother get it? Every champion I ever knew of was extreme, and winning *is* everything. Balance is why Janine is a mediocre runner, and she is the last person in the world I want to be like. Balance is why she doesn't get up until seven. At four a.m. you've got the whole world to yourself, it's yours, it's yours, no one else around you to step over or around you or to get in your way and I stretch and punch straight into my leg to make sure it's still hard and glance over at her again.

Breathing, breathing, so much peace. That's exactly what makes Janine happy to be on the second string, to run at the back of the pack every practice, when for me every day is a race, every time I line up with other bodies and fly over the ground. I can't stand to have anyone in front of me, not for a single sprint, not in warmup, not ever. She's happy, and she smiles all the time. She's so normal, so content, but she's a little fatter than those of us in the first string.

She's got that extra layer softening her edge and by that you can tell she's not as intense, that she's pretty, she's soft. No one would say Janine's fat, by any means, she's just not like us, stripped down, every fiber out there, twitching, carving, working like a muscle should, carving us a space, getting us noticed.

She trails along and is moral support and no one ever talks to her like she matters. She doesn't because if she didn't go to a meet no one would notice, it would make no difference whatsoever in our scores. She always runs with that pack that's just there, hanging on. I'm not sure why Coach wants them around, those nonscholarship girls who'll never beat us. They go to our workouts just to do it. There's no end, no goal, just improve their own times and I don't get it. Here I am up by exactly 4:06, and I've got myself trained to wake up and do this every day and I move through the perfect, perfect quiet. I'm glad no one else gets up, that every day they tell me, "I don't see how you do it," because it's the way I get ahead and it's so simple, you just get up.

So I head for the stairs, wincing a bit from the pain in my right foot. As I put my weight down I can feel that twinge in my hip but it's all right because it'll go away almost as soon as I start to run. I'm out the door and into that rush of cool air and silence that soak over my skin, for at this hour I've even beat the birds. There's such an extreme hush because there aren't any cars, which usually ride in a solid stream so you get used to the noise like a wall of sound always above you pressing you down. But it's not here right now. The wall has opened up and I can move like silver liquid. I head up the street for the first mile of four and within twenty strides all the pain goes and I am cruising starlight, miles, bigger than my own shadow and stretching out like the expansion of a thousand lungs. I fly and fly and everything else drops away.

About a mile in I stop at the same spot, a flat space of ground under the pine trees by the medical center, a corner just back from the road, out of sight. I drop to the ground and hit my first five hundred sit-ups, my back flat and my hands behind my head, knees raised, lifting my chest enough so my shoulders clear the ground but the small of my back stays in place. I feel that plane of muscle in between my hipbones roll tight and then I concentrate on all the squares that run down the middle. They punch in waves like they're supposed to. It's nice, I can count on it, they always respond. I drop my shoulders, relax half a second.

I'm up and back and at about this point the light has started to lift enough that you can make out the shapes that fall out of the path of the traffic lights. Light lifts enough to wake the doves, and their voices wash over me and the air breathes and I'm up again onto the second leg. It has a stop just like this one at the end of it and I hit five hundred more, and the same happens again on the third and the fourth. By the time I pull back up to those concrete stairs with the shaky railings where the iron shakes and squeaks at every step, I've hit two thousand and my stomach feels toned and tight and my lungs worked up and my legs awake and looking for more.

I give them that later. Now I slip through the sticking, ugly door that sort of grates on the way in and I grab my Latin and put on the water to boil for tea.

My roommates won't be up for a long time and I lose myself in declensions for a while and the water boils and I feel the heat of the ceramic cup and hear the hot water soak over the tea smelling of raspberries and lime, and I let it sit until it's very strong and then sweeten it with one pink packet of saccharin I buy in big boxes and the waves of smell and sweetness soothe my head. I forget my foot is throbbing, clean and hot like hungry needles. I forget my hip is more than just a twinge, a pain that sings out clear and bright if I move it, and I let the heat steam over my face and breathe in. I boil another, set a piece of bread in the toaster. I wait one hundred seconds, then pop it out just right, that golden brown that doesn't cry for butter. I get the jar of Smucker's and measure a drop that will cover the bread, give me ten calories more. I bite in. It lasts a while.

I head for the shower and take the stairs one by one, leaning a lot on the rail so I don't have to put too much weight on that hip. I make it down mostly on my good leg and take four Advils right away to dull that pain, shut it up. I make the shower stinging hot but nothing stops the stinging in my foot. It's in the bones of the third metatarsal just under my third toe and as I stand in the heat I can feel it digging at me like I've got spines in there or maybe strips of lead.

I scrub down my hair just the right amount and wait until the rollers are hot. They stay in ten minutes. I touch on a light coat of paint, blend a faint line of blush over the bones along my cheeks, nose, and chin, darken my lashes, brush the curl out, spray it down. Moving slowly, trying to avoid using the hip, I struggle into a short sundress, because though it's only April it's already hot. As I reach back to tie the strings I get a picture in my head of how my back must look, its clean, clean lines, and the cleanness of my legs and I imagine for a minute what my Latin teacher must see when I walk in. I see a steel machine flounced by a dress and who can resist that contrast because my face is soft and beautiful enough and my hair is like rich cotton candy. I feel how the blue strings cross under my shoulder blades, distinct, and I raise my arms flexing the muscle which here at least doesn't hurt. By the time I'm out the door at a quarter till eight my roommates are stirring and I get out quick enough to avoid them, swimming caffeine and endorphins. I try to walk proud but the pain in my foot slows me down.

In Latin sure enough my T.A. looks up when I walk in and he looks at me through lots of declensions. I'm already tan from track work and my hair's bleaching out even a little more white. I look down at my hands, thin like cords of muscle with no protective wrappers, strong hands. I shift my leg, trying not to aggravate that hip, and the muscle curves up nice and the blue skirt rests on it like a gentle hand and as soon as the bell rings I gather my books and try to get up without wincing. I absorb the bright blue shock without showing it on my face; instead I smile and pick up my books and head for the training room across campus.

This early in the morning it's just me and a few of the football players, who are repairing the damage from last fall, trying to catch up before training becomes too intensive this spring. I try to walk straight but it hurts. I find my trainer. His eyebrow twists up, "How is it?" "When I'm running it's fine, it's when I stop." "Well, you don't run all the time." He looks at me as if maybe I do. I look down. "My shoulder's starting to get like the hip, and the pain in the foot isn't better." He says, "You know it won't until you take off more time. I think you should. Remember it's fractured and when you train on it the bones open wider." "Fine," I say, "We've got just another month, it can't get too wide. I can take off a few weeks before cross-country. But why is my shoulder starting to feel like my hip? What can we put on it while I'm in the suds?"

He takes my arm and rotates the bones, and they grind like metal and I wince. "It's bursitis," he says, "just like your hip. I'll give you a cold pack for it while you're in the heat, and then when you're icing your leg we'll give it heat." I shrug my shoulders. "Oh, great, my old favorites, hot and cold. So when will you turn over those drugs?" He grins and pushes my right shoulder, the only part that doesn't hurt. "You'll have to go to Dr. Quack for that—hit the water." I limp to the whirlpool, a vat big enough for twenty bodies. Here I can limp. The pain can show, we all do it. I make a game face, dragging my hip getting in. When I lift it grates like sandpaper over an axle. Laughing, I try to balance legs and heat packs. I look up at the football player across from me, twice as big as me, his leg packed deep in the whirling water.

I ask him, "So why're you in?" and he tells me, "This time it's my knee, it got hit pretty hard and it blew since I planted my foot one direction, got knocked the other." I nod. "That's a little like mine. My foot and hip and now my shoulder. It's the inside leg. It takes most of the weight every turn around the track." He says, "I know, I can feel that in my sprints." We shake our heads and let the heat soak out the pain.

I'm in a long time. I drag myself out and wipe down my leg. The team doctor approaches, looking grave. He rotates my arm around, just as the trainer did, and then my leg, scanning my face for the degree of pain. He nods to himself. He tells me cortisone is the only way to build up the protection around the joints that has been stripped away. It'll cover the bones like a blanket, a coating of oil. I'll finish up practice, the season. Then I can take some time off to rest.

But I can't take time off. I just can't. I think about it as I sit in my car. I head toward practice, and I look down for the tenth time and this time I am sure. My shadow has caught up with me and she's starting to set herself free. She's going to take me over. It's my swollen stomach, yawning like a mouth. All over my legs, big as trunks. I grab a handful of flesh from my thigh. So soft. A sweet sickness twists in my throat, my stomach tightens. It's too loose. It hangs there, dough, like rotting leaves. Fat. I try to straighten a leg out, the one not on the gas. Flex hard. Look. Too much. I know that my thighs touch each other when I stand up. How did this happen? It's the worst in the car. They spread out. They're so big. I pinch them, and something gives. Fat. Dough. There it is.

I've got to do something about this. My stomach is curved. It sticks out. If I go on like this I'll look like them. Like her. Like the lower half of my body is swollen, misplaced. There's this woman on the team. We call her "breadbasket" because her lower abdomen is so swollen and round, sticking out. I can't be her. Not at all. Not one bit. Out of nowhere I think of my mother. Fat at a hundred. Me too. It's what my father would say, "You fat bitch."

I remember looking at her when he says it. Summer and the birds that stop singing, smothered by cotton and everything else I can't hear. It's hot, and it seems like the air conditioner never runs for thrift, so we don't wear a whole lot of clothes.

I look at her, draw myself up, curl my lip. My father is right. I look and think, *you're the most disgusting thing I can imagine* when she is sitting down, warm flesh puffing under a halter top she has made herself. There it is. A roll of whiteness mouthing up. This makes me different. No rolls, no rolls, no rolls. *I'm not you I'm not you I'm not you I'm not you who the fuck are you and how can you stand to be so weak and let yourself get like this how can you stand to sit so still why aren't you up why don't you move how can you just let yourself go?* She weighs 100. My father is hard, like a crust. A solid slab, a blackened shape that takes up space. I can't even see her, except the messiness of her lines. Just the puff. I can't breathe. I've got to get out and I run for the fourth time that day, a quick few miles along the darkening street just to make certain I'm solid, my feet can breathe, my stomach is rippling cuts.

Like now, as I head for the track with my cortisoned feet. I can't stop working out, there's no way.

White Men Can't Run

Amby Burfoot, 1992

The dominance of black runners had been observed for years but considered too politically incorrect to discuss openly—until Amby Burfoot's brave article in *Runner's World*. His well-researched piece did much to clear the air. And of course, it triggered much controversy—the magazine received an estimated 10,000 letters about the article.

This month in Barcelona, for the first time in the history of the Olympic Games, runners of African heritage will win every men's running race. West Africans, including American blacks of West African descent, will sweep the gold medals at all distances up to and including the 400-meter hurdles. And East Africans and North Africans will win everything from the 800 meters through the marathon.

These results won't surprise any close observer of the international track scene. Ever since America's Eddie Tolan won the 100 meters at the 1932 Los Angeles Games, becoming the first black gold medalist in an Olympic track race, black runners have increasingly dominated Olympic and World competitions. An analysis of the three World Championships meets paints the clearest picture. In 1983, blacks won 14 of the 33 available medals in running races. In 1987, they won 19. Last September in Tokyo, they won 29.

What's more surprising is the lack of public dialogue on the phenomenon. The shroud of silence results, of course, from our societal taboo against discussing racial differences—a taboo that is growing stronger in these politically correct times.

A good example: *Sports Illustrated*'s changed approach to the subject. In early 1971, *Sports Illustrated* published a landmark story, "An Assessment of 'Black Is Best'" by Martin Kane, that explored various physical reasons for the obvious success of black athletes on the American sports scene. African-American sociologists, particularly Harry Edwards, wasted little time in blasting Kane's article. Wrote Edwards, famed for orchestrating black power demonstrations at the 1968 Olympics: "The argument that blacks are physically superior to whites is merely a racist ideology camouflaged to appeal to the ignorant, the unthinking and the unaware."

Edwards was right to question arguments attributing sports success primarily to physiology. American blacks fear that such an overemphasis on their physical skills may call into question their mental skills. Besides, sports suc-

From *Runner's World,* August 1992. Reprinted by permission of Rodale, Inc.

cess clearly demands more than just a great body. It also requires desire, hard work, family and social support, positive role models and, often, potential for financial reward.

For these reasons, the University of Texas's Bob Malina, Ph.D., the country's leading expert on physical and performance differences among ethnic groups, has long argued for what he calls a "biocultural approach." Nurture (the overall cultural environment) is just as important as biology (genetics).

Because Edwards and others attacked so stridently, mere discussion of the subject grew to be regarded, ipso facto, as a racist activity and hence something to be avoided at all cost. Last year, *Sports Illustrated* returned to the fertile subject of black athletes in American sports, devoting dozens of articles to the topic in a multi-issue series. Not one of these articles made even passing mention of physical differences between whites and blacks. Likewise, *USA Today* barely scratched the surface in its own four-day special report "Race & Sports: Myths & Realities."

When NBC-TV broadcast its brave "Black Athletes: Fact and Fiction" program in 1989, the network had trouble locating a scientist willing to discuss the subject in the studio. Instead, host Tom Brokaw had to patch through to two experts attending a conference in Brussels. In beginning my research for this story, I contacted one of America's most respected sports scientists. He didn't want to talk about the subject. "Go ahead and hang yourself," he said, "but you're not going to hang me with you."

Fear rules. Why? Because this is a story about inherited abilities, and Americans aren't ready for the genetics revolution that's already sweeping over us. In the next 10 years, scientists worldwide will devote $3 billion to the Human Genome Project. In the process, they will decipher all 100,000 human genes, cure certain inherited diseases (like cystic fibrosis, Tay-Sachs and sickle cell disease), and tell us more about ourselves than we are prepared to know. Including, in all likelihood, why some people run faster than others.

———————————•———————————

Many casual sports fans mistakenly believe that athletic competitions are fair. In fact, this is one reason so many people enjoy sports. Politics and corporate ladder-climbing may be rotten to the core, but sports at least provide a level playing field.

This simple notion of fairness doesn't go very far. Just ask any female athlete. Women excel in law school, medical practice, architectural design and the business world, but they never win at sports. They don't even want to compete side by side with men in sports (as they do in all other areas of social, cultural and economic life). Why not? Because sports success stems from certain physical strengths and abilities that women simply don't have. We all acknowledge this.

But we have more trouble understanding that what is true for women is also true for some male groups. In some sports, certain racial groups face overwhelming odds. Take the Japanese. The Japanese are passionate about sports and surely rank among the world's most-disciplined, hardest-working and highest-achieving peoples. These qualities have brought them great success in many areas and should produce the same in sports.

Yet the Japanese rarely succeed at sports. They fall short because, on average, they *are* short. Most big-time sports require size, speed and strength. A racial group lacking these qualities must struggle against great odds to excel.

Of course, a few sports, including marathoning, gymnastics and ice-skating, actually reward small stature. You've heard of Kristi Yamaguchi and Midori Ito, right? It's no mistake that the Japanese are better at ice-skating than, say, basketball. It's genetics.

———————————•———————————

A scientist interested in exploring physical and performance differences among different racial groups couldn't invent a better sport than running. First of all, it's a true worldwide sport, practiced and enjoyed in almost every country around the globe. Also, it doesn't require any special equipment, coaching or facilities. Abebe Bikila proved this dramatically in the 1960 Olympic Games when—shoeless, little coached and inexperienced—he won the marathon.

Given the universality of running, it's reasonable to expect that the best runners should come from a wide range of countries and racial groups. We should find that Europeans, Asians, Africans and North and South Americans all win about the same number of gold medals in running events.

This isn't, however, what happens. Nearly all the sprints are won by runners of West African descent. Nearly all the distance races are won, remarkably, by runners from just one small corner of one small African country—Kenya.

Track and field is the perfect laboratory sport for two more important reasons. First, two of the most exciting events—the 100 meters and the marathon—represent the far reaches of human physical ability. A sprinter must be the fastest, most explosive of humans. A marathoner must be the most enduring. Any researcher curious about physical differences between humans could look at runners who excel at these two events and expect to find a fair number of differences. If these differences then broke down along racial lines . . . well, so be it.

Second, since running requires so little technique and equipment, success results *directly* from the athlete's power, endurance or other purely physical attributes. This explains why drug-testing is so important in track. If a golfer, tennis player, gymnast or even basketball player were to take steroids or to blood dope, we'd be hard pressed to say that the drugs helped the athlete. In these sports, too much else—rackets, clubs, specialized moves—separate the athlete's physiology from his or her scoring potential.

Runners find, on the other hand, that if they improve the body (even illegally), the performance has to improve. Some scientists even acknowledge that a simple running race can measure certain physical traits better than any laboratory test. The results we observe in the Olympic Stadium are as valid as they get.

———————●———————

The evidence for a black genetic advantage in running falls into two categories: physique and physiology. The first refers to body size and proportions, the second to below-the-surface differences in the muscles, the enzymes, the cell structures and so on.

To appreciate the significance of either, you must first understand that very small differences between two racial groups can lead to very dramatic differences in sports performance. For example, two groups, A and B, can share 99 percent of the same human genes and characteristics. They can be virtually identical. Nevertheless, if the 1 percent of variation occurs in a characteristic that determines success at a certain sport, then group A might win 90 percent of the Olympic medals in that sport.

Over the years, numerous studies of physique have compared blacks of West African heritage with white Americans and consistently reached the same conclusions. Among these conclusions: Blacks have less body fat, narrower hips, thicker thighs, longer legs and lighter calves. From a biomechanical perspective, this is an impressive package. Narrow hips allow for efficient, straight-ahead running. Strong quadriceps muscles provide horsepower, and light calves reduce resistance.

Speaking a year ago at the American College of Sports Medicine's symposium on "Ethnic Variations in Human Performance," Lindsey Carter, Ph.D., observed: "It appears that the biomechanical demands of a particular sport limit the range of physiques that can satisfy these demands." Carter, a San Diego State University professor who has conducted a series of studies of Olympic athletes, concluded: "If all else is equal, can a difference in ethnicity confer advantages in physical performance? From a biomechanical point of view, the answer is yes."

A number of direct performance studies have also shown a distinct black superiority in simple physical tasks such as running and jumping. Often, the subjects in these studies were children (for example, fourth-graders in the Kansas City public schools), which tends to mute the criticism that blacks outrun and outjump whites because society channels black youngsters into sports.

A few studies have even looked beyond simple muscle performance. In one of the first, Robert L. Browne of Southwestern Louisiana Institute showed that black college students had a significantly faster patellar tendon reflex time (the familiar knee-jerk response) than white students. Reflex time is an important variable to study for two reasons. First, because many sports obviously require lightning reflexes. And, second, because classic biological theory holds that faster reflexes will tend to create stronger muscles, which will tend to create denser bones. All of these have been observed in blacks, whose denser bones may make it particularly hard for them to succeed in one major Olympic sport—swimming.

———————●———————

Since the study of black-white differences frightens off many U.S. scientists, it's no surprise that the best research on the subject comes from other laboratories around the world. In the last decade, scientists from Quebec City, Stockholm and Cape Town, South Africa, have been leading the way.

Claude Bouchard, Ph.D., of Laval University in Quebec City, is perhaps the world's leading sports geneticist, as well as a foremost expert in the genetics of obesity. When the *New England Journal of Medicine* published a Bouchard study on human obesity two years ago, it made headlines around the world for its finding that degree of fatness and locale of fat deposition (hips, waist, etc.) was largely determined by heredity.

Bouchard achieved these and many of his other remarkable results through carefully controlled studies of twins who live in and around Quebec City. From such experiments, he has determined the "heritability" of many human traits, including some relating to athletic performance. Bouchard has shown, for example, that anaerobic power is from 44 to 92 percent inherited, while max VO_2 is only 25 percent inherited. From these findings, we might quickly conclude that sprinters are "born" but distance runners are "made," which, loosely, is what track observers have always thought about sprinters and distance runners.

What "makes" distance runners, of course, is their training, and Bouchard has also investigated "trainability." It's surprisingly easy to do. You simply gather a bunch of out-of-shape people, put them on the same training program and follow their progress according to certain key physiological measures. The results are astonishing. Some subjects don't improve at all or take a long time to improve; some improve almost instantly and by large amounts. This trainability trait, Bouchard has found, is about 75 percent inherited.

This means that potential for distance-running success may be just as genetically determined as potential for sprinting success. Which is why many coaches and physiologists have been saying for years that the best way to improve your marathon time is to "choose your parents carefully."

Bouchard is now examining physiological differences between white French Canadians and black West Africans, both culled from the student population at Laval. In one study, the only one of its kind ever performed between these two groups, the researchers compared muscle-fiber percentages. The West Africans had significantly more fast-twitch fibers and anaerobic enzymes than the whites. Exercise physiologists have long believed that fast-twitch muscle fibers confer an advantage in explosive, short-duration power events such as sprinting.

Two Bouchard disciples, Pierre F.M. Ama and Jean-Aime Simoneau, next decided to test the two groups' actual power output in the lab. On a 90-second leg extension test (basically the same exercise we all do on our weight benches), the black and white subjects performed about equally for the first 30 seconds. Beyond 30 seconds, the whites were able to produce significantly more power than the blacks.

This experiment failed to show what the researchers expected—that West African blacks should be better sprinters. It may, on the other hand, have shown that these blacks generally wouldn't perform well in continuous events lasting several minutes or longer.

Of course, a leg extension test isn't the same thing as the real world of track and field. In particular, it can't account for any of the biomechanical running advantages that blacks may have. Which could explain the curious findings of David Hunter.

Two years before Ama and Simoneau published their study, Hunter completed his Ph.D. requirement in exercise physiology at Ohio State University by writing his thesis on "A Comparison of Anaerobic Power Between Black and White Adolescent Males." Hunter began by giving his subjects—high schoolers from Columbus—two laboratory tests that measure anaerobic power. These tests yielded no differences.

Then he decided to turn his subjects loose on the track. There the blacks sprinted and jumped much better than the whites. These results apparently disturbed Hunter, an African-American, whose dissertation concluded that the laboratory results (no differences) were more significant than the real-world results (big differences).

In attempting to balance his results, Hunter noted that a 1969 study in the journal *Ergonomics* found that blacks actually had *less* anaerobic power than whites. What he failed to point out, and perhaps even to recognize, was that the *Ergonomics* study compared a group of Italians with a group of *Kenyans*. Indeed, many of the Kenyan subjects came from the Nandi and Kikuyu tribes, famed for their distance running but scarcely noted for their sprinting (anaerobic power). From running results alone, we would expect these Kenyans to score low on any test of anaerobic power.

I mention this only because I believe it highlights an important point: The word "black" provides little information about anyone or any group. Of the 100,000 genes that determine human makeup, only one to six regulate skin color, so we should assume almost nothing about anyone based on skin color alone. West Africans and East Africans are both black, but in many physical ways they are *more unlike each other* than they are *different from most whites*.

When it comes to assumptions about Africans, we should make just one: The peoples of Africa, short and tall, thick and thin, fast and slow, white and black, represent the fullest and most spectacular variations of humankind to be found anywhere.

———————•———————

Tim Noakes, M.D., director of the Sport Science Centre at the University of Cape Town Medical School, has spent the last thirty years researching the limits of human endurance, largely because of his own, and indeed his whole country's, passion for the 54-mile Comrades Marathon. Noakes's book *Lore of Running* (Leisure Press, 1991) stands as the ultimate compilation of the history, physiology and training methods of long-distance running.

In recent years, Noakes has been trying to learn why South African blacks, who represent only twenty percent of their country's road-racing population, nevertheless take eighty percent of the top positions in South African races. (South African blacks are related to East Africans through their common Bushman ancestors. West African blacks, representing the Negroid race, stand apart.)

In one experiment, Noakes asked two groups of white and black marathoners to run a full marathon on the laboratory treadmill. The two groups were matched for ability and experience. While they weren't among South Africa's elite corps of distance runners, subjects from both groups were good marathoners with times under 2:45.

When the two groups ran on the treadmill at the same speed, the major difference was that the blacks were able to perform at a much higher percentage of their maximum oxygen capacity. The results, published in the *European Journal of Applied Physiology*, showed that the whites could only run at 81 percent of their max VO_2. The blacks could reach 89 percent.

This same characteristic has previously been noted in several great white marathoners including Derek Clayton and Frank Shorter. Clayton and Shorter didn't have a particularly high max VO_2, but they were able to run for long periods of time at a very high percentage of their max. This enabled them to beat other marathoners who actually had higher max VO_2 values.

Among white runners, a Clayton or Shorter is a physiologic rarity. Among black South Africans, however, such capacity may be commonplace. And even though the blacks in Noakes's lab were working very hard, their muscles produced little lactic acid and other products of muscle fatigue. How can they do this?

Noakes speculates that the blacks have a muscle fiber quality, as yet unnamed in scientific circles, that he calls "high fatigue resistance." It's pretty much the opposite of what the Canadian researchers found in their 90-second test of West Africans. Sweden's renowned exercise physiologist Bengt Saltin, Ph.D., director of the Karolinska Institute in Stockholm, has spent most of his professional career investigating the extraordinary endurance performances of nordic skiers, multiday bicyclists, orienteers and distance runners. Since all distance-running roads now lead to Kenya, Saltin decided to travel there two years ago to observe the phenomenon firsthand. He also took a half-dozen national-class Swedish runners with him. Later, he brought several groups of Kenyans back to Stockholm to test them in his lab.

In competitions in Kenya, at and near St. Patrick's high school, which has produced so many world-class runners, the Swedish 800-meter to 10,000-meter specialists were soundly beaten by hundreds of fifteen- to seventeen-year-old Kenyan boys. Indeed, Saltin estimated that this small region of Kenya in the Rift Valley had at least 500 high schoolers who could outrace the Swedes at 2,000 meters.

Back in Stockholm, Saltin uncovered many small differences between the Kenyan and Swedish runners. The results, not yet published in any scientific journal, seemed most extraordinary in the quadriceps muscle area. Here, the Kenyans had more blood-carrying capillaries surrounding the muscle fibers and more mitochondria within the fibers (the mitochondria are the energy-producing "engine" of the muscle).

Saltin also noted that the Kenyans' muscle fibers were smaller than the Swedes. Not small enough to limit performance—except perhaps the high-power production needed for sprinting—but small enough to bring the mitochondria closer to the surrounding capillaries. This "closeness" presumably enhances oxygen diffusion from the densely packed capillaries into the mitochondria.

And when the oxygen gets there, it is burned with incredible efficiency. After hard workouts and races, Saltin noted, Kenyans show little ammonia buildup (from protein combustion) in the muscles—far less than Swedes and other runners. They seem to have more of the muscle enzymes that burn fat and "spare" glycogen and protein. Sparing glycogen, according to a classic tenet of work physiology, is one of the best ways to improve endurance performance. Added together, all these factors give the Kenyans something very close to Tim Noakes's high fatigue resistance.

Saltin believes Kenyan endurance may result from environmental forces. He told *Runner's World*'s "Fast Lane" columnist Owen Anderson, Ph.D., that the Kenyans' remarkable quadriceps muscles could develop from years of walking and running over hills at high altitude. Saltin has observed similar capillary densities among orienteers who train and race through hilly forests, and similar small muscle fibers among nordic skiers who train at altitude.

Of course, Peruvians and Tibetans and other peoples live at altitude and spend all their lives negotiating steep mountain slopes. Yet they don't seem to develop into great distance runners. Why the Kenyans?

The only plausible answer is that Kenyans from the Rift Valley, perhaps more so than any other peoples on Earth, bring together the perfect combination of genetic endowment with environmental and cultural influences. No one can doubt that many Kenyans are born with great natural talents. But much more is also at work. Consider a few of the following:

Boys and girls from west Kenya grow up in a high-altitude environment of surpassing beauty and good weather conditions. From an early age, they must walk and jog across hilly terrain to get anywhere. They are raised in a culture that emphasizes both stoicism (adolescent circumcision) and aggression (cattle raiding). Indeed, the British introduced track and field in Kenya as a way to channel tribal raiding parties into more appropriate behavior. Kip Keino and others since him have provided positive role models, and the society is so male-dominant that Kenyan men are quick to accept their superiority (an aspect of Kenyan society that makes things especially tough for Kenyan women). The financial rewards of modern-day track and road racing provide an income Kenyans can achieve in almost no other activity. In short, nearly everything about Kenyan life points to success (for men) in distance running.

————————•————————

Any close inspection of international track results yields one incontrovertible fact: Black-skinned athletes are winning most races. This phenomenon is likely to grow even more pronounced in the future. Many African athletes, and countries, have barely begun to show their potential.

Yet it would be incredibly myopic to conclude, simply, that blacks are faster than whites. A more accurate—albeit admittedly speculative—phrasing might go something like this: West African blacks seem to be faster sprinters than whites, who are better than East African blacks; and East Africans seem to have more endurance capacity than whites, who are better than West Africans.

Whites, always in the middle. Maybe this explains why whites have managed to hold on the longest in the middle-distance races, where Seb Coe still holds the world record for 800 meters and Steve Cram for the mile. In the past, discussions of racial-group success in sports have largely involved the relative success of blacks in basketball, football and baseball and their relative failure in tennis, golf and swimming. The "country club" aspects of the latter three sports guaranteed that these discussions centered on social and economic status: Blacks weren't good at tennis, golf and swimming because they didn't belong to country clubs. Does an analysis of running add anything new to the discussion?

I think so. Where pure explosive power—that is, sprinting and jumping—are required for excellence in a sport, blacks of West African heritage will excel. The more a sport moves away from speed and toward technique and other prerequisites, like hand-eye coordination, the more other racial groups will find themselves on a level playing field.

The Kenyans and other East Africans, despite their amazing endurance, will hardly come to dominate world sports. As many of us distance runners have learned the hard way—from a lifetime of reality checks on playgrounds and various courts and fields—endurance counts for next to nothing in most big-time sports.

While sports aren't necessarily fair, we can still take heart in the many exceptions to the rule. The truly outstanding athlete always fights his way to the top, no matter what the odds, inspiring us with his courage and determination. In the movie *White Men Can't Jump*, the hero, Billy Hoyle, wins the big game with a slam-dunk shot that had previously eluded him. Billy's climactic shot stands as testimony to the ability of any man, of any race, to rise high, beat the odds and achieve his goal. The marvel of the human spirit is that it accepts no limits.

Of course, *Jump* is only a movie. The Olympic track races in Barcelona are for real.

Evolution of Intelligent Running Ape People

Bernd Heinrich, 2000

Bernd Heinrich is an eminent biologist as well as a former ultramarathon champion. In his book *Why We Run: A Natural History,* he draws on both backgrounds to explain why humans, among all animals, are great long distance runners. In the following excerpt, Heinrich explores the evolutionary adaptations that helped our species compete successfully on the African plain.

> When you experience the run, you relive the hunt. Running is about thirty miles of chasing prey that can outrun you in a sprint, and tracking it down and bringing life back to your village. It's a beautiful thing.
>
> ~Shawn Found, the 2000 American national champion
> at 25 kilometers

The apelike creatures that were our ancestors were a strange breed. They were perhaps at first awkward scavengers on the African plains, who later became bipedal predators. They were neither big nor swift and had to make up for it with sociality and smarts.

The above scenario of our evolution as bipedal savanna hunting apes and ultimately people is like a large house with many rooms in various stages of construction, from rough to nearly finished. It is the result of constant restructuring and elaboration by many builders of a great range of expertise. The various parts were contributed or built by paleontologists, anthropologists, behavioral field biologists, ecologists, physiologists, and anatomists. I will here try to show some of the evidence and logic for the construction of the main frame of the house that contains so much. I will then explore what I think are ramifications relative to our psychological and physiological capacities as endurance predators. In this limited space I cannot here argue all the pros and cons of each specific point. I can only review the scenario as it seems to me to make the most sense. And a central part of that scenario is, I think, our endurance. Furthermore, the key to endurance, as all distance runners know, is not just a matter of sweat glands. It's vision. To endure is to have a clear goal and the ability to extrapolate to it with the mind—the ability to keep in mind what is not before the eye. Vision allows us to reach into the future, whether it's to kill an antelope or to achieve a record time in a race.

———————————•———————————

Our specialty as bipedal runners spans a history of at least 6 million years. It probably began in Africa, when open or semiopen plains were replacing forests and our ancestors began to diverge from other apelike creatures to venture out of the forests and feed on the vast assemblage of herbivores supported by the growing seas of grass. There were many other predators out there and little safety from them in trees. Nor was it easy to hide.

Life on the plains generates arms races between predators and prey. Here we find such sprint champions as the cheetah and the various species of antelopes it hunts. Also on the plains were (and still are) such cooperative predators as pack-running canids and hyenas, which catch prey by capitalizing on the weakness that sprint speed produces, namely compromised endurance. In turn, the sprinting prey species sought and found some measure of safety in numbers. Antelopes are consummate herd animals.

The very first bipedal hominids were undoubtedly not superb runners and they needed alternatives to raw running speed for survival. They would have cooperated to hunt, as some monkeys and apes do today. On the plains, even some normally solitary predators became social in order to hunt. Lions, who live in groups unlike all other felines, are a prime example.

Speed was useful, and necessary as well. We'd never run 60 miles an hour like a cheetah, but a cheetah doesn't need to run for an hour. It needs to run only for a half minute, and it can't run much farther before it runs head-on into the problem of overheating and lactic acid buildup, and must stop. The speed-disadvantaged hominids had other advantages beyond their already existing sociality. Not only did they have grasping hands useful for climbing and throwing, and ultimately for tool use, plus an edge on intelligence, they also developed running endurance while remaining upright.

Human bipedalism in running has been thought enigmatic because it is energetically expensive relative to quadrupedal running. Nevertheless, when used for traveling long distances on the plains, bipedalism was likely a great improvement over the knuckle-walking of hominids' ancestors. In evolution, almost every solution is the result of compromises. Energy efficiency was sacrificed in favor of freeing the hands for other use. For instance, hands were useful not only for throwing rocks and sticks, and later for making, carrying, and using weapons, but also for carrying our babies and prey to our safe campsites. Our progenitors, like chimps today, could likely hurl objects. By standing upright, they could see farther and defend themselves, when necessary, in several directions at once.

British physiologist Peter Wheeler has proposed that our bipedalism evolved in part for thermoregulation under exposure to the blazing tropical sun. As the examples of the hawk moths, bees, and camels demonstrated, reducing heat input or increasing heat loss translates to greater endurance. Wheeler photographed a model humanoid in either bipedal versus quadrupedal posture and found that in the bipedal posture it experienced 60 percent less direct solar radiation. In addition, in that posture the body is better situated to take advantage of breezes for convective cooling. . . .Bipedalism can enhance speed, but even if it did not, and even if it is more energetically costly, it was still a better bargain than giving up our tool-using hands, reducing our visual range, and compromising our endurance in the heat. So, on balance, human bipedalism is not enigmatic at all.

The hominid line to which we belong likely diverged from apelike creatures about 5 to 8 million years ago. The first fossil traces of that hominid line have been found in 4.4-million-year-old rocks from Ethiopia that contain a creature called *Ardipithecus ramidus*. The australopithecines, or "southern apes" (after their discovery in Southern Africa), which were derived from *Ardipithecus*, were small brained relative to us, but as determined from skeletal remains and from footprints, they already walked upright. *Australopithecus afarensis*, of Lucy fame—the three-and-a-half-foot-tall female, was discovered in Ethiopia in 1974—is one of the best-known australopithecine fossils found. Australopithecines were bipedal intermediaries between the apelike and the subsequent *Homo*-like forms and were unlikely to have been able to outrun most large predators. Australopithecines needed other defenses. The endurance running capability that subsequently evolved in humans and that was derived from australopithecines must have been under some selective pressure other than avoiding predation.

Most likely, the australopithecines diverged from forest dwellers to occupy the dangerous plains nor to avoid predation but to seek food there, despite, and perhaps because of, the predation there. Meat was in abundance on the plains for those who could catch it, for those who could take it from such other carnivores as leopards, cheetahs, and lions, and for those who could compete for it against hyenas, jackals, and vultures.

Given the reasonable assumption that the australopithecines were group-living as most present-day apes, it is not difficult to envision a plausible scenario for how they got their food. Traveling in groups and coming upon a predator-killed carcass, they might have chased off the owner with sticks and rocks. Takeovers would have been difficult at night, and it would have been easiest in the middle of the day when the predator had retired into the shade, leaving carcasses untended or at least less vigorously defended.

Intelligent hominids would have quickly learned how to find carcasses. Some years ago, I dropped off a dead horse near my mother's house in Maine to feed ravens. Her two dogs found the carcass with the raven crowd. Ever since then, the dogs have become eager raven watchers. Early plains hominids would have been no less able than circling vultures, my mother's dogs, and myself to recognize and heed signs of a recent kill.

On the African veldt, most predators need to kill frequently, because what they don't eat almost immediately is consumed by scavengers or spoils quickly. There is great competition for scavengers to be there first after a kill has been made, and the fastest come on the wing. In an intact northern ecosystem, Yellowstone Park, it is the same, only there the scavengers that come within a minute or so of wolves' making a kill are ravens, not vultures. Eagles, bears, and coyotes then use the ravens' activity as a cue that indicates the kill, and they also rush in. In Yellowstone, within about seven hours after wolves kill an elk there is nothing left but the bones. In Africa even the bones are eaten (by hyenas), and the carcasses are consumed even quicker.

During my year in Tanganyika (now Tanzania), I found one morning an unattended freshly dead cow in a deep streambed. By noon, when I came by again, there were well over a hundred vultures there feeding, and more were still streaming in all the time from all directions at once. Vultures, too, find carcasses by watching others, and their mobility allows these birds to exploit the diurnal niche of predator-provided meat. Similar competition for predator-killed carcasses would have existed on the grass savannas where our anthropoid ancestors evolved. Then as now, traveling fast and long would have been a great premium for getting to predator-killed carcasses before the competitors devoured it. Ultimately, the hominids' mobility in the heat could have been transferred to getting their own fresh meat, by hunting.

Although the earliest australopithecine-like hominids were probably not swift enough to run down healthy adult antelopes, there were undoubtedly many advantages for them to become ever faster. The races against scavengers and against others of their own species, that is, their closest competitors, could have become the bridge to races with formidable live prey. Once hominids were fast enough, they potentially could run down such weaker prey as calves, the old, and the injured.

Ultimately, what early hominids did routinely may have been less significant than what they could do in the times of greatest need, such as when no dead or injured animals were available. Running ability would have become evermore valuable on the plains after meat became an important part of the diet. By about 2 to 3 million years ago, the bipedal plains hominids already had a leg and foot structure almost identical to our own. The fossilized footprints that Mary Leakey discovered show that they walked like us. It is reasonable to suppose that they could also run even before they evolved to several species of *Homo*, of which *H. erectus* was the first to leave Africa.

Another theory, one recently proposed by Richard W. Wrangham and colleagues, is that the big evolutionary change from australopithecines to *Homo* occurred after the invention of cooking, primarily of energy-rich underground tubers. Cooked food, being easier to digest than raw, increased the available energy supply and freed us up to hunt. If so, then the cooking hypothesis is not an alternate to the hunting hypothesis. Rather, it is one complementary to it; both cooking and meat eating would have promoted reduction of gut size, improved speed, and range of movement, and permitted even more hunting.

At this point in the argument, there will surely be skeptics who will doubt that our ancient hominid ancestors could become specialized enough as endurance predators to outrun swift prey that had *already* evolved to outsprint the world's swiftest predators. To elaborate the hypothesis, it is now necessary first to examine what some present-day apes do routinely, and then to consider the evolution of our uniquely human physiology, social structure, and psychology.

Chimps are generally considered to be frugivores. Nevertheless, they prize meat and hunt monkeys, young antelopes, and other mammals. Studying hunting parties of male chimps at Gombe in 1995, Craig Stanford found them depleting one-fifth of their prey population of colobus monkeys each year. Group hunts are effective. In just a half day of observing olive baboons in Kenya's Amboseli Park, I once saw a troupe of about fifty individuals catch a hare, tear it apart, and eat it with great gusto. Only two or three individuals of the dispersed troupe chased the hare, but the panicked animal was intercepted by others.

Hunting by chimps and baboons is largely secondary to other foraging, but prey is almost routinely taken as opportunity affords. These primates do not rely on meat, nor do they travel long distances in pursuit, yet they eat meat when they can, and sometimes they even hunt systematically and with great vigor. In short, even hominids that are unspecialized for a meat diet are willing and able not only to eat meat but also to hunt.

If our hominid ancestors millions of years ago on the hot open African grass plains *relied* on meat, they would presumably have evolved physiological adaptations to help them obtain it. Animals evolve unique features and capacities when they face unique situations. Of all the insects, for example, only the Apache desert cicada, *Diceroprocta apacha*, has evolved a sweating response. This insect has water available for use because it sucks plant juice, and sweating not only permits it to be active at noon on the hottest days in the hottest season of the year, it also chooses that time to be active, when it escapes its avian predators, because they are forced to yield the field. Similarly, the uniquely heat-tolerant Saharan desert ants, *Cataglyphis bambycina*, become active only when their major predators (lizards) retire from the heat. A similar scenario of taking to the field when the great predators were forced to lie low, and were less able to vigorously defend their kills, likely applies to our hominid ancestors. Humans are unique, as I will show, in having an ample sweating response that allows them to engage in sustained running in the heat, even under direct sun. Furthermore, our 3 million sweat glands excrete not only water for cooling but also toxic metabolic wastes, such as the ammonia and uric acid that are produced when we eat meat.

During my year on the bird-hunting expedition of Tanganyika, I experienced what ancient hunters were up against. I shall never forget my feelings of dreary claustrophobia during the months we spent in wet, dense, dripping mountain forests. These times contrasted with feelings of glorious exhilaration when I was out on the open savanna steppe with its scattered acacia trees and large vistas. On the savanna, to catch even small birds, I had to wander extensively. I wandered half of each day until it was time to return to camp, where my mother cooked our meals and prepared the day's specimens. I never carried water with me, to avoid being encumbered, but I was often forced to slow down or rest due to the heat. Although the heat often made my bird hunting difficult at midday, I could still travel freely. I could cope because I sweat copiously.

Internally generated heat in an animal forced to keep moving or exercising in the heat on the open plains under the African equatorial sun is one of the most potent factors limiting endurance. I could literally feel that fact, and I had shown experimentally that hawk moths, even without solar heat input, are limited to about two minutes of exercise even at modest room temperatures if their mechanism for getting rid of metabolic heat is disrupted. Similarly, jackrabbits, kangaroos, and cheetahs, even without experimental disruption of their heat-dissipating ability, are limited to only a few minutes of running under common field conditions. It is a reasonable assumption that our ancestors would also have experienced selective pressure not only to get rid of body heat by sweating, but also to reduce heat input from the sun in order to maintain sustained physical activity at a time when they had perhaps the most to gain.

Different animals have evolved diverse means of dealing with often debilitating direct solar radiation. In New Guinea, close to the equator as in Central Africa, I found that butterflies heat to lethal body temperatures in as little as one minute if subjected to direct sunshine and prevented from using their wings for shading.

Our erect posture (with our consequent bipedal locomotion) would have been a preadaptation for us in the equatorial sun, both reducing the total amount of direct exposure to solar input and simultaneously increasing the area of exposure of skin to moving and cooling air. The tops of our heads would have been the area where solar input is focused to, potentially endangering the extremely heat-sensitive brain because of its already high internal heat load from metabolism. Thus, although bipedalism reduced overall heat input, it would have accentuated local heating of the most heat-sensitive body part.

A solution to this problem evolved. The human brain has a special network of veins that acts as a heat radiator to dissipate the extra heat load. Vein tracks on fossil skull bones indicate that the gracile australopithecines already had the same blood circulating network; this indicates that they had experienced strong selective pressure to prevent overheating.

Insects have analogous solutions. I heated honeybees on the head and discovered they not only regurgitated liquid for cooling, they also pumped more blood through the head to help carry the heat away. As in other animals subjected to potential overheating from the sun, upright hominids on the open equatorial plains likely would have evolved heat shields to reduce the solar heat input to the brain. Desert ground squirrels shield themselves with their bushy tail, desert beetles use their wing covers, camels have humps and thick dorsal hair—and we are unique in having bushy head hair that covers both head and shoulders from the sun's rays. Head hair probably evolved in part for the very purpose that it now can still serve, although it later could also have become a sexually selected trait. Later still it would also have served as insulation to reduce body heat *loss*, after *Homo erectus* left Africa and invaded the mammoth steppes of the north and became ever more reliant on a meat diet.

That latter invasion occurred recently, only about sixty thousand years ago, and it may have coincided with the inventions of spear throwing and clothing.

Our nakedness and exceptionally numerous and well-developed sweat glands are potent features that contribute to running speed under external and internal heat. Because of sweating, we can tolerate very high heat loads derived from internal metabolism and the exterior environment. But the endurance that capacity buys costs us much water. On a continuous run of over 60 miles on a moderate to cool day, an ultramarathoner may lose nearly 20 pounds of water by sweating alone. Without sweating, running speed and range would be dramatically reduced. Most arid-land animals are compromised in endurance because they are highly adapted to conserve water. The fact that we, as savanna-adapted animals, have such a hypertrophied sweating response implies that if we are naturally so profligate with water, it can only be because of some very big advantage. The most likely advantage was that it permitted us to perform prolonged exercise in the heat. We don't need a sweating response to outrun predators, because that requires relatively short, fast sprinting, where accumulating a heat load is, like a lactic acid load, acceptable. What we do need sweating for is to sustain running in the heat of the day—the time when most predators retire into the shade.

Our ancient legacy as endurance predators is now, in "Western" cultures, effectively masked by recent changes in our ways of living. The Khoisan people of Southern Africa (Hottentots and Bushmen) were well known for being able to run down swift prey, including steenboks, gemsboks, wildebeests, and zebras, *provided* they could hunt in the heat of the day. The Tarahumara Indians of northern Mexico chase down deer till the animals are exhausted, then throttle them to death by hand. The Paiutes and Navajos were reported to do the same with pronghorn antelopes. Australian Aborigines chase down kangaroos, but only by forcing them to reach lethal body temperatures.

Each predator capitalizes on its strengths, brought to bear on the prey's weakness. Most predators catch their prey by a combination of surprise and sprint, or by singling out the young, old, or weak. In turn, prey escape by sprinting. Since they usually will not be pursued for very long, it pays prey animals to sprint fast, a behavioral trait that the human predator can exploit. As the previously mentioned anecdotes from my friend Barre Toelken have suggested, chased deer have little sense of pace. The sprints cost them dearly in the end. If the predator is not induced to give up after seeing the deer's brilliant sprint exhibition, then the accumulated lactic acid and body heat can be exploited. Humans who capitalize on the deer's weaknesses by having a longer vision—a view further into the future—can be a superpredator through the agency of mind power.

It is a truism that animals have evolved to match their morphology and physiology, along with their behavior, creating a coherent unit that fits them to their environment. In Africa, one can distinguish the European migrant birds from the residents by their longer, narrower wings, which in turn indicate greater flight endurance and their behavioral responses of launching themselves biannually on migration. Owls have eyes and ears tuned to detect mice, the unique behavior of hunting by sitting still at night and then pouncing to grasp prey with their feet, and hooked bills for tearing flesh. Kingfishers have sharp, long bills for catching fish, the physiology to digest fish and be nourished by fish proteins, and perhaps more important, the very specific behavior of diving down from a perch at moving objects underwater. Our behavioral and psychological tendencies are also matched to the structure of our bodies, to adapt us to the environment we faced in the past.

The early pack-hunting hominids likely would have been at least as flexible in their hunting behavior as packs of African wild dogs and wolves are today. Specialized skills are required to kill zebras and bison, and learned skills in these canid groups are handed down over the generations. The more learning, the more possible diversity, so we can't draw absolute conclusions.

We are behaviorally much more flexible than most other animals. Proximally we are now so flexible that we get food in any way that we have to; that obscures our innate tendencies. We probably don't work on an assembly line or as a bank teller because that is what we prefer doing above all else in the world. We may not really know what might suit us most of all, because we don't get the exposure to find out and we become culturally biased. I had the opportunity to be out in free, wild nature to hunt. Of course, I no longer shoot little birds with a shotgun, though I still marvel at the excitement I used to feel, and that ornithologists almost universally felt at the turn of the century when they discovered new birds.

I grew up in Maine hunting deer, and that seemed to me the most absorbing activity humanly possible. I still participate in the Maine deer hunt in the fall. Getting my meat from an animal that is wild and has a chance to escape, rather than from one confined in a factory pen and raised for slaughter only, is just part of the reason. Aside from moral considerations, I hunt because of the allure. I wander the woods for days, searching for clues, hoping to see signs, and getting excited by every track. But I'm rarely "successful." Every fall, I hope that I'll get that big buck, but it eludes me. Why do so many of us bother to hunt when the chances of success are so slim? The answer came to me on a recent trip to Yellowstone Park. I saw elk, bison, bighorn sheep, and mule deer from within several yards. As I saw these beautiful animals that were tame, I knew that even if hunting them were allowed, I would have not the slightest desire to do so. The very idea was repulsive. Why? Because simply *shooting* animals is not *hunting* at all. Not even close.

It is not killing that motivates, nor is it the prize as such. The allure is in being out in the woods, in having all senses on edge, and in the chase. The white-tailed deer in the Maine woods are alert to scent, sound, and sight. They are shy, swift, wily.

The qualities that attract us to hunting are precisely the ones that dissuade the other great predators, those that do not have to chase their prey very far. Those great cats and hunting dogs take not that which is most difficult, but that which is easiest—they are very selective, trying to take the old, the young, the weak, the diseased; and the most preferred of all are the already deceased.

We are a different sort of predator. We can't outsprint most prey. We are psychologically evolved to pursue long-range goals, because through millions of years that is what we on average *had* to do in order to eat. To us, even an old deer that had not yet been caught would have required a very long chase. It would have required strategy, knowledge, and persistence. Those hominids who didn't have the taste for the *long* hunt, as such, perhaps for its own sake, would very seldom have been successful. They left fewer descendants.

Our ancient type of hunting—where we were superior relative to other predators—required us to maintain longterm vision that both rewarded us by the chase itself and that held the prize in our imagination even when it was out of sight, smell, and heating. It was not just sweat glands that made us premier endurance predators. It was also our minds fueled by passion. Our enthusiasm for the chase had to be like the migratory birds' passion to fly off on their great journeys, as if propelled by dreams.

A quick pounce-and-kill requires no dream. Dreams are the beacons that carry us far ahead into the hunt, into the future, and into a marathon. We can visualize far ahead. We see our quarry even as it recedes over the hills and into the mists. It is still in our mind's eye, still a target, and imagination becomes the main motivator. It is the *pull* that allows us to reach into the future, whether it is to kill a mammoth or an antelope, or to write a book, or to achieve record time in a race. Other things being equal, those hunters who had the most love of nature would be the ones who sought out all its allures. They were the ones who persisted the longest on the trail. They derived pleasure from being out, exploring, and traveling afar. When they felt fatigue and pain, they did not stop, because their dream carried them still forward. They were our ancestors.

Sometimes I wonder if this ability to have long-range vision, if not also the drive to explore, might not also have been the boost that gave us our *unique* brain power to extrapolate. The currently popular explanation of our unique intelligence is thought to be related to *deception* in the social context. Deception indeed tweaks capacities for mental visualization, and there is little debate that social interactions involve keeping track of individuals, trading favors, paybacks, and possibly deceiving. In support of this idea of intelligence based on sociality, brain size in animals correlates with group size. Did, then, *Homo erectus* live in superlarge groups relative to other animals? That's unlikely; these archaic humans were hunters, likely living in small groups, and their brain size already overlapped with that of moderns. Another hypothesis, also a nonexclusive one, is that sexual selection was a driving force in the hunting syndrome. There is no either-or answer; all factors likely acted in concert, but I'll briefly examine the last hypothesis.

———————•———————

The mere fact that we can run down some of the swiftest ungulates, animals that have evolved to outrun the swiftest predators, indicates that we are indeed highly specialized, physiologically and psychologically, for that particular task. But there is a sexual difference. Curiously, in all human cultures that have been examined, as well as in baboons and chimpanzees, hunting is largely a male activity. Sexual specialization is common in animals. In some hawks, for example, females are larger than males and catch the larger prey, while the males specialize in the smaller prey. As a consequence, the sexes in effect achieve a division of labor in foraging, causing less depletion of the food supply near the nest.

For the protohominid females, pregnant or burdened by offspring who needed to be carried along, hunting for large animal prey requiring long pursuit was even more difficult than it is for present-day apes. Having become naked to increase heat loss, the young could no longer hang on to their mothers' fur but rather had to be held. Through food sharing, a multifaceted male-female symbiosis evolved. Adult men were free to hunt, but women foraged and chose mates. On what basis did they choose?

The females with young could not readily take part in long exhaustive hunts, and they needed to enlist the aid of males to provide them and their families food. Hunters killing large animals had a temporary superabundance of meat, which could not be stored. How could it be used? It was brought home, to be shared in mutual obligations with other hunters, and to trade for sex. Sleeping together and eating together became interrelated. It is an old formula. Chimps trade sex for food routinely, as do baboons. Craig Stanford, who studied the hunting practices of chimps at Gombe, says, "Chimps use meat not only for nutrition; they also share it with their allies, withhold it from their rivals. Meat is thus a social, political, and even a reproductive tool." Similarly, among the Aché of South America, women prefer successful hunters, the meat providers. Similar correlations between reproductive choices and resources exist in most societies where the limiting factor to reproduction in females with young is resources. For males, the limitation is more commonly sex.

For !Kung Bushmen, meat is only a small part of the diet, but it is the food they desire most. The women bring in the bulk of the food, feeding the band from day to day on berries, bulbs, leaves, and roots. The men hunt, oftener than not having little to show at the end of the day. Still, hunting is deemed highly important. Only after a boy makes his first kill of a large antelope does his father perform the rite of the first kill, which marks his passage from adolescence to manhood. A male !Kung who does not hunt remains a child who cannot marry. He cannot expect to have a wife if he cannot bring home meat and skins for his family and parents-in-law. Bushmen males hunt from the time of adolescence until they are old. Often they travel 30 kilometers per day, come home with nothing, and by next morning are off again, impelled by their will to persist, if not their wives' goading. They carry no food or water with them, because that hinders their ability to travel. !Kung hunters might follow a wounded giraffe for five days. This is not work that women carrying infants can perform. Division of labor, though perhaps currently nor politically correct, is an ancient tradition with deep biological roots. And there is nothing wrong with diversity, either between people or between sexes. Division of labor has allowed men to rely on women to feed them, and enabled them to engage in long-range hunts after large prey that required traveling rapidly and unencumbered over long distances.

Contrary to some presumptions and misconceptions, the idea of *man the hunter* as a driving force in human evolution neither denigrates women nor relegates them to a passive role. Misconceptions can be minimized if we read "man" as "humankind." Evolution has not very likely affixed the huge complement of genes that affect growth and development of the brain and human evolution onto the Y (male) chromosome. The different behavioral tendencies of men and women, at least those regarding long-term cooperation to rear children, can best be explained in terms of compromise and cooperation. If "man" is the hunter, then it is because women permitted or selected him to be. They are the other half of the same man-the-hunter syndrome. Women had to become *intelligent* choosers, because choice could not be trusted to appearance alone.

Sexual selection in the animal world often results in such runaway scenarios as the notorious peacock's tail, the elaborate songs of some birds, and even balloon making in flies, which I will discuss later. If the hypothesis that hunting is, in part, also a consequence of sexual selection, rather than merely a device for the fulfillment of caloric requirements, then there are wide repercussions, because with energetics removed as the primary constraint on hunting, there are few limits. If bringing a rabbit back to the group can enhance a hunter's sexual desirability, then just imagine if he kills a mammoth or has the ability to do so, while the woman develops the capacity to evaluate!

———————————●———————————

The strategy of supplying protein to secure mating privileges is the rule in many male birds, spiders, and insects, especially in scorpion flies (*Panorpa*), some grasshoppers, crickets, and cockroaches, and some beetles (Malochidae). Among insects, the nuptial gift food offering may be prey, or in the absence of prey, protein from body secretions. In some mantids and spiders, it is the male's own flesh. Male mantids are legendary suitors, who regularly make the ultimate sacrifice for sex: their own bodies. They are cannibalized by the females with whom they mate. The benefits of offering themselves (usually reluctantly) may go beyond just providing a dietary supplement that ultimately provides nutrition to the eggs he has fertilized. The females first eat the male's head. Males with intact heads mate for only four hours, but the encounters that result in decapitation last up to twenty-four hours. Maydianne Andrade, who studied Australian redback spiders, has shown that being eaten prolongs copulation and increases the amount of sperm transfer. In this spider, allowing himself to be eaten also prevents the female from mating with other males, since a satiated female spider rejects other suitors and the "victim's" sperm thus have precedence in fertilization. Spiders die for sex, and their suicidal behavior has, ironically, evolved because it increases their individual fitness.

These extremes alert us to mechanisms that might otherwise remain hidden in our species. All animals have to pay something for sex. My favorite example, because it is in some ways a caricature of the human situation while at the same time illuminating of the evolutionary process, is that of dance flies (Empididae). These European and North American flies are predators that hunt other flies. Their name is derived from their group gatherings, during which these insects fly up and down and sometimes in distinctive lines and curves, or dances. Females choose mates from among the dancers on the basis of the male's energetic displays and the male's offerings during those dances.

To have a chance of mating, a male must sustain himself in hovering flight while holding a nuptial offering of a fly carcass in his feet. Females size up the lineup, then pick and choose. Couples then drop to the ground, where the males transfer their offering to the females, which then eat their offered prey.

A small fly carcass suffices as a suitable mating inducement in some species of empids. Another step in the evolutionary progression is found in other species, where the male wraps the prey in a fine shiny veil that he weaves with spinning glands on his forelegs. A silk-wrapped nuptial gift is more attractive to the females than an unwrapped one, possibly because it appears larger in size and is more conspicuous than unadorned or unadvertised prey.

The next step in the evolutionary progression seems downright devious. Some males dance carrying an even larger and more conspicuous package, but one that contains a fly that is too little to eat (but easier to carry and thus show off), an inedible piece of debris, or nothing at all. For example, in *Empis politea*, the male carries a great white egg-shaped balloon within which he may or may not enclose a little fly. The female pays no attention to a male carrying a fly. She goes for a big, showy but empty package.

In *Hilaria sartar, S. sartrix*, and *H. granditarsis* the males have taken the final step in deception. They always carry an empty gleaming white oval balloon throughout the course of their ever more acrobatic dance. If a foolish male were to attempt to hoist a balloon containing prey, he would be badly outclassed by dancers with lightweight balloons. Hoisting heavy prey offering would be possible only at high temperatures, when the fly's muscles could achieve the high work output required.

The flies prove the point that, as with the scenario that anthropologists have proposed for humans, it is not the nutritional value of the offering that counts. The showing off does. One difference is that human hunters can't cheat. In the protohominids, the males had to bring home real meat, or demonstrate ability to do so, not just hoist pretty empty packages. Meat was a valued resource that was an important and necessary part of the diet.

As in the dancing flies, vigor or capability can sometimes be evaluated on the basis of physical appearance, but it is more reliably based on *performance*, either in hunting or in symbolic representation. Could the origin of our dances, like our athletic games that provide worthless colored ribbons and metal or fake metal trophies, be symbolic activities that show off our capacities?

A race is like a chase. Finishing a marathon, setting a record, making a scientific discovery, creating a great work of art—all, I believe, are substitute chases we submit to that require, and exhibit, the psychological tools of an endurance predator, both to do and to evaluate. When fifty thousand people line up to race a marathon, or two dozen high schoolers toe the line for a cross-country race, they are enacting a symbolic communal hunt, to be first at the kill, or at least to take part in it.

The real hunt is long out of date to most of us. Very recently (geologically) we eradicated some of the most magnificent creatures that were ever on this globe when we came, as full-fledged hunters, into contact with them in America, Australia, Madagascar . . . We had by then evolved the psychology, physiology, and technology to make us extraordinary hunters. In contrast to those in Africa, our homeland, our new prey did not have time to evolve effective evasive responses to our unique hunting capabilities, which combined physiology and psychology with intelligence, and ultimately also weapons.

It is fortunate that we have now invented some ecologically friendly redirections of our hunting tendencies. We can now chase one another rather than mammoths and mastodons. We can be road warriors, who will have races to run forever. Now we dream not of killing great beasts to be heroes as we provide nourishment for our social band. We may dream—and get the same psychic nourishment that was once necessary to provide bodily nourishment—of winning races or setting records or fulfilling other long-term goals. In the Olympics we witness the biggest hunt. If we can't be part of it, then as spectators we cheer for those who represent us, who are really a part of us, since through our evolutionary time of millions of years we were (and still are) mutually interdependent. There is one main difference, though. In contrast to hunting prey animals, where there is always an end point, in chasing against one another there is no end point. Where can it end? What are the limits?

mind

The mind is a dominant force in any athlete's life and it monitors his every motion, controls his every emotion, allows him superlative productions one night, damns him to embarrassing incompetence the next. It is whimsical, ornery, unpredictable, fractious, inconsistent, easily influenced, controlled with difficulty, and a friend only to those who have attained superiority at their jobs. It is regarded with clichés and surrounded by an aura of mysticism; it is wooed, courted, and pampered . . . .

~From On the Run, by Marty Liquori and Skip Myslenski

I Don't Like to Run Long Distances

Pam Reed, 2006

Races longer than the standard marathon distance of 26.2 miles are called ultramarathons. Pam Reed, one of the top American ultramarathoners, has run races that are eight times the marathon distance. How does she cope with the mind-boggling distances? In this excerpt from her autobiography, *The Extra Mile: One Woman's Personal Journey to Ultrarunning Greatness*, she explains the mental tricks she uses.

People often ask me what I think about when I'm running for so many hours at a time. The answer isn't very exciting. Usually I'm concerned about eating and drinking the right amounts so I don't run out of gas. I never try to keep track of my time during a race. In fact, I don't even want to know what my pace is or whether I'm going fast or slow. For some reason, I do wear a watch that I try not to look at. If I do happen to see it, I feel really frustrated.

An example of this was when I finally did the Hawaiian Ironman in 1993, 3 years after [my husband] Jim and I did the Canadian Ironman. In Canada, I'd done the course in 10:25, which at the time placed me in the top 10 for one of these competitions—that is, in the money. So for Hawaii I was registered as a pro. (This basically was a matter of just applying and paying.) Naturally, I hoped to live up to the designation.

Unfortunately, my swim was not that fast. I'd hoped to get around a 1:08. As I got out of the water, there was a *huge* clock that read 1:16. It was only 8 minutes off my goal, but that totally psyched me out. Mentally, I died. Then, as I got on my bike and went on, a woman pedaling near me started going on about how I was "drafting" off her. She said, "You give pros a bad name." I don't even know *how* to draft. It was just so weird, and it brought me even further down.

My bike time was okay, but not great. In the end, I came in 25th among the pros. The irony is that if I'd just done the race without the pro designation, I'd have placed in my age group. It was that stupid big clock that started my downhill mental spiral. So I tend to avoid looking at the time. I don't want to know.

No matter how daunting a race might be, I start out trying to convince myself that it's "obstacle free." There are always lots of problems if you know where to look for them. And if you can't find them, you can always create them. Then it doesn't take long to turn the problem into an excuse. I try hard to resist making obstacles for myself, because I know it can be a powerful and seductive process. I don't want it to get started.

To illustrate this, let me pick on my husband: Jim woke up one morning and said, "It's really hot in here. We need to turn up the air-conditioning."

I looked at the thermostat. The temperature was about 70 degrees. It certainly wasn't hot, but the process was already under way. From Jim's perception that the temperature was too high, it was a short step for him to reach "I can't believe how hot it is in Tucson."

Next came "We've got to move out of Tucson. We've been here way too long. We're leaving. We're leaving now. Let's sell the house!"

It all started with a little thing, an overheated room—which was completely imaginary, by the way. Once you set out on a path like that, you can go as far as you want. You can feel sorry for yourself. You can blame other people. You can whine. You can quit. You can retire to the North Pole if being cool is what makes you happy.

So I try to stay away from negative thoughts. At the same time, I'm not really into "thinking positive" either. Aside from keeping track of food and drink, my ideal mental state in a race is not thinking about anything. If I can get into a zone where it all seems to be happening by itself, I don't have to call on any special thoughts or feelings to get me through. In order to make this happen, I try to run the race in my head beforehand. I visualize the course and imagine myself at different points. Needless to say, this only works when I know what the course will look like.

On a few occasions, I've been able to get into a zone of running that makes it all seem effortless. In 2001, I ran the St. George Marathon in Utah in 2:59, my best time ever. I felt like I was flying. Just a week earlier I had run 3:09 in a marathon in Portland, so cutting 10 minutes off my time was a real surprise. I wish I knew how to make this happen consistently, but I don't.

It's important for me to try to get into a zone because I have never really liked long distances. And in my own mind, I never really run them.

When I was on the track team in high school, sometimes we'd have to run through the streets around the school for fairly long distances. I used to take shortcuts, not so I would be the first one back, but just because I'd get bored with running. It was just practice, so I didn't feel like I was doing anything wrong. Really, I was just trying to make the run more interesting for myself.

I still like to do that, to play little mental tricks on myself during an event. Now those tricks are not just for fun. They're actually a necessity. I don't think anyone, myself included, can just hit the road and run hundreds of miles again and again and not burn out.

Coming from someone who's done so many ultra events, that may sound surprising. But it's true. In fact, not liking to run long distances is actually why I've been able to run 100-mile races. Along with the necessary physical conditioning, I've had to develop mental tools to overcome my inner resistance to running. I do need to run. That doesn't mean I don't fight it. So I have to psych myself up.

When I compete in a 100-mile race, for instance, I do it 1 mile at a time. In my own mind, I'm not really running 100 miles. I'm running 1 mile 100 times, which to me, as weird as it may sound, is something very different.

I don't think about how many miles I still need to go. Instead, I look at a telephone pole or another landmark up ahead and concentrate on running to that point, and then to another point after that. My mind has to engage in all sorts of negotiations with my body—and both are trying to get the best deal they can!

I think all ultrarunners use some variation of this technique. Without it, I don't think anyone could run extreme distances—certainly not more than once or twice.

Learning how to break down a long distance into a series of much smaller ones is really a key method for getting through any long journey. When a plane flies across the country, for instance, it doesn't just travel in a straight line. It's always being blown off course in one direction or another. So at any given moment, the pilot isn't thinking about how to get from New York to Los Angeles in 6 hours. He's thinking about how to bring the plane back onto the flight path within the next 5 minutes. Of course, the plane will immediately deviate again, maybe in the other direction, and then the correction process has to be repeated. Meanwhile, the overall trip is taking place almost without anyone even thinking about it. The pilot's job is always to look ahead but never to look too far ahead.

This takes mental discipline. It's almost a form of self-hypnosis. Before a long run, there's a sudden realization of how impossibly far you have to go. So you have to step back from the long-range perspective and just focus on letting the first mile happen, or the first quarter mile, or even the first step.

This is a pretty simple concept that takes real mental toughness to implement. I've noticed that young runners have a hard time with it. Even when some people are in their late twenties and thirties, they can't find the patience and perspective that long-distance running demands. They get intimidated by how far they're trying to go, or they get bored with the time it takes, or they follow some other negative idea to its logical conclusion—that conclusion being that their feet stop moving.

Learning to break things down is one of the most valuable lessons I've learned as an ultrarunner. It's helped me when I feel like I can't sit still, and it's also helped me when I feel like I can't get going. When I'm really wired, I convince myself that everything needs to happen at once. The worst part of it is that I actually believe that that's possible. I want everything to happen now, and I can't understand why everybody else doesn't feel the same way. This somewhat irrational impatience is also why I used to get angry with the girls on my tennis team back in college. It seemed so obvious that we should be practicing and that anything else was a waste of time.

The opposite of this comes when I think I can't do anything—not just running, but anything. I'll walk into a room of our house and it will be really messy. Probably, there are just a few things lying around, but to me it looks completely trashed. And it seems like there's nothing I can do about it. I can't even begin to start cleaning it up. I want to, but I can't. It's all too overwhelming and it'll just get messed up again, so what would be the point?

In both cases, the trick is to do less than I think I have to do. I don't have to get to the finish line this instant; I just have to get to that next bend in the road. I don't have to clean up the whole house; I just have to put one object back where it belongs.

Once again, training yourself to think in bite-size bits takes practice and willpower. But it's something you've really got to learn if you want to be a long-distance runner, or the mom of a house full of kids.

I've also developed a way to use this tool in reverse. Instead of tricking myself by making something seem smaller or shorter than it is, I trick myself with the idea of something larger or longer. I'll tell myself, "Well, Pam, you're going to run 15 miles this morning, so you'd better get started."

Then the same old thoughts appear: "Fifteen miles! I must be crazy! I don't even want to *drive* 15 miles!" So I negotiate with myself: "Pam, you don't have to run all 15 miles at one time. That's just too far. So I'll tell you what. You can run half in the morning and half in the afternoon. What a great deal! Go for it!"

Tricks like these can help with the most difficult part of running—the most difficult part of anything, really—conquering it in your mind's eye. If you can mentally convince yourself that you can tackle a task, whether it's running a marathon or cleaning up a room, you can always accomplish it physically.

Well, maybe not always. Almost always. Often. More often than you think. Sometimes, at least. Definitely sometimes!

The Outer Limits/Running Into the Abyss

Steve Scott with Marc Bloom, 1997

In a long career that ran from the 1970s to the 1990s, Steve Scott staked his claim as one of America's greatest milers. He set the American mile record of 3:47.69, a mark that stood for 25 years; he established himself as a consummate professional miler, one of the toughest competitors on the international track circuit; he was a three-time Olympian; he ran 136 sub-4 minute miles, more than any other athlete. His autobiography *Steve Scott: The Miler* ranks as one of the most candid sports narratives. The following two excerpts take us into the mind of a world-class miler.

The Outer Limits

The mile race starts on the bus ride from the hotel where you sit among your competitors and decide, based on how your season is going and how you feel that day, who you'll talk to, acknowledge, or even look at before reaching the stadium. I talk to the milers I know I can beat and avoid the others. I have power over those I can beat; I can shoot the breeze with them, even joke with them, because I have them in my pocket and they know that. Because I don't fear them, I don't worry about showing a soft side of myself or giving them the impression—not true, of course—that I could be weak or vulnerable or not up to the task of running in pain and sprinting the last one-hundred meters as though they're the last one hundred meters of my life. As for the milers whom I'm not certain I can beat—well, I can't let my guard down with them, chat about the weather or the race in Byrkjelo or the knockwurst at the hotel. I can't give my rivals an extra edge by allowing them to think I'm not focused and fight-happy. No, I can't let that happen. So it's as if I'm two different people as I ride with my competitors to the track: nice to those I'll bury, arrogant to those who might bury me. Hey, you gotta learn to survive.

I don't want any surprises, either. I want every detail precise and under control, from the time we arrive at the stadium (where I check in and pick up my race number), to my warmup (which is always the same routine of jogging, stretching, and strideouts), down to how many seconds it takes me to lace up my racing spikes. Everything must be kept to the bare essentials. Nothing can clutter my mind or my space. Because nothing is harder than running the mile.

Nothing. Not the 100 meters or the 10K or even the marathon. The mile, or its metric equivalent, the 1,500 meters, demands the ultimate combination of speed and strength. In training, I run sprints till I drop and I also cover distances as far as 20 miles. I train in pain because I race in pain and if you can't tolerate pain you may as well quit. You won't be a miler.

Just because I can tolerate pain doesn't mean I don't fear it. I do. The pain is like a bad headache that travels through your entire body. Just when you need to speed up, the ache takes over and you want to slow down. Your muscles and joints, tendons and ligaments, heart and lungs all have to work overtime while lacking vital oxygen. That hurts. What I fear is whether I can, yet again, summon the will to peel back each layer of pain and still push my body farther.

My capacity is somewhere beyond my body's perceived limit. Frankly, I don't know if I've ever truly reached it. But each time I race I think I might have to. That's what running the mile is about: the outer limits.

So I sit on the bus, keep to myself, and visualize the race. In one scene, the field goes out comfortably and I have to harness my top speed for no more than the last lap. Very manageable. The pace steadily builds and builds and I'm under pressure for less than a minute. There are tactical strategies to play with, split-second decisions that may decide the race or even define my career, but that's okay.

I see myself winning. I see myself coming from behind and blowing by the leader on the home straight to win. If there's a better feeling on God's green earth, I'd like to know what it is.

In another image, the field flies impatiently from the gun. We are intent on killing each other off. This is not okay. Push too soon and you're in the outer limits with half a race still to go. Hold back too much and you risk losing everything. Someone, maybe more than one, will reach full capacity, set a record, and you won't be there. You'll be up the track when the finish tape is broken, thinking of how you'll explain that to the TV reporters.

Nearing the stadium, I think about the temperature, the humidity, the crowd, and conditions at the stadium. Wind is as important to a miler as it is to a sloop. Flags are the first thing I check when the bus arrives at the track. Still flags, at ease like a relaxed platoon, mean less resistance and a fast race. Uh-oh. I can feel the outer limits creeping up.

Before warming up, I find a patch of grass in the shade and lie down. I try to clear all the clutter out of my system. I am silent, still. At that moment, I'm inanimate. I don't exist. After fifteen minutes, I rise, jog, stretch, take my stride-outs, strip off my sweats, pin on my number, lace up my spikes—the right one first as always—take some deep breaths. I am ready to race.

I want to feel as light as air, and quick. I want my uniform jersey tucked in just so, my number pinned squarely against my chest. I want a little buzz of urgency to keep me bouncy and skittish. I want everything perfect. It rarely is; usually, there's some hiccup: maybe one of your Achilles tendons feels just a wee bit unresponsive as you jog down the track to the start after racing the mile thirty-two times in thirty-two cities this particular season.

Called to take our marks, I'm happy to be given a "dreaded" outside lane on the start line. Most milers like to have an inside lane and rush off with flying elbows into an immediate rumble for the closeup positions. Let them. I like to go out at a measured pace and run two lanes wide if necessary to stay out of traffic before moving to the rail. My trademark is to hold back and come on.

The gun is up and I crouch behind the start, my left foot forward, my arms low, and my gaze pointed straight ahead, like a youngster poised for a challenge-race in the schoolyard. Crack! I let the field draw ahead as I settle toward the rear and gauge the action. I want to conserve energy, pick off one man at a time, and strike for the lead when the frontrunners begin to lose their steam.

That's me: Scottie the Miler, just a kid at heart, racing around the track, the most pure and honest form of work I know.

Running Into the Abyss: The 1984 Olympics

In 1984, lacking the experience of the 1980 Games, I was unsettled by the Olympics. Not only were the Games being held in the United States for the first time in 52 years, but they would be run in Los Angeles, in southern California where I'd grown up, made my reputation, and was considered a favorite son.

The pressure was enormous. I'd never felt anything like it. In the past, if I missed a day of training to go hunting, it was no big deal. Now I thought, I can't do anything but train for the Olympics. When I picked up a little hamstring injury and had to layoff for a few days, I panicked. Oh my God! I missed three days of training! Where had the fun gone?

I had certainly always taken my running seriously. Who else but a serious runner would pace around the house all day until 8 o'clock at night, then run five miles to a steep hill, sprint the hill 30 or 40 times until his legs turned to mush, run the five miles back home, and collapse on the sofa with a beer?

I put myself through workouts like these because I had so much fun running the mile. Even though track was my livelihood, I had learned to mediate the pressures with spontaneity and impulsiveness. Race in New Zealand? Put me on the first flight to Auckland. Go for the run/golf "record"? Gimme my clubs. Run a meaningless road race? Sure. Unlike other athletes, my training was not determined weeks in advance. And I raced everywhere, drawing youthful joy from competition and being careful not to deny the whimsy I brought to the arena.

This was my way of being free. I would try to be the best miler in the world, but I would do it on my own terms. I was not going to map out my life stride by stride, minute by minute, heartbeat by heartbeat, even for something as tantalizing as Olympic glory.

Don't get me wrong: I craved that glory like any other athlete. But now, 28 years old and at the peak of my career, I did not want to feel like a puppet at the mercy of some fire-breathing Olympic beast.

But in 1984, it seemed as if the fun was being crushed by a spirit that distorted the very nature of competition. Now I'm not that naive. I know the Olympics have more to do with corporate largesse than with what Roger Bannister called "the sweat of honest toil." But there was something about the atmosphere in L.A., a kind of rank stupidity, that, for example, made it easy for people to find fault with Carl Lewis after he won four gold medals.

It was common knowledge that many of the people watching us perform in Los Angeles Coliseum were seeing the first track and field competition of their lives. They were not interested in track and field. They were interested in three things: the cachet of attending the Games; American gold medals; and Carl Lewis, by now an icon. The Angelenos did not care about the dynamics of racing or level of performance. They cared about Americans taking victory laps with the flag and standing atop the medal podium as "The Star Spangled Banner" played. Anything else was a waste of their time.

That's why Lewis practically got lynched by reporters (just as sadly ignorant as their readers) when he passed up a few of his long jump attempts to conserve energy for the 200 meters. The folks sitting in the sun with their official Olympic hats and official Olympic pins had no clue that if Lewis pushed too hard in the jump he might not be fresh enough to win the 200, and then wouldn't that be a bad hair day in L.A.?

But this was the American Way. For three and a half years, the masses and most media ignored and even dismissed "Olympic sports" such as track and field. Then, with the quadrennial Games approaching, people woke up and felt it was the duty of athletes lucky enough to make the U.S. team to win big.

At times, the public's ignorance or misconception about track and field reached the absurd. Word spread about spectators who didn't know where races started, which direction athletes ran on the track, what the hurdles were. Anything mildly technical, such as wind readings in the sprints, might as well have been spoken in another tongue.

In just about any other country, with less national arrogance and a more supportive tradition of sports appreciation, track athletes would have been hailed in the proper light. There would have been many gradations of success, not just the gold medal. Simply being an Olympic qualifier would have been worthy of honor.

Oh, how we lacked the Finnish graciousness from the previous summer's world championship meet in Helsinki. The Finns may have booed the slow pace of our 1,500 final in Helsinki, but that was to their credit. They knew we were dogging it.

I was committed to upholding a properly-paced 1,500 in L.A. But I found my path obstructed by the sense that I was no longer running for myself but for a misguided national interest. Every facet of the Los Angeles Games was fed, piece by piece, into some mammoth public relations machine designed to show the might and superiority of America.

The city of Los Angeles, the Los Angeles Olympic Organizing Committee, ABC TV, sports fans picking up on Olympic fever—every source of Games interest delivered the message that victory and nothing less was the American mandate. The Olympics were a convenient political vehicle, and after the U.S. boycott of the 1980 Moscow Games it was time for us to kick some ass. The Soviet bloc retaliated by boycotting L.A.? Screw 'em.

It was muted public interest in the faraway Iron Curtain Moscow Games that had enabled the Carter Administration Olympic boycott to take hold. Now in L.A., people felt a proprietary interest in the swelling us-versus-them ardor, and athletes were treated like one more Olympic trinket to be showcased and then disposed of.

Everything was out of whack. It was like a high school basketball tournament, blown up a billion times, in which the locals who really didn't understand the game were mobilized to feel that their pride, their values, and their way of life was somehow wrapped up in the final score.

I don't know how many times that 1984 season some sportswriter from the football beat or some blow-dried TV interviewer asked me whether I was going to "win the Olympics." I could tell these characters didn't even know basic things—for example, that instead of a mile in the Olympics there was a 1,500 meters, the "metric mile."

The confluence of these forces changed me. A stronger man might have coped better and shucked the pressure off. But I felt I had to win the 1,500 in Los Angeles. Otherwise, I felt I'd be dog poop.

———————•———————

After placing second in the 1983 World Championships—a failure I attributed to the warped, slow pace that obviously benefited the winner, Steve Cram, more than it had benefited me—I sat down with [my coach] Len Miller and devised a new strategy for 1984. We figured that in the tradition of recent Olympic 1,500 finals, the pace would be slow. Every contender, Cram included, would prefer strolling along, conserving energy, measuring the field, and sprinting the last lap rather than fooling with any tactic perceived as risky. Taking the lead and pushing the pace was considered the riskiest way to run. You were a sitting duck waiting to be swallowed whole.

Even John Walker, my early mentor and no slacker when it came to asserting himself on the track, had used a slow pace to his advantage in his 1976 Olympic 1,500 victory. Though he'd become the first sub-3:50 miler in '75, Walker followed the Olympic field in Montreal through a 3:01.2 split for three-quarters, then sprinted to victory. He covered his last 200 meters in 25.4 seconds. Eamonn Coghlan, with less native sprint capacity, ended up fourth, missing a medal by inches. He was devastated.

I knew that could happen to me. Len and I decided early in the season that I could not let a slow pace dictate the final result. Off a slow pace, my talents would be compromised. I wanted to make an honest race of the Olympic final. It deserved that. And I needed to win.

Our plan called for me to do the one thing no other contender would dare do: take the lead early and push the pace. No Olympic 1500 finalist had done that since Kip Keino ran away from Jim Ryun in 1968.

If the prospect of me walking out of Los Angeles Coliseum with a silver or bronze medal had been deemed acceptable to the masses, I would not have changed my running style. I would have been free to go with my instincts—instincts that had served me well for years. I would have trained with anticipation, raced with gusto. Maybe I would have won; maybe I would have run second or third as in Helsinki. If the audience at the Games had understood the dynamics of Olympic racing as well as they did a World Series pitchers' duel, I would not have felt compelled to think of the Olympic final as an all-or-nothing crucible in my life.

But I had to lead, and everything I did and felt in '84 grew out of that rather shaky commitment. My training was based on learning to sustain concentration for longer distances at the front of the field. Two minutes out front in a three-and-a-half-minute race could be an eternity. In L.A., I would have to make every second count.

As the season went on, the plan didn't seem right. I grew uncomfortable with changing my basic nature, my proven running style. I was edgy. I kept checking the papers for track results from Europe. Every time I felt a little ache, I ran to the doctor. That wasn't me. Once, when I couldn't finish a workout, I rushed to get a blood test.

I was so sensitive to Olympic pressure, real or imagined, that I played a cruel joke on my mother when the blood test results came back. Her habit of calling to ask how my training was going seemed like just one more person—my mom yet—telling me it was my job to win. So when the blood workup came in I made up numbers that led Mom, a nurse, to think I was really sick. It was thoughtless and a couple of days later I stopped my scam. But with all the pressure, I had needed to pick on someone, and Mom happened to be in my radar.

There was certainly nothing wrong with me—at least not physically. I was actually in great shape as the Olympics approached. A month before the Games, I did probably the best training session of my life. I ran two sets of a 200, 700, 800, 400, 500, 600, 400. I tried to run every repetition at 55- or 56-second 400 pace, and I did. My 800s were done in 1:52. I pushed my last 400 down to 51.8. As in '82 and '83, I felt capable of a world record.

But I didn't trust the American media to comprehend an athlete's capabilities and the pulse of a championship final. Few reporters covered track as a beat. Most covered track as an Olympic happening, boiling it down to the gold medal and some cute asides. The British press had its faults, but at least they treated track as a major sport.

My race plan, created out of desperation, was not the only issue that had me off-balance that season. My training partner was Tom Byers, also an Olympic 1,500 contender. Tom had the physical ability of a Cram or [Sebastian] Coe but was not known for his acuity on the track. With his erratic racing style and fragile self-image, Tom was like a gifted child incapable of managing his talent. I was still living in Scottsdale and, late in '83, at my urging, Byers had moved nearby. Len welcomed him. He saw Tom's fatal flaws as a coaching challenge.

Tom was a friend and we got along fine, but from a running standpoint our union turned out to be a mistake. I always preferred training partners of lesser ability so that I could dictate the pace. The worst thing I could do in training was compete against another runner. I found that Tom liked to train himself to death. He had no patience. He did not take easy days. He competed, and since we were both in the same event, I was drawn into his intemperate ways. We hammered each other.

I should have known better than to let myself get hooked up with Tom. No runner was flakier or less stable. One year at the Pepsi meet at UCLA, Tom was in great shape but finished last in the mile in 4:12. Right after the meet, to prove to himself he was still good, he ran himself dizzy with a complete speed workout of ten 400s.

Another hallmark of the Byers legend came during one Christmas when he was visiting his folks in Ohio. Tom's dad happened to mention that he'd never seen his son run a sub-4:00 mile. No miler is in any shape to speak of in late December, but Tom went out to the track in wintry conditions and, with his dad watching, broke 4:00.

Tom couldn't stand being away from the track. During periods when I would normally stay off the track for more sedate road work, we trained on the track. Len wanted to kill me. But I was so off balance, I began to think maybe crazy Tom was right: Maybe I should do more intervals, faster intervals; the L.A. Olympics are coming up, right?

———————————•———————————

Because of the Olympics, I cut back my '84 racing schedule. In the winter, I remained home rather than make another trip Down Under, especially with [my second child] Megan on the way. I wish I could have allowed the happiness of Megan's birth to offset my Olympic obsessions. But soon after Megan was born, I was irritable with worry that her late-night crying would disturb my sleep and have a detrimental effect on my training.

A few days before the birth, I'd won the Wanamaker Mile at the Millrose Games. Eamonn Coghlan was injured and did not run. Indoors, I also won the Sunkist mile and the mile at the U.S. Nationals. In all three races, Byers ran second. Great titles, but it was a tepid season.

Byers was my shadow. I opened my spring campaign with a 5,000 at the Sun Angel meet in Arizona, winning in 13:48.66. Byers was inches behind in 13:48.72. Every race was a tuneup for the Olympic Trials, which was a tuneup for the Games. Only one race really counted: the Olympic final.

I showed my fitness was coming along with a victory over a newcomer, Joachim Cruz, in the Pepsi meet at UCLA in mid-May. An 800-meter runner who would win the Olympic gold medal in L.A., Cruz, a Brazilian attending the

University of Oregon, chased me down the homestretch in his mile debut. I held him off in 3:52.99. Cruz ran 3:53.00. A tall, strapping (6'2", 170 pounds) 21-year-old, Cruz was considered an excellent candidate for an 800-1,500 double at the Games. In fact, he would attempt the Olympic 1,500, winning his heat but then withdrawing with an illness.

Even in my victories, I felt an undercurrent of anxiety. Though I was an experienced athlete, I had never experienced the impact of an Olympics. The 1980 boycott took that opportunity away, and as I confronted the pressures of '84 I was like a high school novice running his first conference meet. I had no combat tools. I didn't know how to relax, how to tune out the tumult. In my last race before the Olympic Trials, I ran a miserable sixth in an 800 at the Prefontaine meet in Eugene. That was not a good sign; the Haywood Field track in Eugene had always been a favorite of mine.

Was I the only athlete who'd let a big race get to him? One day at a meet I was sitting around with Jackie Joyner-Kersee, the future heptathlon champion. I asked her how she prepared mentally for the competition. She looked at me blankly and said she did nothing. Her attitude seemed to be: "Don't worry. Be happy." It made a lot of sense. That was the old me.

By late spring, I was training in southern California. I was now sponsored by Nike in addition to Sub-4, and with race earnings my income had grown to around $200,000 a year. The previous fall, we'd purchased a second home a block from the Pacific in Leucadia, California, about an hour's drive from where [my wife] Kim and I had grown up. We called it our "beach house." Kim loved the beach and with me away for much of the summers, the house gave her an outlet and a place for the kids to run around as they got older.

Megan turned into a mellow baby, the opposite of cranky Corey [my son]. I held her and played with her, and if she did cry my embrace seemed to quiet her. Being with Megan was a welcome respite from the track.

I trained without a break at San Diego State for the Olympic Trials, held, like the Games, in Los Angeles Coliseum. Though considered a lock for the Olympic team, I still felt nervous. That one weak 800 in Eugene had rattled me.

I wondered whether I should have taken some rest. Doubts piled up. Where was my confidence? My bulletproof nature? Olympic strategy, race selection, travel plans, training schedule, running partners, body signals . . . nothing was tidy. I had no sense of contentment. The Olympic monster was everywhere.

The other favorites for the U.S. 1,500 team were Jim Spivey, improving fast since winning the 1982 NCAA 1,500 at Indiana, and Sydney Maree, who briefly held the world 1,500 record in 1983. Spivey was funny. He was the most meticulous runner I'd come across. In his training log, which he proudly showed me, Jim would record every run—including his rest periods—in painstaking detail.

Though it was prestigious to win at the Trials, the victory had no consequence and, indeed, Spivey beat me. He ran smartly, timed his kick beautifully, and nailed me on the home straight. The third Olympic berth went to Maree by a hair over Chuck Aragon, who'd taken a year off from medical school to train. Byers, now injured, finished twelfth and last. Afterward, Spivey's assessment was right on the money. He told the reporters, "Steve was training for the Games and I was training for today."

After the Trials, I stayed home instead of going to Europe to compete as I had done every July for seven years. I wanted to keep my travel to a minimum. Another mistake. Racing on the circuit would have sharpened my form, given me back some confidence, kept me away from the Olympic kaleidoscope in California. But I was too uptight to see that. Again I told myself: It's the Olympics, lay low.

I ran some local races, including an 800 in a poor 1:50. In contrast, before the '83 Worlds, I'd run 1:45. Desperate to prove to myself that I still had it, I continued the tin-pot racing, as the British call it, without success.

Through all the anxiety and doubt, I should have leaned more on Len, who was good at keeping an athlete at ease. All summer, Len was holed up in a condo he'd rented in nearby La Costa to work closely with me. I guess I was confused by all these new and troubling feelings and ill-equipped to bring them out in the open. Len was not the type of coach to smother an athlete with his concern, and maybe I took the freedom he gave me as an excuse to hide my weaknesses. . . .

Once the Games began, I became a hermit. Instead of mixing with other athletes and getting out and seeing things, I avoided people, closed myself in, and put more weight on my shoulders. I didn't march in the Opening Ceremonies for fear of expending energy. And the first round of the 1,500 was almost two weeks away.

Two days before the 1,500 started, we dropped the kids at my mother-in-law's and Kim and I sequestered ourselves at a downtown hotel. Len was at the same hotel. I wanted to avoid the Village housing at USC. We killed time trying not to talk about my racing. Instead of looking forward to my Olympic assignment, I shrunk from it.

The hotel turned out to be a terrible location. There was nowhere in the immediate area to run, adding to my skittishness. At least at USC I would have had soft footing to do my casual daily jogging. And I probably would have bumped into Walker and [Ray] Flynn.

I made it through my qualifying heat and semi-final into the final. The three races were run on consecutive days. I wasn't worried about qualifying. But in my semi, crossing the line out front with Jose Abascal of Spain, I felt a bite of tension. A switch clicked in my body and I finished a little short of breath. Our times were 3:35 and change, quick for a semi, but I should have coasted through it.

Suddenly, with the final around the corner, I met with Len to discuss the final, and for the first time I told him I wasn't sure about the race plan. His reaction was not so much to reinforce the plan but to boost my confidence. We agreed as before: I would feel out the pace and if it wasn't to my liking, I would take off.

I remembered that the only time I had done that was one year against Steve Ovett at the Bislett Games in Oslo. The pace was slow so I took off. I ended up eighth.

All three Britons, Ovett included, made the Olympic 1,500 final. Ovett was shaky. He'd finished last in the 800 final, collapsed, and was hospitalized with a respiratory disorder. Considering Ovett's history of suspicious ailments, it was hard to grant him much pity. Still, Ovett ran the 1,500 rounds and took the line for the final. Give him credit for that.

Ovett probably felt the British press would butcher him if he didn't start. They had already pummeled Coe, the defending Olympic 1,500 champion, whose selection to the British team was hotly debated. Coe had not run well in a long while and placed second to Peter Elliott in the British championships. For once I agreed with the British press. I did not consider Coe my competition. In L.A., he first ran the 800, taking the silver medal behind Joachim Cruz. That was nothing to be ashamed of, but it seemed Coe's best form was behind him.

Cram—he was my competition. Cram was stuck in my mind from Helsinki. There were rumors that he'd had some minor injuries, but there was no way to really know. He had not run any big races before the Games. Despite his '83 world title, he expressed concern about meeting me in L.A. Discussing the Games, Cram was quoted as saying, "Steve's going to be on his home patch . . . which is going to make it more difficult for us." Little did he know.

I imagined myself leading the final. I also imagined myself losing. To ease the burden, I tried to come up with a worst-case scenario that would not ruin me. I figured if I died out front, I could still hang on for the silver or, all right, if I really died . . . I would still get a medal, wouldn't I?

A *Track & Field News* preview named me the consensus favorite with Ovett second, Cram third, and Coe fifth. Certainly the thousands of people seated in the Los Angeles Coliseum had me as their favorite. I was the American from southern California. That's all they needed to know.

I did my warmup, sat in the call room, and waited. Would I be able to hold the lead if I took it? Why was it taking so long for us to be called onto the track? Finally an official escorted us out in the sunlight and we were led single file to our lanes. I wanted to jog a few laps and shake out my legs as always. But I couldn't. Olympic procedures confined us to our lane markers. In my fragile state of mind, every bit of pre-race loosening up that was denied me hurt.

Spectators called to me, but I ignored them. I deposited my sweats in the basket provided the athletes and stared blankly down the track. It was time to run the Olympic 1,500 final before 92,000 people in the Los Angeles Coliseum, in southern California, where I'd grown up, run in high school and college, and instead I wished right then I was in Byrkjelo in the fjords with the salmon running upstream at 3 o'clock on a Scandinavian morning.

The gun popped and Coe, carried by momentum, glided ahead in the opening meters before braking and settling in. There were 12 men in the field. Omar Khalifa of Sudan and Joseph Chesire of Kenya went for the lead. Coe slipped into third on the outside. I was back in the middle hugging the inside. It felt like a walk. The 400 split was 58.9—not fast, but not a walk. But I had so much emotion driving me I felt I would explode if I didn't run faster.

In a championship 1,500, after the opening 400, there can be a momentary lull when the field slows a touch while assessing the first lap. The first 400 is nothing more than a prelude. Then, for a few seconds, there's a pullback. In those seconds, you can accomplish a lot. I could not wait.

In one move, just past the 400, I swept brazenly from eighth into the lead. We had two and three-quarter laps left, two and a half minutes of running. My cheeks puffed like bellows. I carried my arms high. My eyes blinked in distress. Coe stuck behind me in second. Abascal was third.

Once you're in the lead, you have to direct your energies down the track in front of you. You can't worry about the action behind: where a certain contender is, who's making moves, what trouble lay in waiting. You must be able to divorce yourself from the field. It doesn't matter if the field is breathing down your neck. You have to be able to make that emotional break. Few men can do it. Could I?

Holding the lead around the second lap, I thought, Okay guys, I'm going, you'll have to catch me. Cram, Coe, Ovett . . . see ya later. . . . But too much of my energy was channeled behind me. I kept listening for footsteps. Where was everybody? My senses were acute. I could feel Coe and the others on my shoulder. My 800 split was 1:56.9 and in desperation I pushed even harder on the ensuing backstretch. But as I willed my body to accelerate, my mind was beginning to lose control.

It's been said that running is 50 percent physical—and 90 percent mental. I buy that. I could never accomplish anything my mind did not embrace. From my first four-minute mile on, I had never doubted myself.

Until now.

Abascal and Coe rushed by me on the far turn with 600 to go. I tried to steady myself, thinking I was finally where I wanted to be: behind, in my comfort zone. Now I would sit behind them and kick them down.

But I had little fight left and one by one virtually everyone else poured ahead. Everyone but Ovett, who dropped out with 400 to go and was taken to the hospital. I ran as hard as I could in a numb state of survival. It was the longest lap of my life. In the biggest race of my career, I faded farther and farther behind, deeper and deeper into the abyss.

Coe outsprinted Cram for the gold medal, and Abascal took third. I finished tenth in 3:39.86. Coe's was a brilliant run, making him the first man to repeat as Olympic 1,500 champion, and his 3:32.53 established an Olympic record. Though I could not focus on the aftermath, I was pleased to learn later that Coe had made a point of rebuffing the British reporters who'd knocked him. "Perhaps you'll believe me now!" he called from trackside.

After the race, I was dazed. Everything was black. It was like wandering around in a dark castle. People tried to make me feel better. They told me I had run courageously, that I ran with honor, but I would have none of it. My competitors gave me credit for, as Coe put it, "taking this by the scruff of the neck." All I felt was total failure.

The linchpin to success in running is emotional control. Up to this time, I had been able to detach myself from the hubbub and psych myself down rather than getting too keyed up. I liked to live below the surface of the hype. That way, at some level deep within me, each race was the same: talent vs. talent. Each race counted the same. That is to say, each race didn't count at all. What counted was not the decoration but the feeling: winning or coming close. And the feeling of training, the adventure of being in shape to win.

At my core, I had managed to keep running as my little secret: a joyful child-like game I was good at, a place in which I could exist that was mine alone for its bliss and purity. Now, at the conclusion of the Olympic 1,500, I was cut open, naked, my little secret undermined by a new and terrible reality.

The Bridge

Frank Murphy, 2000

On June 4, 1986, Kathy Ormsby, a North Carolina State junior and collegiate recordholder, competed in the 10,000 meters at the NCAA championships. With about eight laps to go in the race, Ormsby left the track and ran out of the stadium. She ran another couple blocks, came to a bridge, and jumped off, nearly killing herself. The incident sent shock waves through the running world. What would cause an athlete to do this? In his book *The Silence of Great Distance*, from which the following story is taken, Frank Murphy charts the rise of women's distance running and the pressures that came with it.

Wednesday, June 4, 1986 was a perfect day for an accident. It was a fine day for things to go horribly wrong. Which is not to say that on other days in other circumstances things did not go equally, horribly wrong, nor that on all such days as this they did. It's just that the day had a portentous quality to it. It had high temperatures, a building pressure in the atmosphere, a sense that release was imminent, and a proportionate sense that the release would be, or at least could be, explosive. It was in the air for everyone to feel. It was the first day of the NCAA Outdoor Track and Field Championships in Indianapolis, Indiana. The next morning the local newspaper would report that the severe thunderstorm that struck Indianapolis ignited a $100,000 fire at a west side apartment complex; that torrential rain undermined the foundation of a local nursing home, causing a 30-foot section of the wall to collapse; that rescue efforts in the community were delayed by high water; and that 5,500 Indiana Power and Light customers lost service. The newspaper would also report that the track meet had been delayed three hours at mid-afternoon when the thunderstorm, which sounded like a train coming in, struck the Indiana University Stadium on the campus of Indiana University-Purdue University (IUPU). The newspaper would fail, however, to report at least one other important event that occurred on the evening of June 4, 1986. It would carry no article on the fate of Kathy Ormsby. She missed deadline.

The 10,000-meter run for women was the only championship final scheduled on Wednesday. The event was stuck at the end of an agenda that otherwise included heats and qualifying for events as diverse as the hammer, the men's and women's 400-meter hurdles, women's 200 meter, 3,000-meter steeplechase, men's and women's 800 meters, and the various events that constitute the first day of the women's heptathlon. The scheduled time for the 10,000-meter run was 9:40 p.m. In the days and on the night before the race, Stephanie Herbst

From Frank Murphy, 2000, *The Silence of Great Distance: Women Running Long* (Kansas City, MO: Wind Sprint Press). Reprinted by permission of Frank Murphy.

was a bit more reserved, even, than usual because she had a cold. Slowing down to conserve energy, she nonetheless prepared for an all-out effort. So too did Kathy Ormsby. In the last full week of training, she did precisely what she needed to do. She maintained sufficient mileage to keep her confidence high; she sharpened, and she started a long taper that would leave her rested for the first national competition in which she would be introduced as holder of the American collegiate record.

Arriving in Indianapolis, Kathy met Rollie on Tuesday evening to go over the race plan. Jotted minutes capture the essential message of the meeting: "Get out but not too fast." "Behind but close." "On rail." "Relax." "Watch others: breathing, when will they go? 1000? 800? Last lap?" Kathy clearly planned to follow and kick, a tactic perfectly suited to counter a relentless front-runner like Stephanie Herbst. No one on the North Carolina State team noticed any special apprehension or depression in Kathy as she and Rollie discussed their strategy or as Kathy withdrew to make her final, personal preparations. The next morning, Kathy fell easily into a routine. She always made a list of things to do on the day of a big meet. It helped her relax to have a fixed idea of the day before it began, and there was some assurance in checking the items off one by one—done, done, done—as the important event approached. Otherwise, with time on her hands and no small tasks to absorb her, she might fret and waste nervous energy.

On this race day, the schedule included a short run, stretching, a shower, a starter course of banana and coffee, a walk, breakfast and the newspaper, as well as reading, quiet time, and naps. Later in the afternoon, she scheduled shopping. "Get something for after the race," she wrote to herself. Leaving nothing to chance, she also reminded herself to eat a meal at three in the afternoon and to order a pizza and perhaps dessert after the race, even if the hour was late. Kathy was particularly mindful of nutrition because she had to run a heat of the 5,000 meters on Thursday and could not afford to go without food on the day before that race, no matter how concerned she was about the 10,000 meters.

In the afternoon, Kathy's parents dropped by the hotel for a visit. Later, as evening approached and the time to leave for the track grew closer, Kathy borrowed a tape player. She turned off the lights in the hotel room, rested on her bed and three times played a song by The Imperials: "Not to us Our Lord/Not to us Our Lord/But to thy name give glory/To thy name give praise/As children of a mighty king/we make our lives an offering." Within the song, Kathy sought the eye of the hurricane, a quiet and still place safe within the fury. Kathy also repeated the visualization exercises given to her by the sports psychologist. She encouraged her mind to see the details of a successful, uneventful race.

She could overlook herself standing with the other competitors, experience from a safe distance the start of the race, feel the deep, easy draw of her own breathing, hear the sound of the crowd and the encouragement of her friends, pull from a supply of carefully hoarded energy, enjoy an easy running motion with a composed arm carriage, and she could see—there before her—a swift, complete finish. In caution, however, Kathy also looked squarely to the possibility that "it" would happen again. ["It" was blacking out and not finishing a race, which Kathy had done in three previous college races.] She practiced methods of self-control that might permit her to stave it off. Failing that, she practiced acceptance. Come what may, she would be fine, she reminded herself. To similar effect, she remembered a presentation by the famous University of North Carolina miler, Tony Waldrop, who once said that under pressure it helped him to concentrate on a small, pleasurable detail of life not threatened by sporting success or failure. In his example, the mere prospect of a peanut butter and jelly sandwich could put him at ease. Finally, Kathy tried to relax by getting a clear view of the goal for the evening: she did not have to win. She prayed only that she be allowed to do her absolute best, win or lose. That would be sufficient for anyone who mattered to her. Kathy later summarized her mental state. "I was scared," she said, "but I was trying for all it's worth not to be." She had, in fact, done everything possible to prepare herself, and had no sense of serious danger or impending harm. To the extent she had anything to do with it, she was ready to run no less than anyone else who lined up on the grim, humid night.

Neither Stephanie Herbst nor Kathy Ormsby would have been careless enough to believe the race was between the two of them, however. The field was too strong for that conclusion. Christine McMiken [from Oklahoma State] was there with her low 32 time, faster in fact than Kathy's and missing from the record-book only because it was run in a race that included men. Ellen Reynolds from Duke was entered and still running well. Connie Jo Robinson, sorely missed in Milwaukee, was healthy now and running for North Carolina State, a companionship that pleased Kathy even as she faced the possibility of being the second-best finisher on her own team. Atlantic Coast Conference rival Clemson had a good runner in Ute Jamrozy. In all 24 women would start, and all of them were capable. Wary of such a big field, Stephanie's instructions from her coach Peter Tegen were simple. Stay close but stay back; let the race settle in. Depending on how the race went, he would decide whether she should use a long option, in which case she would move into the lead and drive for the finish line with eight laps to go, or a short option, in which she would move with three laps to go. He would signal at the eight laps one way or the other. Stephanie gave no thought to Kathy Ormsby nor indeed to anyone else in the race. She was waiting for a sound.

When the race started, Stephanie coasted to a spot near but not at the front. From that point, she fluttered through the early running until the field thinned, finally, to four contenders: herself, Ellen Reynolds, Kathy Ormsby, Christine McMiken. The pace was fast but not alarming, at least not to Stephanie.

Despite her cold, she was comfortable, pushing but not pressing. Around her in the tight cluster of runners, she could hear the footfalls and the breathing, mingled with calls from the sidelines and the stands. It was dark and the lights were on. The light was sharp enough to illuminate the scene yet it fell softly over the athletes, enshrouding them in whiteness sufficient to set them apart from those who merely watched. Within the structure of the developing race, Stephanie ran smoothly, almost as softly as the light itself and as ephemeral. Most of the other runners who surrounded her were equally composed and quiet as they concentrated on the work and the passing laps. Only one drew attention to herself by a slight irregularity. It was her breathing pattern, which was odd. The breaths came shallow and quick, almost as if the woman was hyperventilating. With little effort at detection, Stephanie discovered that the runner was Kathy Ormsby. Stephanie paid little attention to the matter; for all she knew, that was normal for Kathy. As the race progressed, Stephanie's attention focused increasingly on the pace, which Christine and Ellen were alternately leading in the range of 78 to 80 seconds per lap, and on the signal that she expected to get with eight laps to go. In preparation for that moment, she drifted up to the front. As she did, either memory or the many retellings of the race convince her that she noticed just a slight shift off the back, and Kathy Ormsby was suddenly gone. That was fine with Stephanie. Whether she saw it or not, she noticed in time that Kathy was no longer with the group, and then she forgot all about it. She had two runners still with her, and eight and a half laps left to get rid of them and complete the job. The signal would come soon. Stephanie braced for it.

She was surprised that it did not come. She just kept on running, of course, but now she was a little curious about what had happened to Peter, who was always so reliable. She could not have known that Peter had troubles of his own, albeit minor. He was standing at a railing in the curve near the backstretch. When he looked up to give the signal, he saw Kathy coming off the track and approaching him, or so it appeared. "I thought she was running directly to me," Peter recounted later. "I thought she may have confused me for her coach. I was wearing red and white, the same colors as NC State. There were eight and one-half laps to go. I know that because I was supposed to give a signal to Herbst then. I missed giving it because I was watching Ormsby." Turning, he watched Kathy continue toward the stands, climb up a full set of stairs, and disappear from view. "It was eerie," he said. "Her eyes were focused straight ahead. She didn't look right or left."

Stephanie remained confused that the signal did not come, but she did not panic. There was time enough. She was, however, on her own. In the circumstance, she decided to act unilaterally. She worked a bit more toward the front, just giving the pace a slight bump. She felt a little guilty about it, though, because she knew that her decision would not have been Peter's. "Well, I figured I better go," she said. "I didn't know what was up with Peter, but I better go because otherwise the strategy won't work. Because I didn't hear the whistle from Peter which would have made me start up, I slowly started increasing the pace, which was very risky, and would not have been consistent with what Peter would like to have done." She was not, however, wholly dependent on the gentle acceleration in rhythm. She still had the short option. Sure enough, with three laps to go she got a whistle and, being prepared for the event, took off again. After the succession of 78- to 80-second laps, many of which had been led by either McMiken or Reynolds, Stephanie's first fast lap was 71.9. With that kind of burst, she immediately detached from Ellen Reynolds and Christine McMiken and went sailing for home. The only problem was that the officials had miscounted the laps. When Stephanie re-emerged in the homestretch after one lap of strong running and with the idea that the board would say "2," it still said "3," a message repeated by a shout from the side: "Three to go." Surely, that is most distressing news for a person measuring energy against distance, and so it was for Stephanie. "I was scared to death," she said after the race. But she also held together. "I just said to myself that I had to keep on going. It didn't make a difference physically, but it kinda did psychologically." Physically and psychologically, what it eventually did make was a national championship for Stephanie and a new collegiate record of 32:32.75. Stephanie's winning effort in Indianapolis beat Kathy Ormsby's old mark by 3.5 seconds. The time also beat the championship record, formerly held by Kathy Hayes of Oregon. Christine McMiken finished second in 32:51.71 and Ellen Reynolds was third in 32:52.52. After the race, Stephanie said that it took a lot of concentration and a lot of praying for the victory, but she also admitted that she never really doubted that she would win. It felt good, she said.

By the time Stephanie crossed the finish line, Kathy Ormsby, the woman whose record she beat, the woman who departed the race as Stephanie took control of it, was already in darkness. After she ran off the track and up into the stands, Kathy came out the other side of the stadium, crossed a softball diamond, found herself confronted by a 7-foot fence, climbed it, and kept running. She ran west down heavily traveled New York Street for two and one-half blocks before arriving at a bridge that crosses the White River. In the late evening of June 4, 1986, with the sound from the stadium echoing behind her and with the lights visible in the great distance, Kathy Ormsby jogged or walked approximately 75 feet onto that bridge. She stopped there. She did not cross the bridge nor would she ever. Rather, she toppled head first off it and fell 40 to 50 feet onto the rain-soaked flood plain below. She landed only 20 feet from the river's water.

Kathy's parents were spectators along with 1,500 other people to the race. They saw Kathy leave the track. When she did not come to them and they did not see her, Sallie Ormsby sought the assistance of a university security officer, who took her description and broadcast it. Rollie, too, saw Kathy leave the track. Under the impression that she was crying when she left the track, he attempted to follow her. When she climbed the fence, she lost him. He returned to the stadium and spoke to a police officer, who arranged to have her paged. When she did not respond to the page, Rollie went back out of the stadium to search. Very soon, he found Kathy where she fell. He flagged down a passing motorist and then clambered down the slope to be with her. When the officer arrived and asked what happened, Rollie could only say what Kathy said. She said she jumped. Only 10 minutes had elapsed from the time Kathy left the track. It was 10:00 p.m. In the fall, Kathy suffered a broken rib, a collapsed lung, and a fractured vertebra in the middle of the back. She was permanently paralyzed from a point just below the shoulders. Stephanie and the other women were still running. Indeed, had they been listening during the race they would have heard the page for the young woman who, by rights, ought to have been among them, and not lost. Had they known the danger she was in, they would have kept her safe. But they did not know. Or, more accurately, they did not immediately know they knew, that deeper knowledge coming only from hindsight and empathy.

Kathy Ormsby knew more, of course, than they did, but even she was and remains mystified by the events that evening, which began with the ordinary act of running a proposed 25 laps of a 400-meter track. She ran well for the first laps. As other runners fell behind, she remained in the lead pack. Eventually she ran with only three other women, Stephanie, Ellen, and Christine. She knew of Stephanie and of Christine, but she knew Ellen personally and liked her very much. She and Ellen had even run together in Durham, where Ellen went to school at Duke. All in all, the race was going well, and she was comfortable. That is, she was comfortable until she began to feel herself slip back from the first three, to sense—again as before—that she could not move. She was running hard but getting nowhere, or so it appeared to her, and she felt again the terror that came upon her in such circumstances. This time however she would not faint or fall because her reaction was different. A volcanic flow of emotion ran through her; and in that flow was embarrassment and frustration and anger. The complex mix was different from anything Kathy had ever experienced and so difficult to understand or explain that, years later, she reduced and simplified it. "All of a sudden—this is the best way I can tell you about it—I just felt like something snapped inside of me," she explained. "And I was really angry. And I felt like it was so unfair. All of a sudden, I didn't feel like this was me because I didn't usually have reactions like that. That was not a reaction I had as a person, ever."

Struggling against the new emotion, the one that was not like her, Kathy ran one more lap and then she could not make her body run any farther. In the moving race, she was thrust aside, a solitary person completely on her own. Incapable now of logic or understanding, she was driven by the single thought that she had to get away, not to any particular destination but to anyplace or anywhere that was not the track. Her memories from that point are, at best, like snapshots. She has no recollection of much of what happened. She only vaguely remembers leaving the stadium, and she reacts with wonder that she was able to climb the fence. "I don't see how in the world I climbed that fence," she says. "Before that happened, I felt like I couldn't run and now I was running harder than I had in the race. I just ran. And I just don't feel like that person was me. I know that sounds strange, but I was just out of control. I just couldn't face everybody. I felt like I had let everybody down. I really don't know how to explain what happened except that I don't think it's something I would have done." Kathy does not remember the run to the bridge, nor whether she stood when she got there and looked over its side, or even whether she saw it was water or land that awaited her. In fact, she does not know that she jumped, only that she suddenly was over the side headfirst, conscious always, and contrite. "I know," she recalls, "that when I went off I was headed down headfirst. But I also know that the part of me, the part that was me, remembers apologizing to God and saying I'm sorry. Because it was like I was watching everything that was happening and I could not stop."

Psychiatrists later opined that Kathy's dreadful experiences in Indianapolis, Milwaukee, Lehigh, and Raleigh were caused by panic attacks, which are related clinically to anxiety and depression, and are often characterized by the feelings of terror that Kathy describes. One of the psychiatrists with whom Kathy worked after the accident described the effect of panic disorders in summary terms as "a sudden feeling of impending doom, of something terrible that's going to happen. There's a fast heart-rate, there's difficulty breathing sometimes, a feeling that you're choking or things are getting unreal." Many times a person subject to a panic attack will hyperventilate, in which case air hunger, lightheadedness, carpal spasms, and even loss of consciousness can result, a frightening set of physical consequences that can make the whole episode that much more damaging. Anxiety and panic disorders are often caused by and associated with serious medical conditions, including a variety of cardiac and seizure disorders, as well as any number of gastrointestinal, respiratory, neurological, and endocrine conditions. In fact, as many as one-quarter to one-half of all people who suffer from panic disorders are also affected by mitral valve prolapse, a condition that causes heart palpitations resulting from the failure of the valve to close properly. Because of the strong organic component in panic attacks, a complete medical examination designed to rule out, or exclude, the various medical problems is often encouraged before a behavioral health approach is taken. Even if a behavioral health diagnosis does result from the medical evaluation, the symptoms often respond well to medication, to relaxation techniques, and simply to an educational process that makes the affected person understand that she is not, in fact, "weak," or "going crazy," or otherwise flawed. Ironically, physical exercise is one of the customary interventions for a person suffering from panic attacks. The release of endorphins—the body's naturally occurring narcotic, by some accounts—is purported to induce a feeling of wellness and euphoria.

———————————●———————————

Because Kathy told Rollie she jumped and because the rail at the bridge was 4-feet tall, some people concluded that she intended the act and its consequences. Many stories even referred to the incident as a suicide attempt. That is far from the truth. By any standard definition, suicide is an act of intention. For example, an old Webster's Dictionary says that suicide is "the act or instance of taking one's own life voluntarily and intentionally especially by a person of years of discretion and of sound mind." Kathy was very young when she was injured. Whether she had enjoyed "years of discretion" is a complex issue, although the best-considered answer is probably that she had not. She may have had the years but not the opportunity for an exercise of discretion. As to the soundness of her mind, only the sliver of time during which she was affected by panic and terror casts doubt on the matter; and then the doubt is limited to that time. On that question, in any event, Kathy has provided the answer. She did not even recognize herself in the person who left the stadium, crossed the field, climbed the fence, and approached the bridge. There is nothing in the act or its description that suggests intention. Surely, a person who intended to destroy herself would have troubled to look over the edge to see whether water or land was below, a thing that Kathy does not remember doing. The question of intention, at least so far as it involves deliberation, is also answered by the notes that Kathy left for herself. Order pizza and maybe dessert. She did neither, of course, but it was her intention to do both. And then, of course, there was the 5,000-meter run. On Thursday morning, Kathy had intended to stand and to run, possibilities now removed from her.

On the known facts, a conclusion that Kathy Ormsby attempted suicide at the bridge in Indianapolis would be unfair and unreasonable. That much should be clear. But what, then, drove her to the act, however haltingly it is measured or understood? Kathy provided part of the answer, or perhaps it would be more accurate to say that she spoke of a single aspect of the incident, which can be understood and appreciated because it is within the experience of us all. She spoke of anger. More specifically, she spoke of an anger directed to unexplained, unaccepted injustice. She was not angry because one thing went wrong on one occasion. She was angry because critical things went wrong repeatedly with nobody and nothing to say why. Was it too much to ask that she be permitted to run one lousy race to the best of her ability—without being interrupted by this nonsense—with her parents in the stands, her coach at the sideline, her teammates hopeful about the result, and best friends at home waiting expectantly? Why must she suffer this attack now of all times? Why again in a national championship? Why not at practices or at home or when she was alone? Why any of this when she worked so hard, studied so hard, did so much, lived modestly, aspired to kindness, and hoped to do good things with her life? Why would she not be permitted so slight a grace as this one race? Why was she being treated in this way? Unfortunately, no answer ever comes to such questions. Injustice is not rational, and no person subject to it finds satisfaction in thoughtful answers. Satisfaction comes, if at all, when the emotions, being permitted to burn, are exhausted. But that is a dangerous and uncertain process. Simple anger is red hot, but it promises to burn brightly and fail. Despair, on the other hand, is a most distorting kind of anger. A stranger to proportionality, it is white hot, the result of many unquenched fires. Those fires burn low and then leap into rage. When despair seeks comfort, it finds only pain, a mocking world that acknowledges no value and no self. Memory submerges; context evaporates; hope recedes; even words lose shape; and soon the idea of jumping off a bridge, for example, becomes no thought at all, but as natural as the next breath, which it neither accepts nor rejects but merely foregoes. From such a world, despair tosses its victims over the edge. "Release me from this dark night" becomes prayer, explanation, and apology in one.

Despair in the face of injustice creates a particularly heavy burden for a Christian who has placed her entire trust in God, for is complaint not a rebuke to Him in His wisdom and His intention? "Oh, for the years gone by when God took care of me, when he lighted the way before me and I walked safely through the darkness, yes, in my early days when the friendship of God was felt in my home." The lesson of Job is our own. To lose hope, to know anger, to doubt, to rail against injustice, even to sulk at offenses committed against us, is humanity itself. For a Christian, only modest acquiescence to God's will is perfection. But it should be remembered that perfection is not a human state, and to aspire too highly, to fail to forgive even ourselves the occasional transgression, is mere vanity. And vanity is yet another sin. So, each of us in our time and place make our peace and move on. Asked to explain the inexplicable, we attempt it, knowing that the alternative is an accidental world, a prospect more frightening than ignorance.

Kathy Ormsby would not run again, neither would she walk. She would spend many hours receiving care and rehab. When she was able, she would finish her undergraduate and professional education, she would become a caring member of the medical community as an occupational therapist, and she would continue her determined effort to be a good person and a good Christian. As the years passed, she would study the events of the night that turned her world upside down; she would search her heart; she would pray to God, and she would accept, if not the act itself then its consequence. She would understand even her parents' admonitions. "Ever since Kathy passed out in her first race," Dale and Sallie Ormsby recounted, "we [had] been very concerned about her well-being. Distance runners as a group tend to be thin, with very little body fat. We felt she was not getting the proper nutrients, and this was substantiated by her need for iron supplements. We must have had a hundred talks about this." And later, after the accident, Kathy knew that her parents served as a lightning rod for other parents with daughters about whom they were worried, girls and young women who wanted to run, and about whom the Ormsbys heard much. "Since Kathy's accident," they said, "several parents of runners and runners themselves have told us of physical changes they had that made them severely depressed for a short period of time, even to the point of not wanting to live. We feel Kathy's problems started from being on a razor's edge physically, with very little reserve to draw on. A lot of things came together at that particular moment, including a burning desire to do well and the fact that the bridge was there."

Kathy agreed that the accident sprang from all those elements and others as well, including her mental, emotional and spiritual status, the pressure, the heat and humidity, accumulated fatigue, the chemistry of her body, and her own sense of responsibility, Highly combustible, they awaited only a trigger. Furthermore, move any element slightly, or change the way they related to each other, and it might not have happened at all. One thing emphatically was not a factor. The accident did not happen because Kathy was disappointed at not winning the race. She wanted only to do her best. She did not begrudge the victory of any runner who beat her, ever. In fact, for the women who ran with her on that fateful night, she worried. She worried in a special way about Stephanie Herbst, who she feared might suffer harm on her account.

In the meantime, it would become an arguable proposition, if not a fact, that what happened to Kathy Ormsby at the White River Bridge in Indianapolis on June 4, 1986, was the most important single event in the developing sport of women's track and field in the United States. To all the women who dared to dream and to hope, to work hard, to sacrifice, to seek the satisfaction that comes from exhausting effort and conscientious training, and to all those who worked with them in the fulfillment of their ambitions, what happened to Kathy was a marker. On the marker were five simple words. For God's sake, be careful.

mentor

The primary reason to have a coach
is to have somebody who can look
at you and say, "Man, you're looking
good today."

~Jack Daniels, running coach

Running for Their Lives

Gary Smith, 2004

Coach Jim White had built a distance dynasty. His Mexican-American boys from the small, hardscrabble town of McFarland had won nine California state cross-country championships. But Coach White's final season before retiring proved to be the hardest, for him, as well as for the unlikely team leader Javier Medina.

There was silence when the footrace ended. Then Ayon threw his arms around the coach's wife and cried, "Why did God do this? I don't know why God did this!" and the boys in red and white each staggered off alone to cry.

They had failed the most successful coach in California schoolboy history. They'd failed the elders who'd walked at their heels to the starting line, reminding them that they had to win the state championship for Mr. White. They'd fallen apart on the old man's last day as a coach, they'd spit on his dynasty and ministry both. *Sixth place.*

Mr. White's wife went to dry their tears. But then she and the elders began crying too, and it was hopeless. No high school sports program in California had ever done what theirs had—won nine state titles—but it had been this team's duty to send Mr. White into the sunset with the untouchable number, the fitting number, the perfect number: 10.

One by one, that autumn day a year and a half ago, the Mexican-American boys awaited their chance to speak to the white man alone. To say, "I'm sorry, Blanco. I'm sorry for letting you down."

Except one.

———————•———————

Eight months passed. Evening fell on the heat-slugged little town. Laundry sagged from plastic lines like skin from the brown dogs' ribs. Workers, home from a long day of picking grapes, sat inside their stucco box houses as if stoned by the sun. Chickens in their front yards gave up pecking at the bare earth. Not a peep came through the doors of El Cha Cha Cha.

Wait. Something just stirred on the southwest edge of town. A plume of dust, out in the almond groves. A herd of brown boys kicking up powder on a dirt road.

A bicycle nipped at their heels. It accelerated if they slackened and made them raise dust again. It moved up onto their flank to protect them against the farm dogs' fangs. It dropped back to round up stragglers. Jim White thought he had passed the torch to his faithful assistant, Amador Ayon, thought he had retired and begun to fade away. But his town and his wife and his gut

From *Sports Illustrated*, March 15, 2004. Reprinted by permission of Time Inc.

hadn't let him, so here he was at 62, weeks before the 2003-04 school year and cross-country season began, sheepdogging his flock through 100 degree heat, chasing state title number 10. Again.

He rose from the seat of the bike and pumped harder, exchanging nods and words as he passed Julio and Baltazar and Octavio and Steven, both Tonys and both Juans, all the boys who'd hoped with all their hearts that the sun wouldn't set on them, that the town's patriarch wouldn't retire during their four years at McFarland High . . . that they wouldn't end up sitting inside those stucco box houses at night for the rest of their lives, dazed by fieldwork and sun.

What were the odds that Ayon or anyone else could take over and keep this magic dust cloud moving? What were the odds that in the annals of California high school sports—all the years chocked with big-city phenoms and rugged valley boys and wealthy suburban programs—the greatest dynasty would be produced by a band of 5 1/2-foot Mexican-Americans at a little high school in a town with no traffic light or movie theater, one of the poorest communities in America? That year after year a blue-eyed man on a bicycle could compel another bunch of teenage campesinos to run eight miles across the fields and orchards where they'd already worked all day harvesting oranges and grapes and almonds and peaches and plums? Every evening? In their *off*-season?

Mr. White tucked his bike behind the front-runner, the fastest one, the unlikeliest leader he'd ever had. The boy who wished that Mr. White had just packed up and left to live his last years in his cabin an hour away in the Sierra Mountains, as he'd planned.

The man and the boy kept pumping their knees. They were both striving for more than number 10, both straining against all the invisible strings that bound them to McFarland. Both struggling to find their way out.

Mr. White drew closer. "Good work, Javi," he murmured.

Javier Medina didn't lift his eyes. He turned his shoulder to his town's legend.

———————●———————

It didn't seem like a hard town to leave. Most people left before realizing they'd ever entered, barreling through the Central Valley three hours north of Los Angeles along Highway 99, a strip of asphalt that separated McFarland's poor West Side from its poorer East Side. The white descendants of the Dust Bowl refugees who had founded the town had no trouble abandoning it in the 1960s and '70s to Mexican immigrants weary of wandering from town to town, crop to crop. McFarland's movie theater became a mortuary, its newspaper was long gone, and all the bars but El Cha Cha Cha were boarded up. The town had two places to go to jail and nine places to go to eat. The population was 9,600 if you didn't count a couple of thousand illegals and the 1,100 behind bars. McFarland was renowned chiefly for its high incidence of cancer, which had afflicted one of Mr. White's nephews and more than 20 other children between the mid-'70s and mid-'90s and scared visiting teams into bringing their own water.

Mr. White loved McFarland.

He arrived in 1964 fresh from college in L.A., took a fifth-grade teaching job and jumped in with both feet, making sure his yard, too, had chickens and rabbits scratching at it. He wanted to get to know people. He wanted *small*. He came from a family of missionaries but had fallen in love with sports: here was his chance to merge duty with passion. He began coaching every school and rec team he could, basketball and baseball and football and track, and when little boys knocked on his front door asking if he'd come out to play tag or ball, he'd say *sure*.

So what if the town turned brown before his very eyes? In college he'd chosen a roommate who was half Mexican, half Native American. So what if Mr. White had never been a runner? The local runts he wanted to coach in cross-country hadn't a prayer on a basketball court or a football field—endurance and slow-twitch muscles were their genetic gifts—and for all his compassion, he needed to win. So what if he had to wait 17 years to get a coaching job at the high school? He'd grown up in a dozen houses in Stockton, moving as swiftly as his father could build a new one and sell the old, and he longed for roots the same way that the weary migrants around him did. Four decades after Jim and Cheryl White arrived in McFarland, the town would be 99.9% Mexican, and that—as their three long-since-departed daughters like to say—was only because Mr. and Mrs. White stayed.

Blanco, his runners often called him. English was their second language, one that bedeviled them in the classroom and kept most of them out of college. Most went to the fields when they reached puberty, stooping and snipping, climbing and crawling and duckwalking through irrigation puddles to supplement their parents' pitiful wages. No one could figure it out, how the runners with the shortest legs and the grimmest lives began winning everything once Blanco took over their program, in 1980. He'd joke that it was the town's notorious water or the beans that McFarland's mamas served. He persuaded the boys that it was the "voodoo juice" oil he'd give them before races to rub on their aching backs and legs, the cleansing teas and the shakes full of complex carbohydrates and the gel capsules full of vitamin E and bee pollen that he'd dole out. But the secret was his vast investment of time and heart.

He'd grip the rawhide hands of the boys' fathers and look in their eyes, convince them that something beyond food, clothing and shelter mattered, that this silly Anglo notion of high school athletics had meaning. He'd fetch their sons in a battered '59 pickup that had been a forest ranger's truck, two lucky lads up front drinking in his stories and 16 crammed in the back where they could keep an eye on the road through the rotting floorboards. He'd haul them into the foothills to run the orange groves. He'd take them to collect old bottles or newspapers, to sell tamales, to hoe cotton fields—*Mexican golf*, the locals called it—raising funds so they could compete all across California.

He'd take them where their own fathers hadn't the energy or money to take them—bowling lanes and Putt-Putt courses and movie theaters in Bakersfield, a half hour away—and farther, much farther, to do things many Mexican boys in McFarland had never done. To set eyes on the ocean, to stay in a hotel, to sleep under a white man's roof and sing Ging Gang Goolie on a 12-hour road trip. To camp at Yosemite and run five miles at sunrise to fish for trout at a lake, then run five back to cook it and roast marshmallows over a fire. To fly in an airplane, as the program grew, to run in New York City and Charlotte, even Germany and China. To see that the flat farmland starting at the edge of town didn't go forever, needn't swallow them if they could just master themselves, just do the simplest, hardest thing: lay one sneaker in front of the other again and again.

He never had a son. He had hundreds of sons. He'd take his runners to the doctor, visit their mothers in hospitals and their brothers in jails. He'd help them study, drive them to college, pay their tuition, feed and clothe them, go to court with them and to the wall for them even when, long after graduation, they strayed off the path. "I need you to come back and run with us, buddy," he'd tell fleshy 25-year-olds through prison bars. Cheryl, who'd grown up watching her mother, a minister's wife, do such things for her husband's Church of Christ congregations, showered the boys with homemade cookies and hugs, heart-to-heart lunches and handwritten notes signed "Mrs. Coach." Mr. White, following the calling of his cousins and uncles, had served as a minister in his church in McFarland; his sister and an uncle had served missions overseas: He knew no other way to run a team.

He rarely raised his voice. He'd stumbled upon the sorcerer's stone of coaching: Give so much of yourself that your boys can't bear to let you down. They won the first state cross-country championship held in California, in 1987, and their town gussied them up in foam antlers and had them pull Mr. White through the streets, scrunched in a red Flyer wagon and wearing a Santa hat. They won 22 of 24 league titles and 15 sectional championships, beating schools with enrollments seven times as large as theirs. The first 15 years that California held championships, they won nine, all in Divisions III and IV, but some years they likely would've taken the whole tamale against the megaschools in Divisions I and II as well, if only they'd gotten the chance. They became McFarland's treasure, their ranks swelling each year as graduates circled back to push them and chide them and mentor them, to chorus Mr. White's wisdom to the next wave. They became so much like a family that one day even Javier Medina decided that he wanted in.

———————————•———————————

Something takes a part of me.
Something lost and never seen.
Every time I start to believe,
Something's raped and taken from me.
~Lyrics from "Freak on a Leash" by Jonathan Davis of Korn

Javier lay in his bedroom, listening to Korn howl the lyrics to "Freak on a Leash." He was in eighth grade. It was 1999. He was teetering. His sister, Corina, had already tumbled into drugs and darkness, tattooing her wrists with SURE-ÑAS LOCAS—Crazy Southerners, the female subset of a McFarland gang. Their father kept vanishing, into jail for half a year for hitting Corina, or God knows where for months on end after drinking and raging and being thrown out of the house by Javi's mother.

Javi cranked the music—*Sometimes I cannot take this place/Sometimes it's my life I can't taste/Sometimes I cannot feel my face*—and put on his game face. It wasn't easy. His eyelashes were too long, his eyes too soulful, his stack of books too high for punkhood. He yanked on his blue Korn T-shirt, grabbed the notebook that he'd driven a screw into and headed to school, late again.

He had tried to honor his favorite anarchy-rock band by ducking into the locker room during Mr. White's gym class at McFarland Middle School and sandpapering KORN onto the brand-new lockers. It had nearly gotten him expelled and—as he tried to talk his way out of it—into perhaps deeper trouble still. "*I'm* going to run for Mr. White one day," he'd blurted to the startled vice principal, one of White's assistant coaches and former runners, David Diaz.

Even Mr. White snorted when he heard that one. *Javi?* The smart aleck who'd flunked Mr. White's phys-ed class because he refused to suit up, suddenly grunting out 10 half-mile repeats straight uphill at a 2:45 clip? *Yeah, right.* The sulker with the 0.9 grade-point average in seventh grade, the school's Snail Award winner for most days tardy, setting his alarm clock for 6 a.m. to run along the irrigation canals? *Sure.* The younger brother of Salvador Jr., who had smart-mouthed and drag-assed his way through high school while running for Blanco just a few years before? Mr. White's life's work was retrieval, salvage, salvation and so, of course, he'd give Javi a shot, but . . .

Javi went home, lay in bed and, for the third time, read *Banner in the Sky*, a book about a fatherless boy who climbs a mountain that no one believed could be climbed. Javi went outside as darkness fell and lay in the back of his father's pickup truck, staring at the sky while his dad sat in a plastic chair nearby and drank beer in silence.

They couldn't talk. Salvador Sr. spoke Spanish, insistent on remaining Mexican. Javi spoke English, determined to be American. Each was too stubborn to speak the words he knew in the other's tongue. When Salvador, a third-grade dropout who didn't read or write, saw his son disappear behind another book, he'd bark, "Go out and play! You'll hurt your eyes!" He had smuggled himself into the U.S. twice as a teenager, the first time beneath the hood of a pickup truck, the second, for keeps, in a footrace with the border patrol, one of 25 desperate men who darted across the desert. Only two had made it. He believed in work, not words, but he wouldn't let Javi work with him in the grape or rose fields, denied him his share of McFarland's bitter drink. "You're too soft," Salvador said. On summer mornings Javi would watch his older brother and the other boys in town climb into pickups and head off for the fields with their fathers; then he'd return to his books and his bedroom.

Salvador crushed his beer can and rattled it into the bucket of empties. Before the *snap* of the day's first pop-top, he'd vacuum and mop the house and wash every dirty dish, and when he went on errands he couldn't pass a stranger stranded on the road without stopping to help. That was the man Javi loved. Some days he would hide his father's beers in a kitchen cabinet. Others, he was so hungry for approval that he'd be the first to his feet to fetch Dad another cold one. Korn was correct: Life was pathetically mucked up.

Salvador sipped and stabbed a callused finger at the stars. "Los Siete Osos," he murmured. The Seven Bears. Javi nodded. Salvador pointed and murmured again. "El Camino de San Diego." The Road to San Diego—the swath of stars that Mexicans on foot followed at night on their way to San Diego, America, hope. Javi nodded again. Those constellations, these moments beneath the night sky, were what he and his father had. When adults asked what he'd like to be when he grew up, Javi had begun to say the most astonishing thing for a McFarland boy: an astronomer.

But how could he reach the stars from a town like his? Just one man there had stretched that far: the tall, handsome white man bicycling down the road, herding his family every single day. Something about Mr. White's steadiness, his resolute pursuit of the highest goals, struck Javi even as he defied the man in gym class. Maybe, too, it was the twinkle in Blanco's eyes as he mangled Spanish, the silly dances he'd do and the pranks he'd play, smuggling cookies into a teacher's purse and then clucking in disbelief over her gluttony, or crooning "Jose can you see . . . any bedbugs on me?" to every Jose in town. Somehow, Blanco was both a remorseless taskmaster and a big, goofy kid—and one of the few gringo teachers who didn't commute from Bakersfield, who'd lived among McFarland's Mexicans for nearly four decades, showing them the surest way out of town . . . but never taking it.

Javi showed up one day at a rec department cross-country practice directed by one of Mr. White's former runners, a proving ground for prospects. *I'm going to show Mr. White something he won't believe*, Javi told himself. He gasped and quit running and had to walk to the finish. But he came back for the next practice and the next, and by the end of eighth grade—*too soft, huh?*—he had run faster than anyone believed a boy with a chip on his shoulder could: a 4:55 mile!

He joined the fleet trying to stay in front of Mr. White's front tire. He muttered an obscenity during a team outing, and Mrs. White walked him off alone and said, "Oh, no, no, no, not in this family." He apologized, and his life began to fall into a groove. "Running bolts my head on," he'd explain. "I know who I am by running. It puts me into reality, so I don't float off into space. I forget my problems. I say, 'I run for McFarland,' and people are like, 'Wowww!' Deep down I want people to think of me as part of something, even though I pretend that none of that matters. Jeez, man, without this program, I'd have no personality, I'd be . . . nothing."

He made his first true friends, a brotherhood of sweat and pain with runners Juan Gonzalez and Steven Cavazos. He loved bumping fists before and after each practice with his teammates and all of Mr. White's former runners, *los veteranos* who still trained with the team and became a battalion of big brothers to Javi. He loved arriving at meets on the bus and watching the other schools' runners' heads swivel and their eyes cloud and lips move: *McFarland's here.* He loved closing ranks for the team prayer and feeling his stomach knot at the sight of taller, wealthier boys on the starting line. "They're all white," a new kid on the team would sometimes say, and Mr. White would reply, "Yep . . . and they're all bigger. But I guarantee you they aren't as tough and don't work as hard as you do. Let's go take them down."

Mr. White was right. State title number 8 came in Javi's freshman year, when he ran with the frosh-soph team. *Omniscient* wasn't a word he'd toss around with the guys, but that was the word, he decided, for Mr. White. *Just follow him,* Javi told himself, *and good things will happen.* He followed Mr. White across the country, felt the thunder of Niagara Falls on a running trip, looked *down* on a cloud from atop the Golden Gate Bridge, saw water at Lake Tahoe that was bluer than any in a dream . . . and began to fix his eyes on college *somewhere else*. He scratched his way to No. 5 varsity runner in his sophomore year on a team that, midway through the season, clawed all the way to the No. 1 ranking in the nation among small schools and to No. 4 overall. Anyone who came to the races could see that Javi wasn't too soft to work in the fields, could see his grit as he rubbed out opponents in the last quarter mile . . . anyone at all. But his father never came.

"Oh, how your father brags of your achievements to his relatives," Javi's mother, Sylvia, would tell her son. But never a word from Salvador to Javi, even when his sophomore season ended with the ultimate ascent, up the ladder with his teammates as their names were painted in white letters on the ninth black silhouette of California on the school gym's outer wall, the display that opponents gaped at when they visited cross-country's Mecca.

Of course, the Snail still crept in late for some practices, skipped some and moped through others. Javi still was a boy missing something, one who could get lost searching for it in the spaces inside his head. He remembered to get his eyebrow and ear pierced and his hair dyed blond, but he forgot to bring his running gear to a meet. An excellent idea, he thought it was, to sign the Whites' guest book JAVI BAD A** in gangsta graffiti bubble lettering. Then he had to Wite-Out the words to remove the red from Mr. and Mrs. White's eyes. That was Javi. Ten years from now, a *veterano* wondered aloud, would Javi be in astrophysics . . . or in jail?

Mr. White was the weight that could tip the balance. Javi would do almost anything to please that man. He'd set up tables and sell concessions at rec department races to raise funds for the McFarland program, slice fruit for the peewee runners and act as their rabbit to improve their times. His grade-point average rocketed to 3.5 his first semester in high school, then to 4.0, then 4.17. He affixed the watch Mr. White gave him to his bedroom wall—he couldn't risk wearing it on his wrist. He taped Mr. White's photograph amid the pictures of planets that orbited his room.

One day late in his sophomore year, the planets moved, the solar system shifted. Javi heard the rumor: *Mr. White's leaving.*

———————————•———————————

How do you leave a place where you've taught and coached and loved for 38 years? How do you tell a couple of dozen Mexican boys that it's time to give your children's children what you didn't have time to give your own children: *you.* How do you tell teenagers what you owe your wife after four decades of flying out the door at dawn and trudging back in as she falls asleep? How do you explain to field hands' sons that you've worked so many years that your annual retirement pay would total 96% of what you'd get if you kept working . . . that you're human, not a saint?

You don't. You don't explain. You don't call a team meeting and make a big wet fuss over this being your last year and how much they've all meant to you. Not when you're Mr. White, and your life leans on actions rather than words. Not when the words might stick in your throat. You just take aside your trusty disciple Ayon and tell him that you're going to start pulling back and letting him emerge as the leader during this transition year, because that's your goal: to pass the torch without extinguishing the flame.

The rumor festered. The family gathered, as always, at Mr. White's home for their evening runs that summer of 2002. Javi peered at the dark windows of Blanco's weather-beaten stucco box house. Where was he? Off in Texas or Long Beach visiting his daughters, Ayon would say. Off at his new cabin up in the mountains, building the wraparound deck of his wife's dreams. He'll be back to coach this year, don't worry about what happens after that, and c'mon, now, guys, let's pick it up. Javi slogged toward the almond groves. Who had sat all the boys down beneath the orange trees and, in the dulcet voice of a pastor, reminded them over and over how important it was, every day, to show up? Who had said he'd *always* be there for them?

Every time I start to believe . . . .

Somehow it didn't seem so urgent anymore to throw one foot in front of the other. Somehow, as summer ground on and no one knew when to expect the coach, it no longer seemed imperative to show up. Mr. White would act as if nothing was wrong, no big deal, when he did appear, full of pleasantries and wisecracks—as unaware of the effect on Javi of his looming departure, it seemed, as Javi's dad had appeared to be all those times he'd left.

But Javi couldn't confront Mr. White any more than he could his father, and so he began to do things that seemed to have nothing to do with the hurt. He began staying up late, emptying a few beer cans of his own and drifting into practice late because he was walking a girl home from school, kissing off Mr. White's age-old warning that nothing would pull a butterfly back to the caterpillar pile faster than a girlfriend. He didn't need Mr. White's voodoo juice before races anymore. He'd hear the other runners beg Mr. White to change his mind about retiring, but Javi wouldn't do it. *If someone wants to leave*, he kept thinking, *then I don't need him*. It wasn't easy being the one who saw through the armor of the town's white knight. But Javi had gone it alone before, and dammit, his second father wasn't going to lay a finger on the wound left by his first.

The Whites felt him slipping through their fingers but kept giving him another chance. They were old pros at this, at rescuing runners who'd dropped out or impregnated girlfriends or slept on plastic lounge chairs because their parents couldn't afford a bed. But Javi was different from the other lost boys, more intelligent, more sensitive, more perplexing . . . always just out of Mr. White's reach. His long eyelashes would flutter and his face contort for a half minute before he'd reply to the simplest query, agonizing over how much to drop his guard.

Mrs. White took him out to lunch for one of her heart-to-hearts, but only one heart was put on the table. Mr. White went to Javi's house to talk to Javi's father but couldn't penetrate the beer and language barriers. He tried teasing Javi back into the fold, then tightening the screws. "Look, everyone, we have a new kid running with us today," he'd say when Javi showed up after a few days' absence. "Got your brain on today, Javi?" None of it worked, none of it could, because Javi was waiting for the man to show his feelings, not his needle.

More than for their town or their school, the boys had always run for Mr. White, a tie so strong that it bordered on dependency. Now that rope began to unravel. The team split into cliques. The boys yo-yoed. One day they would speed up, at *los veteranos'* insistence: It was Blanco's final year! The next they'd crawl: It was Blanco's final year. Yet by sheer force of habit McFarland ran well enough, as the state championships approached, to be favored to win number 10—and a fourth straight crown.

Javi, who had become the team's No. 2 runner, could see it in *los veteranos'* eyes: He'd be marked in his town forever if he failed. It jabbed at his sleep like the bedsprings coming through his mattress. The day before the state meet, Mr. White opened *The Bakersfield Californian*'s sports page and shuddered. *What?*

"We realize that second place is just not going to happen," said Javi in the article. "We're going to win, and that's it. We're not competing against other teams. We're competing against ourselves and trying to get a personal record." Javi had turned his terror inside out.

Ayon pulled the boy aside, aghast. "No McFarland runner," he growled, "has ever been as blunt as you." Silence filled the team van on the ride to Fresno that gloomy Saturday. Thirty former McFarland runners awaited the boys at Woodward Park, reminding them of their obligation to Blanco even as they braced at the starting line. The gun sounded, and the alumni took off as if it were their race, crunching through the dead leaves outside the ropes to keep a bead on the boys.

It was too much cargo to bear. Javi crossed the line in 16:41, 23 seconds slower than his best time on the five-kilometer course he'd run so many times. McFarland's top five runners ran their worst races of the year, and the team's sixth-place finish was its worst ever in a state meet. The boys were still weeping into their mashed potatoes at a buffet an hour later, still sobbing when they stumbled out of the van back in McFarland. Javi went straight to his bedroom and wouldn't come out.

The boys walked into the team banquet two months later as if they weren't good enough for the tuxedos Mr. White had rented for them. Blanco apologized to the town, took the blame for what happened and couldn't beat his tears to the end of his farewell speech. Javi didn't cry, as his mother and the others did. Javi never saw Mr. White give his speech. He'd turned his chair to face the other way.

———————•———————

Sixth place sat in Mr. White's gut like a pit from one of his backyard nectarines. Retirement tasted like the pesticide on a summer breeze. Instead of pride over all the migrants' sons he'd transformed into teachers and administrators and coaches, uneasiness settled over him as he gazed at the mementos of his coaching career. All his life he'd played to win, even if it meant bumping the Ping-Pong table in mid-rally, pinning down an opponent's arm as he went up for a rebound or wreaking havoc as a flag football coach by instructing one of his players to *almost* leave the field during a mass substitution, then streak up the sideline unnoticed to snag a touchdown pass.

What, he kept asking himself, had gone so wrong on his final day? Forty-two years earlier his varsity basketball coach had burned him at Magic Valley Christian College in Idaho, banishing him to the jayvee for his defiance of a decree that students attend no other church but the one on campus. He'd *never* do such a thing when he became a coach, he'd vowed—he'd bend over backward to be fair to his kids. But maybe, in his final year, he'd violated his golden rule. Maybe he'd cheated his runners by his absences from summer practice, the furnace in which his teams were always forged.

His wife smelled his uneasiness, and she wasn't so sure that she was ready to retire as Mrs. Coach. Cheryl approached the school board president, Linda Genel, and told her that she'd had a dream in which her husband got the thing he'd been giving boys for decades—a second chance. The idea caught fire with the school board, and a contract was cobbled together that would permit Mr. White to receive his retirement pay yet be kept on as a full-time substitute gym teacher at the middle school for one more semester, so he could sing his swan song again with the boys of McFarland High. Mr. White agreed. All the runners seemed thrilled.

Except one.

Javi spiraled down . . . down . . . down. It was so easy, in a town plagued by gang violence and drug problems, to end up with your mug on a pickle jar on the counter at the Chevron station, soliciting donations to pay your burial expenses. But when the gunfire hit Javi's family last spring, it was his 22-year-old cousin, Ruben Juarez Jr., who died, and it was Ruben himself who pulled the trigger rather than surrender to police and face a third conviction that likely would've sent him to prison for life. Javi froze. He had grown up playing tag in the dark with Ruben. He stopped eating and studying, cut classes and track practices, piled up detentions and flunked history. He shut himself in his bedroom and let the confusion in his house howl around him.

"Go see Mr. White," begged his mother.

"I can't," muttered Javi.

"Why not?" asked his brother, Salvador.

"He doesn't care about us anymore," said Javi.

He entered a 5K road race in June and, before Mr. White's disbelieving eyes, crawled to the finish in 21 minutes. This was his next leader, his fastest returning senior, the one that Blanco's season of redemption would hinge on? Maybe, Mr. White and *los veteranos* began to suspect, working the fields—which Javi had never done—was more important than any of them had realized. Maybe the fields were what had burned the *will* into their runners all those years, and there was just no way this boy who read books could ever muster it. "Not bad, Javi, only five girls beat you," Mr. White fumed after the race. "Were you waiting for somebody, or just counting the flowers? What's a McFarland runner doing back there? You need to step it up. You need to *wake* up."

Ayon could see it coming, another slap to his hero's face, and could bear it no more. He invited Javi to a Chinese restaurant, waited until he lifted his fork over his beef and broccoli, and then cut loose, freezing that fork in midair for five minutes. "If you can't cut it, I don't care if you're a senior!" Ayon hissed. "You won't be on this team! What happened last year *can't* happen again. You've got to be a leader!"

Who's to say just when or why a boy begins to become a man? Maybe the death of his cousin finally cried out its counterpoint to Javi: *Don't waste your life. It's too precious.* Javi made a promise to God that he wouldn't waste it. Maybe it was seeing Mr. White show up on July 1 for the summer's first evening run, and every night after that, and the words Mr. White spoke to him after one evening run. "I know how you felt last year," he said. "But I'm going to be here for you this year, every day. I'm going to give everything I've got, and I'm hoping you're going to give everything too." Javi still harbored doubts, still wondered if Mr. White was returning out of obligation rather than desire. But he stopped brooding and decided to give the coach that second chance, becoming resolute in his evening training, adding six-mile runs three mornings a week, hitting the weights in the afternoons and running in a wet vest in the pool. He wrote down his teammates' phone numbers to make sure they'd show up too.

Mr. White assessed his squad: a young one, teeming with promising freshmen and sophomores but lacking a single junior and crying out for leadership from the three seniors—Javi, Steven and Juan, introverts all. A state title? A tall task.

"We're going to low-key everything," declared Mr. White. "I want to enter the state meet under cover."

"We're not going to talk about doing it for Mr. White this year," Javi said. "We'll just see what happens." But privately he set three lofty goals: a sub-16-minute 5K; a top 10 state ranking for McFarland among all schools, regardless of size; and state championship number 10.

Two days before the season's first meet, gunfire erupted again, and two of Mr. White's former runners dropped. Jose Velasco, a pal of Javi's brother, died in a drive-by gang murder, and Jose's brother Aurelio survived a bullet in the neck. The Whites went to the Velascos' house on the double, still distraught over the stabbing death of another former runner just weeks earlier. Javi felt as if he were going to throw up. At night he stayed home, warned by his brother that retaliation was in the air and that more bullets might soon be too.

Three weeks later, at the Bell-Jeff Invitational in L.A., Javi led his team to a sweeping 2-3-7-8-10-11 finish as McFarland thrashed 58 schools—33 of them from higher divisions—to gain the No. 2 overall ranking in the state. Their cover was blown. They were in the headlines.

Then came trouble. Freshman phenom Julio Olvera fell hard for a girl, tumbled all the way into the caterpillar pile, then inflamed a nerve in his hip and ended up having to run for a month in a swimming pool. Juan Gonzalez hurt his knee and was finished, for all intents and purposes, for the season. Now McFarland was down to two seniors and a slew of raw freshmen and sophomores. Ninth-grader Baltazar Topete, the No. 5 varsity runner, informed Mr. White that he'd be retiring when Mr. White did because all this pain was pointless without him, and Cheryl kept asking, "Are you sure you want to leave, Jim? Are you sure you're ready?" until the old coach, too, began to wonder whether the torch could ever be passed.

Javi, too, had begun feeling the gravitational pull of a poor Mexican-American town. None of Javi's senior friends spoke of moving on, as if the next phase were a betrayal. "Go to college wherever you want," his father said when he learned that Javi was applying to UCLA, UC Santa Barbara, UC San Diego and San Diego State. "We just won't visit you." It was a leathery Mexican fieldworker's way of saying, "I'm going to miss you, it hurts to think of you going away," but how was Javi, for all the reading he did, ever to read that deep between the lines?

Somehow everything was connected. Somehow McFarland's pack mentality and Javi's own fear of pulling away clutched at him even when it was time to leave everyone behind in a meet. Week after week he led his team across the finish line, but his times remained a half minute slower than his goal. "Kindergarten times," he snorted. "I'm holding back, running *with* people and not grinding them up. I'm looking for someone to go with, like Steve or Juan, someone I *know*."

And yet, barely realizing it, he'd begun imploring his teammates with the same words that Mr. White had once used on him: He was becoming a leader. Mr. White saw it one day in practice when he instructed his boys to cover a 4 1/2-mile steep uphill climb in 33:30. "No, we're not gonna run 33:30 like Mr. White said, we're gonna run it in 31:30," he heard Javi tell them, and then he watched Javi stay with the trailers, talk them through their pain and sheepdog every one of them home in 31:30. "He's just a different kid this year," Mr. White told people. "He's fantastic. He doesn't have that sad face anymore. He's talking, encouraging all the other kids and working his butt off."

The town bid its formal farewell to Mr. White at midseason. It draped banners for each of the championship years over the hoods of nine shiny new pickup trucks, filled them with runners, past and present, and enthroned Mr. and Mrs. White in a red Porsche at the front of the procession, waving regally while horns honked as if every virgin in town had just been married off. Then everyone sat down to celebrate a life, and Mr. White knew in his bones that he had to leave, this time for good.

In the second-to-last meet of the year, Javi's breakthrough race came at last, a blazing 16:07. "I actually believed in myself," he marveled. "It's peculiar. The fastest race I've ever run felt the easiest."

But there was no time to revel. Every day, every race, was little more than a prelude to what really mattered, the state championships two days after Thanksgiving. A countdown to Take 2 of Mr. White's final day.

———————•———————

Word went out to the vets. Don't spook the boys this time. Don't even mention that it's Mr. White's adios. No need even to show up in Fresno, matter of fact. Mum's the word, men. No Churchill from Blanco. Just another stroll in the park.

The old Javi reared his head. He showed up for McFarland's final practice a half hour late, well after stretching time, when team meetings were held and the leader might be expected to talk from the heart.

He slept in his mother's bed on the eve of the race, a night of freedom from his bedsprings, but still he tossed and turned for hours. A 16:01 or better would place him among the top 10 runners in McFarland's storied history and might pull the freshmen and the sophomores into the 16:30-to-16:45 range required to topple their more experienced foes. A loss, and Javi might go down as the runner who smothered *both* of Mr. White's last hurrahs. It wouldn't be easy, not with the team's leading freshman, Olvera, barely recovered from his hip injury, and not with Carmel and Oak Park, the other two favorites in Division IV, coming in loaded with seniors.

Mr. White and his boys each dropped to one knee and prayed, the runners' white shorts and singlets stark against their brown skin and against Woodward Park's blaze of autumn oranges and yellows and reds. They all locked arms, and their eyes began to mist—exactly what Mr. White had been determined to avoid—as Juan Gonzalez stammered out how much he loved them all and how sorry he was that, because of his knee, he couldn't go to war with them. They walked to the starting line, where 184 other boys in other colors waited to take them down. Javi looked back. There, for the first time, stood his father.

The boys tapped fists. Mr. White and Ayon watched in silence. The gun sounded, and the two men hurried through the mass of spectators and across the creek to catch the boys at the first mile marker. Javi flew by it in 4:52, among the top 10, and his six teammates all managed 5:07 or better . . . not bad, not bad. Blanco's eyes clouded at the second mile marker—they'd bogged down too much in the hills!—then he bolted toward the finish to rally the final kick of his coaching life.

Six runners funneled through the chute, then Javi—he'd done his job, or near enough, with a 16:10 and seventh place, the second-fastest 5K of his life. He whirled at the finish line and squinted, waiting to glimpse the next flash of white breaking from the tree line . . . and waiting . . . and waiting, hope vanishing with every tick of the clock. Finally, at 16:51, they began to arrive, each nearly a half minute too slow, gasping their apologies to Javi.

He reeled away, no time to think, and wrapped his arms around his father and pulled him to his chest.

———————●———————

No one cried after Mr. White's last race. Blanco wouldn't let them, moving from runner to runner to let each one know that third place, behind Carmel and Oak Park, was no disgrace. "You couldn't do it all," he told Javi.

Javi looked up at his coach in a mournful daze. "Are you doing O.K., Mr. White?"

"I'm doing fine, Javi."

It was all over, and now Javi entered no-man's-land, waiting to see if his dream of studying astronomy and running in college would come true. Waiting to find out if he'd really do it, really walk away and reach the other side of the almonds and oranges and grapes, or if this season was the peak of his life, as it had been for so many other runners, and now he'd struggle the way they had when there was no Mr. White to run for.

No, he sensed. A boy couldn't *walk* away from McFarland, he had to run, and so he got up the next morning and ran six miles, and a few days later he upped it to eight, sometimes even 10, as if the season had never ended. "If I don't stop," he said, "I'll keep going."

The team's last night together came at their banquet seven weeks ago. Javi wouldn't go to the podium, just couldn't do it, to express the team's feelings about Mr. White, leaving that to Juan. But Javi hung on every sentence from Mr. White, and when tears streamed down the coach's cheeks and he croaked, "I felt like I deserted the boys a little last year," the words went inside Javi and melted one more layer of ice.

"It felt like a victory, no, not a victory . . . a breakthrough," Javi said. "Something more than 'good job,' because we've heard plenty of 'good jobs.' Something from his heart. I know I should've been more understanding of him. I know I lost a relationship with a good man. And so as I was leaving I told him . . . uh . . . 'I just *hope* you won't be a stranger and I won't be a stranger. I hope I see you more often,' and Mr. White said, 'Yeah,' and . . . and it's not anything big, but I gave him a hug. I know it sounds like something small, but I'd never done it before, and for me it felt *big*. Maybe it wasn't as big for him as it was for me, but I . . . I was just trying to tell him something."

Mr. White got it. He walked away feeling wonderful about Javi and the deep shelf of talent he was leaving behind, vowing to the boys that he'd be back to watch them run, then drying his eyes and heading for his mountain cabin with Mrs. Coach.

And Javi? He lies in bed at night now staring at the planets on the wall, wondering if he'll ever sort the whole thing out. He had reached none of his three goals—not the state title, not the top 10 ranking, not the sub-16 5K—but his final season had given him something else, fruits he hadn't even thought to reach for. In those last two races he'd finally learned to run without the McFarland pack: He'd become a *racer*. And up on his wall hung that hug with his father, a picture splashed across five columns of The *Bakersfield Californian* that brought tears to his dad's eyes and kept bringing him back into Javi's room to peer at it in the moonlight while his son slept. And in Javi's heart hung that other hug, with that other man, that moment when at last he didn't run.

Lornah and Her Camp for Girls

Lori Shontz, 2002

Lornah Kiplagat is one of the world's greatest distance runners. She has won world-class marathons, has won the World Cross Country Championships, and currently holds four world records. However, for Kiplagat, these facts pale besides this one: In her homeland of Kenya, the career opportunities for girls are limited. For Kiplagat, her true mission in life is not world records; instead it is this: Change Kenya one girl at a time.

Iten, Kenya—Like everyone else, Lornah Kiplagat got the word from the newspaper. That's what made her so angry. She didn't understand how the Kenyan Amateur Athletic Association could possibly announce in the *East African Standard* that it had canceled a 10-kilometer race—the one *she* was organizing to celebrate the one-year anniversary of *her* running camp—without warning.

Lornah didn't become the only Kenyan woman to open a training camp for runners—while continuing a successful competitive career—without having the guts to stand up for herself. Within hours of reading the paper that November day, she was on the phone.

First she called the reporter and demanded a retraction.

"The Kenya 3A, they are not doing anything for the women athletes in this country, not at all, and if I do something they want to complain," she said. "The Kenya 3A cannot say it is canceled. It is my place and my house, and the K3A cannot cancel it."

Next she tracked down the mobile phone number for the athletic association's chairman, Eljiah Kiplagat (no relation). By the time she reached him, television news had reported that the association might ban Lornah and anyone who ran in her race from competing for Kenya in international events.

When the chairman answered his phone, she said brusquely, "This is Lornah Kiplagat. What is going on?" When he didn't answer immediately—Kenyan men aren't used to having a woman take such a tone—she filled in the dead air. "Why are you threatening me? I haven't killed anyone."

Recounting the incident—after she had agreed to change the date of her race to avoid a conflict with an association-sponsored event, and after he had accepted an invitation to attend her race and stay for lunch—Lornah shook her head and laughed at her audacity. "Sometimes I say things," she said, "and later I am so embarrassed."

But she just can't help herself, an attribute that enables her to be a voice for young women who aren't yet prepared to speak up for themselves.

"I don't think I am different," Lornah said. "We all think the same, but because of oppression, well, not oppression, but because they don't like to talk about it, they don't like to tell out the truth. And I can't say anything else."

The truth, according to Lornah, is this:

- Some parents won't allow their daughters to pursue a running career because they believe a daughter is more valuable for the dowry she can bring as a bride.
- Some girls compete but are taken advantage of, financially and sexually, by male coaches, agents and athletes.
- Some successful women athletes have failed to reap their rightful monetary rewards because their husbands have squandered their earnings.

The solution, according to Lornah, is for Kenya and its athletic federation to stop neglecting the country's girls.

In case they aren't sure how, she is providing an example. She has spent all of the prize money she has earned since 1998 on her camp, which aims to give girls a chance to work toward a brighter future. And not just in sports.

Lenia Cheryiuot, who dropped out of running as a teenager because she got pregnant and married, spent a year at the camp and then won several thousand dollars on the European road-race circuit this past summer.

Jane Kiptoo, described as undisciplined and uncoachable by her male secondary school coach, finished second at 3,000 meters in the 2000 junior world track championships.

Hilda Rotich didn't run fast enough to distinguish herself in Europe, but she is studying physical therapy at a school in the Netherlands, and Lornah is paying her tuition.

Florence Komen, who lagged behind the other girls in training but read voraciously when she finished her runs and chores, is now the camp's assistant manager. Lornah is sending her to computer classes, and if Florence wants to continue studying at a university, Lornah will make that happen, too.

"We're not trying to give them a running career," said Lornah's husband and agent, Dutchman Pieter Langerhorst. "Just a career. A future."

Camp Culture Shock

Lornah's camp—officially, the High Altitude Training Center—is nestled on a brilliant green hillside at 8,000 feet, surrounded by clay huts and situated next to the weather-beaten Impala Inn (read: "bar"). The camp stands out because of its cream-colored concrete walls, its brick-red floors, which are scrubbed daily and painted regularly, and its blue-green metal roof.

And because of its size.

An entire family lives in each of the neighboring one-room huts. Lornah's camp has 20 rooms, and only two people live in each one.

The camp also has electricity, a common room with seating for scores of people, a desktop computer, a store and, most difficult for outsiders to believe, a shower in every room.

"I never thought I would do something that big," Lornah said. "I think it's about six times, seven times what I had in mind. When I decided to do it, it came into my mind that, 'OK, if you have decided to do it, you are going to do it right.'"

That meant building 20 shower stalls—and buying a hot-water heater—even though the Kenyan girls at the camp are content to take bucket baths.

Lornah did this to make accommodations more comfortable for the European athletes who train occasionally at the camp—and who, unlike the Kenyan girls, pay for the privilege. She also wanted to cushion the culture shock for the Kenyan girls who end up competing in the United States or Europe.

Young Kenyan women with athletic potential who have graduated from secondary school can live and train at the camp for free. Europeans pay $20 a day for room and board and provide the camp's primary source of income. Some Kenyan boys are admitted, too, most of whom also pay.

Runners train twice a day, once at 6 a.m., again around 4 p.m. The rest of the day they help the cook prepare meals, keep the camp clean, run errands and wash clothes—including those of Lornah and Pieter, who stay in one of the camp's dormitory rooms because they are saving money to build their own house in Kenya someday.

Everything about the camp has broadened the horizons of the girls who live there.

Most hadn't met white people. Most hadn't seen a relationship like Lornah and Pieter's. Most hadn't met a woman like Lornah, who is comfortable being in charge.

"She's very, very different from the normal Kenyan woman," said Vivian Ruijters, a Dutch runner who has periodically trained at the camp. "Kenyan women still serve the men dinner. She does take care of Pieter, but Pieter also takes very good care of her. Their relationship has an equality. It's good for the girls here to see that."

Even the chores take on deeper meaning because the girls and boys share the work. They take turns washing dishes, they wash their own laundry, and they divvy up other daily tasks. One of the first girls to live at the camp was so shocked to see a boy scrubbing the floor that she averted her eyes.

Lornah made her look. "I told her, 'That's why you are here, to learn,'" she said. Lornah laughed. "Now she tells them what to do."

Thank-You Notes From Lornah

Lornah, now 28, absorbed such lessons at a young age.

She grew up on a *shamba*, a farm, in the heart of Keiyo territory, a part of the Kalenjin homeland so remote that she doesn't go home for a visit unless it's a sunny day.

It is too far to walk from the camp, and only a four-wheel drive vehicle can get there if it rains because the road turns into a ribbon of mud. This quasi-road—which passes the childhood homes of an Olympic champion, a world junior cross-country champion and a handful of other running stars—ends before it reaches the *shamba*, anyway. Lornah needs to cross through several fields to get home.

Lornah grew up in two huts much like the others that dot the Kenyan highlands. Her family was different, though. None of the neighbors knew what to make of the Kiplagats, who moved there in 1964, just after Kenya became an independent country.

They appeared normal enough, although they were wealthier than many. Lornah's father owned 300 acres of land and the area's only cheese store. As befitting his station in life, he had two wives.

But Kiplagat's sons, unlike the other boys in the village, couldn't just toss their dirty clothes on the floor to signal that the women should wash them. If they wanted their sisters to wash their clothes, they had to say please. And the sisters—no one could believe this—had to agree.

As for Kiplagat's daughters, well, no one thought they would ever find husbands. Kiplagat refused to have them circumcised. Custom dictated that a girl wasn't ready for marriage until undergoing this painful and potentially dangerous initiation ritual, in which an old woman of the tribe uses a knife to split open the clitoris, making a young woman "clean."

Kiplagat didn't care. "I have a lot of farm," he used to say. "If anybody doesn't want to marry my daughters, they can stay home. I have enough place for them."

Lornah doesn't know where her father got such ideas. He wasn't a feminist; sometimes he refused to give his daughters money for school fees, and they had to devise ways around his whims. Lornah succeeded in doing so and finished secondary school in 1993, at age 20.

She spent the next four years confounding her family and friends.

"I do my own thing," Lornah said. "I don't know why."

She received a scholarship to study medicine in India and turned it down because a cousin had embarked on a similar program and returned three years later with mental problems. "Up to now, he is completely nuts," Lornah explained. "If that could happen to a nice guy, a quiet guy, it might happen the same to me."

She left home three months after graduation without saying where she was going or what she planned to do, and traveled two hours to the city of Nakuru to turn herself into a world-class runner—even though she had never advanced beyond local competition in secondary school.

Lornah's cousin, Susan Sirma—who in 1993 became the first Kenyan woman to win a medal at the world track and field championships—gave her a place to live, and one of Sirma's friends offered Lornah a job looking after her children.

Lornah provided her own motivation.

She improved her times so much that the late Kim McDonald, one of the world's leading agents, offered her a plane ticket to Europe, where she could compete for prize money. She turned him down.

"My friends were asking, 'Are you normal? You must be crazy,'" Lornah said. "I said, 'No, I'm just going my own way.' I just started running and I'm not at the top, so I won't want to start at the top and come down. I want to start down, and then I go up."

Lornah eventually went to Germany and succeeded on the European circuit. She then turned her attention to the United States, where there are bigger prize purses.

Lornah first attracted the attention of Pieter, her future husband, when he was director of marketing for Saucony, a company that manufactures sporting goods. Pieter sent her some running equipment in 1995 after a friend alerted him to a young woman posting good results, and a few days later he received a thank-you note.

He was stunned, especially when the notes kept coming. "Every time I sent a pair of socks, she thanked me," Pieter said. Most runners, "you send them five pair and they say, 'Can I have six?'"

She spent the paycheck from her first major victory, the 1997 Los Angeles Marathon, the way most Kenyans do, on a new house for her parents. Next to the two one-room huts on the *shamba*, Lornah built a four-room house with brick she scavenged from the nearby ruins of "the *mzungu* house," so called because it was once occupied by white people.

An engraved silver platter, her first-place award from the marathon, hangs on the white-washed living room wall.

"Nothing Can Stop Her"

As Lornah's relationship with Pieter turned into a romantic one, he became her agent. She moved to the Netherlands, and Pieter began accompanying Lornah on visits to Kenya, eventually winning the approval of her family and paying her father the traditional brideswealth—five cows, five sheep.

Lornah began to talk about how much female running talent was being wasted back home. The stories of Lornah and her friends got Pieter thinking, and he helped Lornah turn her impulse—to help the girls back home—into plans for a full-blown athletic training facility.

Pieter also nurtured the qualities within Lornah that enabled her to attempt something so audacious.

"She had to get used to men and women being equal," Pieter said. "It was always in her mind, but they tried to push it down. I treat her the same, and she's changed a lot. It gave her a lot of confidence.

"She was always different—that's the reason I really liked her. But if something is in her mind now, my God, nothing can stop her."

In 1998, Lornah bought an acre of land just outside the town of Iten, where she had trained for a while at St. Patrick's, a Catholic boys school that sponsors running camps. She couldn't yet afford to build anything, so every time she returned to Kenya, she went to her land and sat on it. "I looked at it and thought about what it would look like," she said. "It really was a dream."

By the end of 1999, Lornah had won enough prize money to hire builders. She put more than money into the camp, however. She sketched the original plans, coordinated fabric for bedspreads, curtains and chair cushions, and even insisted on a few feminine touches, such as full-length mirrors in all of the rooms.

The villagers heard rumors that Lornah was building something, but they weren't sure what it was. A hotel, most figured.

"It went up so fast, all of a sudden there was a camp in their midst," said Brother Colm O'Connell, an Irish Catholic priest who helped build St. Patrick's into a running powerhouse. "For most buildings like that, it takes years. But Lornah and Pieter knew what they wanted to do. They had a plan, and they did it."

Even before the camp officially opened, runners were living and training there—and Pieter was helping them enter races in Europe.

Lornah continued to compete, and as she became more successful, she earned more prize money and more publicity for the camp. She began to do newspaper and television interviews, and her camp was firmly established well before its official opening in November 2000.

By its one-year anniversary this past November, the camp had become a phenomenon. So many Kenyan running stars attended the 10K race to celebrate the occasion that the introductions and speeches lasted two and a half hours.

The most special guests, of course, were the country's growing number of women stars, including half-marathon world-record holder Susan Chepkemei and marathon world-record holder Catherine Nidereba. They all listened as Patrick Sang, the 1992 Olympic steeplechase silver medalist, evoked the famous John F. Kennedy quote: "Ask not what your country can do for you, ask what you can do for your country."

Sang said, "Lornah has asked herself, 'What has sport done for me?' And she has said, 'I want to do something for the sport.' For that, Lornah, we thank you very much."

Lornah enjoyed the tribute—and the attention—but got right back to work.

When a reporter/photographer from the *Daily Nation of Kenya* showed up at the camp one day, she spent hours talking with him, explaining her vision and detailing the problems that girls must face. When he wanted to take a picture of her and Pieter standing in front of the camp, she balked.

She insisted that the photo include the runners, too.

"This place is not ours," Lornah said. "It is for the girls."

The Man

Kenny Moore, 2005

Bill Bowerman was one of the legendary track coaches. In his 24 years as coach at the University of Oregon, Bowerman trained 12 American record holders and won 4 NCAA titles. His book *Jogging* helped trigger the running boom, and his famous experiments with waffle irons and running shoes led to a new company called Nike. Possessed of a vigorous mind and forceful personality, Bowerman left an indelible impression on his athletes. One was Kenny Moore, who gives us a glimpse of this unique coach in the following story from *Runner's World*.

> A guru gives us himself and then his system; a teacher gives
> us his subject, and then ourselves.
>
> ~Adam Gopnik, in his eulogy for art historian and football
> coach Kirk Varnedoe, in *The New Yorker*

In the spring of 1964, Bill Bowerman gave me his subject, and stood back to see if I deserved it. Bowerman, then 53, had coached six sub-four-minute milers at the University of Oregon and had won the 1962 NCAA Track and Field Championship on the very field where he now stood, signaling me over. I was 20, a sophomore two-miler, just finishing my first training run after being out with the flu. He put two fingers to my neck, taking my pulse from my carotid artery.

"Easy day?" he said.

"Easy day. Absolutely."

"Twelve miles?" As if he were my physician, he tilted my head back so he could look me in the eye. He was 6'2" and over 200 pounds, with a powerful upper body.

"An easy twelve," I said.

We had vexed each other that year. I had never won a race in high school, had never broken 9:15 for two miles, but was determined to run the 100 miles a week his good friend Arthur Lydiard assigned his New Zealand Olympic champions.

"Are you in this simply to do mindless labor," he said, "or do you want to improve?"

"To improve."

"You can't improve if you're always sick or injured."

"I know, but Bill, it was an *easy* twel . . ."

He closed great, callused hands around my throat. He did not lift me off the ground. He did relieve my feet of much of their burden. He brought my forehead

From *Runner's World*, December 2005. Reprinted by permission of Rodale, Inc.

to his. "I'm going to ask you to take part in an experiment," he said with menacing calm. People five yards away thought we were sharing a tidbit of gossip. "For three weeks, you are not going to run a yard except in my sight. You will do a three-mile jog here every morning, and our regular afternoon workouts. If I or any of my spies see you trotting another step, you will never run for the University of Oregon again."

"Bill . . ."

"Are we agreed?"

"*Bill* . . ."

"Agreed?"

As I was feeling faint, I submitted.

————————•————————

Some of my afternoons remained exactly the same. I was allowed our regular hard-day sessions of four three-quarter-mile repetitions at 67-second-per-lap pace, then a five-mile run through the hills and rhododendrons of nearby Hendricks Park and four fast 110-yard strides before showering.

It was the easy days that were humiliating, reporting to Bowerman morning and evening on the sawdust trail inside the hallowed old Hayward Field track, having him count my laps, barely feeling warmed up before he called, "Three miles. In. In."

I was tempted to do secret, defiant runs, but he had enlisted the rest of the team and half the town; every friend was a possible traitor. And the potential cost was too great. No one who knew me doubted that I desperately wanted to be an Oregon runner. No one who knew Bowerman doubted he would back up his ultimatum.

As I learned a season earlier, even when Bowerman went out of his way to be welcoming, as at the annual team picnic at his house in September, it wasn't safe to relax. For freshman runners, the intimidation started with his hillside view, which spread to the snowy Cascades. Below, the McKenzie River carried fishermen in boats through spangled light. Beyond lay a soft-edged shire, stretching past farms to the mill town of Springfield and the university in Eugene. We were greeted by platinum-haired, unexpectedly beautiful Barbara Bowerman, who guided us to tubs of corn, roasts of beef, wheels of pie. The sight closed our throats because standing behind them, magnanimously pouring cider, was our coach.

Bowerman seemed in leathery profile to have been through some mythic struggle. He spit when someone called him coach, because the football coach he most hated had demanded it. "Just call me Bill," he said, but few would, or could, at first.

We gathered in the living room. The house had no trophies, just varnished fir beams, high windows, and a tall, rock fireplace Bowerman built himself. There was a wood stove in the kitchen, beside Barbara's spinning wheel. Bowerman stood. The river and mountain behind him now were filtered through Barbara's bonsai and sprays of orchids. This accorded with why we were here. We were to be cultivated, refined. Bowerman was about to ask us to put aside the things of the child. Not by accident did he begin, "*Men* of Oregon . . ."

"Take a primitive organism," he continued, his voice oil and sweet reason, "any weak, pitiful organism. Say a freshman. Make it lift or jump or run. Let it rest. What happens? A little miracle. It gets a little better. It gets a little stronger or faster or more enduring. That's all training is. Stress. Recover. Improve. You'd think any damn fool could do it, even . . ."

He turned, squinted, went far away somewhere, and turned back. "But you don't. You work too hard and rest too little and get hurt. You yield to the temptations of a liberal education and burn your candle at both ends and get mono. Every angelic, lying face I see here is poised to screw up, to overtrain, to fall in love, to flunk out, to play the guitar until three in the morning in the Pioneer Cemetery . . ."

There were hoots. Senior Archie San Romani reddened.

"We have no hard and fast training rules," Bowerman went on. "The vicissitudes of life usually teach an intelligent person what he can handle. It helps to have someone wise in the ways of candles to steady you as you grope toward the light. That would be me.

"But I regret to inform you," he added, his tone not the least regretful, "you cannot just tell somebody what's good for him. He won't listen. First . . . first you have to get his attention."

Upperclassmen nodded. Bowerman didn't have a central organizing principle. He had this, a central organizing parable.

"Farmer can't get his mule to plow," he said. "Can't even get him to eat or drink. Finally calls in a mule skinner. Guy comes out, doesn't even look at the mule. Goes in the barn, gets a two-by-four, and hits the mule as hard as he can between the ears. Mule goes to his knees. Mule skinner hits him again, between the eyes.

"Farmer drags him off. 'That's supposed to get him to plow? That's supposed to get him to drink?'

"'I can see you don't know a damn thing about mules,' says the skinner. 'First you have to get their attention.'"

In the hush that followed, Bowerman's grin was not far from fiendish. This was his allegory, his rationale, his fair warning. He was our mule skinner, and all he will do to us—including booting us from the team to make a point—constitutes the two-by-four he will use to crack open our mulish skulls, that lessons might be inserted.

At the time, of course, I didn't know the details. Leaving that first meeting, I felt only baffled disquiet. Even men who had trained under him for years were edgy. "Bowerman," said Keith Forman, a 3:58.3 miler and a keen psych major, "is ruled by a need to unsettle, to disturb. The man lives to get to you."

———————●———————

That first fall, Bowerman's urges seemed to war with each other. His own competitiveness was barely containable, but anyone racing in cross-country practice found himself working out alone. He affected countrified ways ("You run like a turkey in a plowed field"), but just as often quoted Scripture, the classics, or the Epic of Gilgamesh. He was a difficult, dignified professor of kinetics, but cracked up at jokes that began, "Two guys were peeing off a bridge . . ." He raised funds for the Bach Festival, but when a trucker kept flattening his mailbox, he booby-trapped it to puncture the guy's tires. For 25 years, Oregon freshmen asked each other the same thing. Was Bowerman here to teach us to overcome a cold, hard world? Or was he one of its coldest, hardest terrors?

In theory, as a coach, he should have been as interested in motivating the lazy as in mellowing the mad, but he wasn't. He regarded that most frustrating athlete, the gifted but casual, as beyond real help. He would juggle their roommates to give them an example of ambition, but took no further steps to inspire. He never gave a pep talk. "I'm sorry I can't make them switch brains," he said. "But I can't."

That left him free to be absorbed by the eager. He examined and reexamined what we ate. What we wore. What we did (and with whom we did it). He rethought our gifts, our goals, and the blind spots that kept us from reaching them. And yet, no matter how he permeated our lives, he always kept a kind of officer-and-troops distance, never trading intimacy for intimacy. The better you knew him, the less you could let down your guard. He confounded friend and foe alike; he was completely unreadable.

Bowerman thought of himself as an educator. He scorned recruiting and almost never gave full scholarships. "Anyone can be taught," he said. "Those who don't expect a handout best of all. I'd sure rather be teaching than blowing smoke up some spoiled brat's ass."

He loved language, and loved it if you loved it too. When he forced those easy days on me, I called him a tyrant, and he would never let me forget that. Once when I was too weak to trim some ripple soles he'd glued to my shoes, he took the shears and felt my hands and called them "philosopher's hands." And later he came in the sauna and put a big claw on my tender thigh and grinned that fiendish grin and said, "Now, Kenny, *this* is a horny hand. Feel a truly *horny* hand." I decline to call that "mentoring."

He didn't believe that a paternal concern for our feelings was his job. Athletes who'd depended on father-figure high school coaches were always in for a shock. When we were new, he'd assign a track workout and time us civilly enough, yet ignore us otherwise. Was our form correct? His only answer was to stonily lift his gaze to the swallows in their flight above Hayward Field.

"He speaks to us as does God," said my roommate, Bruce Mortenson. "Intermittently."

Disdainful of the leaden weight and nonexistent cushioning of running shoes in the 1950s, he had taken up cobbling and made us three-ounce spikes that lasted one race. We had no inkling that these were the beginnings of Nike's vast success, but we knew we had better shoes than anyone else. When Bowerman satisfied his academic curiosity about whether middle-aged professors and townspeople might be trained to actually trot a few miles, we had no idea jogging was about to inspire a sea change in American habits and health. But we knew there was only one man who could make both the professors and the mill foremen get out and run. Bowerman held our town together.

His training system rested on the deceptively simple truth that all runners are different. He might forget our names (he was famous for long and sometimes futile pauses when introducing even seniors at the Monday Oregon Club lunches), but he never forgot who strengthened more after intervals and who after long runs, nor whether we showed up fresh and ready for more work the next day, or stiff and sour. In the 1950s he'd learned to tailor the nature and intensity of workouts—and especially recoveries—to individual needs, and had been rewarded with Jim Bailey's 3:58.6 mile in 1956, the first sub-four on American soil. A steady green line of national champions and Olympians followed, from Otis Davis, the 1960 Olympic 400-meter champion; through Bill Dellinger, the bronze medalist in the 1964 Tokyo Olympics 5000 meters; to Steve Prefontaine, holder of all seven American distance records, from 2000 to 10,000 meters, at the time of his death in 1975. In the sprints, jumps, and throws, Bowerman was just as good. He coached NCAA champions in 15 of college track's 17 individual events.

———————•———————

Our desire to join that lineage was almost demented. I, for one, was so wild to remake myself into a champion that I rolled my eyes at Bowerman's patient studies of our strides and metabolism, and especially his damn easy days. It felt demeaning to just rest. Work was righteous; rest was weak-willed, ignoble.

And so I rammed into a classic paradox. "To run a world record," said Australia's Herb Elliott, world record holder and 1960 Olympic 1500-meter champion, "you have to have the absolute arrogance to think you can run a mile faster than anyone who's ever lived; and then you have to have the absolute humility to actually do it." Elliott was a god to me then. I took him as an example of maniacal effort. But if that sentence urges anything, it urges balance. You must balance the arrogance of your ambition with the humility of your training. If that was a hint to rest more, I ignored it.

Bowerman understood that very paradox—the need for both abandoned effort and ironclad control—because it was his own. He told us of being turned from youthful rebellion by Ercel Hedrick, the Medford School superintendent, who terrified him into channeling his energies. Bowerman knew and loved and distrusted us as he had been known and loved and distrusted himself.

When he talked with us about goals and hopes, he asked us, though never in so many words, to balance the hunger that is in all runners with some grasp of what our predecessors had achieved. The thing was not to blindly disregard limits but to understand the odds, even as one refused to accept them. He asked us, therefore, to leave open a tiny window of possibility. "If you go out to race," he said, "and know you'll lose, there's no probability involved. You'll lose. But if you go out knowing you will never give up, you'll still lose most of the time, but you'll be in the best position to kick on that rare day when everything breaks right."

———————————•———————————

He said that on May 4, 1964, when my three weeks of tyranny were over and he sent me out to run the two-mile in a meet against Oregon State. He said to begin no faster than 4:30 for the first mile and not chase after their animal, Dale Story, the NCAA cross-country champion, who ran barefoot and was 30 seconds better.

Stripping down, our filmy, Bowerman-designed racing shirts and shorts made me feel battle naked. My sharpened steel spikes sank into the cinders with a gnash that evoked Jim Bailey years before. On the starting line, Story's shirt looked heavy, almost like wool, and something hit me of the care with which Bowerman had prepared me. I gave myself completely to his plan. I hit 4:30 for the first mile. Story ran 4:19 and led by 70 yards. Bowerman, on the infield, said, "He won't hold it. See what you can do."

I began to gain, and the crowd, Bowerman's crowd, ten thousand strong, saw me coming and got up and called. With half a mile to go, I had no real will left. All control had passed to that thunder that would not let me slow. Into the last turn, Story still had 10 yards. Then he looked back, his shoulders tightened, and I experienced for the first time the full savagery of my competitive heart.

I outkicked him by a second in 8:48.1, ripping 27 seconds from my best, finishing in bedlam, crowd and teammates pressing the air out of me, shouting that everything was possible now, the Olympics were possible now.

Bowerman was there with wild blue eyes and a fiendish grin, and I knew what he would say. "See!" he'd crow. "I told you! You just needed rest!"

But he didn't. He whispered in my ear as he had when he strangled me. "Even I didn't think you could run that fast, Kenny," he said. "Even I."

He had given me his subject. I had found myself. It finally began to penetrate my thick skull that I had to rise above the world's fixation with sheer work. I had to attend to my own eccentric physiology. I accepted easy days into my life. I stopped counting miles.

Over the next eight years, the one long run he permitted me every 10 days would turn me into the fourth-place finisher in the 1972 Olympic Marathon. It was the lesson of my life and forces me now to consider—with a shiver—whether anyone besides Bowerman could have gotten through to me.

Running With Ghosts

Mark Wukas, 1997

What provokes our first forays into running? Who are our role models, our mentors? To what extent do we live up to their expectations? Writer Mark Wukas packs a lot in this personal narrative about his father and his coach.

I saw a ghost today.

Two miles into a long run in Lincoln Park, my eyes drifted to the two dozen high school girls stretch striding on a soccer field at the foot of Cricket Hill. Their coach was a squat woman whose bleating exhortations and shrill whistle pierced an otherwise perfect September afternoon of summer temperatures and autumn color. Next to her stood an older, tall, stoop-shouldered man with skinny legs who swung his hands low into a clap in front of his waist. He looked amazingly like Jack Bolton, who coached me when I was in high school. I remembered how well I ran under his tutelage and wished I was running half as well today.

My life as a runner began more than 25 years ago on the day that my father challenged me to a race around the block, about a quarter mile. We'd had relatives over for Easter dinner, and when the conversation finally turned to the kids, an uncle asked what sports I was interested in.

"Track," I said. I'd never taken so much as a step in an organized race, but that morning I'd read an article about Jim Ryun and his excellent prospects for a gold medal in the 1500 meters at the Olympics in Mexico City.

"Let's race around the block," he said. It was as much an order as it was a challenge. I was surprised. Although dad was fairly coordinated, he never was an athlete. When we would shoot at my hoop in the alley or play one-on-one, he always looked like what he was: a 42 year-old man stiffly chasing his 13-year-old son who was running rings around him.

We stood alone on the sidewalk in front of our house on a cloudy April afternoon; none of the family, not even my uncle whose question had sparked this contest, was interested enough to watch. Dad gave the ready-set-go, and we took off. I sprinted to a quick lead, running scared from the sound of his footsteps. He expected, I think, to catch me before the finish, but he never did. Dad pulled up at 300 yards and walked the last half block to where I stood panting and grinning in front of our house.

"Good run," he said sincerely as he shook my hand, something he never did after basketball. This was a significant moment for us: His handshake gave me a taste of what every son wants from his father, respect, in a way that my easy victories at my alley hoop never did.

From *Sport Literate,* Spring 1997. Reprinted by permission of Mark Wukas.

"He beat me," dad laughed in embarrassment as we rejoined the family. I'd dealt a blow not only to his pride but his mortality as well.

In May of the following year, a notice in my neighborhood newspaper announced that anyone interested in trying out for the Marquette Park Track Club, a summer squad, should be at the track the following Monday evening. Dad gave me a ride to the meeting. We were met by a man with a ruddy complexion in his early 50s who introduced himself as the coach and spoke with a Welsh accent.

"Ye want to be a roonnerrr, then, eh?" he asked me.

"Yes, sir," I said.

His name was Jack Bolton, and he looked like a runner. He was tall and thin and stood like a flamingo on his long, spindly legs. Deep-set, piercing blue eyes peered from above a bristly silver stubble of beard.

My first workout, Bolton said, was three laps of the track with another runner who had come out for the team, followed by a fourth lap as fast as we could. Dad stood next to Bolton, intently watching me trot my three laps. With visions of Jim Ryun in my head, I tore a blistering final lap and left the other fellow in my dust. Once I'd recovered, I went over to Bolton, who gave me a curt nod and told me to come back the next night.

"You sure left that other guy on that last lap," dad said as we walked to the car. Dad was never long on praise, but his remark gave me a flash of gold-medal triumph.

And so it began. I joined Bolton's pack of distance runners from sundry South Side high schools who each summer formed the Marquette Park Track Team. As a coach, Bolton instilled in us his strong work ethic which he tempered with distant affection, and I learned more about running from him than anyone else in my life. My high school coaches were all well-meaning teachers who picked up the sport to make a few extra bucks to supplement their meager parochial pay. None of them knew anything about running. But Bolton knew—first-hand. The older guys told us that he would have run for England in the 1940 Olympics in the 1500 meters if it hadn't been for World War II.

Bolton emphasized teamwork in what was essentially an individual's sport, insisting that we always run as a pack. When one of us would drop off the pace, he would pump his arm like a boxer throwing repeated uppercuts and urge the laggard to "go ooon, pick it ooop." We in turn would encourage one another with a panted, "C'mon, stay with me," when we, too, were steps from complete collapse. He urged us to "rrrun thrrrough" any and all pain, knowing that it would be easier going on the far side, and he constantly harangued us to have "the goots" to fight through a workout, to fight off an opponent during a race, and to fight ourselves no matter how much our bodies wanted to quit.

A few nights during those summers, my body simply quit mid-workout, and I shamefully went home without a goodbye. I would return dutifully the next night, wondering whether I still had a spot on the squad. Before sending us out for that night's run, he would turn and say, "Yer not going to quit on yerrrself tonight, arrre ye now, Marrrk?" I would shake my head but say nothing. He'd give me one of his sharp, signature nods. "All rrright then."

Bolton's praise was rare, and therefore savored; his criticism was sharp but always to the point, which was familiar enough to me. Like dad, he loathed self pity and sharply deflated any swelling pride. "Marrrk, yer rrresting on yer laurrrels" was Bolton's most stinging insult. In his eyes, we were only as good as our last races and then only until the next practice. "Grrrandstand finish," he'd growl if we'd blaze across the finish line after loafing earlier in the race. Or if we'd run a consistently mediocre pace without bothering to kick home, he would accuse us of "feeling sorrry for yerself," another of his mortal sins.

Every Friday before Labor Day, Bolton would bid us farewell until Memorial Day. "Good luck this fall, then, eh," he would say as he looked around affectionately at all of us. "Worrrk harrrd, and don't forrrget to keep up the frrriendships—that's what it's all about, y'know." He'd clap his hands, give us the nod—and that'd be that.

After cross country season in the autumn, winter was down time. I would run a couple nights a week so as not to lose my edge and also because it provided me with a welcome escape from the rigors of adolescence. On still winter nights when there was little or no wind, dad would offer to accompany me on the three-mile circuit. I would set the pace, and he would ride his bicycle alongside as we'd glide from pool of light to pool of light from the street lamps along the park's recreation drives. Dad would ask some perfunctory questions about school, comment on my form, but otherwise said little else. What we most enjoyed, I think, was being together in the winter solitude, each with private thoughts but happy in the silent company of the other.

Dad rarely came to see me run in meets, maybe one each season, but I'm glad he watched me run the best race of my life.

Every Thursday night during those summers Bolton would take us to Stagg Field at the University of Chicago for open meets. I had finished my sophomore track season without breaking 5:00 in the mile. I'd run a 5:00 flat, but anything faster eluded me, and I wondered if I'd reached my physical limits. My parents drove me up to 55th Street and Cottage Grove for that Thursday's race, and there was a mile on the card.

The gun went off, and after the crowded jostling of the first turn I found myself leading the pack, a lead that I held for two laps. After the first 880, two runners passed me, one a teammate. I had pushed the first two laps so hard that by the half I wasn't sure whether I had the energy to keep the pace, let alone finish the race, so I drifted a few steps behind the new leaders.

"Go with 'em, Marrrk," Bolton barked from the sidelines. "Show some goots."

I looked over and saw he was pumping his arm—the "go" sign. I put my head down in pursuit and strained to keep pace. I passed the three-quarter mark under 3:45, which Bolton told me I had to beat in order to break 5:00. Hearing that time, realizing that I had the chance for a sub-five, I threw everything into my last lap. Never mind that the two runners ahead of me were pulling away. Never mind that my lungs were burning for more oxygen. Never mind that I could barely control my legs. Blinded with sweat, I could only hear Bolton shouting as I turned down the home stretch.

I staggered across the finish line in 4:53.7, my best mile by more than six seconds, and it felt like a world record. I wanted to cry for joy, and I might have if I hadn't been so dizzy and dehydrated. As I trotted a warm down lap, my legs felt like I was running on pillows. My parents came down from the stands to say hello to Bolton, who gave them the nod and said, "He did all rrright tonight."

I beamed.

On the ride home I asked dad what the race had looked like.

"When I saw you leading after two laps, I figured you had something going," he said.

That was it.

I stopped running with Bolton after my sophomore year of college. Most of the guys I'd run with in high school had not returned, and Bolton was preoccupied with a new crop of younger (and faster) harriers. But I kept running laps of the park or 440s up the sledding hill—old habits die hard—and sometimes I'd see Bolton at the track coaching or just talking with the regulars. I'd stop, say hello, and while I was confident he recognized me, I don't think he remembered my name.

"Marrrk," I'd say, faintly echoing his accent. "From Quigley."

Bolton would give the old nod and grin. "I rememberrr ye," he'd say.

I've never stopped running, although seven-minute miles, which I once thought impossibly slow, now leave me as wrung out as five-minute miles once did. I was recovering from a broken ankle the winter my father was diagnosed with stomach cancer. I would spend weekends at the hospital, helping him take a lap of the floor and pushing his IV tower as he pushed his walker. We'd talk a little about the future, about his life after recovery and rehabilitation, but like those winter runs in Marquette Park more than 20 years earlier, we communicated best through our silence. He was dying, and we knew it, but some days he would find the strength, the guts, to press harder, to walk a second lap, fighting the pain with a determination that I have never seen in my life.

As dad weakened, mom asked me to move back to the South Side to help her care for him. Dad died the night before I moved home.

I promised mom that I would stay with her until she sold the house. Moving back to the old neighborhood meant that I could run the old paths in Marquette Park. I had expected to feel a home-turf exuberance that would restore old energy, quicken my stride, but I'd lost too many steps, and the park was too full of ghosts, including my own. For the next year, I ran uninspired laps of the park, sometimes taking the sledding hill or stopping at the track to run some anemic intervals. I looked for Bolton every time, but I never saw him. I figured he'd died, too.

When I moved back north, I resumed running in Lincoln Park and found a four-mile circuit with varied terrain. Yesterday I felt strong and daft enough to attempt interval 220s up Cricket Hill. I'm not sure why I felt compelled to thrash myself that way, but I think it had to do with wondering whether I still had the "goots" to run such a gruelling workout. Foolish thinking these days, but ingrained nonetheless. As I started the first 220, I remembered the man who taught me to run hills and said, "God bless ye, Jack Bolton, whereverrr yer roonning." I ran all eight 220s as hard as I could.

In an effort to reward myself for that agony, today I decided to take a slower run and enjoy this perfect autumn day. I spotted Bolton's Doppelganger as I was passing Cricket Hill and decided to trot a little closer.

Sure enough, it was the man himself. I could scarcely believe it. I stopped running and walked toward him.

"Mr. Bolton?" I called. He looked over and gave the old Bolton grin and nod. He looked a little worse for the wear but still fit, not unlike a Volvo with 300,000 miles on it. Same sharp eyes though, and the same silver beard stubble on his ruddy complexion.

"Mark," I said, extending my hand. "I ran with you twenty-five years ago in Marquette Park. I went to Quigley."

Bolton nodded and shook my hand firmly. He turned to the female head coach and jerked his thumb at me, saying, "One of me old roonnerrrs." She was not the least impressed, but he seemed awfully pleased.

Bolton said he's still coaching during the summer, but in a suburb south and west of the city where he has a one-mile loop with a hill nearby, which didn't surprise me. Wanting him to know that his lessons remained ingrained, I told him that I was running hills right here only the day before. Another nod and grin, as if to say, "Good forrr you, laddie."

Bolton looked busy, so I excused myself with a grateful handshake, told him it was good to see him and resumed my run. I just laughed with joy for the next mile at finding him alive, albeit a little more frail.

After the run, I was still smiling as I pulled a beer from my refrigerator and held it to my forehead. My knees ached and my stomach churned as I slouched against the wall on my back porch and remembered how much easier this used to be. Suddenly I felt very old. I thought of Bolton, still out there in his late 70s, and then I thought of Dad, dead at 68.

As I slowly recovered in the late afternoon sunlight, the moisture on my cheek turned from sweat to tears. Running into old Bolton had been the next best thing to seeing my father alive again.

race

The gun goes off and everything
changes . . . the world changes . . .
and nothing else really matters.

~Patti Sue Plummer,
Olympic distance runner

Four-Minute Mile

Roger Bannister, 1955

The sub-four-minute mile loomed as an irresistible goal for the milers of the early 1950s. For 10 years the world record had been stuck at 4:01, and it was just a matter of time before the "barrier" would be broken. John Landy of Australia, Wes Santee of the U.S., and Roger Bannister of Britain were all knocking on the door. Early in the 1954 track season on a windy day in Oxford, Bannister made a preemptive strike on the record. In the following excerpt from his autobiography *The Four-Minute Mile*, Bannister tells the story of this historic race.

> Now bid me run, And I will strive with things impossible.
>
> ~Julius Caesar

I expected that the summer of 1954 would be my last competitive season. It was certain to be a big year in athletics. There would be the Empire Games in Vancouver, the European Games in Berne, and hopes were running high of a four-minute mile.

The great change that now came over my running was that I no longer trained and raced alone. Perhaps I had mellowed a little and was becoming more sociable. Every day between 12:30 and 1:30 I trained on a track in Paddington and had a quick lunch before returning to hospital. We called ourselves the Paddington lunch time club. We came from all parts of London and our common bond was a love of running.

I felt extremely happy in the friendships I made there, as we shared the hard work of repetitive quarter miles and sprints. These training sessions came to mean almost as much to me as had those at the Oxford track. I could now identify myself more intimately with the failure and success of other runners.

In my hardest training Chris Brasher was with me, and he made the task very much lighter. On Friday evenings he took me along to Chelsea Barracks where his coach, Franz Stampfl, held a training session. At weekends Chris Chataway would join us, and in this friendly atmosphere the very severe training we did became most enjoyable.

In December 1953 we started a new intensive course of training and ran several times a week a series of ten consecutive quarter-miles, each in 66 seconds. Through January and February we gradually speeded them up, keeping to an interval of two minutes between each. By April we could manage them in

61 seconds, but however hard we tried it did not seem possible to reach our target of 60 seconds. We were stuck, or as Chris Brasher expressed it—"bogged down." The training had ceased to do us any good and we needed a change.

Chris Brasher and I drove up to Scotland overnight for a few days' climbing. We turned into the Pass of Glencoe as the sun crept above the horizon at dawn. A misty curtain drew back from the mountains and the "sun's sleepless eye" cast a fresh cold light on the world. The air was calm and fragrant, and the colours of sunrise were mirrored in peaty pools on the moor. Soon the sun was up and we were off climbing. The weekend was a complete mental and physical change. It probably did us more harm than good physically. We climbed hard for the four days we were there, using the wrong muscles in slow and jerking movements.

There was an element of danger too. I remember Chris falling a short way when leading a climb up a rock face depressingly named "Jericho's Wall." Luckily he did not hurt himself. We were both worried lest a sprained ankle might set our training back by several weeks.

After three days our minds turned to running again. We suddenly became alarmed at the thought of taking any more risks, and decided to return. We had slept little, our meals had been irregular. But when we tried to run those quarter-miles again, the time came down to 59 seconds!

It was now less than three weeks to the Oxford University v. A.A.A. race, the first opportunity of the year for us to attack the four-minute mile. Chris Chataway had decided to join Chris Brasher and myself in the A.A.A. team. He doubted his ability to run a 3/4-mile in three minutes, but he generously offered to attempt it.

I had now abandoned the severe training of the previous months and was concentrating entirely on gaining speed and freshness. I had to learn to release in four short minutes the energy I usually spent in half an hour's training. Each training session took on a special significance, as the day of the Oxford race drew near. It felt a privilege and joy each time I ran a trial on the track.

There was no longer any need for my mind to force my limbs to run faster—my body became a unity in motion much greater than the sum of its component parts. I never thought of length of stride or style, or even my judgment of pace. All this had become automatically ingrained. In this way a singleness of drive could be achieved, leaving my mind free from the task of directing operations so that it could fix itself on the great objective ahead. There was more enjoyment in my running than ever before, a new health and vigour. It was as if all my muscles were a part of a perfectly tuned machine. I felt fresh now at the end of each training session.

On 24th April I ran a 3/4-mile trial in three minutes at Motspur Park with Chataway. I led for the first two laps and we both returned exactly the same time. Four days later I ran a last solo 3/4-mile trial at Paddington. Norris McWhirter, who had been my patient timekeeper through most of 1953, came over to hold the watch.

The energy of the twins, Norris and Ross McWhirter, was boundless. For them nothing was too much trouble, and they accepted any challenge joyfully. After running together in Oxford as sprinters they carried their partnership into journalism, keeping me posted of the performances of my overseas rivals. They often drove me to athletics meetings, so that I arrived with no fuss, never a minute too soon or too late. Sometimes I was not sure whether it was Norris or Ross who held the watch or drove the car, but I knew that either could be relied upon.

For the trial at Paddington there was as usual a high wind blowing. I would have given almost anything to be able to shirk the test that would tell me with ruthless accuracy what my chances were of achieving a four-minute mile at Oxford. I felt that 2 min. 59.9 sec. for the 3/4-mile in a solo training run meant 3 min. 59.9 sec. in a mile race. A time of 3 min. 0.1 sec. would mean 4 min. 0.1 sec. for the mile—just the difference between success and failure. The watch recorded a time of 2 min. 59.9 sec.! I felt a little sick afterwards and had the taste of nervousness in my mouth. My speedy recovery within five minutes suggested that I had been holding something back. Two days later at Paddington I ran a 1 min. 54 sec. half-mile quite easily, after a late night, and then took five days complete rest before the race.

I had been training daily since the previous November, and now that the crisis was approaching I barely knew what to do with myself. I spent most of the time imagining I was developing a cold and wondering if the gale-force winds would ever drop. The day before the race I slipped on a highly polished hospital floor and spent the rest of the day limping. Each night in the week before the race there came a moment when I saw myself at the starting line. My whole body would grow nervous and tremble. I ran the race over in my mind. Then I would calm myself and sometimes get off to sleep.

Next day was Thursday, 6th May 1954. I went into the hospital as usual, and at 11 o'clock I was sharpening my spikes on a grindstone in the laboratory. Someone passing said, "You don't really think that's going to make any difference, do you?"

I knew the weather conditions made the chances of success practically nil. Yet all day I was taking the usual precautions for the race, feeling at the same time that they would prove useless.

I decided to travel up to Oxford alone because I wanted to think quietly. I took an early train deliberately, opened a carriage door, and, quite by chance, there was Franz Stampfl inside. I was delighted to see him, as a friend with the sort of attractive cheerful personality I badly needed at that moment. Through Chris Brasher, Franz had been in touch with my training programme, but my own connection with him was slight.

I would have liked his advice and help at this moment, but could not bring myself to ask him. It was as if now, at the end of my running career, I was being forced to admit that coaches were necessary after all, and that I had been wrong to think that the athlete could be sufficient unto himself.

In my mind there lurked the memory of an earlier occasion when I had visited a coach. He had expounded his views on my running and suggested a whole series of changes. The following week I read a newspaper article he wrote about my plans, claiming to be my adviser for the 1952 Olympics. This experience made me inclined to move slowly.

But Franz is not like this. He has no wish to turn the athlete into a machine working at his dictation. We shared a common view of athletics as a means of "recreation" of each individual, as a result of the liberation and expression of the latent power within him. Franz is an artist who can see beauty in human struggle and achievement.

We talked, almost impersonally, about the problem I faced. In my mind I had settled this as the day when, with every ounce of strength I possessed, I would attempt to run the four-minute mile. A wind of gale force was blowing which would slow me up by a second a lap. In order to succeed I must run not merely a four-minute mile, but the equivalent of a 3 min. 56 sec. mile in calm weather.

I had reached my peak physically and psychologically. There would never be another day like it. I had to drive myself to the limit of my power without the stimulus of competitive opposition. This was my first race for eight months and all this time I had been storing nervous energy. If I tried and failed I should be dejected, and my chances would be less on any later attempt. Yet it seemed that the high wind was going to make it impossible.

I had almost decided when I entered the carriage at Paddington that unless the wind dropped soon I would postpone the attempt. I would just run an easy mile in Oxford and make the attempt on the next possible occasion—ten days later at the White City in London.

Franz understood my apprehension. He thought I was capable of running a mile in 3 min. 56 sec., or 3:57, so he could argue convincingly that it was worth while making the attempt. "With the proper motivation, that is, a good reason for wanting to do it," he said, "your mind can overcome any sort of adversity. In any case the wind might drop. I remember J.J. Barry in Ireland. He ran a 4 min. 8 sec. mile without any training or even proper food—simply because he had the will to run. Later in America where he was given every facility and encouragement, he never ran a fast race. In any case, what if this were your only chance?"

He had won his point. Racing has always been more of a mental than a physical problem to me. He went on talking about athletes and performances, but I heard no more. The dilemma was not banished from my mind, and the idea left uppermost was that this might be my only chance. "How would you ever forgive yourself if you rejected it?" I thought, as the train arrived in Oxford. As it happened, ten days later it was just as windy!

I was met at the station by Charles Wenden, a great friend from my early days in Oxford, who drove me straight down to Iffley Road. The wind was almost gale force. Together we walked round the deserted track. The St. George's flag on a nearby church stood out from the flagpole. The attempt seemed hopeless, yet for some unknown reason I tried out both pairs of spikes. I had a new pair which were specially made for me on the instructions of a climber and fell walker, Eustace Thomas of Manchester. Some weeks before he had come up to London and together we worked out modifications which would reduce the weight of each running shoe from six to four ounces. This saving in weight might well mean the difference between success and failure.

Still undecided, I drove back to Charles Wenden's home for lunch. On this day, as on many others, I was glad of the peace which I found there. Although both he and his wife Eileen knew the importance of the decision that had to be made, and cared about it as much as I did myself, it was treated by common consent as a question to be settled later.

The immediate problem was to prepare a suitable lunch, and to see that the children, Felicity and Sally, ate theirs. Absorbed in watching the endless small routine of running a home and family, I could forget some of my apprehensions. Charles Wenden had been one of the ex-service students in Oxford after the war, and some of my earliest running had been in his company. Later his house had become a second home for me during my research studies in Oxford, and the calm efficiency of Eileen had often helped to still my own restless worries. Never was this factor so important as on this day.

In the afternoon I called on Chris Chataway. At the moment the sun was shining, and he lay stretched on the window seat. He smiled and said, just as I knew he would, "The day could be a lot worse, couldn't it? Just now it's fine. The forecast says the wind may drop towards evening. Let's not decide until five o'clock."

I spent the afternoon watching from the window the swaying of the leaves. "The wind's hopeless," said Joe Binks [journalist and former mile great] on the way down to the track. At 5:15 there was a shower of rain. The wind blew strongly, but now came in gusts, as if uncertain. As Brasher, Chataway and I warmed up, we knew the eyes of the spectators were on us; they were hoping that the wind would drop just a little—if not enough to run a four-minute mile, enough to make the attempt.

———————●———————

Failure is as exciting to watch as success, provided the effort is absolutely genuine and complete. But the spectators fail to understand—and how can they know—the mental agony through which an athlete must pass before he can give his maximum effort. And how rarely, if he is built as I am, he can give it.

No one tried to persuade me. The decision was mine alone, and the moment was getting closer. As we lined up for the start I glanced at the flag again. It fluttered more gently now, and the scene from Shaw's *Saint Joan* flashed through my mind, how she, at her desperate moment, waited for the wind to change.

Yes, the wind was dropping slightly. This was the moment when I made my decision. The attempt was on.

There was complete silence on the ground . . . a false start . . . I felt angry that precious moments during the lull in the wind might be slipping by. The gun fired a second time. . . . Brasher went into the lead and I slipped in effortlessly behind him, feeling tremendously full of running. My legs seemed to meet no resistance at all, as if propelled by some unknown force.

We seemed to be going so slowly! Impatiently I shouted "Faster!" But Brasher kept his head and did not change the pace. I went on worrying until I heard the first lap time, 57.5 sec. In the excitement my knowledge of pace had deserted me. Brasher could have run the first quarter in 55 seconds without my realising it, because I felt so full of running, but I should have had to pay for it later. Instead, he had made success possible.

At one and a half laps I was still worrying about the pace. A voice shouting "relax" penetrated to me above the noise of the crowd. I learnt afterwards it was Stampfl's. Unconsciously I obeyed. If the speed was wrong it was too late to do anything about it, so why worry? I was relaxing so much that my mind seemed almost detached from my body. There was no strain.

I barely noticed the half-mile, passed in 1 min. 58 sec., nor when, round the next bend, Chataway went into the lead. At three-quarters of a mile the effort was still barely perceptible; the time was 3 min. 0.7 sec., and by now the crowd was roaring. Somehow I had to run that last lap in 59 seconds. Chataway led round the next bend and then I pounced past him at the beginning of the back straight, three hundred yards from the finish.

I had a moment of mixed joy and anguish, when my mind took over. It raced well ahead of my body and drew my body compellingly forward. I felt that the moment of a lifetime had come. There was no pain, only a great unity of movement and aim. The world seemed to stand still, or did not exist. The only reality was the next two hundred yards of track under my feet. The tape meant finality—extinction perhaps.

I felt at that moment that it was my chance to do one thing supremely well. I drove on, impelled by a combination of fear and pride. The air I breathed filled me with the spirit of the track where I had run my first race. The noise in my ears was that of the faithful Oxford crowd. Their hope and encouragement gave me greater strength. I had now turned the last bend and there were only fifty yards more.

My body had long since exhausted all its energy, but it went on running just the same. The physical overdraft came only from greater willpower. This was the crucial moment when my legs were strong enough to carry me over the last few yards as they could never have done in previous years. With five yards to go the tape seemed almost to recede. Would I ever reach it?

Those last few seconds seemed never-ending. The faint line of the finishing tape stood ahead as a haven of peace, after the struggle. The arms of the world were waiting to receive me if only I reached the tape without slackening my speed. If I faltered, there would be no arms to hold me and the world would be a cold, forbidding place, because I had been so close. I leapt at the tape like a man taking his last spring to save himself from the chasm that threatens to engulf him.

My effort was over and I collapsed almost unconscious, with an arm on either side of me. It was only then that real pain overtook me. I felt like an exploded flashlight with no will to live; I just went on existing in the most passive physical state without being quite unconscious. Blood surged from my muscles and seemed to fell me. It was as if all my limbs were caught in an ever-tightening vice. I knew that I had done it before I even heard the time. I was too close to have failed, unless my legs had played strange tricks at the finish by slowing me down and not telling my tiring brain that they had done so.

The stop-watches held the answer. The announcement came—"Result of one mile . . . time, 3 minutes"—the rest lost in the roar of excitement. I grabbed Brasher and Chataway, and together we scampered round the track in a burst of spontaneous joy. We had done it—the three of us!

We shared a place where no man had yet ventured—secure for all time, however fast men might run miles in future. We had done it where we wanted, when we wanted, how we wanted, in our first attempt of the year. In the wonderful joy my pain was forgotten and I wanted to prolong those precious moments of realisation.

I felt suddenly and gloriously free of the burden of athletic ambition that I had been carrying for years. No words could be invented for such supreme happiness, eclipsing all other feelings. I thought at that moment I could never again reach such a climax of single-mindedness. I felt bewildered and overpowered. I knew it would be some time before I caught up with myself.

Get the Hell Out of My Race and Give Me Those Numbers!

Kathrine Switzer, 2007

In many races today women runners outnumber men, so it hardly seems possible there was a time not long ago when women were not allowed in races. They literally had to fight for that right. One of the pivotal moments in their battle came in 1967, when the Boston Marathon was still a male-only race. A 20-year-old college student named Kathrine Switzer wanted to run, so she submitted her entry as "K.V. Switzer" and received her official race number. Little did she know that the story of her race would make national news and help ignite the women's running movement.

The 1967 "American Marathon Race, under the auspices of the Boston Athletic Association," better known as the Boston Marathon, was on Wednesday, April 19, Patriot's Day in the State of Massachusetts. (A few years later, when the federal government moved major holiday observances to Monday, the Marathon was run on the third Monday in April.) I thought it was neat that folks in Massachusetts got a special holiday commemorating the young American patriots who fought the British in the first battles of the American Revolution, at Lexington and Concord in 1775. The marathon was made a part of Patriots Day in 1897, the year after the revival of the Olympic Games in Athens.

Several young men from the BAA participated in the Athens Games and returned home fascinated with a romantic new event called the marathon. Since the marathon in Greece commemorated the historic run of a messenger, the BAA Marathon would commemorate the historic midnight ride of the messenger Paul Revere. For a long time I thought the Boston Marathon course must have been the same route as Revere's ride but Arnie [Briggs, my training partner] said it was not. In any case, the revolutionary history was significant to me and I felt proud to be a part of it. Every American school kid can tell you about "the shot heard round the world" and quote some of Longfellow's poem, "Paul Revere's Ride." We had visited the main historic sites on a family vacation to New England when I was a kid and here I was going back to them, and to being a part of the oldest American race, the biggest one, and the most famous. I was going to be a part of history!

Still, I told no one else until the day before, and then only under duress. I'd decided to cut all my Wednesday classes with no explanation, but I had to tell Dr. Edmund Arnold, my graphics arts professor, as we were having a test on Wednesday and I needed to request a makeup. Since honesty worked best with the doctor at the infirmary, I decided to tell Dr. Arnold the truth, swearing him first to secrecy. I did not want this spread all over campus and Dr. Arnold was a chatty guy, quite an enthusiast about everything. I was pleased with his unequivocal support, and then he said, "Well, I remember the days of the great Clarence DeMar!" Boy, this guy DeMar must have been something, I thought.

As I was packing up my stuff on Tuesday afternoon, I decided to tell my roommates, who were wondering where I was going anyway. Since I didn't actually know what might happen to me—I mean, we could have a car crash or something—I thought *somebody* should know where I was. Jane, Kaye, and Connell had all moved on from the first days of my running in October, when they'd mildly ridiculed me and called me "Roadrunner," to a kind of acceptance as a good-natured eccentric. I was incredibly independent and not totally uncool after all, and as these were all women who abhorred conformity at all costs (with the exception, of course, of turtlenecks, jeans, and Winston cigarettes) they had all rather come to like me. I had to explain what a marathon was, trying to be offhand when I told them that I might be the only woman. I begged them for secrecy, as I didn't want any fuss at the last minute. They sat on their beds, smoking, thinking, and then just said, "Okay, cool," as if, who could we tell even if we wanted to?

Arnie picked up John [a runner from our cross country team], Tom [my boyfriend], and me, and we hit the road at about three in the afternoon for the five-hour drive to Boston. It was a blast of a trip, mostly because Tom was in a great mood; he told jokes and we all acted silly. I'd noticed that when Tom was grumpy it made everyone around him tense, not just me, and when he was pleasant, we'd all be so relieved we would fall into a kind of silly glee. I felt confident enough to ask Arnie who Clarence DeMar was in front of Tom, and for a moment the fun was almost over. Before Arnie could answer, Tom smacked his head in disbelief. "How can you not know who Clarence DeMar was? Hell, he was the *greatest*. He won the Boston Marathon seven times!" Even John knew who Clarence DeMar was. Then Arnie said kindly, "Yeah, but he ran a million years ago," which meant that Arnie, like so many people, only go on and on about those heroes of their own generation. Anyway, you had to hand it to Tom, he knew about every sport and just about every athlete in it.

That was the mood in the car and it was great. We shared the driving and the costs for gas and dinner, and we found a motel with a vacancy sign in Natick, about nine miles east of Hopkinton, where the race was to start. I thought it was amazingly chivalrous that the three guys took one room and gave me one by myself and we still split it four ways. After dinner, Arnie insisted on showing us the course even though it was already nearly ten at night—it was freezing cold and rainy outside, pitch black, and as we drove along in Arnie's old rattletrap with bad windshield wipers, we couldn't see a blessed thing. Arnie was all excited at every landmark, saying things like, "Now here's Wellesley College! Here are the Wellesley hills!" The windows were completely steamed up, there was nothing to be seen, and the ride seemed to last an eternity. I had a feeling of impending doom. Here we were, driving at forty miles an hour, and it was taking *forever.* Finally, we all said it was hopeless, what did it matter, we had to run it anyway, let's go back and get some sleep, and Arnie reluctantly turned the car around for the journey back to the motel, which seemed to take most of the night. Ever since then I've never driven over a marathon course the day before the event. It is demoralizing when you see how far twenty-six miles actually is.

I was spooked by this experience, and when I called my parents it was late, but they were always up. As I had to my roommates, I had to explain first what a marathon was, and then why I was in Boston, ending with, "I am nervous about being able to finish. It is important for me to finish the race." My dad was acute when it came to any anxiety on my part; I never reached out with a lack of confidence unless it was serious. And he delivered perfectly. "You go get 'em, kid, you can do it!"

"It's twenty-six miles, Dad."

"Aw hell, kid, you can do it. You're tough, you've trained, you'll do just *great.*"

It was exactly what I needed to hear. My dad knew I didn't jump into things untrained; he'd watched the running progress in high school, and although this marathon thing was a surprise, he had no doubts. I knew he had no doubts, and I felt good but just a little sad when I hung up. What I couldn't explain to him, what nobody knows unless they've done one, is that the marathon is unpredictable, anything weird could happen, and anything could happen to *me!* I could get diarrhea! I could get hit by a dolt opening his car door. Arnie had told me about that happening to a guy once. Eventually, I got too tired to worry about the kinds of things I could not control. The thing I worried about most was courage. Would I have the courage to keep running if it really hurt, if it got harder than I was used to, if Heartbreak Hill broke me? Yep, that was it, I was worried about maybe not having the courage if it got awful.

So I decided to have a word with God, for whom I felt I'd shown plenty of respect and appreciation well in advance of this race, so this was no last-minute panic plea. I thought it was selfish of runners to ask God for things like, "Please make sure I finish," or "Please don't make it hurt." If you've done the work, I don't think God is up there making those kinds of decisions anyway. But I do think he (or she) does help us out if we ask for things to better our character, so I felt it was fair to ask for the courage to make the right decision when it got hard. Because it was going to get hard. The marathon was always hard. It took me a long time to boil down my fears to this, but once I realized what my fears were really all about, I slept soundly.

I also thanked God that the Boston Marathon starts at noon, as we all got to sleep till eight and were eating breakfast at nine. Arnie said to chow down, we really needed a lot of fuel because it was a long day and cold outside. He wasn't just kidding—it was freezing rain, really pelting down, with sleet and wind. So we ate everything: bacon, eggs, pancakes, juice, coffee, milk, extra toast. I was excited to see other people in the little roadside restaurant wearing gray sweat suits just like us.

In addition to allowing us a great breakfast, the noon start gave me time for a significant poop, which was always an issue on early-morning long runs that started before breakfast. Today the system never felt better; I crossed "getting diarrhea" off my worry list. No period, no diarrhea, there were two of the big ones. Oddly, the weather didn't concern me; we'd trained for months in weather like this. It was annoying, though, as I had wanted to look nice and feminine at the start in my newly ironed burgundy shorts and top. Now that would have to wait until later, when I'd warmed up and chucked off my sweats, as Arnie said we would.

We went back to our rooms, packed our stuff, and I carefully put on makeup and gold earbobs, and coated my feet in Vaseline. For what it was worth. My feet hadn't totally healed from our trial marathon run and I just hoped this Vaseline would protect them for as many miles as possible. Tom banged on my door, holding out a sanitary napkin bag from the back of the toilet and a big safety pin. "Here, we're pinning these on the back of our gloves. They're perfect for holding dextrose tablets. See, you put four tablets in the bottom of the sack, rip off the top, fold it over, and pin it to your glove. Then when you need the dextrose, you rip it open."

"Why do you need dextrose?" I asked.

"It's sugar, for energy, get it?" he said in that tone that made me feel stupid again. Tom always had a system, knew there was a vitamin or something magic that would make you better. I had no idea that sugar per se would give you energy, I mean any more than, say, a piece of bread. I'd been hungry and tired plenty of times on a run, but I never craved sugar or equated it to energy.

"I don't need sugar, we never needed it before," I said. It was just another complication. I hated fussing with equipment anyway; we had enough to worry about.

"How do you know? Just pin it on, already." I shrugged my shoulders. It was easier to do it than argue. Besides, Tom was now assuming his experienced-athlete-and-coach role and was acting bossy. He was starting to get hyped; I'd seen him before competitions as he stomped around and snorted, and this was no different. Still, I felt idiotic, but when I got to the car with my suitcase I saw that Arnie and John had the sanitary napkin bags pinned to their gloves, too. What a team!

As we drove to Hopkinton, the rain at times turned to snow, with giant flakes that splashed into slush on the windshield and onto the pavement. It wasn't cold enough to be icy slick, but it was penetrating. The temperature was 34, and I knew there was no way I was taking off my sweats. It was plain awful outside, even by Syracuse standards, and inside my sweats, which had been worn down to soft flannel over the hundreds of miles of training and laundering, I felt as cozy as if I were wearing pajamas. To hell with looking great, I thought, I've got to keep warm and loose to run, that is my first priority.

We got to Hopkinton High School and parked right beside it, an unthinkable thing nowadays, where there are thousands and thousands of people who have to come in streams of special buses just to sit around for hours to wait for the start of the race. Arnie told John and me to wait in the car where it was warm while he got the envelope with our numbers and pins. Since we'd preregistered as a team and sent our papers in together, the race organizers would put all our stuff together for pickup by the team coach or captain, just as they always did for a track or cross-country meet. Tom went in with Arnie, since Tom had to take the physical. A few minutes later, Arnie came out with the envelope and two number bibs each to pin on our fronts and backs; they looked like cardboard license plates. We looked up our names in the printed start list and smiled at each other nervously; seeing "K. Switzer" in print beside "261" gave me a little frisson. There were 733 people listed on the program, a huge race. Arnie grumbled about it getting out of control.

I pinned my numbers on my sweatshirt and not my burgundy top. It was the final commitment to wearing that sweatshirt for the whole race and I was pleased; the sweatshirt had been a buddy in Syracuse for a few hundred miles and would live on another day rather than dying at the roadside on the way to Boston. Not so for the big hooded warm-up sweatshirt, however, that I'd worn during blizzards in Syracuse. This was the one with "U.S. Naval Academy, Annapolis" on the front. Dave had given it to me at my request for Christmas three years ago and it had been my pride and joy. Now it was going to get jettisoned forever—like Dave. That made me glad, too.

We got out of the car and started warming up as we waited for Tom. Everyone was darting about in different directions, all in gray sweat suits, some with hoods up, some with nylon windbreakers over them, some barelegged, and some with shorts over the pants, a method of wearing sweats I never could understand. If you had cast your eye over the whole scene, we all looked alike, like ragtags.

As runners jogged past us, most kept their slightly nervous eyes ahead, lost in pre-race concentration, but plenty did double takes, and when they did I'd smile back or wave a little wave. Yep, I'm a *girl,* my look back said. Many of these guys turned right around and jogged over to me, all excited. "Hey! Are you gonna go the whole way?" "Gosh, it's great to see a girl here!" "Hope you know there are hills out here—are you ready?" "Can you give me some tips to get my wife to run? I know she'd love it if I can just get her started." Arnie was kind of holding court, saying, "Sure she's going all the way!" Then he'd start on his "This girl ran me into the ground!" routine. He was shining. "See? I *told* you you'd be welcome at Boston!" he said. And indeed, I felt very welcome. I felt special and proud of myself. I knew something other women didn't know, and I felt downright smug.

It was getting close to noon and Tom had not appeared. We still had to park the car for the day and get to the start. Suddenly he burst out of the doors of the high school in his bright orange Syracuse track sweatshirt and ran over to us, practically punching the air. "Stupid jerks!" he said. "They weren't going to let me run, said I had higher than normal blood pressure! Of course I have higher than normal blood pressure! I am getting ready to run the goddamn Boston Marathon, what do you *think,* you asses! So I had to sit down and get calm and convince them I was okay to run and they took it again and said it was entirely up to me but they wouldn't recommend it." Arnie said, "C'mon, c'mon, let's get the car parked," and he drove around the village square and over to St. John the Evangelist Catholic Church and parked in the lot there, apparently his regular place. It was a two-minute walk to Hayden Row, where the race started.

Incredibly, with twenty minutes to the start of the race, Tom and Arnie decided they had to go inside to pray. John and I wailed to the sky. "Oh come *on,* why didn't you pray last night when you had time!" I implored. I wanted to say it doesn't count if you wait until the last minute like this, but not really being an authority, I said, "Come on, just pray as we walk, you don't need to go into a church for heaven's sake, God hears you no matter where you are!" I was frantic and it was useless. I wasn't Catholic so of course I wouldn't know that maybe it counts more when you're down on your knees with a crucifix and all. John and I jogged in circles around the parking lot and I swear to you Tom and Arnie were in there ten minutes if they were in there a second.

When they came out Tom was pumped. "I'm ready! I'm psyched! Hey, where's Bikila*? Bikila, ha!!" And he spat in joking contempt.

"God, you are wearing lipstick!" he said to me as we jogged over to the start.

"I always wear lipstick! What's wrong with that?"

"Somebody might see you are a girl and not let you run, take it off."

"I will *not* take off my lipstick," and that is how we arrived at the start. There was a mob of runners in every getup imaginable funneling into a penlike area that was a block off Hayden Row surrounded by snow fencing. At the gate of the funnel were clipboard-holding BAA officials wearing long overcoats with blue ribbons on the lapels, and felt dress hats. Everyone was sodden, and hats were gathering snow, as were the shoulders of the runners who had been standing in the pen a while. It was pretty disorganized and the officials were agitated. They were checking off the bib numbers of the runners as they came through the gate. I lifted up the big outer sweatshirt so they could check off my number and the official put his hand on my shoulder and gently pushed me forward saying, "C'mon runners, let's move on in, just keep it moving here!" We worked our way into the back of the field, and Arnie said, "See? No problem!"

All around us the men were excited and pleased to have a woman in their presence. I tried to stay low key. I didn't want any attention especially at this moment, but I tried to be accommodating, even when one runner insisted on having his wife, who was on the other side of the fence, take our photo together. Then the crowd quieted, someone up front must have been making announcements. We moved close together, and the smell of liniment was so strong my eyes stung. I pulled off the heavy top sweatshirt and threw it over the fence, the gun went off, and we were away at last. At last!

---

*Abebe Bikila was the legendary runner from Ethiopia who won the Olympic Marathon barefoot in 1960 and then returned to win again in 1964, this time in shoes.

Boston was always a Mecca for runners, and now I, too, was one of the anointed pilgrims. After months of training with Arnie and dreaming about this, here we were, streaming alongside the village common and onto the downhill of Route 135 with hundreds of our most intimate companions, all unknown, and all of whom understood what this meant and had worked hard to get here. More than ever before at a running event, I felt at home.

When you are a slow runner like we all were, the first few miles of every marathon are fun, when the running is easy, the crowd noise exciting, and your companions conversational and affable. You know it's going to hurt later, so you just enjoy this time. So it was with us as we stayed in our little group, running four abreast, joking and saying thanks to the many well-wishers who passed us with encouragement. Arnie and Tom were in their element hearing all the positive encouragement directed at us; running with me—a girl!—was giving them attention they had never had before. Tom ran with his chest stuck out and Arnie pranced; it was nice to see.

Then there came a honking of horns and someone shouting, "Get over, runners move to your right!" There was a lot of shuffling and some cursing as a big flatbed truck lumbered by on our left, forcing us all to the right side of the narrow road. Following close behind the truck was a city bus. The truck was the photo press truck; on the back of it were risers so the cameramen could each get a clean shot of the race as the vehicle pushed up to the front of the field. I thought at the time that it was incredibly poor organization, dangerous even, to allow moving vehicles behind a pack of seven hundred runners, especially in a world-class competition like this one. We were pretty slow, but up front were good guys and it's pretty risky to beep at Olympic athletes in full flight and expect them to move over. I was thinking this when I realized the press truck had slowed to be right in front of us and were taking our pictures. In fact, they were getting pretty excited to see a woman in the race, a woman wearing *numbers*. I could see them fumbling with their programs to look up my number and name, and then shoot again. We all started to laugh and wave. It was our "Hi Mom! on the nightly news" moment and it was fun.

Then suddenly, a man with an overcoat and felt hat was in the middle of the road shaking his finger at me; he said something to me as I passed and reached out for my hand, catching my glove instead and pulling it off. I did a kind of stutter step, and we all had to jostle around him. I thought he was a nutty spectator, but when I passed I caught a glimpse of a blue and gold BAA ribbon on his lapel. Where had he come from?

Moments later, I heard the scraping noise of leather shoes coming up fast behind me, an alien and alarming sound amid the muted thump-thumping of the rubber running shoes. When a runner hears that kind of noise, it's usually danger—just like hearing a dog's claws on the pavement. Instinctively I jerked my head around quickly and looked squarely into the most vicious face I'd ever seen. A big man, a huge man, with bared teeth was set to pounce, and before I could react he grabbed my shoulder and flung me back screaming, "Get the hell out of my race and give me those numbers!" Then he swiped down my front, trying to rip off my bib number, just as I leapt backward from him. He missed the numbers but I was so surprised and frightened that I slightly wet my pants, and turned to run. But now the man had the back of my shirt and was swiping at the bib number on my back. I was making little cries of aa-uh, aa-uh, not thinking at all, just trying to get away, when I saw tiny brave Arnie bat at him and try to push him away, shouting, "Leave her alone, Jock, I've trained her, she's okay, leave her alone!" And the man screamed, "Stay out of this, Arnie!" and swatted him away like a gnat.

Arnie *knows* this maniac, I thought wildly, as I tried to pull away. The only sound was the clicking whirr of motordrive cameras, scuffling sounds, and, faintly, a Japanese cameraman yelling, "eeechai yawoow" or something. The bottom was dropping out of my stomach; I had never felt such embarrassment and fear. I'd never been manhandled, never even spanked as a child, and the physical power and swiftness of the attack stunned me. I felt unable to flee, like I was rooted there, and indeed I was, since the man, this Jock guy, had me by the shirt. Then a flash of orange flew past, and hit Jock with a cross-body block. It was Big Tom, in the orange sweatshirt. There was a thud—whoomph!—and Jock was airborne. He landed on the roadside like a pile of wrinkled clothes. Now I felt terror. We've killed this guy Jock, it's my fault, even though Tom that hothead did it, my God we're all going to jail. And then I saw Arnie's face—it was full of fear, too; his eyes were goggled and he shouted, "Run like hell!" and boy did we! All the adrenaline kicked in and down the street we ran, flying past the press truck, running like kids out of a haunted house.

I was dazed and confused. I'd never been up close to physical violence; the power was terrifying and I was shocked at how helpless I, a strong woman, felt against it. Tom's precise execution, the way he took out Jock and only Jock, was sublime athleticism but I was not grateful for the save, I felt sick at heart, it was awful; it had gone too far. I wished Tom was not there; I wished I was not there. Everyone was shouting. I could hear the journalists on the truck behind us yelling to the driver, "Go after her, Go after her!" The driver accelerated, popped the clutch, and I heard the truck buck and what unfortunately sounded like photographers, tripods, and crank cameras crashing down in a cursing melee.

Everyone was cursing, most loudly Arnie, the mild-mannered sweetheart, who proclaimed he was going to Kill That Jock Semple Who Should Know Better Being a Runner Himself! (Arnie actually *ran* with this maniac?) Tom really looked as if steam was coming out of his ears. He was still in full bombastic mode, and each of his curses was accompanied by a jab or a challenging look over his shoulder. John looked bewildered. I felt puke-ish, afraid that we had seriously hurt this guy Jock Semple, and maybe we should stop and get it sorted out. But it was clear that Jock was some kind of official and he was out of control, now he's hurt, we're in trouble, and we're going to get arrested. That was how scared I felt, as well as deeply humiliated, and for just a tiny moment, I wondered if I should step off the course. I did not want to mess up this prestigious race. But the thought was only a flicker. I knew if I quit, nobody would ever believe that women had the capability to run the marathon distance. If I quit, everybody would say it was a publicity stunt. If I quit, it would set women's sports back, way back, instead of forward. If I quit, I'd never run Boston. If I quit, Jock Semple and all those like him would win. My fear and humiliation turned to anger.

The press truck caught back up to us and hovered alongside with its engine droning only about three feet away. Off the back and side of the vehicle the journalists began firing aggressive questions and the photographers hung out very close to us to get face shots. It felt very weird to try to answer someone's question when there was a clickety-clickety apparatus practically up your nose. And oh, how quickly their tone had changed! Now it was, "What are you trying to prove?" and "When are you going to quit?" Consequently, my tone changed, too. I was polite but no longer friendly. I made it clear that I was not trying to "prove" anything except that I wanted to run, I'd trained seriously for the distance and I was not going to drop out. They wrote down what they wanted to write. Clearly, they didn't believe me, as they stayed alongside us even when I stopped answering their questions and tried to ignore them. They thought it was a prank and didn't want to miss the moment when I'd give up. This only strengthened my resolve. In fact, it actually infuriated me.

Then the bus came by. Standing on the floorboards and holding on to the outside door rail was Jock Semple! My God, he's alive! I thought. I was so relieved! But the bus slowed as it came alongside us, and Jock, teeth bared again and shaking his fist, screamed in a Scottish brogue, "You all ere een beeeeeggg troooouble!" All around us, men gave him the finger and shouted obscenities back at him, and Arnie shouted "Get out of here, Jock! Leave us alone!" I put my head down—I was not going to say a word. My mom had always told me not to say *anything* to unreasonable or aggressive people, and she'd been right so far. And with that, the bus accelerated with a huge cloud of stinking exhaust in our faces and sped away, blaring its horn for the runners to get out of its way.

Eventually, after fifteen minutes or so, the press truck gave up on me when they saw I was not talking anymore and was not going to give them the satisfaction of dropping out to suit their photo ambitions. With a smoother shift of the gears, it accelerated and drifted up toward the front of the race, where it should have been anyway. Our chatter died down, and without the sound of the truck motor and cameras, it seemed very quiet. It started to snow again. We were all deep in thought, and mine were moving all over the place, including wondering why girls first get embarrassed over confrontational situations and only later get angry, and guys can react instantly. I was a little envious of that and glad to feel anger now, because I believed that this was not over, not by a long shot. I said quietly to Arnie, "You know that guy Jock has gone up ahead and is probably arranging for one of those big Irish cops to arrest us when nobody is looking." I'd never seen such big, burly policemen. They made even

Tom look small. "So, if it happens, I am resisting arrest, okay? And something else." I turned to Arnie and looked him in the eye. "Arnie, I'm not sure where you stand in this now. But no matter what, I have to finish this race. Even if you can't, I have to, even on my hands and knees. If I don't finish it, people will say women can't do it, and they will say I was just doing this for the publicity or something. So you need to do whatever you want to do, but I'm finishing."

"Well, the first thing we're going to do is to slow down, then. Forget about time, just finish!" Arnie was now the army sergeant. "Okay everybody, listen up!" he said to everybody in hearing range. "Let's get it together. Slow it down, just relax, we've got a long way to go. Shake it out, shake it out!" We dropped the pace down, dropped our arms, shook our hands. My left hand was wet and freezing; losing that glove was bad. You can have a lot of your body uncovered while you are running and be okay, but if your hands are cold, you are miserable all over. I pulled at the sleeve of my sweatshirt and tried to cover my hand but the sleeve wasn't long enough.

We were just falling into the rhythm of Arnie's stride and beginning to relax when Tom, still fuming, turned to me and blurted out, "You're getting me into all kinds of trouble!"

It was out of the blue.

"What are you talking about, Tom?"

"I've hit an official, and now I'll get kicked out of the AAU. I'll never make the Olympic team and it's all your fault."

I felt really sad, but I was angry, too. "I didn't hit the official, you hit the official, Tom." I said it quietly. It was pretty embarrassing having an argument in front of Arnie and John, and for that matter anybody else running near us. I thought it extremely crass of Tom to pick a fight in public with me, his steady girlfriend. Everybody looked embarrassed.

"Oh great, yeah, thanks a lot for nothing. I should never have come to Boston," he answered loudly.

"I told you not to come to Boston! It was your idea to come to Boston!" I was whispering now, trying not to go on in front of all the people who couldn't help but hear us, and feeling sickish again, as if I were swirling out of one nightmare into another.

"Just stop it, you two," said Arnie.

Tom ripped the numbers off the front and back of his sweatshirt, tore them up, threw them to the pavement, and shouted, "I am *never* going to make the Olympic team and it is *all your fault!*" Then he lowered his voice and hissed, "Besides that, you run too slow anyway." And with that, he took off and disappeared among the runners in front of us.

I couldn't help it. I felt so ashamed I was crying. Once again Tom had convinced me I was just a girl, a jogger, and that a no-talent like me now had bumbled the Olympic Dream out of his life. I thought I was a serious girlfriend to him, and so I guessed that was over, too. It was a helluva race so far, that's for sure, and we still had over twenty miles to go.

"Let him go. Just let him go. Forget it, shake it off!" scolded Arnie. Dutifully I dropped my arms like I'd done a million times in practice and shook my hands. I kept my head down. I didn't want to see anyone, as this was the only way I could lick my wounds in public. I felt myself go into a deep trough of fatigue; actually, the three of us began to go under together, I could feel the downward pull. Even I knew the adrenaline had gone. God, what I'd give to just go to sleep for a while, I thought. We had such a long way to go, but I didn't care anymore, not about Tom, not about anything but finishing. I didn't care how much it hurt or how long it was going to take or if I got put in jail or even if I died. I was going to finish no matter what. We were all quiet for a long time.

A couple of miles later, we slowly began to notice things, the way you do when you first come out of anesthesia. The energy was coming back; by letting ourselves go into the trough we had rested and now we were getting strong again. It was an amazing sensation. First we heard a few feeble cheers; this was really nice and we waved back. There were hardly any spectators. It was such a rotten day that nobody was waiting around for the back-of-the-packers like us. I felt I was still going so slowly, that my soggy long pants must be dragging me down, so I went over to the roadside, pulled them off, and tossed them away. As I did this, a boy of about eight ran for the pants and grabbed them up, swung them around his head, and screamed in glee at his souvenir. The three of us looked at one another and made a face as if to say, "Can you imagine what his mother is going to say when he brings *that* home!?"

We came upon a great scattering of orange peels in the road, a sight incredibly weird to me. When I asked Arnie, he said "Oh those are for the elite runners."

"You mean, the elite runners get *orange slices?!*" I was astonished at this privilege. "Why don't they have orange slices for everyone?"

"They are only for the guys up front, the *real* competitors."

"So, when you were racing in the fifties, you got orange slices?"

"Yep. And sponges and water, too."

"Everyone should get those things. If I ever organize a race, I'll make sure of that."

"Well, everyone does get beef stew at the end," said Arnie. John and I both laughed. "Why do I think we will not be getting beef stew, Arnie?" I said.

He grinned sheepishly. "It's not very good anyway. It's Dinty Moore's, out of a can."

"Oh yuck, I hate beef stew out of a can!" said John.

"Who wants beef stew at the end of a marathon anyway?" I said.

"I wonder where they got that idea."

"It's some kind of old tradition," said Arnie. "And you're right. Plenty of guys on a hot day just get kind of sick when they eat it."

There was a lot about this great race that was just plain wacky to me.

In Natick Center, at about ten miles, we were comfortable again, even telling jokes and stories. I saw a truck parked along the road with a big sign on the side: SNAP-ON TOOLS. For some smutty and very childish reason, this was just hilarious to me, and I got John laughing so hard we both got side aches. Arnie didn't get it, which made it even funnier. From the crowd on the sidewalk a youngish man came running toward us shouting, "Arnie, Arnie!" and jogged alongside us in his raincoat and street shoes. It was Jimmy Waters, one of Arnie's former running pupils from a few years before, when Jimmy was studying at Lemoyne College in Syracuse. Jimmy was now living in nearby Wayland, and the way he treated Arnie you'd have thought Jesus himself was strutting down Natick's Main Street. After chastising Arnie for not telling him we were coming to Boston, Jimmy proposed that he pick us up at the finish and get us back to our car. By any stretch, this was a generous offer, and we readily accepted, especially since Arnie apparently didn't have any kind of plan to get us back to Hopkinton. Then Jimmy ran ahead of us, turned around, and took a fast photo.

Now we entered the famous Wellesley Hills, where, in one of Arnie's theories, "the race began." I was wondering how I'd do on the hills—if the girls at Wellesley would cheer for us and what they would make of me—when I saw a flick of orange go over the top of the next hill in front of us. No, it couldn't be . . . could it? For a while on this stretch, we could see the road ascend, descend and ascend again, and the tableau was so gray, and so wet that the only color was in store signs or in odd bits of spectators' clothing, and there weren't many spectators. Orange anywhere was definitely eye-catching. I couldn't think of anything else but what was going to happen when I got to the top of the next hill, and before I knew it, we were there. We looked down and saw runners running away in front of us, and one big one, in an orange sweatshirt, walking.

Shoot, another disaster, I thought.

"Hey! Is that Tom up there?" chirped Arnie.

"That sure looks like Tom," John added, all singsongy.

I didn't say anything. Of course it's Tom, you jerks, I saw him a long time ago.

Because I said nothing, Arnie then said loudly, as if I were deaf or something, "Hey, I'll bet that really is Tommy!"

Jesus, Arnie! I wanted to smack him. Still I said nothing. Getting the message, the guys went quiet. Tock tock tock went our feet. The orange sweatshirt got closer and closer.

Arnie couldn't stand it. He finally declared, "Yep. That is *definitely* Tom." I slowly looked over at Arnie and gave him a look that said, "Oh, puh-leez," and he said, "Okay, okay!" We ran the next half mile in total silence, and then we were upon Tom, passing him.

"Hey, Tom, how ya doin'?" we all said, trying to be casual.

Tom jumped as if we'd stuck him with an electric prod. Then he started to run, pretending he'd been running all along. I almost laughed out loud at his not knowing we'd been watching him walk for the last mile.

Then he sputtered back to a walk, saying, "Whew! I'm tired! I just need to walk a little."

"It's long way," I said dryly. The guys didn't say anything. Since we kept running, Tom had to jog again to try to catch up.

"Hey!" he said breathlessly, "Walk with me. I'll be okay in a minute."

"Don't walk! Don't you walk!" Arnie whispered to me furiously.

"I'm *not* going to walk, Arnie, for heaven's sakes!" I whispered back. Tom was walking again. I was drifting ahead.

"Hey, Tom, I can't walk with you," I said apologetically.

"Oh, c'mon, I'll get it back!"

"Tom, I can't walk! As slow as I'm going, I have some *momentum* here." Since I said this last thing quite sarcastically, I added a bit more kindly, "You're a talented athlete and you can get it back. If I walked I'd *never* get it back again." Even this sounded patronizing, and it was. Frankly, if you are walking at the thirteen-mile mark in a marathon, you should call a taxi. You're never going to get it back.

Tom tried to run again and then just went "pffffft." I was running backward now, still talking to him, and said, "Look, there's a sweep truck that comes along and picks up the wounded and the lame. Now, since you are a talented athlete" (I couldn't resist saying that again), "you will probably get it back and pass us again. But if you don't for some reason, catch the sweep truck and we'll see you at the finish!" And I turned around and caught up to Arnie and John. I looked back over my shoulder and Tom was walking along like a petulant child. Then presto, we were gone. A while later, I heard him shout from a long echoing distance, "I'd never leave yoooouuuu!!!"

The rest of the race came in remote vignettes, as I was deep in thought, lost in the rhythm of the long run. This had been an eventful day, and I had a lot to think about and needed the miles to work it all out. I could feel my anger dissipating as the miles went by—you can't run and stay mad!—and, as always, I began tumbling it all over, reliving the moment, trying to twist it this way and that until I got an answer. Why did Jock Semple pick on me like that? Just because I was a girl or because he was tired and overreacted? Naw, it was because he thought I was like one of those goofy guys pulling a prank, making a mockery of his race. Well, he should have known better, I was running there, not wearing a sign that said Eat at Joe's or something. So he's all furious, huh? We're probably going to get nabbed by one of those cops just at the point where we're too tired to fight. He'd know the spot. Got to keep a sharp eye out. So I wonder why I am the only girl in this race, anyway. Girls just don't *get* it! Girls just aren't interested, that is why there are no girls' intercollegiate sports at Syracuse and other big schools. And that is why there are no scholarships, no prize money for us. God, they drive me crazy. So if they aren't even interested in basic fitness, they sure aren't going to be interested in running marathons! Well, if they only knew how good they would feel running they would do it. And if there were enough of them, we could have our own race! Yeah, right. So how come I am interested, how come I want to push my physical limits, and they *don't?* Why am I so doggone special? I don't feel very special today, that's for sure.

We'd just gone over the hill at sixteen miles that crosses Route 128. It shook me out of my thinking because it is a sharp hill, and I said, "Shoot, that's not even Heartbreak Hill," and Arnie said, "No, not by a long way."

Often, we'd pass or be passed by men with whom we chatted amiably for a while, all of them happy to see us, even if they were having a bad day. Sometimes we'd run together for a mile or two; mostly we'd just exchange words of motivation. Each one gave me a special word of encouragement; their positive sincerity was very touching. All these guys felt like my best friends; there wasn't one of them I wouldn't trust with my life, that is how strongly I felt. They *understood.* Maybe this is what war is like, only we're not hurting anybody. Better, this is what a quest is like, that's it, we're in search of a kind of Holy Grail. I couldn't find the exact words that would fit. I still can't, but all of us who do it understand.

Occasionally a die-hard spectator would cheer outrageously for us, and this would shake me out of my reverie. Very occasionally it would be a woman, screaming, "C'mon, honey, do it for *all* of us!" Most often though, the women who saw me looked stunned; they didn't know how to react. Almost always the men they were standing with would cheer heartily, but the women would stand there, hands suspended in mid clap as if they were afraid to voice an opinion. I wanted to say, "Yes, it's eighteen miles and I've run that far, and yes, I will go twenty-six. Women *can* do this." But why weren't they here running, too? Those women's faces covered a sweep of emotions—fear, anger, propriety, disbelief, joy, inspiration, hope—and I got lots of messages. A light went on. Those women weren't in the race because they actually believed all those myths about women's fragility and limitation, and the reason they believed them is because they had no opportunity to experience something else. That is why I seem like a creature from outer space to them; I represent something unimagined. And yet, I look just like *they* do!

Gosh, I wasn't special! How stupid of me to ever think that, how totally, utterly stupid. I was just lucky! I was lucky I lived in America and not some place where women have to cover their faces and bodies! I was lucky that my dad encouraged me to run and my mother had a career. I was lucky that my high school had a girl's field hockey team. I was lucky to be asked to run the mile in Lynchburg. And boy, was I lucky to find Arnie. When most girls got to be twenty years old, it would never occur to them to do something so physically challenging, because when they were eight, they were told not to climb trees anymore, and when they were twelve, somebody would whisper stuff about how they'd get damaged if they exercised, and then somebody else would tell them it was more cool to fawn over the guys than do something for themselves. All they needed was an opportunity to actually *do* it. To understand this freedom and power, they had to feel it, they had to feel the Secret Weapon, it doesn't work just talking about it, you can talk until you are blue in the face but you can only *feel* this kind of victory. If they could just have a running opportunity that was welcoming, acceptable for women, not intimidating, regardless of how slow they were to start, that would do it. I've got to do that, I thought.

Running has done a lot for me. I've got to tell them all about it! It is important to pass on this discovery. Dad said that to pass good stuff on is the best way to say thanks. And besides, I feel obligated, responsible. There will be a little noise from this. I didn't intend for that to happen but it turned out that way, and now I will have to make good on this by finishing this race and creating opportunities for women to run. It won't be easy, since the women don't yet know they need the opportunities; they are talking about them in other areas—like jobs—but running is a surefire way of really getting it quickly at a gut level. I'll have to be a kind of Johnny Appleseed, going around and spreading the word, putting together races and other things.

Even though my body was beginning to grind, my mind was just whirling, as if I'd drunk a gallon of coffee. For so many hundreds of miles in training, I was always amazed at how pieces of my past, long-forgotten memories of childhood, or some imaginary scenario, would flash in front of me like a slide show. Today it was all different. As I dissected the day, my mind threw back new images: of the future, of possibility, of an astonishing sense of destiny. I could see my life spread out ahead of me, like a road map.

I felt both light and very old. Finding the solution was wonderful, but I knew I had a lot of work to do. That included becoming a better runner. Nobody was going to take me seriously as an athlete at this pace, and there would have to be a lot of training to bring the time down. Arnie always told me I could be really good, but that was just Arnie giving me a pep talk. I didn't think I could ever be good, but I knew I could be better, and dammit, I was going to try. I was already twenty, and people were telling me I was too old to start serious running. Although I didn't believe that for a minute, I knew I didn't have a lot of time, either.

Jimmy Waters rushed onto the course again with his camera, took our picture, and gave us a big cheer. We laughed and waved. I was back in reality again, realizing that my hips were beginning that deep ache. I could feel the jelly wateriness in my arches and knew some very big blisters would soon have to burst. But I could handle that, pain was nothing. *Nothing.* It was part of what made you a hero, doing this, overcoming it, relegating pain to the incidental for a higher purpose. Arnie said Emil Zatopek, the legendary Czech runner, would keep going until he passed out. Now that's something, but I'm not sure what. Crap! How much longer? I didn't want to ask, it sounded sissy, so I said, "Arnie, when are we going to get to Heartbreak Hill?" Arnie looked startled. "Why, you passed over Heartbreak a long time ago!"

"We *did?* Gosh, I missed it. Why didn't you tell us?" I actually felt disappointed; I thought there would be a trumpet herald or something at the top. In fact, nowadays there is a guy who is a self-appointed archangel on a megaphone telling you "You've done it! You're at the top of Heartbreak Hill!" but on that day it was so unremarkable I didn't know it from any of the other hills.

Arnie was smiling and shaking his head. "You've got to be the only person not to know they just ran over Heartbreak Hill!" He sounded very proud of me, but in fact wherever it was, Heartbreak was a piddly hill compared to those we ran over in Pompey in our workouts or, for that matter, compared to the one here at sixteen miles.

We turned from Commonwealth Avenue onto Beacon Street and now it really did seem endless. There was block after block of identical row houses. There must have been a hundred sets of trolley tracks; I was afraid I'd catch my foot in them and break my ankle, and every time I broke stride to mince over them my blisters squished and stung like hell. The cops had let traffic out on the course, and although they were monitoring it, and although there were plenty of runners behind us, I felt like we were holding up the show. It was another disappointing organizational detail about Boston. I had heard the road was closed for the race and it really wasn't. "I can stay home and run in traffic," I carped. We were frozen. John groaned and rolled his head. Together Arnie and I said, "C'mon John. You can do it." I was amazed at John. What a guy, to hang in like this!

On a street corner, a boy with a stack of newspapers held one up and cried out, "Read all about it! New Zealander wins Boston Marathon!"

"Do you believe *that?*" I said. "Jeez, just imagine. He finished hours ago! He's had a hot shower! He's had a press conference! Shoot! He's on his second beer *right now!*" We had a good laugh, but it was pretty eye-opening. I couldn't even imagine how fast that was. But hey, it was also inspiring. A year ago I couldn't run more than three miles, and here I was at Boston, running twenty-six. I couldn't ever be like those guys, no matter what Arnie said, but I bet I could be better. Those guys are my heroes!

Someone from the sidelines shouted, "One mile to go!" And Arnie snapped quickly, "Don't listen to them, they are all wrong. We have at least three miles to go." John groaned again. I tried not to think about it, but it was hard, because for twenty-five minutes along Beacon Street people kept shouting, "Only one mile to go!" Finally, even Arnie wanted to believe them. A nice cop directed us up Hereford Street, and Arnie got agitated. In his day, the finish had always been up Exeter Street, and he began to protest; I think he and I were both worried that maybe we were getting misdirected at the last minute on purpose. But up at the top of Hereford, we rounded the corner onto Boylston, and there it was, the long slope down to the front of the Prudential Building to a line painted on the street: FINISH. Nobody had misdirected us, nobody had arrested us, and we were going to do it.

John said, "Let's let Arnie finish first," and Arnie said, "No, we'll all finish together," but John winked at me, and at the last moment we slowed and pushed Arnie in front of us. We three had run every step together, we never walked, and we never doubted. Then we hugged, but only briefly, as we didn't want to get all gooey about it. Golly! We'd just run the Boston Marathon!

The finish line crowd consisted of about a dozen water-logged people, none of whom clapped for us. Half of this group converged on us, a few kindhearted souls throwing army blankets over us and the rest peppering us with questions and writing down stuff in their reporter's notebooks. They were very crabby, which is what I would have been if I had had to stand out in this freezing wet for four hours and twenty minutes, which is what one of them said our time was. And they were crabby at *me,* since it was my fault for keeping them waiting so long. Plus, I could tell, they felt indignant at having to cover a *girl*. Being a journalism student, this amused me most. Here you are a big shot sports reporter and your editor tells you to wait for the *girl*. *Na na-na na na.*

"What made you do it?" (I like to run, the longer the better.) "Oh come *on*, why Boston and why wear numbers?" (Women deserve to run too. Equal rights and all that, you know.) "Will you come back to run again" (Yes.) "They will ban your club if you come back." (Then we'll change the name of our club.) "Are you a suffragette?" (Huh? I thought we got the right to vote in 1920!) All of the questions were asked in such an aggressive way that it put me off to be suddenly challenged again. After all the miles, I'd worked out the anger and was now quite mellow. Plus, I felt so *great*. Really, except for the blisters, I felt like I could have run all the way back to Hopkinton. There was only one journalist who asked interesting questions, and asked them politely. He was a young man, about my age, covering his first Boston Marathon. His name was Joe Concannon.

A BAA official came over insisting that I report to the ladies' locker room and have the podiatrist check my feet. This "locker room" was in the garage of the Prudential building; it was freezing cold and damp, devoid of towels, heat, water, or anything that would actually constitute a locker room. The podiatrist was real, however, but very grumpy at pulling this detail, and when I took off my shoes he nearly fainted. My socks were blood-soaked. He lanced and bandaged and lanced and taped and then left. Now what am I supposed to do, I thought? I waited a while, no one came, and I certainly could not get my shoes back on. So I pulled the socks over the bandages and I hobbled back upstairs to the finish line area. I was now really frozen, chilled through, and I had to walk in my socks and bandages through the icy rain puddles. Arnie was frantic wondering where I'd gone. "I think I was removed from the press guys," I muttered.

Jimmy Waters was there to take us home, but there was no sign of Tom. We huddled in our blankets waiting. It had already been over half an hour and we began asking around. Where would official vehicles drop people off? Nobody knew anything. We waited another fifteen minutes, and Arnie kept saying, "Where could he be, where could he be?" If he's smart he's someplace warm and dry and probably gave up on us thinking we'd never finish anyway, I thought. God, now we're just dead frozen and we're gonna have to spend the whole evening looking all over Boston for Tom. We weren't accomplishing anything now, we decided, and got ready to leave when John shouted, "There's Tom!" And sure enough, up at the top of Boylston Street, we saw a figure in an orange sweatshirt, lumbering and lurching forward in a shuffling walk. At first, I didn't even recognize him except for the orange shirt. All recognizable body movement and body type had changed. He looked so, well, *thin!* But it was Tom, and for a moment we were all motionless, thinking the same thing: He had actually finished the Boston Marathon! Then we croaked out our cheers, as loud and long as we could. Honestly, it was one of the gutsiest things I'd ever seen. "C'mon Tom, you're gonna do it, way to go Tom, all the way, all the way!" and hearing us he burst into a little jog to the finish, crossed the line, bent over gasping, his hands on his knees. He sounded like he was having an asthma attack, but we rushed him, clapping him on the back. "You did it, Tom, you really *did* it, gee I'm proud of you!" I shouted. Tom kept gasping and then spit out, "The goddamn sweep truck never came!"

We went back to Hopkinton to get Arnie's car, and on to Jimmy's house, where we took wonderful hot showers, and his wife made us a superb steak dinner that we just inhaled, we were so hungry. How she managed to find a grocery store open on a holiday I'll never know, but I'm grateful to this day. We laughed ourselves silly, drinking beer and telling and retelling stories of the day's adventures, and then it was past ten and time to begin the long drive back to Syracuse. With our spirits at an all-time high, it didn't even occur to me to phone my parents to tell them how I did. In hindsight, I can see how children by their very nature drive parents crazy.

Arnie did the driving and we took turns talking to him to try to keep him awake. In the backseat, Tom was ebullient with his new athletic success—after all, running a marathon is not something too many hammer throwers can do!—and he got all lovey-dovey with me, whispering endearments. I felt pretty darn good. We'd had a tough time, but in the end we'd done it, did it as a team and lived to laugh about it. In this endorphin high, neither Tom nor I had a memory of any hard feelings, and somewhere on the Massachusetts Turnpike, in the darkness around Pittsfield, we decided to get engaged. Surviving your first marathon together is as good a reason as any, I guess.

Albany was halfway home, and it was around midnight when we stopped along the New York State Thruway for gas and coffee. We were so stiff we could barely unfold ourselves from the car. In the restaurant, there was only one person at this hour, a man sitting at the U-shaped counter, reading a newspaper. We sat in a row opposite, yammering away, when my eyes became fixed on the man's newspaper. "My God!" I shouted and ran over to the man, babbling, "Excuse me, sir, excuse me, please let me look at your newspaper!" I was so frantic that he thrust it at me like it was on fire.

All over the front and back covers were our photos. The three of us—and the man, too, who suddenly realized it was us in the photos—gathered around gasping as we went from page to page. Everywhere it was girl running, girl being attacked, girl being saved by boyfriend, girl continuing to run, angry officials and race director, bedraggled girl in rain in socks. Sandwiched in between were photos of the front runners, the winner, Dave McKenzie, and Roberta Bingay (now Gibb), who had run the previous year. We hadn't even known the name of the winner or that Roberta had run until that moment. When had they taken so many pictures? Finally, we just looked at each other and I handed the man his paper. "Keep it! Oh please, I insist, keep it!" he said.

There was surely no danger of anyone falling asleep at the wheel after that. The guys were in heaven; they sounded like roosters in a barnyard all the way back to Syracuse. I laughed at their jokes, but my revelry had turned into quiet musing. I've stepped into a different life, I thought. To the guys it was just a one-time event. But I knew it was a lot more than that. A *lot* more.

Me and Julio Down by the School Yard

Marc Bloom, 1986

In 1966, Andrew Jackson High School and Boys High were the premier two-mile relay teams in the U.S. At the end of the season that year, they dueled to a virtual dead heat and a national high school record that would last for 36 years. Marc Bloom, who had covered the historic race as a young reporter, wrote this article for *The Runner* on the 20th anniversary of the race. When the article appeared, it struck a nerve in readers, many writing that it captured the high school track scene like no other story.

Chapter 1: The Season of Glory

It was 1966, and I was a teenager in love.

I was 19, just starting out as a journalist, and infatuated with something called High School Track.

College friends said, "Get a date, we'll go out."

"No," I said. "I have a meet to cover."

They did not understand of course. I explained: "The meet lasts all day, then I have to compile the statistics, and make some calls, gather my data, and rush a report to *Track & Field News*."

Still, they did not understand, and secretly I was glad that they didn't. Imagine what they would have thought if they did.

Try to tell them that instead of going out on a Saturday night you preferred to watch Julio Meade and Otis Hill run the quarter at a dank military armory on the fringes of Harlem, then write effusively about every nuance of the race to assure that the local athletes were duly recognized and credited by anyone who cared as much about this sort of thing as you did.

Oh, the memories, sweet and lasting: One indelible image is of the sprint relays that were part of the indoor meets at the "Armory," the 102nd Engineer's Armory, a huge installation used by the National Guard in upper Manhattan. Track in New York is black, especially the sprints, and for a white kid barely wet behind the ears in the early '60s, watching an all-black final of an 880-yard relay on the slick, wood Armory floor took your breath away. Even the warm-ups were captivating. Four young men with shaved heads and dress sweats would jog in unison, cool and dignified. Towels rested around their necks, tucked into their sweat tops. I always wondered what they were for. Long strips of tape were affixed to the jersey of the leadoff man. Homemade starting blocks.

In the tight balcony rimming the track, teammates and friends swayed to the rhythms of radios, harmonized lyrics of encouragement and reached over the guard-rail to pound the balcony beams with their fists. Sprinters' soul music. When I ran, no team from my school, Sheepshead Bay, would dare answer an early call for the 880-yard relay and risk being thrown into a qualifying heat with, say, DeWitt Clinton of the Bronx. The 880 final always had fury and style and filled the cold arena with tension and heat. For a minute and a half, the place rocked with riveting athletic expression.

But these were kids. So was I, and I was awed by them, thrilled by them and, as a fellow competitor, certainly intimidated by them. Even before I wrote about them, I had absorbed their performances in some odd, personalized way, rooting for them perhaps even more than they rooted for themselves. I wished I could be like them, be that fast.

I saw, even then, a certain nobility in running track. At the high school level the sport was at its purest, unadorned by frills, unadulterated by the seamy side of athletics, largely uncomplicated by privilege. To succeed you had to overcome. To run indoors at the Armory, you had to survive its treacherous, splintered floor. You couldn't just be fast: You had to be smart, tough, impervious to pressure.

It was too much to ask of a kid. But some were men. One was Julio Meade, another Otis Hill. They were rivals in 1966, the two best quarter-milers in the country. Meade attended Andrew Jackson High in the borough of Queens, in New York City. Hill was from White Plains High in the Westchester suburbs. They dueled often that year, on relay legs and out of the blocks.

———————————————●———————————————

I covered them closely. You could say I idolized them, especially Meade. Like me, he turned 19 in '66. Meade had the grace and good looks of a young Sidney Poitier; he had the regal bearing of an Edwin Moses.

He also had Hill's number that season. In one unforgettable indoor 300 Meade beat Hill despite taking an elbow from Hill and almost falling. There was nothing Meade could not do and when he raced I paced and fretted like an expectant father. I tried not to show Meade my awe. After all, I was a reporter, or trying to become one. We were both after the same thing: his success.

His success would become my success. It was that way with Hill and all the others, too. They were stories, and I wanted to write them. They broke records, and I wanted to compile them. Their excellence nourished me—nourished all of us who had a reason to be on the circuit and cared—and out of this grew a communal family that shared, week in and week out, a burning desire to see kids run fast.

When half-miler Jim Jackson of Boys High hit the scene as a sensational sophomore in '65, that's all anyone talked about. All you'd hear was how fast he could run, how great he could be. When he turned in a knockout performance, I could live off that for a week. All was right with the world when a kid ran fast.

I claimed any new and virginal talent as my own in a proprietary way. It was *us* versus *them*. Emotionally I was aligned with the athlete, in overcoming silly rules, competitive hardships, neighborhood traps, any injustice that got in the way of success. When they hurt, I winced.

Frequently *them* might be other runners from Texas or California, whom we Noo Yawkers felt could not really have run as fast as *Track and Field News* said they had. California distance runners had it too easy, we believed, and Texas sprinters had the wind at their backs. Let 'em race Jim Jackson at the Armory!

I was so proud of Jim that I told my younger brother Les about him, and one day Les came to meet him and see him run. More than anything, I think, he was curious. We didn't have many black kids at our high school.

I must admit I'd been curious, too. When I was running, especially indoors at the Armory, I was gripped with the dizzying fear of exposing myself for two laps around a splintered 220-yard oval more suited to a square dance than a one-mile relay. My team always screwed up. We dropped batons, fell, arrived late and missed our race. Kids from Boys High did not. They had other problems, but when they ran and competed they were aristocrats. I couldn't fathom how they dealt with the pressure.

I'd seen how they lived. When I was in high school my father was a soft-drink salesman with some customers in the Bedford-Stuyvesant section of Brooklyn. On school vacations I'd help him out. It was like going to the Armory and being thrown into a new, threatening culture, one that bred a magical energy and courage and needed track as an outlet.

What I'd succumbed to, I realize now, these kids had been trained to thrive on. And they sang about it as well, with cheering chants at the Armory, a gospel if you will, passed on like street games. James Jackson's eventual rival in the half-mile, Mark Ferrell of Andrew Jackson High, emerged from this *joie de vivre*. While sheer power propelled Jim, Mark was moved by an inner spirit that drew upon language, melody and nuance. Jim was the slugger, Mark the artist.

Indeed, Mark saw running—the running experience—as an art form. When we talked 20 years later, he could still livingly imitate the anthems of the Armory grandstand: "Jackson's got a heat wave, hoo, hoo . . . Boys High Mambo, olé, olé . . ." He smiled. "That's all we knew."

But it was plenty, and I sensed he knew that, too. You could not divorce the running from the man. Out of the track grew something that struck the heart in a profound way, a kind of freedom, and in Mark and others I saw that early on. For me, goodness and hope and passion were somehow embodied in that select little world. It would help me follow my own lights when it mattered most.

Later on, after I'd become a kind of secretary of state for high school track in New York and its environs, the *Albany Times-Union* described me as, "New York State's consummate track nut, who lives in a world of stopwatches, split times, weather factors and deadlines." *The NY Times* called me "a cross-country star." In high school I was so weak in cross-country that I ran in what was then called the "scrub" division. But previewing one Sunday piece I wrote, *The Times* said, "You'll like the Views of Sport by Jimmy Breslin, Roger Kahn and cross-country star Marc Bloom, who says he hates the Super Bowl."

My high school coach, Dick Lerer, must have gotten some laugh out of that. "C'mon, Bloom, blossom!" he'd yell as I huffed and puffed my way up the hills of Van Cortlandt Park in the Bronx. I never would.

Instead, I became the official unofficial chronicler of high school track and field and cross-country in New York State. With my record-keeping, newspaper coverage (primarily for *The New York Times* and *Long Island Press*) and publication of newsletters and yearbooks, I became The Source. College coaches picked my brain for recruiting purposes. Meet directors wanted me on their seeding committees.

Yet I had my detractors. Coaches from public schools said I favored teams from parochial schools. Coaches from the city said I favored teams from the suburbs. Coaches from Long Island . . . . well, you could never satisfy coaches from Long Island. They tried everything, including bribery. Checking into a motel with my wife for an upstate meet, I was presented with a bottle of champagne from a Long Island coach. "Now, maybe we'll get ranked," he said.

I enjoyed having such influence because I felt I could make a difference in the lives of these young athletes. The exposure provided opportunities and led to college scholarships.

When Mark and Julio went off to Kansas University, I missed them. We wrote. They sent me colorful K.U. stickers, which I affixed to my car. If the high school kids did not show well in college, I took it personally. I brooded when Jim Jackson, at Purdue, couldn't nail his four-minute mile. Today, he says, he has no regrets. He got his degree. But still . . .

Early one spring morning in 1966 a call came from the chairman of the selection committee of the Golden West Invitational high school meet in Sacramento, California. This was—and is—a kind of national championship for high school seniors. There is no greater plum than an invitation from Golden West. I'd been bragging to the meet officials about the athletes in the New York area who warranted their attention. In the midst of their final selections, the meet committee decided to phone me. It was midnight on the coast, 3 A.M. in New York. I grabbed my color-coded notebook and spoke to them for an hour. Every athlete I recommended, including Mark, and Julio, was invited.

I went with them. You don't think I'd let them go without me? Once there, we took a bus trip to San Francisco. We rented a station wagon, drove to Tahoe and dipped our toes into the frigid lake. We took pictures of one another with our Instamatics. When they raced, my heart raced.

That was the year, 1966. It was, best of all, the year Andrew Jackson High and Boys High, both of the New York City Public Schools Athletic League, set a national scholastic record that still stands today. It was set in the two-mile relay and, for all we know, may never be broken.

It happened on June 7, 1966, 20 years ago this month, the jewel in a season of glory.

Chapter 2: The Race Takes Shape

The Catholic schools league of New York City held a relay carnival during the '60s at the end of each spring season, to provide an opportunity for good teams to break records. The meet was needed because the rules governing

New York track at the time, essentially restricting athletes to one event per meet, prevented the top schools from running "stacked" relay teams when the runners were at their best.

In 1966, all year long, there was talk about when and where that season's remarkable collection of athletes would get their shots. I was a primary instigator, keeping athletes and coaches apprised of the various national relay records. The record for the two-mile relay, a favorite New York event and a hot one in '66, was vulnerable. It was decided the race would have to be run as a special event in the Catholic schools Relays at St John's University in Queens, which had the only all-weather track in the city. Even Randall's Island, where the AAU Nationals were held that year, had a cinder track.

Today, no one seems willing to take credit for setting up the race. "I didn't bring the idea up," says Milt Blatt, the Andrew Jackson coach. "Doug Terry made the offer. He wanted someone to push him. I said 'Sure, let's have fun. We'll see if we can beat you.' He laughed."

Twenty years later, Terry, the Boys High coach, laughs again. He insists it was not he who initiated the showdown.

The meet director, Jack Donovan, seems to recall being contacted about the special two-mile relay by Marty Lewis, the PSAL track chairman. "I had nothing to do with it," says Lewis. "I wasn't even there."

Whether from memories dulled by time or differing points of view, such discrepancies were not uncommon in my recent conversations with the principals of the record-setting race. I decided, in researching that day of 20 years past, not to pursue disputed facts to the point of corroboration, but to let comments ride. While my own memory, like that of others is selective, I did have the benefit of a scrapbook full of old clippings.

First I sought to find the eight runners and two coaches. Coaches Milt Blatt and Doug Terry were easy. I had their phone numbers. Seven of the eight athletes came to light rather easily, too. I started with James Jackson who, as the current Boys High coach, I saw from time to time. One contact led to another. On the Andrew Jackson side, Julio Meade was in Kansas, while Mark Ferrell, Sam Thomas and Bill Jacobs were all in New York. From Boys, John Henry was in New York while Mike Randall was living in New Jersey. Each was delighted to hear from me, excited that the record was being excavated like buried treasure. A few could not believe the record still stood. Others had kept up with the sport and were even aware that last year a team from Illinois came within two seconds of the mark.

To have known such runners as teenage prodigies is to have seen them, perhaps at their finest: as innocents seeking the nobility of success, offering, to anyone who really looked, a privileged glimpse into the souls of raw youth.

It has never left my mind that the record still stands, and I've always felt a sense of duty to tell what happened. I also wanted to satisfy my need to find the men as bright and devoted as they were as youths, and I was not to be disappointed. They still show respect for one another, and an appreciation for the lifelong growth they trace to their origins on the track.

"There was nothing but success," says Julio Meade. "Those were very, very good times." His best friend, Mark Ferrell, says it was Julio who taught him pride and self-esteem. "I'm still learning from him," Mark says.

Mike Randall of Boys, now a man of letters and philosophy, dropped me a note after I'd first contacted him, to say he was proud of *me*. It had never occurred to me that I could be important to anyone of *them*. Perhaps, as adults, our roles in the renewed relationship have now merged onto the same plane.

The missing person was Boys' Mark Edmead. Originally from Trinidad, he seemed to have disappeared. No one had seen him in years. "He lived in the fast lane," says Terry. Others agreed. I spent hours checking obscure sources. I placed an ad in a West Indian weekly published in New York. It turned up nothing. Then, at the Millrose Games in February, I saw Edwin Roberts, the former Trinidad Olympian. He directed me to a local college coach, also from Trinidad, who told me Edmead was living in Brooklyn. Finally, I found him, but not until we were going to press, by which time little about him could be included.

Jackson and Boys were great athletic powers, not only in track but also in basketball and other sports. In track a pungent rivalry existed because the two teams would clash just about every week throughout the school term. "We had respect for the Boys High team," says Julio Meade. "They were always the team to beat in the city champs."

In the winter of '66, as a prelude to their outdoor match, Boys, with Andrew Jackson assisting, went for the indoor record in the two-mile relay. Archbishop Molloy of Queens, the perennial Catholic schools power, had run 7:49.1 on the Madison Square Garden track in '64. Boys and Jackson raced in the Armory, a good second slower per man. Running with its best unit, Boys ran 7:54.2, but creamed Jackson, which clocked 8:01.7. That race left Andrew Jackson wounded, but it also gave Boys a deadly false impression of its rival's potential strength in the event.

While Boys marched mechanically from victory to victory, the Jackson kids were having their own fun. They hung out together, supported each other, developed bonds.

"On the way home from school." says Mark Ferrell, "we'd stop at Julio's for plantains, then we'd stop at my house for something else to eat, then stop at Bill's house and play ping pong."

"We had a lot in common," Bill Jacobs says. They even made music together. Through Ferrell's older brother, Jacobs got hooked on jazz. He played marimbas and was asked to join a dance band. Julio was also a member. He played congas.

"Mark and Julio were very intelligent, mature young men," says Jacobs. "I was not like that then. Their good habits rubbed off." It was not all so serious. "We'd do things like tease dogs so they'd chase us. Any excuse to run. We knew we were good." Good enough to believe there was nothing they could not do. "After school," says Meade, "we'd go over to Mark's house and basically dream about running fast and breaking records."

One day, in '65, they wrote out the dream. At lunch, Bill jotted down how fast he thought he, Mark, Julio and a fourth could ultimately run the 880; added up, it came out in the mid-7:30s for the two-mile relay. "I know I was dreamer," says Bill. "It was a college time, but Mark said it could happen."

They did not relate this calculation to Blatt until '66. A miler and two-miler, Billy the dreamer kept letting Blatt know that he wanted in. At first Sam Thomas was not a part of the dream. A year behind the other three, he had not yet developed and, as a younger student, was not as close. "I was very impressed with Julio and Mark," Sam says. "They were people I wanted to be like." And he would.

When on June 7, 1966, the Jackson kids assembled to run the race of their dreams, they were the decided underdogs. Boys had four proven half-milers. Jackson had two half-milers, a sprinter and, alas, a distance runner. Every top team in the area was there, including Molloy, which had held the national record of 7:43.8 in 1964. In '65, the record was lowered to 7:42.9 by East High of Wichita, Kansas, a team anchored by Jim Ryun, and then to 7:42 by Proviso West of Hillside, Illinois.

The day, a Wednesday, was pleasant and, by necessity, without serious wind. I rushed over from college. It was finals week, and I had rescheduled an exam, desperate to make the meet. White Plains High (the best all-around team in the country that season set the tone by first running 1:25.4 to slash the national record in the 880-yard relay. Otis Hill ran anchor. This time Julio Meade, the sprinter, could not join him. Coach Blatt had named him to run leadoff in the two-mile.

"Lots of character," says Blatt. "He could handle any event. He didn't worry about it one bit."

"Julio was the key," says Doug Terry.

He meant the key to the Boys High record. A strong leadoff by Julio would spur Boys High and keep them, quite literally, on their toes.

"We were so experienced. I had these guys for two years, we knew exactly how to run, how to make moves," says Terry, still dazed about it after all these years. "This was our baby."

"We were there to push them," says Blatt. Oh, baby.

Chapter 3: Coach Milt Blatt

"Coach Blatt was very special to the many lives that he touched," says Julio Meade. "He would sit with you and say, 'You can do this, you can do that.' Not only in track but also in your studies. He took an interest in developing the total individual. To this day I am very thankful to coach Blatt, because he basically changed my life."

When Milton Blatt retired from the school system in 1972, after 42 years as a teacher and 26 years as a track coach, a dinner was held in his honor. Athletes, students, those whom he'd touched and given light, came from all parts of the country to pay him tribute. As the athletes filed past the museum-like display of scrapbooks and trophies, picking out their names and remembering, I could see love in their eyes. When Milt addressed the gathering, the stillness was palpable.

Milt Blatt did not aspire to sainthood. What he aspired to do was teach young men to achieve. His approach was simple. "I treated them as if they were young friends of mine. Any problem, I'd get them to talk about it." He was not a disciplinarian. "I didn't have to be," he says.

We are in the living room of the Blatt's modest home on Long Island. Milt is in good health and even at 76 boyish and keen. He tenderly spreads out 20-year old frayed clippings and photos and recalls the high notes with a reverence not for himself but for the young men, especially those of the two-mile relay. "They were ideal trackmen." He says. In Milt Blatt's heart, you could do no better than possess the qualities—the decency and desire—of an ideal trackman.

Blatt began teaching English at Andrew Jackson when it opened in '37. When the track coaching spot became available in '46, he took it. By then, he was also a grade advisor, counseling students on college. Many of his own would do particularly well. Books they would write shine with warm inscriptions from the walls of his home.

Blatt carried big teams, 50, 60, 70 kids, almost unheard of today. He had no assistant coach. Even while spreading himself thin as the sole mentor of a large group, Blatt created an environment in which relationships would prosper. "There was a special camaraderie," says Mark Ferrell. "I haven't seen it duplicated. Milt Blatt made it special. And he stressed that if we performed well, we could get a college scholarship."

He also stressed speed over distance. "If we did 40 miles a week," says Ferrell approvingly, "it was a lot." Twenty years ago, spurred by the impatience of youth, Ferrell wanted more. He read about Jim Ryun, whom he would join in college.

"Look at the workouts Ryun is doing," Ferrell complained to Blatt. "We're doing nothing here."

"Your body's not ready for that," Blatt told him.

Facilities were typical of city schools. Jackson had a five-lap-to-the mile dirt track. Indoors, there was a hallway, about 100 yards long. "It was not ideal, believe me," Blatt recalls. "But it was like interval training."

"It was dangerous," says Meade with some pride. "You ran, touched the wall, and came back. You'd see how many laps you could do without falling apart. I enjoyed it."

If you could hold up to such a challenge, you developed an edge. "Any time a visitor would come to practice, he couldn't believe how we ran indoors," says Sam Thomas. "But you got a workout. I remember crawling out of that school; I couldn't wait to get into bed. It was a good feeling."

During Blatt's tenure, Jackson teams won 16 consecutive Queens borough outdoor track titles and a total of 14 PSAL city championships in track and cross-country. Blatt's individual stars included Vinnie Mathews, a 48 second quarter-miler in '65. He was PSAL champion that year. In 1972, he won the Olympic gold medal. Milt always referred to him as "Vincent." I loved to hear that. It sounded so respectful.

Blatt is not given to fancy analysis of what works and what doesn't. Never was. He coached by instinct. He imparted good sense and high standards, instilled trust, clutched his stopwatch and saw his kids run like the wind. Still I wondered, how did he do it? "Ideal trackmen," he says.

But Milt Blatt was a teacher. When you're a good teacher, kids produce. "Athletes respected him and liked him," says Larry Ellis of Princeton, the 1984 Olympic coach. When Blatt was at Jackson, Ellis coached at Jamaica High. "He did wonders training people," says Ellis. Yeah, hallways.

When Blatt's ideal trackmen needed help, he was there. "If you couldn't get to a meet, he'd come to your house and pick you up," says Sam Thomas. "He prodded me into certain courses to make sure I'd get into college."

Bill Jacobs, at first, was not an ideal trackman. He fell in with the wrong crowd. "Thank God for Milton Blatt," he says. "I felt as though someone had put their arms around me."

Blatt knew his track, too, the names, the stats: He was a real fan. Mark Ferrell caught some of this. He put clippings on his bedroom wall. He went over to St. John's to watch Tommy Farrell, the '64 Olympian in the 800 meters, work out. Two years later, on that same track, on the anchor leg of a two-mile relay, Mark would run his greatest race ever.

An ideal race, you could call it, by ideal trackmen. The ideal coach had something to do with it, too. "He wasn't just a coach, he was a friend," says Ferrell. "He was Uncle Miltie."

Chapter 4: Coach Doug Terry

Doug Terry was raised in the Bedford-Stuyvesant section of Brooklyn, a few blocks from Boys High, and as a young athlete was dying to go there. He was an excellent student, however, and his mother insisted he attend Brooklyn Tech, a leading academic school with an entrance exam. Terry captained the Tech track team and won the city 440 title, indoors and out, in 1954, his senior year. A decade later as a student at St John's and at 28 the old man of the track team, he got to know the Boys coach, Ken Gibson, who was on campus taking graduate courses. Gibson had accepted a college coaching position and asked Terry if he might be interested in the Boys High coaching Job. Terry said, "Yeeeaaahhh!"

He had a ready-made team. "Better quality than I'd seen in college," he said. The next decade—from Terry's first year in '65 to his last in '74—Boys probably had more top-notch runners than any high school in the U.S. They had sprinters, quarter-milers, half-milers, distancemen, and hurdlers. And did they ever have relay teams. In the '66 record two-mile relay the Boys "B" team took fourth in 7:53.2 (*Track & Field News* called it a "world record" for a second-string team), and Boys had a third string capable of about 7:58.

Those guys were high-stepping, in-your-face swoopers. Terry needed to protect his turf, as he explains from the den of his home in Providence, Rhode Island, where he's lived since he took the head coaching job at Brown in 1974.

Boys was an all-male school and therefore "special": You could attend Boys from outside the district; or, if you live in the district, you were permitted to go elsewhere, say, to Erasmus Hall over in Flatbush. Terry's mission was to keep the local runners from Bed-Stuy at Boys, then to sharpen the instincts they'd already acquired from ghetto life.

On the rough streets of Bed-Stuy there was not the stability Blatt enjoyed in the Cambria Heights section of Queens, a black middle-class community and home, then, to celebrities like Count Basie and Brook Benton. Terry built his young men less on fatherly warmth and more on pragmatic toughness. He did not want to excise the neighborhood from the athlete; the athlete *was* the neighborhood. "They knew how to survive, to make life work," he says. They needed to run with that.

Mark Ferrell of Andrew Jackson got a taste of it. In his junior year, he took an after-school job in his brother-in-law's pharmacy in Bed-Stuy. "I remember one day coming back from a meet with a trophy we'd won and trying to figure out a way to hide. I thought someone would ambush me."

Terry took risks. In '65, his first year, he put the soph Jimmy Jackson, who'd never run a half-mile, on the anchor leg of the two-mile relay in the national scholastic indoor meet at the Garden. "I was the duck," says Jackson. But he ran 1:56 and his team won. He didn't know he wasn't supposed to.

That same winter Uncle Miltie pulled a fast one on Terry—about as fast as they come. Boys was after the national indoor record for the 880 relay, at Blatt's suggestion according to Terry. "Milt told me he'd put Julio on leadoff to push." Julio Meade, then a junior, had just won the city 100-yard dash title in record time. "But when we got to the line," Terry says, "there was no Julio."

Blatt had Julio Meade running anchor. He had Vincent running third. Upset city? Meade touched off a good twelve yards behind the Boys anchorman, Leroy Foster. It was an impossible distance to make up. Impossible . . . Meade jetted after him, and on the home straight performed a miracle, defying gravity and—dare he—Boys High. I saw it, and it looked as if his legs were running away from his body. He came within a half-step of catching Foster. Boys got the record, running 1:30.1. Jackson ran 1:30.2. Blatt looked at his watch, tapped it, looked again, shook his head. Could it be? Meade's split was 21.3! Carl Lewis couldn't run that fast in the Armory.

"I was angry," says Terry. "They tried to steal my record."

One day they would, and Terry would blame himself.

Terry's teams won the PSAL outdoor title seven times and the indoor title six times. Six times they won championship races at the Penn Relays. Five times they won Eastern States team titles. His two best runners were Jim Jackson and Bill Dabney, a decade apart. Both started as sprinters and developed into 1:50 half-milers. "My two killers," Terry called them.

"Coach Terry knew how to motivate people," says Jim Jackson. "If he said you could do something, then you could do it. He provided guidance. You could not be on the team unless you were doing well in class. He was the total coach."

"Tradition," says Terry. "That's what motivated them, gave them confidence. We were king of the hill."

"Did that add to the pressure?" I ask him.

"If anything," he says, "my teams would relax me. I'd be on the edge of my seat, sweating, and they would say, 'Coach, what are you worried about? Don't worry about a thing.'"

Terry trained his team much as Blatt did. The half-milers ran sets of 220s, 440s, 660s, based on pace. "Modified intervals," Jim Jackson called them.

He made it sound easy, but it wasn't. "Jack used to hate me," says Mike Randall, the team captain. "I worked him too hard. I was gung-ho. Like Frank Burns on M*A*S*H."

"When we went to practice," says John Henry, "we went to war. Guys would be throwing up. But it was fun. It was our whole life."

Henry had run with Jim Jackson in junior high and was awed by what he found at Boys. But he recognized the possibilities. "You could come in with nothing and Terry could make you into something, if you dedicated yourself."

That was not all you got out of Boys High. "You went to Boys to get girls," says Randall with irony. "Wherever we went girls died for us. Why? It was the charisma of the athletic school. It was an academy for athletes, the best in the city."

For Terry, now 49, that changed in '74 when a federally funded college-bound program was dropped. "Kids didn't want Boys High, and the pool of talent shriveled up."

He went to Brown. From Bed-Stuy to the Ivy League. "At Brown, I had to relax *them*," he says. Despite the culture shock, Terry's teams did well, but he would grow disenchanted with the university because of what he termed inconsistencies in the admissions policies regarding athletes he recruited.

In 1984, after ten years, Terry quit. Before then, he'd gotten involved in civic affairs. He started a black newspaper. He hosted a TV show. He ran for Providence city council (and lost). Currently he teaches and lectures on black issues and participates in a number of black development programs.

He says, "I used to tell my athletes that you've got to do the right thing educationally, then come back and straighten out the community. It was a self-help philosophy. We never depended on anybody. That's what we were about in '66."

Chapter 5: Leadoff Leg

Julio Meade, Jackson vs. Mark Edmead, Boys

Julio Meade probably was the most extraordinary track athlete to come out of New York City. He was one of a kind, a premier sprinter who could also run distance. He was the best quarter-miler in the U.S., winning the Golden West title in 46.8, but he'd also run cross-country, and quite well. Cross-country? Most sprinters would not dare.

"No one ever worked harder to develop a talent," says Mark Ferrell. "He was a *runner*. He'd run anything."

So Milt Blatt figured, why not the 880? Julio had run a 2:04 half-mile as a freshman. When the special two-mile relay was being assembled, he was game. "I knew I could run the 440 in 47 and I knew the leader would not come through the quarter any faster than 54," he explains. "I could stay behind and not be bothered by the pace."

We meet at his spacious home in Lawrence, Kansas, where Julio became a successful businessman after college. I find him much as before: uncommonly handsome, articulate, confident, pragmatic, and with a strong sense of duty. He always saw possibilities, even in the absurd.

Julio was born in San Cristoval, the Dominican Republic, and lived there for 10 years with his maternal grandparents. His mother and father left for New York when he was an infant. When they could afford it, they sent for their children. "It was just country," Julio says. "No electricity, no formal schooling. We were considered wealthy because we had a radio."

Julio's grandfather had a sugar cane crop. Julio helped him in the fields, with his horses and served as his grandfather's messenger boy, which is how he developed endurance. He ran barefoot, three miles each way, to deliver messages to a relative. He did this regularly for five years.

At Jackson he was an immediate hit, almost making the team's two-mile unit for the '63 Penn Relays. "It was Mark Ferrell who moved me down to the shorter distances," says Julio. "He wanted me out of his event."

By his junior year, in '65, a legend was building around him. He'd won the Eastern States outdoor 100 as a soph, impressing 220-man William Walker of Englewood, New Jersey. Going into the Eastern 220 in '65, Walker was possessed by Meade's threat. He was quoted as saying, "I went to the dentist the week before the meet. He gave me gas, and when I woke up he told me I kept repeating over and over, 'Beat Meade, beat Meade . . . .'" In fact he did beat him. Julio Meade was not yet invincible. Remember, Vincent was on the team. But the best sprinter that season was Otis Hill of White Plains, also a junior, who ran the 440 in 47.3.

Julio had one goal his senior year: "To beat Otis."

Thus began a rivalry like no other, especially indoors at the fabled Armory. You didn't need anything else, just Julio and Otis. "Otis was muscular, very intimidating," says Julio. "I made it a practice never to look at him."

"It was serious," says Mark Ferrell. "Like a hit man going out on a job."

"I would focus on it the night before. I would talk to myself, I would imagine it," says Julio.

Word of the rivalry spread, drawing gamblers. Julio remembers it: "Ten guys from Brooklyn would come to the Armory strictly to bet against Otis. They'd come and tell me, 'Meade, I got so much money on you today.' A hundred, two hundred. They'd say, 'How do you feel? You gonna kick his butt?' I'd tell them I'd do the best I could."

Julio won all four races that winter, two 300s and two 440s. One, a 300, lives on. People who didn't see it say they did. After taking an elbow from Hill that put him ten yards behind ("I almost fell on my face") with only 150 yards to go, Julio went into third gear, as he described it, and nipped Hill at the wire. "I always felt, if I could see you, I could catch you."

"He went around that turn as though he were blown through a glass tube," says Ferrell. "If you really want to see Julio perform, put him at a disadvantage."

Otis was the least of it. Julio's father did not believe in sports. "You go to school, you go to work," says Julio, stating his father's command. "I was not allowed to participate." At one point, in junior high, he was working three jobs after school. While at Jackson he'd sneak into the house after practice before his father, a longshoreman, returned from work. Even when Julio's running became obvious, his father would never accept it. "Coach Blatt would pick us up for a meet, and I was scared to death my father would say, 'You're going to work.'"

Julio's parents never once saw him run. That, he says, is what motivated him. "I wanted my father's approval. I figured the better I did . . ." The memory makes him pensive. "He did give in. He would carry my clippings. But he never said to me, 'You ran a good race.'"

When the gun cracked for the record attempt in the two-mile relay, Mark Edmead of Boys went for the lead. He didn't get it. Julio sprang to the front. Edmead tucked in behind him. "I figured his strategy was to burn me out," says Mark. "I thought he would fade." The two West Indians raced away from the other teams, establishing the tenor of the race for good.

Edmead had solid competitive range and had won the PSAL indoor 1,000-yard title, beating Jackson's Sam Thomas. "An import," coach Terry called him. "Fast."

"He was different than the rest of us," says John Henry. "He liked to have fun, talk to the girls, but he was dedicated to the sport in his own way."

"I cracked jokes, tried to keep everybody loose," says Mark. Two years before, Mark had come to Brooklyn with track experience from Port-of-Spain. He felt more worldly than the others and sought to mediate the tension with humor. He helped himself as well, coping with Julio despite a bad back that still plagues him today.

Mark ran smartly, but was visibly wary of the sprinter who dared to lead. Julio floated. His stride had wings. At the 660, precisely as Blatt had instructed, Julio took off. "It was automatic," says Julio. Mark couldn't respond, but he did not die.

Julio brought it in first, in 1:54.3. It is the fastest leadoff 880 ever run by a high school runner, before or since. Mark was seven yards behind, in 1:55.3, his best time.

"Julio complained that I held him back," says Blatt. "It was unbelievable. I should have known. He could have run 1:52."

Doug Terry loved it. "When I looked at my splits, I knew the record would go." He feared nothing, thinking, "No problem, babe, 'cause I got my killer on the end."

Chapter 6: Second Leg

Bill Jacobs, Jackson vs. John Henry, Boys

"Julio told me he was gonna give me the stick in first, and that I better run my buns off," says Billy Jacobs. "I told him, if you bring it in first, I'll bring it in first."

Blatt prayed he could get under two minutes, that's all. "We were concerned about Billy," says Julio. "He was a two-miler. Perhaps he didn't have the leg speed."

As a youngster, he was the fastest kid on the block. "As soon as we ventured off the block, I got to see that my block was kind of slow," he says. At the Jackson track tryouts, he was overwhelmed by the size and speed of the others and decided not to run his freshman year.

He returned as a soph and ran a fine practice mile. "Fantastic," Blatt told him. It was 5:32. Bill had done some jogging in his neighborhood. He'd been warned not to. "I had an enlarged heart and a murmur. The doctor told me not to run," he says. "But I was a rebellious kid. If you told me I couldn't do something, I'd do it."

He ran, looked up to Julio and Mark, wished he were fast, and fell in love with the two-mile relay, though he rarely ran one. "The 880 was the shortest distance I could run and help the team," he says. It wasn't a sprint but it was close enough.

His opponent, John Henry, *was* fast. But Boys had more sprinters than it knew what to do with and Terry threw Henry into the half. He accepted it, with Jim Jackson as his role model.

At Boys, Henry ran mostly relays and by the winter of '66 had worked his best half down to 2:02. A junior that year, he still felt like a small fish in a big pond. Jacobs, on the other hand, ran individually in the distances, becoming a 4:24.8 miler (with a resting pulse of 38) who took third in the city indoor championships. But the dreamer wanted action in the two-mile relay. He had a sense of destiny.

That season when Boys and Jackson went for the indoor record, Jacobs was chosen for the second leg. He was hungry. John Henry was lucky. Selected for the send leg, too, Henry recalls, "I was thankful to God I even made that team. I don't know how coach Terry ever picked me."

Henry put Jacobs away, running 1:58.7 as Boys won easily. Jacobs ran his best, "close to two minutes," but it was not good enough. "From that point," says Jacobs, "I wanted Henry. And I wanted that race to be run again."

First, Bill had a revealing match up with Doug Terry's killer, At New York's Brandeis Relays, Jackson and Boys tangled in the distance medley. Boys did not run its best unit and, going into the mile anchor leg, Jacobs had a huge lead over Jimmy Jackson. "When we were lined up waiting for the sticks," Jacobs recalls, still in wonder, "he told me, 'I'm gonna get you.' I wasn't used to someone being so cocky."

Jackson tore after Jacobs, somewhat recklessly, a prodigious talent stained by style. "I turned and I saw this guy coming like blazes. And I thought, 'You're running the *mile*; what do you think you're doing?'" Jackson passed Jacobs before the half. But, sensing Jackson was burnt out, Jacobs hung with him, had more to give in the stretch and won. His split was 4:32.8. Jackson had run 4:23.8.

By June 7, the day of his dreams, some of Jacobs's passion had given way to contentment. The regular season was over for him, he'd gotten a college scholarship, was working, learning to drive . . . and . . .

"I forgot about the race." A jazz musician and composer today, Jacobs was at work at Alexander's department store elsewhere in Queens when he realized that at that very minute he should have been warming up over at St. John's for the race that he'd dreamed about, fought to be a part of, indeed helped to create through the sheer force of his will.

He rushed off, ran for a bus, arrived late, zipped up his sweats and saw Julio. "He was looking at me, like what the hell . . . I didn't go to Milt. I went to Sam. He had my number." Jacobs's entire warm-up, aside from his run for the bus, consisted of a 220 jog.

Henry, too, was on edge. He had the experience and 49-second 440 speed to run a dazzling half, but felt the pressure and was not apt to risk an untested move. On the first lap, he cut into Jacobs's seven-yard lead, and stayed put. "I held back. I didn't want to blow it," he says.

"I felt him breathing down my neck," says Jacobs. "We bumped. I was glad to see him on my shoulder. He was the Boys High man who'd beaten me indoors. I would not let him pass."

Henry tried at the 660, but Jacobs, the distance runner, drew upon speed that was not his own, as a musician finds a rhythm through the beat of others.

Jacobs handed off first, running 1:57.3. Henry ran 1:56.6 trimming the Jackson lead to two yards. Henry plopped into the infield grass and heard people say, "If they keep this up, the record is gone." Jacobs collapsed in the pole vault pit where he watched it happen.

Chapter 7: Third Leg

Sam Thomas, Jackson vs. Mike Randall, Boys

"The one who ran the best race was Billy Jacobs," says Julio Meade. Of the Jackson runners it was Jacobs, given his recent competitive emphasis, who'd come closest to realizing his full potential that day. For Boys, the same could be said of Mike Randall.

Like Bill, Mike was a little guy with a big heart who ran distance but preferred the 880. "Mr. T never gave me a chance to run open halves," says Mike. "I never knew what I was capable of. But I was the team captain. I was supposed to be selfless."

Sam Thomas had no such conflicts. He was comfortable in the half and, a year behind his teammates, had Mark Ferrell's records to shoot for. "It was beautiful," says Sam. "When I came to Jackson, Mark knew I was after his soph record, and he encouraged it."

As a junior in '66, Thomas turned in a 1:55 for third in the city champs. He was unfamiliar with Randall, who was the city mile champion. Randall had established himself as a top half-mile prospect at Boys and in '65 had run a 1:55 relay leg. In '66, that's where his best still stood. Longer races blunted his speed. "I wasn't sharp," he remembers. "I should have been at 1:51."

Sam could feel safe. He sought only to hold the lead he was given. He feared for Mark Ferrell. "We still had that madman, Jim Jackson, on anchor. He could do anything."

It was Randall who'd contributed to that. At Boys he won the award for being the most physically fit athlete, showing skill in tumbling, calisthenics and body building. At track practice, no one worked harder. "Jack had to come along with me. I was the man. We became the guys to run with—or avoid, depending on how you looked at it."

As a leader, Randall was an exemplary team captain. And while he credits Terry with being an outstanding coach who "taught me a lot about running on an intuitive level," their minds did not always meet, and not only regarding Mike's preferred racing distance.

"He never told me what was going on. I didn't know diddly. On the day of the race, I didn't even know we were going for the record," Perhaps Terry took Randall for granted. He'd always come through, as he did at the '66 Penn Relays with a marvelous 3:06 three-quarters leg. "I had the suspicion Jack knew everything. He was consulted. I wasn't. I had problems with that."

Randall quit the team. He said that on top of everything Terry had words with him over a girl he'd been dating. Randall said a teammate started a rumor that he'd been "fooling around" with a girl, and that Terry told him to cut it out. After Randall quit, he said, Terry took him to dinner to patch things up. Soon, he was back.

But not in the half-mile, and on the day of the big race Mike felt strangled by lack of speed. "I envied Sam," he says. Sam's head was not as cool as Mike thought. "To calm down," Sam says, "I warmed up by myself."

With the two-yard lead to play with, Sam jumped out assuredly but within reason, hitting a tempo that left room for a strong second lap. Sam had no idea about the impression he left on the man behind.

"Sam was crisp. I mean, if you touched him, you'd get cut," says Mike. "He took off, knees high. He was smoking. I'm thinking, how can he handle this? Then, on the backstretch, he took off like a bat out of hell."

Mike was stunned. So was Doug Terry. "He sighed, 'Oh, no.'" says Mike. "I could hear him."

Still, Mike held on, calling up his miler's reserves. Billy Jacobs watched from the pole-vault pit. "Mike was a great athlete. Watching the way he stuck with Sam clarified that for me."

Sam was dazzling, clocking 1:52.7, a time few high school half-milers could run. Mike, amazingly, ran 1:53.1. Andrew Jackson had a five-yard lead on Boys going into the anchor leg.

Milt Blatt could not believe his eyes. All logic had left since Julio's 1:54 lead-off. He kept hitting his stopwatch. The numbers looked funny.

Doug Terry was in heaven. "These guys are knocking off 1:54s, 1:52s. And my stuff ain't there yet? I'm gone." A coach's fantasy: Everyone on a relay running his best. It happens maybe once in a lifetime.

"And I got my killer?" said Terry, "Wooooooooo!"

Chapter 8: Anchor Leg

Mark Ferrell, Jackson vs. James Jackson, Boys

Just talking about '66, Mark Ferrell seems to feel it as he felt it then. He summons the vibrations, fresh and soulful "When you're doing it, out there performing, it's a high you can't find anywhere else. It's euphoric. It's being so nervous before a race you get sick: then the gun goes off and you're in a different dimension. Like Alice in Wonderland."

Such transcendence never occurred to James Jackson. "Jack," they called him. He was The Man. The crazy wonder of the track was not to be his, not in '66, his junior year. By then they were out to get him. "Everyone was getting better because I was taking the pace. It was burdensome," he says.

Jack's tactics belied his sobriety. Charging ahead with his sprinter's speed for out-of-sight times, Jack looked the imprudent showman, brash, out of control. Daring? Yes. But he was nobody's fool. He was dead serious, targeting himself straight ahead, never looking back or sideways. "I was diligent, I worked hard, I liked to win," he says.

"He was very forthright," says Doug Terry. "No nonsense. He wanted to achieve. Only problem was that he tried to tell *me* what to do." Terry laughs. "I'd come a few minutes late to practice and he'd say, 'Coach, where you been?'"

Hey, you gotta survive, man. Be on your own. When James Jackson grabbed the baton for the most important half-mile of his life, he was on his own. Mark Ferrell wasn't. Under his skin, at his core, flared the unity and commitment—the responsibility—forged by his friends. "Julio, Bill, and I—we were the unholy trio. A lot of pride was involved. That was all Milt's 'fault,'" he says. At Boys the pride was inbred. "Like West Point," says Mike Randall.

Ferrell did not want the lead. "When Sam was coming down the straight, I'm saying, 'Oh, my God! Five yards on Jack?'" Raw meat for a piranha. Ferrell cut out cautiously to draw Jackson toward him. "I wanted to run with him, know where he was, how he was breathing."

"Mark worried more about me than I did about him," Jackson says. He had to: Jackson was a thoroughbred from the moment he put on his first pair of flats.

He began running at age 10, a sprinter first coached by Fred Thompson of the Atoms Track Club, then a kind of farm system for Boys High. Jackson had a rep and entered Boys with street smarts and speed galore. He'd once gone to the Penn Relays on his own just to hang out and smell it.

In '65, his first year at Boys, he became a half-miler only with the promise from Terry of a spot on the mile relay at Penn. "He could handle the workouts," says Terry. "Right away." Only a soph, Jackson ran a nationally ranked 1:53.7 880.

Two years before, Ferrell had run a 2:02 half-mile to set a New York State record for freshmen. As a soph, he ran 1:58. In '66, even while Jackson beat him, Ferrell made it close. Their first big matchup in the 880 came at the indoor city championships. Jack beat him by inches as both ran 1:55.2, a national record for races run on a "flat floor," that is, without the aid of spiked shoes or banked turns. Jackson also set records in the 600 and 1,000. He lost only one race all winter.

"James Jackson may become the finest prep middle distance runner in history," announced *Track & Field News*.

Yet it was Ferrell who soaked up the atmosphere of the Armory, whose pulse jumped with the intrinsic thrill of competition. He says, "Those races were hot. When the gun went off, all hell broke loose."

In the spring Jim Jackson continued his rampage through the record book. After the Penn Relays, where Jack led Boys to the distance medley title with a 4:14.4 anchor mile, the next stop was an upstate meet in Schenectady. I went up on the Boys bus and heard talk about an attempt at the national 880 record, 1:48.8 at the time.

Conditions were ideal, and Jackson's first quarter was a sizzling 53.2. "Whoa," thought Ferrell, who laid back. After all, who was *he*? But Jackson was shaken by the hard pace and ran 1:51.5, still his best and at the time the fastest in the country for '66. Ferrell was second by a long yard in 1:51.8. But he was *there*.

Could Jack be taken? "That race proved to me, I was going to get him," says Ferrell. Doug Terry realized Jack's rhythm was ragged. He was trying too hard on the second lap. "He told me if I stayed smooth, I'd still have my kick," says Jackson. "I'm sure the 1:48 was within my grasp."

As Ferrell and Jackson circled the St John's track, passing through the first quarter together, no one was thinking about the record any longer. It had turned into a race, not a time trial. Boys vs Jackson. The Kangaroos vs. the Hickories. Jack vs Mark. The Slugger vs. the Artist. The battle of Brooklyn, Queens, the city, the world. One lap to go.

"We were running all over the place screaming at Mark," says Julio. "There was a commitment that day not to let anybody beat you. The four of us had gotten together at Mark's house to psyche each other into running the race of our lives."

Terry was still cool, deceived by logic. I know Mark is worried, I know Jack is ready. He's got the best sprint of anybody. Everything's perfect."

Ferrell led Jack around the turn and onto the backstretch. Ferrell was slink-thin, an eel. Jack was beefier, solid. Nearing the 660, Jack took off. "It's the move no one could stop," says Terry, gesturing. "Pffffft." Jack had five yards, then seven. "Mark had sort of given up," Jackson remembers. Says Terry, "You could see it on Mark's face. That was it."

It should have been. But in this crucible of the track each man found a new and guiding emotion, abetted by the other. Jackson turned inward, seeking retribution. Ferrell faced the challenge squarely; this was no ambush in Brooklyn.

There was a tangible reason for this. The previous week, in the city championships, Ferrell had finally beaten Jackson in the 880. First Mark threw up, then he beat him.

"It was a letdown for the whole team," says John Henry. "Till then, Jack was invincible. He was affected by it. He was gonna pay Ferrell back. It was understood."

"Jack was obsessed. He wanted to 'hurt' Mark," says Mike Randall.

Jackson admits it. "I didn't like losing. I do think it affected the way I ran the special two-mile relay."

Terry has gone over it again and again since. "That is where you learn when something means more to someone else than it means to you. You have to be able to assess that as a coach. Jack was personally after Mark Ferrell. I was after my record. That's when we lost each other."

Seven yards weren't enough. Jack went for more. "I tried to put him away," he says. On the last turn he picked up the pace unnecessarily and tightened up. Ferrell, given a second chance, came on.

Bolted out of his slumber in the pole vault pit, Billy Jacobs could not believe the developments. Mark was ahead. He had a yard, not more. Jack was on the rail, Mark on the outside. They were on the home straight with less than 100 yards to go.

"I was wiggly," says Jackson. "I was thinking, let me get my body back together."

Ferrell's sprint was gone, too. "I was heavy. It was a matter of holding him off."

They ran straining, hurting . . . 50 yards . . . 40 . . . Jack found a small spark of life. He caught Mark 20 yards out. They were swimming. Mark inched ahead. Jack pulled up to him. "Both dealing," as Terry put it. A stand-up runner, Jack, thrust across the line. Mark leaned.

Andrew Jackson won.

After considerable deliberation, the Hickories were declared the winners. It was so close Boys was awarded the same time: 7:35.6.

The third-place team, Molloy, was a good 100 yards back. The national record had been broken by 6.4 seconds. Both Jackson and Boys would receive credit. Boys didn't care. Its runners felt they'd won. They still do.

"I know we won," says Jackson, whose split was 1:50.6. He claimed his torso, as the rules require, hit the line with Mark's head, and that the judges did not detect the difference. Mike Randall and John Henry agree: "Jack nipped him."

"I knew I had it won," says Ferrell, pointing to his torso. His split was 1:51.3. He could still see it today.

Jack says that before the decision was reached, "Milt was politicking" with the officials. Randall says the same. "Milt was celebrating. It was his show. Nobody challenged him. We were in shock."

I ask him if he means Blatt had influenced the officials' decision. "No doubt about it," says Randall.

I ask Milt. "That's ridiculous," he says. "I was sitting in the stands and stayed put. I never once interfered with the officials in all my years of coaching."

The officials I could find did not remember the details. In my search for finish-line evidence, l came to believe that the race was destined to live on only in the memories of its makers. Neither coach still has his notes from that day. *Track & Field News* no longer has the account of the race I'd sent. I no longer have my carbon. The meet director's file is gone. It appears that not a single photographer of merit shot the race. The only pro who might have, Manning Solon, has passed on, and I've been unable to unearth his files. A Jackson high jumper, John Bivins, always took photos at meets but says he arrived late to this one and did not shoot it. Bill Jacob's father took movies of the race but they didn't come out.

"I always regretted we never had a movie," says Blatt. "But who knew this was going to be the greatest race ever?"

While Blatt and his runners were drunk with success ("l walked around in a daze," says Jacobs), the Boys camp was stunned, naked, mad at themselves for not blasting the opposition away.

Terry stood silent in the infield with his mouth open. "I was totally disappointed. I had me a 7:28." He is referring to Jack's anchor. "Just run it cool. He had a 1:48 in him easy."

"We had a philosophy at Boys High," says Jim Jackson. "Don't allow it to be close." He repeats it again, the legacy of his race: *"It should not have been close."*

Says Randall, "I didn't fault Jack. He got himself in a hole, but he came out of it. That was the most incredible thing of all"

"They ran a perfect race," says John Henry. "We didn't."

"There was talk about a rematch," says Julio Meade. Twenty years later, they may get their chance.

Chapter 9: Track in Trouble

The conditions that led to such excellence in New York City high school track and field two decades ago have significantly eroded. I saw for myself in March at the PSAL indoor city championships, at the Armory.

Rumors of the Armory's demise always struck the track community with dizzying fear. Either the National Guard was fed up with servicing track at its installation, or the neighboring hospital complex was going to take it over, or a tennis concession was going to buyout valuable space. What has really happened is far more poignant. The Armory has become a city-run shelter for homeless men.

The hallways where runners would change and psyche each other out smell not of muscle liniment but of urine. The whole place reeks of squalor. Hundreds of beds are piled high in the arena infield, obscuring the view of the backstretch from the other side of the track. Beds are everywhere, even near the "hole" where kids at the start would inhale the hot dog aroma wafting in from the food concession. This year not a single college recruiter from the previous night's TAC championships at the Garden shows up. Where two years before I sat in a row waiting for my heat in the one-mile relay, banks of lockers, jammed into every corner, stand as testaments to the destitute.

It is quiet. (The homeless regulars, who number over 1,100, are not allowed in the track area during meets.) There are few spectators, thin fields, no excitement—not a single chorus of Boys High Mambo. All you notice are beds and lockers, the fetid smell and Armory workmen tending to mundane chores. Kids run, and a few run fast, but it has all the feeling of a dual meet.

The hurdles are chipped, bent and lined up unevenly. No reporters are present. No track nuts scurry after the twelfth place time in the two-mile.

Fact is, few meets and practices are held in the Armory anymore. Coaches and parents don't like the idea of youngsters spending the day there. Once the cathedral of indoor track in the northeast, the Armory is now an anachronism. But as pathetic as it is, the Armory is still desperately needed. It's an old story grown more insistent: In a city willing to pour hundreds of millions of dollars into professional stadia, there is not a single facility to house high school track. The circuit has spread to West Point, Princeton, Yale and Harvard. New York? Forget it.

"How do you argue against a shelter for the homeless?" says Ed Bowes, track coach of Brooklyn's Bishop Loughlin High School and director of the Loughlin Games, the only remaining major invitational at the Armory. "My argument is that we should do all we can to prevent today's kids from becoming the homeless of tomorrow."

"Remember what kind of meet this used to be?" sighs Henry Junk. Junk retired in 1984 after 38 years of coaching track at Brooklyn's East New York High. Like Milt Blatt and Doug Terry, he brought out the best in young people.

Coaching, like teaching, is no longer attractive. Moreover the PSAL is a unit of the Board of Education, which requires a coach in any sport to have a N.Y.C. teaching license. "That stinks," says Jim Jackson. He feels there are club coaches who can do the job in the schools. He also blames the PSAL for lack of supervision of negligent coaches, who have allowed programs to deteriorate.

Marty Lewis, the former PSAL track commissioner and coach, feels the main culprit is lack of funding and traces the problems to the budget cuts of the '70s. "Coaches' salaries were cut. The junior varsity program was knocked out," he says. "You know what coaches do all the time? They raise money for transportation to meets."

Teenagers have changed too, hardened by a cruel fate. "You can't get them out for sports anymore," says one track coach carrying only six athletes this year. PSAL rules require a minimum roster of 18, but many of the league's 79 teams have fewer. Drug use, unstable families, high dropout rates have all increased. Track practice? "Kids are too entrenched in the cycle of poverty," says another coach. Many of today's best runners are "immigrants" from the

Caribbean, who have yet to become victimized by the worst influences of their environment.

There has been some help from outside the schools. Tracy Sundlun, president of the metropolitan association of The Athletics Congress, has developed a series of meets, with primary funding from Manufacturer's Hanover, that provide competitive opportunities for city kids. The high school girls program, only a decade old, has been enriched by the Colgate Women's Games. In addition, Sundlun has been working to win city and state funding for a new track facility and feels approval may come some time this year.

The Armory used to be a refuge from mean streets. It is now a reminder of them. On my recent visit I was overwhelmed by melancholy and had to get out.

Chapter 10: "We Were Baadddd!"

"How did we ever run so fast?" says Julio Meade, an immigrant himself. In '66, 7:35.6 (an average of 1:53.9 a man) was considered beyond a high school team. "I thought they must have miscounted the laps," says Marty Liquori. In 20 years, up to this spring, only six other high schools have broken 7:40. Now, high schools run the metric equivalent, 3,200 meters, about 20 yards short of the full two miles. When York High of Elmhurst, Illinois, ran the 3,200 last year in 7:34.8, it jarred those who forgot to add the conversion factor of 2.6 seconds. Thus, York's "true" time was 7:37.4, still 1.8 off the mark.

Meade arrived in New York in 1957. From Jackson, he went to Kansas University in Lawrence. Already married and running track, Meade began to sell insurance on the side. He was good at it. He remained in Lawrence after graduation, sold insurance full-time and acquired real-estate holdings. In 1979 he started his own financial consulting business, which has done so well that Meade, 39, plans to retire at 45—to play the guitar and relax after working all his life.

As he looked after Mark Ferrell and Bill Jacobs, Meade now presides over an extended family. He and his wife Renee have one natural child, 13-year-old Kendall, and another on the way. Kendall is an exceptional athlete and artist. The Meades also have two adopted sons, one the offspring of his sister. In addition, two of Julio's nieces live with them while attending K.U. Julio has helped finance their education. "I'm the godfather," Julio says. He wants to write a book and call it *Only in America*.

His peers have also gone far. Mark Ferrell went to Kansas and roomed with Julio until Julio got married. Then the rebellion of the artist sprouted. Mark drifted into campus activism, developed an interest in photography, quit school after two-and-one-half years and joined the Navy. After the service he bounced around, worked in photography as a "lab rat" and toured with rock groups as a lighting director, finally settling in New York again in 1982. He is a partner in a photo lab and still searching, it seems, for the harmony he first found in his running.

Sam Thomas had an outstanding senior year in '67, running on the victorious Jackson mile relay at Penn and hitting a nationally ranked 1:53.8 open half-mile.

After that, he "got lost for a while," spent four years in the army and persisted after a college degree, which he received from Long Island University in '82. He worked as a market analyst for the Stock Exchange, and when we met he looked elegant, trim and still a mite bashful. Recently he left Wall Street to buy his own business, a grocery near the beach in Rockaway, Queens. He is nervous about the new venture. "Like running in the Armory," he says.

Bill Jacobs went to Emporia State in Kansas, married young, left school, had a child and got divorced. "The real world slapped me out of my dream," he says. He witnessed the dreams of others: As a spectator at the '68 and '72 Olympics, he saw his Queens compatriot Bob Beamon and former teammate Vincent Matthews win gold medals. In due time, he says, "I was able to find the God of my understanding." He is the founder of Ensemble, a jazz history program geared to schools. Jacobs, who also works for the local school board, is a mallet percussionist and a jazz composer, arranger and performer. "I teach that jazz is American classical music," he says.

In 1967, his senior year, Jim Jackson ran the half-mile in 1:50.8 (2nd best in the country), the mile in 4:09.1 (breaking the N.Y. State record) and anchored Boys to victory in the two-mile relay at Penn. Still, he had not fulfilled his enormous potential, which both he and Doug Terry felt was a four-minute mile, just as Marty Liquori had run in high school that year. "I was doing twelve halves in two flat with a two-minute rest," says Jackson. "I was ready." However, he was stifled by state rules that prohibited him from running in "open" competition, as Liquori had done to his benefit under New Jersey rules. "When Jack got to be king of the hill," says Terry, "there was nowhere to go."

Jackson went on to Purdue and became the first member of his family to earn a college degree. A teacher, he succeeded Terry as Boys coach in 1975. Like Terry, Jim won't tolerate poor academics and has suspended runners for not going to class. As a sideline, he is the Police Athletic League track coordinator.

Mike Randall has done a little of everything, and quite well. As an educator, he's taught African literature, composition, mysticism and computers. As a writer, he's composed stories, plays and poems. As a geocosmic analyst, as he terms it, he has counseled on meditation, psychohealing and astrology. Randall received bachelor's and master's degrees from the University of Nebraska. Currently he teaches computer literacy in a junior high, and writes every chance he gets. One of his poems, "Staring Into The Eyes of My Soul," was published in the anthology of the American Poetry Association.

After high school John Henry spent 2 years at Kentucky State. Despite good grades, he left school when he became disenchanted with the track program. After two years in the navy, he went to work for the post office as a letter carrier, which he has continued. He and his wife are president of the married couples' fellowship at their church.

None of the men ran with great success or conviction in college. Many found unwelcome athletic environments. There was no coach like Uncle Miltie or Mr. T, no team chemistry like that at Jackson or Boys, no program like the one they were weaned on in New York.

At Purdue, Jim Jackson barely improved his times. He said he couldn't get quality workouts, and that the coach discouraged him from running the mile. "Was it racial?" I asked him. "It's not important," he says. "I wanted to get my degree."

John Henry said his college coach would have the half-milers do an interval workout consisting of two hundred 220s. I did not believe him. He swore it was true. "I guess we did them in about 30 seconds each," he says.

At Kansas, Meade and Ferrell ran for Bob Timmons on a team with Jim Ryun, whom Timmons also had coached in high school. Both were hurt by collegiate rules that restricted freshmen to a handful of competitions. While training harder than ever, they had no way to channel it the first year. Ferrell ran 120 miles a week. "I got strong as a horse, but the workouts robbed me of my speed," he says. He cut his half-mile best to 1:48, on a relay.

Forced to double and triple for team points, Meade's quarter did not go under 46 seconds. One year he made the 440 finals at the NCAA indoor championships. He felt his college event should have been the 880 and, had history been allowed to repeat, it might have. Once Timmons needed a fourth for a big two-mile relay and held a time trial, which Meade won. "I begged him. I said, 'Let me lead off.'" Meade was put in a sprint relay instead.

After college, Julio had one more chance to become a world-class half-miler. A former K.U. assistant coach, Tad Talley ("He knew my race was the half"), agreed to train him for the '72 Olympics. But in '71 he popped an Achilles tendon in a calisthenics drill and was in surgery the next day. "Even to this day," he says, "if I try to run hard on it, it hurts."

But he would. There is talk of a rematch: now, this year, on June 7 at St. John's—20 years to the day after the record was set. "I'll do it again," Julio says nonchalantly. Jim Jackson is running 40 miles a week again and says he could knock out a 1:56 if he wanted to. When I tell that to Mark Ferrell he laughs. Mike Randall's in fine shape. John Henry says he's game. So is Sam Thomas. "I'd love it," he says. Billy Jacobs was scheduled for minor foot surgery but looked tough from lifting his musical instruments. One more time? Maybe . . .

When the shock of defeat wore off, the Boys runners grew to savor the record as well. Like the Jackson quartet, all four Boys runners ran their fastest times that day. Even given the factors that contributed to such success, that kind of collective peak experience just doesn't happen in running, especially with young people.

Mike Randall feels the explanation lies with astrology. His theory goes like this, "Most athletes will have Mars in the mid-heaven in the astrological chart of their birth. On the day the record was set, Mars hit exactly between six and eight degrees of Gemini, the sign of the winged foot." In other words, says Randall, it was definitely a prime day for athletes.

Mark Ferrell also has a theory: "We were baaaddddd!"

I don't know a lick about astrology, but I trust the stars on this one. Ideal trackmen? It *was* fantasy. It *was* perfect.

"I feel humbled by it," says Randall. "The significance is awesome. At the time people still believed that blacks couldn't run distance, or middle-distance. We snapped that myth."

And, by example, the larger myth of mean streets and their devilish hold on young people. Given a chance, virtue will prevail. It just needs air to breathe. You can't do better than be what these men are.

"I look at the old clips and medals at my mother's house," says Mark Ferrell. "The track taught me so much about myself, how to set goals and work for things. It's unbelievable to me that we were running that fast, and how much fun it was."

"Now I understand it," says Billy Jacobs. "Unconsciously back then, I was doing some of the right things. Today, I'm achieving success and have a good attitude about life. I was involved with winners. By being with winners, I became one."

That's what can happen when you're a teenager in love.

The Dream Mile

Marty Liquori and Skip Myslenski, 1979

It was May 1971. Jim Ryun, once the world's top-ranked miler, was attempting a comeback after almost two years in retirement. His challenger was Marty Liquori, the brash Villanova University senior who had assumed the mantle of top miler in Ryun's absence. Their match race in Philadelphia was billed as the Dream Mile, and it lived up to all the hype. Liquori and sportswriter Skip Myslenski tell the story of this great duel.

The mile has traditionally been the Hope Diamond of track and field, and many of the sport's most illustrious names have been connected with the event. There was Paavo Nurmi in the twenties, Glenn Cunningham in the thirties, Gunder Hagg and Arne Andersson in the forties, Roger Bannister and John Landy and Ron Delaney and Herb Elliott in the fifties, Peter Snell and Jim Ryun and Kip Keino in the sixties, and now Filbert Bayi and John Walker. It was the English standard of measure, everyone understood how far it was; it could be divided into four quarters, everyone could easily follow it; and it presented an elusive barrier, everyone thought of the magical four minutes. It was long enough to involve the spectator emotionally, and it was short enough to keep the spectator from getting bored, and it soon acquired an aura all its own.

I believe that is changing now. I think the mile's glamour has faded, but when I first started running I was acutely aware of it. I was from the East, and the indoor season was a special time there, and the mile was the special event of that time, and I dreamed often of breaking its world record indoors, I never even thought of accomplishing that outdoors. It was the heavyweight championship fight, especially at the Millrose Games in Madison Square Garden, and it was surrounded by theatrics, dressed in superlatives, and draped in tradition. I remember my first experience at that meet. I was impressed that my race was different; at ten o'clock exactly the National Anthem was played and the mile was run, it didn't matter if the meet was behind schedule or if there was a war in progress. Everything else stopped, there were flamboyant introductions, a spotlight fell on you as you stepped forward and waved to the cheering crowd, in the far corner there was a band, and that band played faster and faster as the race moved toward its conclusion. You were on stage. You were a star in the city that acknowledges nothing less.

———————————●———————————

I covered one of the most significant miles of my life in May of 1971, during the Martin Luther King Games at Franklin Field in Philadelphia. No title was at stake, no record was set, it was early in the season, yet the race itself was soon called The Dream Mile and then compared to the Kentucky Derby, to the Indianapolis 500, to Frazier against Ali, to Namath against the Colts, to David against Goliath. Two years earlier I had beaten Jim Ryun in Knoxville, two years earlier Jim Ryun had stepped off the track in Miami and faded into retirement, and now we were going to meet again. He had been mentally defeated then, and so this confrontation loomed as a psychological challenge to him. Many were anxious to see if he had conquered his depression. I had assumed his place as the world's best, and so this confrontation loomed as a physical challenge to me. Many were anxious to see if I were truly his equal. I honestly felt that I wasn't—he still had done so much more work than me—but I fought those thoughts. I kept remembering a single point: that he could be beaten. Many were once again in the rut they had traveled before, they were viewing Jim Ryun as infallible, and even I experienced flashbacks that portrayed him that way, especially when people prophesied my demise. I respected him, I knew he could easily win, but his reputation really meant little to me. I did not fear him. I had felt him on my shoulder, and I had felt him drop off, and I realized better than anyone that he was vulnerable. These circumstances prompted the hyperbole, but in fact it was not going to be a Dream Mile, it was merely going to be the first momentous mile of the year, and it was not going to be an end in itself, though many insisted on that characterization. It was, simply, an important race. It was Jim's first major challenge since his return, and it was my opportunity to gain the legitimacy many had denied me.

———————●———————

Although I was ranked number one in the world, many people never accepted me or that fact. Jim was an American, Jim was in retirement, Jim wasn't racing, Jim was waiting in the wings, and all those who had viewed and admired him over the years begrudged me my position. I received a batch of letters after I first defeated him, most from his home state of Kansas, and their messages ranged from disparaging to downright nasty.

It would have been different if I had replaced a runner from Africa, but here I resembled Joe Frazier while Muhammad Ali was in exile. In 1970 an article on me appeared in *Sports Illustrated* and afterward the author was continually queried by people who should have known better.

"Do you actually believe he's that good?" he was asked.

"Do you really think he's better than Ryun?"

"Do you think he'll beat Ryun when Ryun's in shape?"

"You're going to look bad when Ryun's back in shape."

"I thought you knew something about track."

It is never easy to follow a phenomenon, which Jim Ryun had been, and it is less easy to assume his throne, which I did. "I got a kid training down in Louisville and he's just as good as Ali," a man could now say with accuracy. "You're crazy," the public would reply. "No. It's impossible."

No American miler had reached the top in thirty years, and then Jim did, and then I did. I was then saying, "Look, you have two at the top."

"No, it's not possible," people said back.

———————●———————

From the beginning of his career Jim Ryun was superior. He was first a man running against boys, then a superman running against mere men. He was never tested—he dominated with his overwhelming talent; and he was never exposed to reality—he emerged from a sheltered home and was guided by a paternal coach. But, "There has to be a point where a really gifted person turns away," says Dr. Bruce Ogilvie, the noted sports psychologist. "Many athletes turn away from the teacher or instructor, much to the chagrin of the teacher, who feels rejected. That's the nature of excellence. Some of the overcompensatory greats have run for the coach who turns out to be a daddy, who will love them like the daddy they never had. That's fraught with all sorts of potential dangers. Usually it blows up." I believe this was a conflict that affected Jim Ryun, especially after his marriage, and then he was forced to face another: He had to struggle with the clash between his natural introversion and the runner's natural aggression. This was no problem when he was winning easily; when he was challenged, though, belligerent reactions were suddenly necessary.

This inner strife bedeviled Jim Ryun in 1969, and it defeated him in Miami, where he stepped off the track and finally started to examine his own emotions. He was then sitting in his hotel suite, four hours after his disappearance, and as he talked he frequently reached out and tenderly touched his wife Anne. "The Jim Ryun of a few years ago is dead as of today," he said. "I've tried very hard to be The Jim Ryun in what hasn't been a serious year of running. I would like to have enjoyed this year, but I'm not programmed that way. I just exert too much pressure on myself.

"You have to understand, there is always the fear of losing. I am afraid of losing—I can't think back to the day when I wasn't scared. It's when that fear of losing becomes so overwhelming, then it's time to quit. The problem is that the world I lived in before was one of fantasy. All I've done is win. It's a new thing to lose. The Jim Ryun before was a person who, because of circumstances breaking his way, made it to the top in a short time, without knowing how to lose, without knowing how to finish a strong second.

"There has to be a new Jim Ryun. I have to exemplify my new self instead of the old one. I am anxious to compete, but I have to realize I can't control races like before. What happened out there today was more mental than physical. It's not a question of making excuses. It's just a question of explaining it, and I don't know how to do that now. But if I don't get over this pressure I put on myself, that fear of losing, I may never step on a track again. I made a mistake by quitting, I realize that. I think I grew up today. I think the life Anne and I live from now on will be a lot more real and with a lot more feeling. It's not a pleasant thing, losing. Yet it makes everything more real. Actually, we've always been down with the Joneses. But before, no one would admit it."

————————•————————

All distance runners can be conveniently fitted into one of three basic categories. They may be like Dave Wottle, who was a great sprinter and wanted every race to come down to the final hundred yards. They may be like Ron Clarke, the Australian, who pushed the whole way at an even pace that would bring him to the finish near the world record. Or they may be like Nick Rose, the Englishman, who surges throughout his run and hopes to lose his competition.

When I was in college and racing in the United States, I was superior enough to play the cat, and I would lay back until the final 220 yards and then kick and win. But my natural talents were not truly shaped for the mile. Even in high school [my coach] Freddy Dwyer told me I would eventually be a 5,000-meter man, and so I was forced to employ singular tactics when I competed internationally. Then I began my attack 600 yards from the finish, moving steadily and swiftly, but always with something in reserve, and I aimed to drain the sprint from my opposition, hoping we both headed down the final straight in oxygen debt.

————————•————————

A Kenyan named Wesley Mayo once tied up badly during a race and afterward he was trying to tell us exactly how he felt. He was having difficulty, and finally someone smiled and said, "The bear jumped on your back, huh?"

"No," he said quizzically. "We have no bears in Kenya."

The questioner was speaking analogously, of course, for the bear is the runner's nickname for oxygen debt, that drained condition you often reach at the end of a race. Through most of your run you are operating aerobically; oxygen is passing through your muscles and out, and more oxygen is coming in, but finally you face that most difficult of interludes when you are in pain and your muscles are fatigued and you feel stifled and you must run through sand. Scientists say you can cover three hundred yards in this state, and this is why a runner like Filbert Bayi can present such problems. He has trained at altitude, he can go out quickly and not be affected, but if you attempt to match his pace, you will be in this condition much too soon.

When I ran the mile I wished to reach it in the final hundred yards and I wanted my competitors there too, for I knew that most were better pure sprinters than me. I was robbing them of this talent. I was negating the variables and making it all a matter of courage. I was willing to take a chance on my mind. My opponents were then like the aging Muhammad Ali in the final rounds of his later fights, when he was no longer able to dance and to prance and to escape the punches, but was forced to stand there and trade blows. I wanted that. I wanted it to come down to the simple matter of who desired it more.

————————•————————

I returned from a meet in Fresno, California, lay down, and as soon as my head hit the pillow, I started to think of that Sunday afternoon seven days in the future. I'd always looked forward to this kind of race, I'd looked forward to this meeting with Jim Ryun for a month now, but I'd always had one race or two races yet to go. Now there were none, and I found myself wishing for just one more.

On Monday and Tuesday and Wednesday I answered phone calls, endured interviews, posed for photographers, and as those days slowly passed, my personality was transfigured. I am normally calm and self-contained, but here I was nervous, agitated; I am normally measured and calculating, but here I was skitterish, nonplussed. On Tuesday I thought of going to a movie, which I hadn't done in years, and on Wednesday I attended a going-away party for a priest, I just had to get out, and on Thursday I ran into Patsy Smithwick, a close friend of [my girlfriend] Carol's. She said hello, quickly noticed my agitation, and asked, "What's wrong?"

"I guess I'm nervous," I said.

"Why?"

"I don't know," I said, then I shrugged my shoulders. She began talking, just chattering aimlessly, and after some time I smiled at her and said, "Okay, it's worked. I haven't thought of the race for fifteen whole minutes."

Jim was enduring similarly at his home in Eugene. One afternoon he opened his door and found a television crew on his front doorstep. "We just happened to be in the neighborhood. Do you mind if we drop in?" one of the crew said to him.

"In the neighborhood?" Jim said with a laugh. "In Eugene?"

"As a child I can remember wanting to participate in something spectacular, something real special," he said later. "I didn't want to be a hero, I just wanted to be on the inside to see what was happening. Well, I'm involved in something that is supposed to be spectacular and I'm wondering what the athletes involved in all those other spectaculars must have been thinking."

At midweek he flew to his in-laws' home in Cleveland and there he found relief, ate strawberry shortcake, and took long, slow runs. By midweek my emotions were leveling, and on Thursday I had dinner and a few beers with a friend, and on Friday I was anticipating Carol's arrival from her family's home in New Jersey. "It's funny," I told my friend, "but I'm finally starting to get back into my normal routine for a race. You know, worrying about Carol getting down here. It's been a year and a half since I've seen Jim and only three weeks since I've seen her and, with no offense to Jim—he's good-looking and a nice guy and all—but I'm looking forward more to seeing Carol than I am to seeing him."

Jim arrived in Philadelphia on Saturday. He was soon placed behind a table and a battery of microphones, and he stared out into a room crowded with faces. "What kind of time will you be happy with tomorrow?" he was asked.

"A winning time," he said.

"Do you think it's a dream mile?"

"I'd like to see it called the mile sometimes."

That night he went to Bookbinder's Old Original Restaurant for dinner, considered lobster, ordered steak, then returned quickly to his hotel. "I think it's great that there's a lot of interest in the sport," he said, "but I think a lot of people are trying to see a lot of things in this race that just aren't there. Until now, my comeback, if you can call it that, has been fun. But now this, all the pressures of publicity—" His voice tailed off and he shook his head.

Carol and I went out for a steak sandwich, a pepperoni pizza, and ice cream, then stopped by the Main Point to hear singer-composer Jimmy Webb. He'd written "MacArthur Park," "Wichita Linesman," and "By the Time I Get to Phoenix," relaxing songs, but this night he offered medleys of protest songs. I was disappointed, and I hoped the experience wasn't an omen, for I looked at tomorrow as a day when I had nothing to gain and everything to lose. If I won people would say, "Well, Ryun's not in shape yet." If I lost, those same people would say, "See, we told ya so. If Ryun had been around, Liquori would never have won all those races he did."

———————•———————

A heavy rain drenched Philadelphia on Sunday morning, and that afternoon the air was still damp and the sky was still overcast. Twenty-two thousand people were at Franklin Field, shivering, and at three o'clock Jumbo Elliott was scurrying by the southwest stands of the stadium, looking for his assistant, Jack Pyrah. "What time is it? Are we on time?" he shouted when he found him. "That mile better go off a four twenty. I don't want Marty warming up for nothing."

[My teammate] Ron Stanko was fifty yards away from them, talking to a reporter. "Marty's been nervous," he was saying. "Very nervous. A funny thing came over him. Ordinarily, he doesn't say very much, but he's been cracking jokes for the last two weeks. I mean really bad jokes. But I had to laugh. You know, what are friends for?"

Hurdler Erv Hall, a former teammate, was standing near Ron and he was with yet another reporter. "I just flew in from Los Angeles and they're talking about this mile there," he was explaining. "They're talking about this everywhere."

I was in a dressing room huddled next to a heater, and my legs were tucked up under me. At 3:20, an hour before the race, Jumbo walked in, sat down next to me and said simply, "Go out before the last quarter."

Minutes later I arose, appeared momentarily in front of the audience, then left the stadium. I warmed up in solitude, along the streets, and I thought only of the race, without distraction. I did not return for forty-five minutes, and then I did some strides a half lap away from Jim, who had already removed his warm-up jacket and left it with his wife and their baby girl, who were in special seats at the lip of the first turn. Just before the introductions I passed Jim, nodded, walked over to Anne, said hello, then admired the baby. "Did you see that?" my mother later said to a reporter. "That was sincere. People always say Marty's cocky, but they're looking in their own rearview mirrors. They forget that this is Marty Liquori. This is the way he is. He is not Jim Ryun. He is not somebody else. Maybe he is cocky. Show me someone who has great confidence who's not. But Marty's also a gentle person. I wish someone would write about that."

I removed my sweats, waited nervously, and finally Jack O'Reilly, the public address announcer, leaned into his microphone and said: "This young man needs no introduction. This is Marty Liquori." Most of the crowd cheered, but many booed, even though I went to school in their city; I knew people either loved me or hated me, so I was not surprised, and I was pleased when I heard the clapping increase, trying to drown out the critics. Jim's name was greeted with loud roars of approval. Then they quieted and we approached the starting line. Herm Mancini, the clerk of the course, walked up to me. "Marty, make them eat their words," he whispered.

"Don't worry," I said.

———————•———————

Jim Ryun was a legend, he had assumed heroic proportions for many in the public, and when I blossomed and began chipping away at his monument, those people cast me as a villain. He was admired by even the casual observers of track, even they were awed by his accomplishments, and then I arrived, and I started nipping at his heels, and I defeated him, and they were upset. I was young, I was loquacious, I spoke my mind, and I appeared cocky, and they wanted to hang onto their old favorite rather than tie their emotions to a flashy new kid from the East. They thought I was from a different planet. I was not the traditional American hero, and in the end they kept trying to shoot me down because I had beaten Jim, who matched their visions perfectly.

It was a situation that I couldn't help, it was a moment that had to eventually occur, but now I reflect on that time and am often sorry that it couldn't have unfolded differently. I feel bad about the image I received, I feel bad that people didn't recognize that my accomplishments had merit on their own, I feel bad that I had to be the first. I sometimes dream of how people would have viewed me if Jim hadn't existed, and I sometimes think that I would have been more inclined toward the mold if he hadn't secured it first. Even now many do not understand that I never said I was better than Jim Ryun. I only said that neither of us would win every race if we ran ten times.

———————•———————

There was one false start, we were regrouped and reset, and finally the wait was over, finally there was no more nervous anticipation, there was just the moment, the battle at hand. I settled into fifth place and Jim settled into seventh, we were a pair of boxers feeling each other out, and Joe Savage, a freshman from Manhattan College, led the pack through a sixty-second first quarter. This was slower than either of us wanted, and Jim moved by me along the backstretch of the second lap, burst on the far turn and dropped in behind Morgan Mosser of West Virginia, the new leader, and I followed in his wake, and we were only strides apart when we passed the half in a slow 2:03.

I was ready to jump to the front, but Jim did it first, and I tucked in behind him, and we circled again toward the backstretch. "I thought the pace was too slow," he said later. "I hadn't done much speed work and I didn't think I was ready for an all-out 220 at the end. I guess Marty had the same thoughts. We both figured the way to win was with a long, fast, last half mile."

He was in full flight now, and he looked strong, and the crowd was on its feet, responding to his spurt, and I knew that any runner's confidence grows when he surges into the lead and hears this reaction, and so I suddenly transformed myself into a barroom brawler. He had thrown the first punch and I instinctively threw a counterpunch. I wanted to keep that confidence from building, I wanted him to do some wondering. "Oh, yeah," my actions said. "You think that's something? Well, you ain't seen nothin' yet. You want to pick it up? Well, let's really pick it up."

As soon as we came off the turn I passed him, I pushed even harder, and seven hundred yards from the finish we were both sprinting like a pair of kids running from the cops.

———————————●———————————

Immediately before the Knoxville race in which I first defeated Jim Ryun, I was sick, and Jumbo relieved the pressure by not stressing the necessity of victory, by merely talking tactics. "No one beats him with a last-minute kick," he told me, "so jab at him. Start moving after the half and force him to move with you." Even then I had enough international experience to know that he was right. I realized I couldn't outsprint a top runner over the last hundred fifty yards, and so I followed the plan. I slowly, slowly stretched Jim's rubber band, and that time he snapped.

I've entered this confrontation with the same design in mind, and in the weeks leading up to it Jumbo has trained me for a long and sustained drive. I've done little speed work—that will be irrelevant here—I've instead been enduring repeat half miles at faster than race pace, preparing for the torturous journey toward the finish. It is a luxury I cannot always afford; I cannot aim my training for one person unless I know with certainty that the race will come down to two individuals in a private war. Even when this is obvious, many coaches and many runners don't alter their approaches—they follow a set pattern—but I'm like the football team that each week adjusts its offense to take advantage of an opponent's weakness, that each week adjusts its defense to negate its opponent's strengths.

If I'm going to race Filbert Bayi or someone who employs tactics similar to his, I practice running in oxygen debt, I do workouts until I tie up and then try to cover two hundred more yards; I know that in the competition itself I will have to react when my legs feel like lead. If I'm going to meet an opponent who's in better condition than I and who is anticipating a fast race, I'll be prepared to surge past him and then slow the pace, hoping to win on the final sprint to the finish; this is especially effective indoors, and I know I've won more than one national title with this tactic.

Of course, these preparations are not possible when you're going to compete in a high-caliber meet, in the Olympics or against a world-class field. There are then too many good runners to consider, and you succeed only if you run your own race and squeeze every second from your body. In fact, even an anticipated confrontation can disintegrate during a race itself, and you must always be ready for alterations. After I beat Jim in Knoxville I prepared myself for a rematch in Miami, and I was content to stay with him far behind the leaders, but then he stepped off the track and I had to hurry like hell to catch the leaders, which I did not manage until the final drive to the tape.

———————•———————

I forced the pace up the backstretch, pulling Jim with me, and then I glanced over my shoulder and spotted him gliding smoothly along. It was a specter I'd imagined often in the past. He looked controlled, under no strain; he was a preying panther awaiting his moment. "My God," I thought. "It's still too slow."

I accelerated an imperceptible notch, rounded the corner, flew by blurred images in the stands and through the three-quarter mark in three minutes flat. "He's just sitting on my shoulder waiting to pounce," I thought. "Any minute now he's going to eat me up. More pressure. More pressure."

"I was running scared," I admitted later. "That damn slow pace. It suddenly came to mind how he had blown so many other people, mature people like Kip Keino and Bodo Tummler, right off the track. I was afraid the same thing was about to happen to me."

———————•———————

The third quarter of any distance race is traditionally the slowest, and the most difficult mentally. The nervous excitement you felt at the start is then drained, and the moment for your final rush has not yet arrived; you try to float through it, to relax, to gather yourself for your kick to the tape. Not many runners have ever attacked from farther than a quarter mile out, and so my tactic struck at my opponents not only physically, but also mentally. They were conditioned to acting at the gun. I was forcing them to alter ingrained habits.

It was then a matter of moving as fast as I could without the throttle full open, of keeping my fist right in their faces, of sowing doubt in their minds, of risking rigor mortis in the final hundred yards. In that final stretch I knew that I might start to fall apart, I knew that my knees might not come up, that I might stumble, that my arms might flap, that my face might tighten, and I knew also that I might have to be prepared to throw myself at the tape. But I had trained the whole year for that one interlude and I had experienced exhilaration through it, when twenty-five thousand frenzied people were caught in my peripheral vision, and I was completely abandoned, totally concentrated, and I was moving effortlessly, on all cylinders, like a perfectly tuned race car. Many people claim they play tennis for that one millisecond when their stroke is perfect and the action sends a positive feeling through their bodies. For me that emotion could last for thirty seconds, for forty-five seconds, and then I ran downhill, I was racing little kids from my block.

I didn't know if that moment would come here. I didn't even know if I would make it to the finish line. I did know that we would both be dead at the end.

———————•———————

The crowd was now on its feet and noise was rushing down on us from the deepest caverns of this stadium, and we rounded the penultimate turn and headed up the long backstretch for the last time. I peeked once, twice, then again, I didn't want to kick too soon, I wanted him on my shoulder so I could surge and, I hoped, discourage him. "Be ready, be ready," I kept thinking, but still he didn't come, he remained a stride behind. We hit the final turn, we were enveloped by shrieks and squeals, and we headed off of it, and suddenly Jim Ryun was right there, on my right shoulder. "Aw, shit, here he comes," I thought. "Hold him off, hold him off."

"He's dying now," he thought. "He's coming back to me."

"It looked like Jim would take the lead at the break of the turn," his coach said later.

My head was tilted slightly starboard, and my mouth was open, greedily sucking gulps of air, and my face was a white mask, and my hair was blown back, and my arms were cutting furiously through the air, and inside I was dying. For two strides we were together and then suddenly I was half a stride ahead. "I was dead," Jim said later.

"Where is he?" I thought. "Dammit, where is he? Be ready. Be ready."

"There's nothing left," he thought. "Whoever's standing at the finish line will win."

"Where's the finish line?" I thought.

Then I saw it, twenty yards away, but when I reached that point there were still ten more yards to go. "My God, we're not through yet," I thought. "He's still going to get me." I was worried, I could do nothing but reach down and find something and throw myself forward, and I hit the tape with a funny expression on my face. I felt incredible, but I didn't want to seem too happy, I restrained myself. "Hell, that's not me," I finally thought. Suddenly, I was very happy.

———————•———————

If you could capture the emotion of that moment and bottle it and hand it to a young runner, he would spend the next ten years of his life striving for a similar achievement. It was no ephemeral reward, it was not something that would last for five minutes, it was instead a final coming of age.

This is where I feel sports supersede all other ventures and why I feel sports are something special. You may spend thirty years trying to prove you're the best writer in the business and you may gain that recognition only after a long and unfair struggle, or you may never gain that recognition since you are quiet and do not publicize yourself. But in running no one can deny you; you train, you receive your opportunity, you achieve and you are immediately granted your reward.

Many analysts sit in their quiet and cloistered studies and claim that athletic competition is no more beneficial than an intense endeavor in any other field; I disagree. There are few fields where the effort is so energetic and where the benefits accrue so quickly, even if you're just a jogger. Competitive sports are even more special, they compress the selection process into a compact time and space, and the young athlete must face in only a few hours all those pressures that occur over a number of years in the life of an achievement-oriented individual. I always thought that I could go into business and there confront situations and challenges that could replace those I experienced in track, but I didn't. Business did not supply immediate satisfaction, it often didn't even offer that much of a challenge. I am now convinced that it *is* something special to work for ten years and then have your gratification arrive in the space of ten seconds.

Duel in the Sun

John Brant, 2004

The 1982 Boston Marathon featured one of the epic duels in American running. For 26 miles and all the way to the finish line, Dick Beardsley, a journeyman marathoner on a roll, battled Alberto Salazar, the world record holder and the country's premier distance runner. John Brant tells the story of this great race and its lasting effects on the two combatants.

In front of some audiences, Dick Beardsley never even mentions the 1982 Boston Marathon. In fact, he barely touches upon his running career at all. When he's delivering one of his regular talks to a twelve-step group, for instance, he simply begins, "Hi, I'm Dick, and I'm a drug addict," then launches into the rending story of his disease and recovery.

When Beardsley finishes speaking, and the people are wiping away their tears and settling back into their seats after a standing ovation, then the host might explain how Dick Beardsley is the fourth-fastest American marathoner of all time, and that his race with Alberto Salazar at Boston twenty-two years ago remains one of the signature moments in the history of distance running; perhaps, in the history of any sport.

But other audiences, such as this one at the Royal Victoria Marathon in Victoria, British Columbia, know all about Beardsley's athletic career, and are eager—even hungry—to relive his legendary "duel in the sun" with Salazar.

There's a considerable amount of preamble first. Beardsley is not good at leaving things out. He tells the crowd of two hundred about getting creamed at his first high school football practice, quitting the team, and turning out for cross-country without knowing quite what it was. "Do they tackle you in cross-country?" he asked a friend. He explains how he ran his second marathon in a brand-new pair of running shoes that he didn't want to get dirty by breaking in, and that he prepared by fasting for four days because he'd read somewhere that fasting worked in ultra marathons, so he figured. . .

Beardsley is blessed with the fundamental trait of the born entertainer: a complete lack of self-consciousness. He strides back and forth in front of the podium, laughing right along with the audience, as delighted as they are by his own buffoonery. His voice—honking, booming, unabashed—rolls around the conference hall in overpowering waves. Wearing jeans, a red pullover, and a blue fleece vest, whip-cord lean and with a lilt to his step, Beardsley might be mistaken for an athlete in his prime, rather than a man of forty-eight. You have to sit close to notice the hard miles showing around his eyes.

From *Runner's World*, April 2004. Reprinted by permission of Rodale, Inc.

The crowd's laughter drowns out the canned rock music blaring from the expo next door. But when Beardsley shifts gears, traveling back to Hopkinton, Massachusetts, on the sunny noon of April 19, 1982, the room falls raptly silent.

Which only seems appropriate, because the 1982 Boston Marathon was great theater: two American runners, one a renowned champion and the other a gutty underdog, going at each other for just under two hours and nine minutes. Other famous marathons have featured narrow margins of victory, but their suspense developed late in the race, the product of a furiously closing challenger or rapidly fading leader. At the '82 Boston, by contrast, Beardsley and Salazar ran in each other's pocket the entire 26.2 miles, with no other competitor near them for the final nine miles. They were so close that, for most of the last half of the race, Beardsley, while in the lead, monitored Salazar's progress by watching his shadow on the asphalt.

Neither man broke, and neither, in any meaningful sense, lost. The race merely came to a thrilling, shattering end, leaving both runners, in separate and ultimately Pyrrhic ways, the winner. The drama unfolded in the sport's most storied venue, at the peak of the first running boom, when the United States produced world-class marathoners in the profusion that Kenya does today.

"An Epic Duel;" "The Greatest Boston Marathon;" "A Display of "Single-Minded Determination and Indefatigable Spirit;" read the next day's headlines. Since Beardsley was just twenty-six and Salazar twenty-three, everyone assumed that this would be the start of a long and glorious rivalry, one that would galvanize the public and seal American dominance in the marathon through the 1984 Olympics and beyond.

But rather than a beginning, Boston '82 represented a climax. After that day, neither man ran a marathon as well again. And from that day since, incredibly, only two more of the world's major marathons have been won by a native-bred American man. On that day 156 runners, virtually everyone an American, finished the race in a time of 2:30 or faster. At the 2003 Boston Marathon, by contrast, just twenty-one runners logged 2:30 or better. So some of the younger members of the audience—including the elite runners who will lead tomorrow's Royal Victoria Marathon—listen to Beardsley's story with a mixture of curiosity, envy, and awe. Others in the crowd, those closer to Beardsley's age, listen on a different frequency. They know the enormous toll that Boston exacted on both Alberto Salazar and Dick Beardsley. If the glory of their marathon bore a heroic quality, so did their suffering afterward.

———————•———————

At Nike corporate headquarters in Beaverton, Oregon, Alberto Salazar descends to the ground-floor cafe of the Mia Hamm Building for a quick lunch.

For the last several years, Nike has employed Salazar as a kind of coach-at-large, chartered to deliver that most endangered of species— The Great American Distance Runner—from the brink of extinction. On this drizzly October Tuesday, Salazar has spent the morning training the professional athletes in Nike's ambitious Oregon Project. This afternoon, he'll supervise the cross-country team at Portland's Central Catholic High School.

Both teams, he reports, are thriving. The Oregon Project's Dan Browne has met the qualifying standard for the 2004 Olympic marathon, and Central Catholic's Galen Rupp should repeat as the state cross-country champion. Meanwhile, other parts of Salazar's life are in similar bloom: his oldest son, Antonio, plays wide receiver for the University of Oregon football team, and his younger son, Alejandro is a star striker for the University of Portland soccer team.

At forty-six, Salazar appears every bit the proud, happy family man and flourishing professional. His brown eyes are clear, calm, and bright, and his cheeks have lost a marathoner's hollowness. He no longer resembles "the young priest fresh from seminary whose face drives all the housewives to distraction," as one writer described him twenty years ago. Now Salazar looks more like a fit-but-comfortable middle-aged monsignor, a man still true to his religious vocation, but also at ease in the worldly realm of fund-raisers and cocktail parties.

A Japanese visitor approaches and politely asks for an autograph. Salazar graciously complies. "After Boston I was never quite the same," he says, after his fan has departed. "I had a few good races, but everything was difficult. Workouts that I used to fly through became an ordeal. And eventually, of course, I got so sick that I wondered if I'd ever get well."

Salazar's warm smile briefly returns wintry. For a moment, his poise falters and he seems like a traumatized man who, after exhaustive therapy, can finally talk about his past. "It took me a long time to connect the dots," he says, "and see that the line stretched all the way back to Boston."

Monday, April 19, Patriots Day, broke warm and blue over Boston, perfect for just about anything except running 26.2 miles.

After driving out to the start in Hopkinton, Beardsley and his coach, Bill Squires, avoided the high school gym that served as the staging area for elite athletes. For the last four months, Beardsley had spent all of his waking moments, and some of his sleeping ones, thinking and dreaming about Alberto Salazar. Squires wanted to keep Beardsley as removed from the race excitement as possible.

So they camped out in the house of a town matron. Squires went into his usual patter. "How do, missus, beautiful day, lovely home, let me introduce Dickie Beardsley here from Minnesota. Dickie's a dairy farmer, got hay stuck in his teeth, but don't be fooled. In a few minutes he's gonna run the Boston Marathon, and just between you and me, he's got a shot to win it if he sets his mouth right and does the hubba-hubba on the hills . . ." While Squires and the grandma yakked, Beardsley stretched, sipped water; made a half-dozen trips to the bathroom, and listened to a Dan Fogelberg tape. He punched ventilation holes in the white painter's cap that Squires had given him to ward off the sun, and tried not to jump out of his skin.

At a quarter to twelve he heard the call for runners. He jogged out to the street, heading for the section at the front of the starting area roped off for elite athletes. But thousands of citizen-athletes stood between him and the starting line. He tried to fight through the crowd but couldn't make any progress.

Beardsley panicked. He felt as if he were caught in one of those sweat-drenched nightmares, in which he was desperately trying to reach a critical destination, but couldn't move. (Decades later, after detox, Beardsley will be haunted by a similar nightmare: He's been in another accident. He's lying on a hospital bed and nurses are hooking him up to an IV drip attached to huge pouch of Demerol. He tries to scream at the nurse to stop, but not a sound comes out of his mouth.)

So Beardsley reverted to character. He started to make noise. "Hey, let me through! I'm Dick Beardsley for crying out loud! I gotta get up to the front!"

The other runners, immersed in their last-minute preparations, eyed him coldly. Then someone recognized him, and word rippled through the crowd: "Look out, we got Dick Beardsley, here! Make way, Dick s coming through!"

The crowds parted, and Beardsley, his nightmare dissolved into a dream, followed a clear path to the starting line.

Throughout the winter of 1981 and '82, as he had sat in front of the TV in the evenings, Beardsley pounded his thighs with his fists 1,500 times. He had read somewhere that pounding your muscles made them tougher. If he thought it might gain him a few seconds on the downhills, Beardsley would have tried curing his quads in a smokehouse. He knew that the marathon would be decided on the course's three long hills rising between miles 17 and 21. If he had any chance of beating Salazar, he would have to fly down the hills like a bobsled racer; capitalizing on the fact that Salazar outweighed him by twenty pounds. Conceivably, a series of rocketing descents might pummel Salazar's legs to the extent that Beardsley would be able to pull away from him before mile 25. If that plan failed, and the race came down to a kick at the end, then Salazar, with his superior short-range speed, would do the pummeling.

Fifteen hundred punches, each thigh.

Born in Havana but raised in the Boston suburb of Wayland, Alberto Salazar, the world's greatest and most charismatic distance runner, was coming home from Oregon to run his first Boston Marathon. It was one of the most eagerly anticipated sports stories of 1982. He was fit and prepared, he announced to reporters upon arriving at the airport with his wife, Molly. If there were no injuries or unforeseen developments . . . well, the facts were plain: he was the fastest man in the race.

Six months earlier, Salazar had won his second consecutive New York City Marathon in a world-record time of 2:08:13, which had earned him, among other honors, a White House audience with President Ronald Reagan. In March, he had finished second at the World Cross-Country Championships. And just one week before Boston, he had run a blistering 27:30 in a ten-thousand-meter match race with the great Kenyan runner Henry Rono at the University of Oregon's Hayward Field.

The ten-thousand had been Salazar's idea. He had lined up the appearance money for Rono, who had shown up in Eugene looking fat and blowsy, in the early stages of the alcoholism that would eventually destroy his career. But once the race started, he ran with his trademark ferocity. For twenty-five laps around the historic track, Rono and Salazar belted away at each other. Rono outleaned Salazar at the wire, by the width of his jiggling belly, the wags in the press box joked.

Rono's brilliant victory was essentially ignored. But Salazar's draining, world-class effort, just two seconds off Craig Virgin's American record, raised eyebrows. Occurring only nine days before the Boston Marathon, it violated every code in the sport's training canon.

Salazar didn't care. At the age of sixteen he had determined that he would become the fastest marathoner in the world. Instead of the standard training—laying a foundation of endurance, then adding speedwork— Salazar did the opposite. He first honed his track speed to match that of a Henry Rono, then built his strength so he could maintain that pace over the length of a marathon. His goal was to demolish his competitors, run so far out in front of them that there could be no doubt of his greatness.

"I viewed every marathon as a test of my manhood," he says. "It wasn't enough for me to win the race; I wanted to bury the other guys."

At mile 5, the lead pack passed a pond where a couple was floating around in a canoe, enjoying the beautiful afternoon. Bill Rodgers poked Beardsley. "Hey, Dick, wouldn't you love to be out there right now?" As if they were two young executives commuting into the office, looking out the train window.

Then, a few miles later, Ron Tabb and Dean Matthews threw a rogue surge. It was way too early for a serious ante, but not so early that the contenders could afford to ignore it; they had to burn precious energy reeling in the pair. Beardsley laughed it off, but Salazar was genuinely steamed.

The crowds were huge. Most of the spectators cheered for Salazar, the native son. When Salazar waved at his fans, Beardsley did likewise. He waved and grinned as if this were the Fourth of July parade back home in Rush City, Minnesota, and the folks were cheering for him. Salazar was not amused.

Salazar wasn't finding much of anything amusing. He was booming along in the lead pack, looking strong, yet Beardsley sensed that he wasn't quite in sync. He also noticed that, despite the gleaming sun and seventy degree temperatures, Salazar never drank.

There weren't any official, fully stocked water stations. You had to accept cups of whatever a spectator might offer. As often as he could, Beardsley would grab a cup, pour whatever it contained over his painter's cap, take a swallow, then offer the cup to Salazar. But he always refused it.

On the morning of November 13, 1989, snow was forecast for the dairy-farm belt of central Minnesota. Before the storm arrived, Dick Beardsley, recently retired from his professional running career, needed to milk his cows, store the corn that he'd harvested the day before, and pick the corn remaining in his fields. He rose at a quarter to four, blitzed through milking, skipped breakfast, and went to work loading the harvested corn in a grain elevator.

Like much of the machinery on a family farm, the elevator ran on a device called a power take-off, a revolving steel rod connected to the tractor engine. Normally, Beardsley sat in the driver's seat to engage the device; but today, trying to accomplish several jobs at once, he stood on the slippery tractor drawbar. The engine turned over unexpectedly, catching Beardsley's overalls leg in the power take-off. For a horrified moment, he watched his left leg disappear into the maw of the machine. Then he was caught in a whirlwind.

The shaft of the power take-off curled Beardsley's leg around it like a string around a spool, casting him into a devastating orbit. It crumpled his left leg, and flung his skull against the barn floor with each revolution. Beardsley screamed for help, but his wife, Mary, was in the house, too far away to hear. His head hammered into the floor as if it were a rag doll's. On each revolution he desperately reached for the shut-off lever, but it remained just a few inches beyond his grasp.

Beardsley started to slip away. It was an iron-gray morning, spitting snow, but he saw a brilliant light.

Somehow, the tractor engine died. Beardsley pulled his crushed leg out of the machine and crawled out to the yard, where Mary finally found him. Beardsley was relatively lucky; power take-off accidents kill more farmers than they maim. He came away with a punctured lung, a fractured right wrist, broken ribs, a severe concussion, broken vertebrae, a mangled leg, and a monkey on his back.

That first rush of Demerol in the hospital was unlike anything the straight-arrow, teetotaling Beardsley had ever experienced. He rocketed into another world—one without stress or strain or worry. It was so wonderful that if some higher power told him that he could go back, avoid the accident, but never take Demerol, Beardsley wouldn't hesitate—he would turn down the offer flat.

Past the thirteen-mile mark, and past Wellesley College and its gauntlet of shrieking women, the lead pack melted down to Rodgers, Ed Mendoza, Beardsley, and Salazar.

At age thirty-four, the great Rodgers, four-time winner of the Boston Marathon, had lost a step, and the front-running Mendoza would inevitably fade. The only concern was Beardsley, whom Salazar pegged as a talented journeyman. True, he'd run a few good marathons—a 2:09 at Grandma's in Duluth, the win at London the previous year—but he had no credentials on the track. Beardsley's best 10-K was a full minute and a half slower than his own.

And look at him there in his silly little painter's cap, slurping water from every kid he passed. Beardsley lacked gravitas. So let Beardsley and Squires think they could break him on the hills. Salazar knew they were dreaming. He was faster, tougher, and had prepared more thoroughly. The hills belonged to him.

A few feet away Beardsley was thinking the same thing. He had spent the winter training in Atlanta, not to escape the northern cold, but because Georgia, unlike

Minnesota, had hills approximating Boston's. In early April, he left Georgia to finish preparing in Boston, where he could familiarize himself with the marathon course. Shortly after his arrival, however, a northeaster blew into town, bringing heavy snow and a howling wind. Beardsley was scheduled for a key workout on Heartbreak Hill: up one side and down the other, eight times. Squires looked out the window and told him to forget it.

"Come on, coach. Let's give it a try."

"I don't think I can even get us to Heartbreak, let alone have you run there." But Squires finally relented. He drove at a creeping pace through the deserted streets, delivering Beardsley to within three miles of Heartbreak.

"For chrissakes, Dickie, look at this snow. Let's go home. You're gonna slip and fall and kill yourself."

"Let me give it a shot, coach."

Beardsley got out of the car and started running toward Heartbreak. He ran gingerly at first, but after a few steps picked up the pace. His footprints cut lonesome notches in the unblemished drifts; the icy wind scorched his eyes. Beardsley closed his eyes, moving on touch and sound and instinct, imagining—knowing— that at this desperate moment, Alberto Salazar was running someplace where it was warm.

He completed eight round trips over Heartbreak, just as planned. At the end of the workout, he quietly reported to Squires that he was ready. The hills belonged to him.

In the weeks and months following the 1982 Boston Marathon, Alberto Salazar's decline was so gradual that it barely seemed like a decline at all. In the summer of 1982 he set two American records on the track, in the five-thousand and ten-thousand-meters. In October, he won his third consecutive New York City Marathon. His time was a few minutes slower than at Boston, but he appeared to be his elegant, imperious self—the finest distance runner of his time.

But privately, Salazar worried. Before Boston he'd relished his workouts, ripping through them with the barest hint of fatigue. He was able to follow hard days and weeks of training with even harder ones; the ceiling for one training cycle became the floor for the next. But after Boston, the workouts yielded less and less pleasure. His legs felt heavy, his breathing shallow. It took him days instead of hours to recover from a maximum effort.

Salazar tried to convince himself that he hadn't blown it at Boston; that despite drinking so little, and running so furiously, he hadn't done himself lasting damage. He scoffed at the media for making such a fuss about his "duel in the sun" with Beardsley.

Throughout 1983, Salazar suffered one heavy cold after another. Deep, racking, bronchitis-style colds, one a month, lining up like winter storm fronts off the coast of Oregon. Consistent high-level training became impossible, and he entered the crucial Olympic year of '84 in dire shape. At the Marathon Trials, he struggled to a 2:12, second-place performance. It earned him a berth in the

Games, but for Salazar, finishing second—especially in a race restricted to other Americans—was like finishing last.

He had a chance to redeem himself in Los Angeles, but the colds and malaise continued all summer. On the last night of the Games, it was Carlos Lopes of Portugal who ran into the Coliseum before the world's admiring eyes. Salazar finished an exhausted fifteenth.

Still, he was only twenty-six, with many marathons and Olympics seemingly ahead. But the illness and weakness did not abate. Doctors failed to identify his malady, and Salazar, desperate to fight, remained impotent before an invisible enemy. He experienced insomnia, and went to the Stanford Sleep Clinic. He visited a cardiologist. He underwent surgery. He tried training in Kenya. Nothing worked.

But he stubbornly refused to stop running. Because running was how Salazar defined himself. Running was the means by which he proved his manhood. At the same time, on solitary long runs or during exacting workouts with close friends, the sport provided a shelter, a place to escape the pressure of constantly proving himself. Now, in his physical prime, his only outlet was denied him. He couldn't run, yet he couldn't stop running. Salazar reached the point where the best he could do was cover four or five miles in a crabbed shuffle.

"For much of the last ten years, I hated running," he confessed to a reporter in 1994. "I hated it with a passion. I used to wish for a cataclysmic injury in which I would lose one of my legs. I know that sounds terrible, but if I had lost a leg, then I wouldn't have to torture myself anymore."

Just past mile 17, just before the firehouse at the base of the Braeburn Hill, Rodgers started to fade; just beyond it, Mendoza dropped away. Now it was down to Beardsley and Salazar. Beardsley stepped to the lead he would hold for the next nine miles.

As the hills unreeled, Beardsley launched one gambit after another. He would drive hard for four hundred yards, then back off for two hundred. He'd repeat the cycle two or three times. But after a third fast four-hundred, he'd slow down for only one hundred yards. Then, hoping to catch Salazar flatfooted, he would surge. But Salazar covered every move. He stayed plastered on Beardsley's shoulder, throwing his own combinations. The sun was behind them, so Beardsley could watch Salazar's shadow on the pavement. When the shadow began to move forward, Beardsley speeded up just enough to stay ahead of it. Psychologically, he could not afford to let Salazar take the lead.

Heartbreak Hill came and went. The two runners remained joined.

By the summer of 1995, Dick Beardsley was taking ninety tablets of Demerol, Percacet, and Valium a day. He photocopied physicians' stationery, forged the prescriptions, and filled them at a dozen pharmacies in and around his home in Detroit Lakes, Minnesota. With meticulous care, Beardsley recorded his drug transactions in a small notebook, disguising the entries as bait purchases for the fishing-guide business he bought after recovering from his farming accident.

When Dick and Mary visited a friend's house for dinner, Beardsley excused himself from the table, went to the bathroom, and rifled his host's medicine cabinet for pain pills. He did the same at the house of his father, who was dying of pancreatic cancer.

Beardsley no longer drank water with the pills; he had trained himself to gulp them down dry, as if they were M&Ms or sunflower seeds. He spent all his waking moments thinking about pills— acquiring them, concealing them—much in the way that, years earlier, in the winter before the 1982 Boston Marathon, he spent all his time thinking about Alberto Salazar.

Amazingly, Beardsley was able to hide his disease, live a double life. Nobody in Detroit Lakes harbored suspicions. He appeared to be the same great guy as always: friendly, generous, outgoing, forthright, not in the least bit pompous despite his past as a world-class athlete. His fishing-guide business was thriving. He had become a popular motivational speaker for youth groups.

At the bait shop, or on a boat with a client, Beardsley never slurred his words or stumbled. He drove with obsessive care. He hid his pills in a secret place in his pickup truck, and floated around in a private, secret cloud that insulated him from all trouble and anxiety. He was a week or two away from dying.

"After I got caught, during detox and treatment, the doctors just shook their heads when they found out how much I was taking," he recalls. "It was enough to kill an elephant. The doctors said that thanks to my running, I had a tremendously rapid metabolism, and an incredibly strong heart. Still, it was only a matter of time until one morning I just wouldn't wake up."

At home in the evenings, Beardsley would often nod off over his supper plate. One night, Mary said to him in frustration, "Do you think you could force yourself to stay awake and watch a video with me tonight?"

Worried that his cover might be fraying, Beardsley willed himself to watch the entire movie. The next day, while returning the video to the rental shop, he decided to surprise Mary with another movie. He spent a long time combing the aisles, studying various titles. Finally he found a film he was sure she would like. At home, when he delivered the surprise, Mary stared at him. The video he had brought her was the same one they had watched the night before.

After watching the early part of the race on TV, and discovering that an extraordinary contest was in progress—two runners, stripped down to bone and will, relentlessly moving down the streets of their city—the citizens of Boston turned out of their houses to witness the finish. Fathers lifted their children up on their shoulders and told them to pay attention, as an estimated crowd of two million turned out to watch some part of the 1982 Boston Marathon.

Beardsley had come off Heartbreak with Salazar breathing down his neck. The crowd pressed so close there was barely a path to run through. They were screaming so loud he couldn't hear himself think. He couldn't feel his legs. They seemed to belong to somebody else.

Twenty-one miles into the eighty-sixth Boston Marathon, and he was running a stride in front of the great Salazar, who must be hurting too. Because if Salazar wasn't fried, he would have blown past him by now.

Five more miles was unthinkable. Beardsley decided he'd just go one more mile. That would be easy—or at least possible. Stay ahead of Salazar for one more mile. After that—well, he'd think of something.

He couldn't feel his legs. One more mile.

Meanwhile, Salazar was hurting. Shards of pain splintered up from Salazar's left hamstring. Sometime during the last few miles he had stopped sweating. His singlet had stiffened, as if covered in dried blood.

All that mattered now was not losing. That made things simple. He could forget about his time and focus on that single and sovereign goal. He might lose a ten-thousand-meter race to a Henry Rono, but he did not lose marathons, especially to a palooka in a painter's cap. Any moment now Beardsley might blow up and drop away like a disintegrating booster rocket. If he could maintain the pace, then it would simply be a matter of outkicking him.

Alberto Salazar feared no opponent, at least none that he could see.

Jose Salazar, Alberto's father, was a passionate man. Journalists never tired of writing about Jose's romantic Cuban background: the fact that he'd been a close friend and fellow revolutionary of Fidel Castro; that he d grown to hate the Communists and, in exile, had dedicated his life to overthrowing his former comrade.

In 1988, Jose's church in Wayland hosted a guest from Europe bringing strange but exciting news: six teenagers in the Balkans of Yugoslavia had been visited by an apparition of the Virgin Mary. A devout Catholic well disposed toward saints and miracles, Jose was fascinated. He undertook his own pilgrimage to the distant town, called Medjugorge. Upon his return home, Jose started sending Medjugorge literature to Alberto in Oregon. Alberto was the most devout of his four children, but also the one most in need of grace.

After a failed bid to make the 1988 Olympic team, Alberto Salazar had started a business career, owning and operating a popular, eponymous restaurant in Eugene. Despite the fact that he'd grown increasingly distant, surly, and abstracted since his running had declined, he regarded himself as a happy and prosperous man. He didn't need any of his father's Virgin Mary moonshine.

But one day in 1990, Salazar picked up a tract that his father had sent him. Within a few months, he was on a plane to Yugoslavia, embarking on his own pilgrimage. While in Medjugorge, Salazar was interviewed by a local priest. At long last, the former champion acknowledged his pain and emptiness.

He told the priest he was once presented with a wreath of genuine green laurels after winning a marathon. "My father took it with him and preserved it as a memento in a safe place," he said. "Several months later, this beautiful wreath, which marked a great victory, had lost its entire beauty.

"For sport is not simply a discipline," Salazar continued. "Sport can become a compulsion, another god. So long as one depends on it, he forgets everything else. If he loses this god, he has nothing else."

He flew home to the United States, sold his restaurant, moved his family to Portland, and went to work for Nike. A doctor finally determined that his chronic health problems were largely due to his overheating at the '82 Boston

Marathon. The doctor prescribed Prozac, which resolved the worst symptoms of the pernicious strain of exercise-induced asthma and lifted Salazar's decade-long depression. At age thirty-four, he resumed training. In May of 1994, Salazar won the fifty-four-mile Comrades Marathon in South Africa. Soon afterward, with nothing left to prove, he retired from competitive distance running, and began to coach.

Dick Beardsley still couldn't feel his legs. Mile 24 had passed, so his one-more-mile scheme seemed to be working.

He kept watching Salazar's shadow. Suddenly, it loomed huge on the asphalt. Beardsley wondered if he was hallucinating. But it was the press bus roaring past to the finish line. The crowds were so thick that the bus had to travel the same line as the runners. As the bus went past, its mirror clipped Beardsley on the shoulder. Beardsley punched the bus in frustration. Then it was gone.

By the twenty-fifth mile, Beardsley didn't need to look for the shadow anymore. They had been running together their whole lives. He felt Salazar's presence more palpably than he did his own ruined legs. My God, *he thought,* one more mile, and I'm going to win this thing.

A half-mile to go. Continuing to move in a disembodied, dreamlike cloud, Beardsley flashed on his father. For his high school graduation present, his father had given him an IOU plane ticket, good one day for a trip to the Boston Marathon. Tears started to well up. Beardsley told himself to cut it out, get into this, attend to business.

Beardsley tried one last surge, but as he bore down, a shout of pain arose from his right hamstring. The leg turned to rubber. You could see the knotted muscle bulging.

Salazar blew past him. This was wrong on every conceivable level.

Then the motorcycle cops roared past, following Salazar, forming a phalanx around the new leader. The motorcycles massed together and for the first time all day, Dick Beardsley lost sight of his opponent.

On the morning of October 1, 1996, Dick Beardsley attempted to fill a forged prescription at the Wal-Mart pharmacy in Detroit Lakes, just as he'd done scores of times over the last few years. The pharmacist was a fishing buddy. They always kidded around when Beardsley came in for his pills. But on this day, the pharmacist wouldn't make eye contact. Beardsley knew right away that he was in trouble. He did not flee, and he did not dissemble. He was booked on felony narcotics charges. His shocking arrest made headlines across the country.

Beardsley avoided a prison sentence, but he hardly escaped punishment. He underwent a long, harrowing detox and treatment that entailed methadone, lengthy stays in psychiatric wards, and rigid adherence to a twelve-step program. Mary and Andy, Dick and Mary's son, stood by him, as did his friends in Detroit Lakes and the national running community. Through excruciating work—and the dispensation of grace—Beardsley regained his health, the trust of his family, his business, his public speaking career, and his sport.

In 2002, he ran five marathons, and six more the following year, with a post-accident personal record of 2:45:58 at the Toronto marathon in October 2003. Each September, he puts on a popular half-marathon in Detroit Lakes. In 2003, the special guest at the race was Beardsley's good friend Alberto Salazar.

Just when Beardsley thought nothing more could possibly go wrong, something did. A moment after losing sight of Salazar with less than a mile to go, he stepped in a pothole. That tore it, he thought; the best he could do now was crawl in. But somehow, instead of worsening the pain, stepping in the pothole stretched out the hamstring, straightening out the knot.

Beardsley started to sprint. He put his head down and pumped his arms. He found another gear. He felt like angels were lifting him up. A hard right turn onto Hereford Street. He caught a glimpse of Salazar, like a glimpse of the pope in a motorcade, twenty yards ahead, then put his head down again.

At the top of the hill there was a hard left turn before the final straightaway. Salazar and the motorcycles made that turn and the crowd at the finish line went wild, screaming in their hometown boy.

Beardsley had to weave his way through the motorcycles. The cops thought he was finished, but here he was back from the dead. They looked pie-faced and astonished as he pushed past them.

Salazar glanced back over his shoulder, also thinking that Beardsley was gone. But instead he was right there, on his shoulder, bearing down on him. Salazar's eyes grew as big as headlights. He turned to the finish line, the last hundred yards, with Beardsley in hell-hound pursuit.

Up in the TV booth above the finish line, Squires kept screaming, "Dickie! Dickie. Dickie!"

It was all clear to Salazar: There was nothing else to consider but the finish line up ahead, somewhere in that insane jumble of people and police barriers and motorcycles. The fact that he did not lose was as ineluctable as a law of physics.

Hail Mary, full of grace. The pain and the jumble and a dry-ice cold all over. My God, Dick Beardsley was tough, but Alberto Salazar did not lose.

The cafe at Nike's Mia Hamm Building is just about deserted. Alberto Salazar's quick lunch break has turned into a two-hour retrospective of his life and career—just a few minutes less than it once took him to run a marathon.

Finally, Salazar rises from the table. In the lobby, before riding the elevator up to his office, he says, "At the time of the Boston Marathon, I didn't know Dick very well. And to be honest, for a long time after it, I sort of resented him. Well, that passed, like a lot of my stuff passed." He gives a terse shake of his head.

"Then in 2002, the Boston Marathon brought us back for the twentieth anniversary of our race. We got to know each other. Now, among all the guys I ran with or against, Dick might be the one I feel closest to. I'll pick up the phone every few months and give him a call. I think he and I have a special bond. All that he's gone through. . . I'm not saying I can understand it, but maybe I can come close.

"We both give a lot of talks, to all kinds of groups, all over the country," Salazar continues. "Sooner or later, someone always asks about the '82 Boston. I don't mind—I like talking about it, and so does Dick. That's because we never discuss the race in terms of running a 2:08, or beating the other guy. It took us both a long, long time, but we finally realized that that's not what the marathon is really about. It's not what it's about at all."

"After the race, people came up to me and said, 'Gosh, Dick, if you hadn't had to fight through all those police motorcycles, you might have won,'" Beardsley recalls for his audience at the Victoria Marathon. "But I don't look at it that way. I ran the race of my life, 2:08:53. Alberto happened to run two seconds faster. All I know for certain is that I left everything I had out on that course. I didn't give an inch. Neither did Alberto. The way I look at it, there were two winners that day."

The crowd erupts in applause, as if they were at the finish line at Boston. Beardsley lets the cheers wash over him for a moment, then holds his hands up for quiet.

"Tomorrow, at your marathon, you're going to give it your all," he says. "When it's over, you can look back on a job well done. You'll be able to relax. You'll be finished.

"Well, the race that I'm running now, I can never relax, never be finished," Beardsley goes on. "The day I say that I've got my addiction beat, I'll be in greater danger than when my leg got caught in that power take-off. I can't let that day come. I just celebrated my seventh year of sobriety. These have been the seven hardest, and the seven most wonderful, years of my life. Every morning I feel like I'm getting up to run the Boston Marathon all over again."

Mary vs. the Soviets

Frank Murphy, 2000

In a career that spanned three decades, Mary Decker set 36 national records and 17 world records in events ranging from 800 meters to 10,000 meters. The pinnacle of her career came in 1983 at the inaugural World Track and Field Championships. Decker arrived at the Helsinki meet on a record tear, but she was considered no match for the Soviet athletes who had long dominated women's distance running. Decker had to face the two-time Olympic champion, Tatyana Kazankina, in the first race, the 3,000 meters, and then the world leader, Zamira Zaytseva, days later in the 1,500 meters. Author Frank Murphy calls these two great races, which came to be known as the Decker Double.

One day separated the heat from the final, a time for rest and a time for figuring. Decker and Kazankina were in [the final], of course. The way they finished the heat, side by side, combined with the way Decker had run in the weeks prior to Helsinki and with the fact that Kazankina was running at all made them objects of fascination and interest for the final. Where had Kazankina been? Was she fit? Could she run 3,000 meters as well as she had the shorter distances, which had been her specialty? Could Decker hold together in her first major international championship? Was it possible for her to take on the Soviets, virtually unchallenged since 1976, when Decker sat sadly on the sideline? What of [Svetlana] Ulmasova? Was she not the world-record holder? Surely, neither Decker nor Kazankina could stay with her? And finally, what of the third Soviet, Natalya Artyemova, who barely qualified for the final? Might she be a rabbit planted in the field to assure a fast pace for her two teammates? It was the kind of roiling possibility that made a rest day uneasy and edgy, as coaches and athletes anticipated events.

Decker settled on a strategy. She would lead the race and accelerate progressively in the later stages in order to control the tempo and take the sting out of her rivals' kicks. The progressive acceleration was a suggestion from Bill Bowerman, which [Mary's coach] Dick Brown and Mary Decker accepted. When the gun sounded, the strategy unfolded. Decker headed to the front, unmindful of the clustered runners behind her. Later, she said that this had been "a good feeling compared to being way out front. You can't make mistakes, and you sure keep alert." She led rhythmic laps of 66,70,71,71,71,70, a little faster initially than she wanted and then a little slower, but still close to her targets and likely to have the effect she wanted. The field began to separate

From Frank Murphy, 2000, *The Silence of Great Distance: Women Running Long* (Kansas City, KS: Wind Sprint Press). Reprinted by permission of Frank Murphy.

until only the two top Soviets, Brigitte Kraus of West Germany, Wendy Sly of Great Britain, and Agnese Possamai of Italy remained in contention. The first kilometer split was 2:51 and the next two runners through were Kazankina (2:51.27) and Ulmasova (2:51.51). As the pace slowed slightly in the second kilometer, Decker went through in 5:48.89, followed now by Kazankina and Sly at 5:49.13. Ulmasova was still close in 5:49.35 as was Kraus in 5:49.73. When the field approached the bell, conventional wisdom said that Decker was finished. She had jackals at her back and she had done all the work for them. Food for the kill, that's what she was.

Nothing was further from the truth. Decker had worked her plan to perfection. The pace had been steady if not sensational, and Decker had accelerated at the 600-meter mark. The bunched runners behind her at the bell, including Wendy Sly who was almost abreast with her, and Kazankina, Kraus, Possamai, and Ulmasova, were tired by then, and when Decker accelerated again going into the last 400 meters, she tormented them, sending little pinpricks of pain through already enervated legs and arms. Nevertheless, they responded, no one dropped back, and everybody who ever had a chance, still did. On the backstretch, Kazankina was boxed on the inside by Wendy Sly, and Ulmasova was boxed by Possamai and harassed by Kraus. Less experienced runners would have been unnerved but the Soviets were patient. They knew that one of two things would happen, that an opening would appear or that they would force one. They waited as long as possible in the hurrying crowd for the first eventuality, the one they expected and preferred, but nothing happened, no gap, no failure of will from the leader, no fallen runner; so finally, on the last homestretch, with no distance left to spare and time running out, Ulmasova sprang from her fifth-place position into an open outside lane. It was late and she would have hoped for better, or at least for sooner, but, no matter; she had a clear path in front of her to the tape and Decker was in her sights. Kazankina, responding to the late bustle, was even better positioned. When Wendy Sly finally fell away, Kazankina moved through. She was on Mary Decker's shoulder with 50 meters to run. The race was Kazinkina's after all. She and not Ulmasova would handle the usurper. In the crisis, the announcer permitted expectancy to enter the call of the race: "and—here—comes—Kazankina!" drawn out as herald, and then quickly to prevent the message from being overtaken by the event, "here/comes/Kazankina," "here/comes/Kazankina." Self-congratulation entered the voice of the announcer, as it must have done. Did he not tell his listeners before the race that this would happen, that Decker would fold before the Soviet onslaught. And now the time has come, and it must be described: in deep, quick tones with greater urgency as the runners come up the straight together, the words rush fast enough to keep pace with the race, then the single word that tells all: "Kazankina! Kazankina!" Horseman, pass by. War, famine, pestilence, and death, the end of Decker's short reign arrived in the presence of the one runner who was too strong for her, the runner she would never beat. The great Kazankina emerged at last, ready to strike. Kazankina the totalitarian to make order from chaos.

Was it the Russian Pavlov, one of the two major influences on the Soviet sporting theory, who made dogs salivate by repeating patterns and rewards? "And—here—comes—Kazankina!" they had said in Montreal, and two times Kazankina had run around the field to victory. They had said it again in Moscow, "And—here—comes—Kazankina," and she had finished like fierce wind across an open prairie. And it came therefore to pass that in Helsinki in 1983, as Kazankina poised for just the barest second on Mary Decker's shoulder, there wasn't a dry mouth in the house. Pity Mary Decker, exposed in a low, flat place with no shelter.

Just then a strange and illogical thing happened. How could it be explained? For Kazankina came to the precipice, close enough to see, really, what was possible, and then she hung there, so briefly, before being knocked back by a force that she neither saw nor felt, but which occupied the field next to her own. Mary Decker "took a deep breath, relaxed and went." Could it really be as easy as that? Decker's stride was smooth, level, and unexcited, all her energy was directed to forward motion, and she blew away to a shocking victory. Stymied and surprised by Decker's speed, strength, and courage, Kazankina faltered near the end, and Brigitte Kraus passed her on the line. That remarkably, it was over, quick as an execution or a coup bubbling up from the people. The Soviet distance runners had been toppled by two women from the West, two democrats. Decker's final time was a relatively slow 8:34.62 with a last lap of 60, while Kraus took 8.5 seconds off the West German national record by running 8:35.11. Kazankina ran 8:35.13 in her first big 3,000, while Ulmasova, who lacked the last-lap punch of the other women, finished fourth in 8:35.55, a long way behind her world record of 8:26.78. After the race, Kazankina was forthright. "I was sure I would win it. But I lost in the final sprint to the American Mary Decker, who proved to be stronger at the finish." Decker herself professed never to have doubted the result, saying, "I wasn't worried when Kazankina came up on me in the stretch because I know I have a good kick."

The Western media reaction to Mary Decker's victory was instantaneous and enthusiastic. One of our own had brought down the bullies. Said one major report, "Mary Decker proved two important points in this race: that, given the ability of course, it is still possible in a major championship to run the legs off your rivals from the front . . . and that even the great Soviet women runners are not unbeatable. What an inspiration the 25-year-old American is to Western girls who for so long have suffered from an inferiority complex toward the Eastern Europeans, and what a marvelous advertisement she is for the sport."

The marvelous advertisement for the sport still had a race to run in Helsinki. All along she had said she would run the 1,500 meters for fun, but if anybody ever believed that before, they no longer did. The fun would come in the winning, and after easily advancing to the final with the fastest qualifying time (4:07.47), she lined up with the Soviets again: Zamira Zaitseva, Yekaterina Podkopayeva and Ravilya Agletdinova. All three had the potential to win the world championship, as Zaitseva had run 3:56.14, Podkopayeva had run 3:57.14, and Agletdinova had run 3:59.13. After a false start by Zaitseva, the field sprinted up the first turn, hesitated slightly looking for a leader on the backstretch, and then deferred to Mary Decker as she took her now-customary position. She passed 400 meters in 64.1, 800 meters in 2:11.0 (66.90), and 1,200 meters in 3:16.7 (65.7). The pace was fast without being withering and the Russians were still in attendance, all of them reassured that they were each at least one second faster than Decker in an open 800 meters. At the bell, Decker led and Zaitseva followed closely. Too closely, Decker said later, "She hit me practically every stride the whole way. Not obviously, but just brushing elbows, touching shoes." Still, Decker controlled herself and the tempo, accelerating into the penultimate turn and heading for the backstretch, making it impossible for any but Zaitseva to get to the front and making it hard even for Zaitseva to manage it. Nevertheless, the race looked once again set up for Decker to falter. She was in front, in contact, had led the whole way, and the pursuer had the advantage of both surprise and superior 800-meter speed. The conclusion, foregone but unfulfilled in the 3,000 meters, was sure to happen on this day. The patient Soviet would explode past the even-tempo leader and dash away from her on the homestretch. In her discouragement, the leader might even find herself prey to the last-minute attention of the dashers behind her and end up out of the medals, disconsolate and discouraged, full of self-recrimination for having been bold enough, audacious enough, to try twice in a major championship the tactic that never works, leading from the front. The foolishness of such a thing was evident and Zaitseva was its proof. There on the backstretch, she was awaiting her moment, not running smoothly but jagged and rough—like a person who could jolt into top speed and come with a rush.

And she did. On cue, Zaitseva did rush past Mary Decker approximately 170 meters from the finish line, did jump her for a quick lead of five meters coming into the homestretch and did sprint ferociously toward the end, her legs driving powerfully, her face contorted in determination, her one good chance for a world championship set out in front of her, and no obstruction in view. The hand that held the dagger had stuck it in the back of her neighbor, to paraphrase an even more outrageous act of plunder. If you asked Mary Decker, she would say Zaitseva's five-meter lead and her clear view of the finish line was ill-got gain, the profit from cutting her off on the last turn. "I don't think it's personal. It's just the way they're trained. . . . She was running with me and leaning on me and I had to back off." When Zaitseva cut in on her, the chop in Decker's stride, necessitated by the nearness of Zaitseva's move to the pole position, was barely detectable, but running at speed is a precision sport. Even a minor adjustment can cause a major decline in speed, cadence, and momentum. It would have been possible, of course, for Decker to fend Zaitseva off a bit, just touch her slightly to warn her of the encroachment at the critical stage, but she dared not, "It was a mistake, letting her cut me off. But I didn't want to have to make a sudden move. I stay more relaxed if I move into my sprint gradually. So I had to let her get a little lead, and then she surprised me by cutting in." Making the decision of the moment—the decision not to touch Zaitseva and not to protect herself from the interruption in her race—was Decker's fear of disqualification and her fear that she might overreact, "If I was more aggressive," she said, "we'd be punching (each other) through the turn." So, in that moment, the moment when Decker fell victim to her inexperience and her apprehension, the race was decided. Decker had, in fact, run her race for fun, refrained from fisticuffs and physical battle, and now it was completed. Silver was good, and Zaitseva was a forceful and dynamic victor even if she was Soviet! That is what the eyes and the mind said as Zaitseva fled for home—except, that is, for the one detail that began slowly and then with gathering momentum to reveal itself. Decker was sprinting.

In the rough stride that took Zaitseva past Decker, a role reversal occurred instantaneously. Decker the pursued became Decker the pursuer. Decker the defender became Decker the attacker. That the reversal occurred in just that way was a credit to Mary Decker, for in almost every other case the reversal takes another form, as the bold leader becomes a defeated, straggling follower. How was it possible for Mary Decker to shift mental gears so fast and attack once beaten? In part it was her disposition, in part it was an aspect of her physical gift, in part it was because Zaitseva's move had been anticipated in Decker's race planning, and in part it was her anger. Zaitseva had broken the rules—she had cut in early—and she must not be allowed to get away with it. Two meters down as they entered the stretch, Decker's sprint closed the gap to one with 20 meters to the finish line. Remarkably, Decker held her smooth stride, maintained its length neither too long nor too short, and increased her turnover ever so slightly, looking down at her legs a time or two to see that all was going well, grimacing slightly in concentration and, within a long reach of the line, closing her eyes and pulling mightily with the last one or two arm swings before she was across the line. Zaitseva did not withstand the counter attack. When Decker came back at her, Zaitseva instinctively lengthened her stride, lost control of it, and jumped down as much as out toward the line, for all the world a child in an apple tree who reaches toward the fruit in the tallest branch, loses her balance, and tumbles to the ground. When she fell, Zaitseva maintained second place only because she rolled across the line. Decker's winning time was 4:00.9 while Zaitseva was 4:01.19, a gap that illustrates the difference between sprinting across the line and rolling across it.

Mary Decker was the two-time world champion. Her race at 3,000 meters had shattered the myth of Eastern Bloc invincibility, and her victory at 1,500 confirmed the earlier result. The races established Mary as not just a fast, strong runner but as a competitor of the highest order. The victories had great value in and of themselves and should have been savored. In fact, they were celebrated and praised and recounted in high words and glowing terms, but they were not truly savored. They were not treasured in their own right. Instead, they were almost immediately set in shadow. The object that shadowed Mary Decker's triumphs in Helsinki was the Olympic Games scheduled for Los Angeles, Mary's hometown, in 1984. When Zaitseva rolled across the line, the

Soviets began to speak of 1984. "Mary has prepared very well this year. I think we will change our tactics and find something new. We will change," said a translator speaking on behalf of either Zaitseva or Podkopayeva, depending upon which account you read. And Mary herself fed the fire with statements emphasizing how special it would be to run in Los Angeles at the Olympics. Asked what her strongest impression was from the competitions in Helsinki, she answered, "Well, I have a lot more confidence for next year, for the Olympics.". . . Mary's reaction and that of other people to her Helsinki victories was normal, predictable and unavoidable given the warping significance of the Olympic Games, but it is saddening as well. One would wish for a champion to have at least one triumph that is truly final, one that satisfies all debts and answers all questions. Unfortunately, sporting accomplishment is by its nature transitory, and the highest triumph often provides the platform for the longest fall.

bonds

Any friendship that is based on running is, in essence, about accrual—of time, of miles of intimacy built over a lot of small steps forward.

~Sara Corbett,
writer and distance runner

Chasing Justice

Kenny Moore, 2004

Mamo Wolde is considered one of Ethiopia's greatest runners, a three-time Olympic medalist in long-distance events. The author Kenny Moore ran against him in the 1972 Olympic marathon, losing to Wolde in the final stages of the race. Their paths crossed again years later when Moore visited him in an Ethiopian prison where Wolde had been held without charge for three years. In this story the Olympic ideals of peace and brotherhood are put to the test.

There's a story all Ethiopia treasures, in which I learned I played a bit part. It's how the country's primal champion, Abebe Bikila, having won the 1960 Rome Olympic Marathon barefoot (symbolically avenging Mussolini's invasion of Ethiopia in the 1930s), and having won the 1964 Tokyo Olympic Marathon in a world record, set out in the thin air of Mexico City in 1968 to win his third gold medal in a row.

Then 24, green and idolatrous, I ran at Bikila's side in the early miles, through a claustrophobic gauntlet of screaming, clutching Mejicanos locos. Bikila, protecting his line before a turn, even gave me an elbow. I wanted to tell him that there was no way I'd ever drive him into that crowd, but I knew no Amharic. He had tape above one knee.

Any Ethiopian child can tell you that Bikila was running hurt. After 10 miles, he turned and beckoned to an ebony wraith of a teammate, Mamo Wolde, the 10,000-meter silver medalist and a fellow officer in Emperor Haile Selassie's palace guard. Wolde wove through the pack to Bikila's side. Thirty-four years later, I would learn what they said.

"Lieutenant Wolde."

"Captain Bikila."

"I'm not finishing this race."

"Sorry, sir."

"But Lieutenant, you will win this race."

"Sir, yes sir."

"Don't let me down."

Wolde, thinking some runners were out of sight ahead, took off. None was, but until the tape touched his chest, he couldn't be sure. He took the gold medal in 2:20:27 by a masterful 3 minutes.

I got blisters. I'd wrapped our trainer's new "breathable" adhesive tape around the balls of my feet, where it came unstuck and rolled up into ridges of fire. I sat down in Chapultapec Park, took off my shoes and ripped off the

From *Runner's World*, January 2004. Reprinted by permission of Rodale, Inc.

tape—and my skin. I got my shoes back on, hobbled until I bled out and went numb, and finished 14th in 2:29:50.

Thus I was in the stadium tunnel when Abebe Bikila emerged from an ambulance. He caught Wolde's eye, came to attention and saluted. Wolde, mission accomplished, crisply returned it. Wolde's victory meant his country hadn't produced a lone prodigy, but a succession. Wolde had made the marathon Ethiopia's own.

Wolde went home, had his portrait enshrined among the Olympic rings atop his national stadium, and eventually would inspire Olympic champions Miruts ("Yifter the Shifter") Yifter, Derartu Tulu, Fatuma Roba, Gezahegne Abera, and Haile Gebrselassie. The tale of Captain Bikila's order to the good soldier Wolde became legend in Ethiopia, but I didn't hear about it until April of 2002, when Wolde recalled I was one of the runners he passed to reach Bikila's ear. What took so long? A simple matter of the champion being made to rot in Ethiopian Central Prison for 9 years.

You are quick to ask why. We'll get to that, to Wolde's great purgation, but let's linger with him as long as we can back before the fall, before he was overtaken by the monumental anguish of his nation.

In the Munich Olympic Marathon in 1972, Wolde and I ran almost stride for stride. With 5 miles to go we were dueling for second, a minute behind Frank Shorter. Wolde was as soft of foot and breath as an Abyssinian cat. The only way I knew he was there was that distinguished widow's peak bobbing at my shoulder. Occasionally our shoes brushed. "Sorry," Wolde said each time.

On a rough path in the English Garden, a cramp shot up the back of my right leg. Wolde watched me slow and grab my hamstring. He ran on. Then he turned and gave me a look I would never forget. His face filled with regret. It was as if he were saying this is all wrong, we were supposed to race together, and the stronger take the silver and the other the bronze. Instead, Belgium's Karel Lismont caught us both and finished second. Wolde took the bronze. I followed in fourth, 30 seconds behind.

Shorter, stunned at his triumph, embraced me. "I thought at least I had bronze," I croaked. "Wolde took my bronze."

Then Wolde and I shook hands, departed the terror-stricken Munich Olympics, and returned to absurdly opposite worlds.

———————————•———————————

Mamo Wolde returned to Addis Ababa, was promoted to captain, and promised a nice house. He never got it, because in November of 1974, Emperor Haile Selassie, age 83, was suffocated in his bedchamber, and his 60 top ministers, admirals, and generals were lined up against a prison wall and machine-gunned.

For the next 17 years, a fanatic paranoid named Mengistu Haile Mariam changed Ethiopia from a feudal empire to a Marxist dictatorship known as the Dergue (Amharic for committee). Revolutionary Guards killed tens of thousands suspected of disloyalty. To claim the body of a loved one, a family had to reimburse the government for the bullets used in the execution. More holes meant more revenue, so death squads observed a two-bullet minimum.

Wolde, being Imperial staff, seemed in mortal danger. His Olympic and many championship medals saved him. He was ordered to take a lowly position in a local kebele, a sort of neighborhood council that Dergue officials used to spy on, detain, or torture counter-revolutionaries. He married Aymalem Beru, and in 1976 they had a son, Samuel. Aymalem died in 1987, and 2 years later, Wolde married young, adoring Aberash Semhate. They had two children, Adiss Alem Mamo and Tabor Mamo.

In 1991, the Dergue was overthrown by the forces of the Ethiopian People's Revolutionary Democratic Front. The new government caught 2,000 suspected authors of the Red Terror and created a special prosecutor's office to try them. Wolde was caught up in this sweep and locked up in Ethiopian Central Prison.

Wolde sat for 3 years without the western world's notice. Then in 1995, Amnesty International reported that he had been imprisoned without even being charged with a crime. Amnesty appealed to the prosecutor to either charge or release him. Ethiopia did neither, refusing even to say what he was suspected of. When the International Olympic Committee (IOC) demanded an explanation, it was told to back off and "await the verdict of the court."

I remember Shorter, a friend and a lawyer, wondering just how well we knew Wolde. I felt we knew enough. A gold medal doesn't guarantee moral integrity, but what is more basic to the Olympics than forsaking violence? Ideals were involved here. The only way to know was to go find out.

An indispensable ally was 1972 Olympic 800-meter bronze medalist Mike Boit, who was then Kenya's sports commissioner. He urged me to come down to Nairobi, where he got me an Ethiopian tourist visa. And so, on a rainy day in August 1995, the photographer Antonin Kratochvil and I landed in Addis Ababa.

First, we called the special prosecutor's office. Spokesman Abraham Tsegaye blandly said Wolde was going to be charged with "taking part in a criminal act, a killing."

I went queasy. I had come all this way on the strength of a backward glance. Suddenly it seemed childishly sentimental.

"Did Mamo Wolde have access to a lawyer?"

"Not now. Not until he is charged."

"If I was detained for 3 years without charge, I'd sure have a lawyer."

"Well, in your country, every time you shake hands with someone, you need a lawyer. In Ethiopia it's not such a way."

He said he had no authority to let me visit Wolde, and hung up. Kratochvil took a look at my waxen face and asked a question that turned everything around. "Does Mamo have a wife?"

Did he ever. Slender, doe-eyed, and resolute, Aberash Wolde-Semhate, then 24, welcomed us into their mud and stick home off a rocky lane, behind a sheet-metal wall. Son Tabor, then three, gave me a brave, cold, trembling little handshake. Adiss Alem, Mamo's 5-year-old daughter, showed us his gold and silver medals from Mexico City.

The wood floors were smooth and clean. Frankincense was in the air. Aberash poured us glasses of home-brewed beer and apologized for Wolde not being able to welcome us himself. We looked at a photo album and she sketched his history. He was born in 1932 in Ada, south of Addis Ababa, and was of the Oromo tribe. She had met him when she was 17 after his first wife died. "When I was in school, I ran a little, not seriously," she said. "But I read about them both, our heroes, Abebe Bikila and Mamo."

When asked, Aberash explained that Wolde was being framed. On a night in 1978, Wolde had been ordered by a top official to put on his uniform and go to a nightclub. At the club, Aberash said, he saw a group of officials with a teenage boy, hands tied behind his back, who might have been in a youth group that fought the Dergue. The officials shot the boy, then ordered Wolde to shoot the body again (the ghoulish two-bullet policy). According to Aberash, lots of people saw him purposely miss. At a hearing in 1992, many witnesses testified that Mamo hadn't killed anyone. "Only one accused him," said Aberash. "The official who shot the boy wants to blame Mamo to save himself. The prosecutors say they have to keep him in detention until they bring charges, but they never do."

Meanwhile, he'd had bronchitis, hearing loss, and liver problems. Prison meals were terrible, but families were allowed to bring in food. Aberash suggested we come along for a visit.

———————————●———————————

The aptly nicknamed End of the World Prison was 10 blocks of post-apocalyptic depression. Rusty metal walls surrounded cement barns. In the shelter of a crumbling plaster watchtower, guards lounged in thin blue overcoats, their eyes locking instantly on us, the faranjoch, the foreigners. We joined perhaps 200 visitors in an open shed. But when we moved with Aberash toward the gate, Kratochvil's camera was seen, and we were encircled by guards yelling that foreigners were never allowed in a prison. It was a national security offense. One guard, a man with a crippled hand, kept shouting we were cunning foreigners and that it was their duty to ignore everything we said and arrest us. We were ordered through the gate and put on a bench in the courtyard as higher authority was summoned. "Now we are detained," said Kratochvil.

We waited 6 hours, the man with the crippled hand whining ever more hysterically for our heads. They kept asking for our passports, to prove who we were. We'd left them at our hotel. Finally, we were given an escort there, a huge armored vehicle with six guards. You should have seen the face of the Hilton doorman when we all pulled in. I diverted the officers, while Kratochvil went to his room and flushed his film of the prison. A Major Neguesse confiscated our passports, and said, ominously, we would talk the next day.

The next morning, we didn't wait. We went to the dreaded Ministry of Internal Affairs and threw ourselves on the mercy of its chief, a Ms. Mahete, a sour, angular, Tigrayan woman in a red dress. When our interpreter said I had run against Wolde in the Olympics, Mahete's expression softened. She held up a hand, made a call, and dictated a letter. In a stroke of impossible luck, we had permission to visit Wolde.

At the prison we held up the letter like a cross before a vampire. The gate rolled open. The guards who had terrified us before shrank back against the walls. Major Neguesse begged to be forgiven. We were led down a rocky path toward a two-story building. Guards were coming down a staircase. Among them was a slender man dressed in a green-and-white sweater, and with a distinguished widow's peak. We fought through our guards, and embraced on the steps. He was bony but warm, strong, and excited.

"It all comes back," he said. "You had a goatee. Oh, thank you from my family for this! Remember me to the Olympic brothers."

"You are remembered," I said, and poured out the good wishes of the International Olympic Committee, including a standing invitation to run or be grand marshal of the Honolulu Marathon, in Hawaii, where I now live.

Wolde, thunderstruck, said, "These are words from God."

We had maybe 8 minutes together. Then he grabbed my forearms. "It restores my soul," he said. "It is something I can feel in my body, that people outside the country remember." They led him back upstairs.

Watching him go, I thought of what a slender thread had brought me there. But this time it was my turn to look back and cry out that this was wrong, this isn't the way things should be happening.

———————————•———————————

After the 1995 trip, I wrote about Wolde's plight in *Sports Illustrated*. As a result, that Christmas cemented my faith in human nature. Every mail brought copies of letters people had sent to the prosecutor, reminding him that justice delayed is justice denied. Schools and churches adopted Wolde in letter-writing campaigns. Athletes United for Peace, headed by Olympic long jumper Dr. Phil Shinnick and former 49ers quarterback Guy Benjamin, flooded the United Nation's Human Rights Commission with appeals, as did the National Council of Churches.

The most unexpectedly galvanized was Bill Toomey, the 1968 Olympic decathlon champion. Toomey has never been accused of taking life too seriously, but something clicked. As president of the Association of U.S. Olympians, Toomey recruited two-time 800-meter Olympic champion Mal Whitfield (who had coached Wolde in Ethiopia) and former Assistant Commerce Secretary Carlos Campbell to urge the U.S. State Department to press for Wolde's release on bail.

Toomey then postponed his honeymoon, went to Switzerland, and hit up IOC president Juan Antonio Samaranch for help. Samaranch made Toomey the IOC point man on the Wolde case, gave him a check to take to Aberash, and wrote a letter appealing for Wolde's freedom and inviting him to be a guest of the IOC at the 1996 Atlanta Olympics.

Toomey ran with it, stopping in Nairobi to pick up 1968 Olympic 1500-meter champion Kip Keino, arguably Africa's greatest sporting ambassador. In May of 1996, they descended upon Addis Ababa. Toomey called to report.

"The minister of justice was almost in tears at the sight of Kip Keino in his office," Toomey said. "And Kip set it up beautifully. He said, 'In 3 months, 3 billion people are going to watch the Atlanta Olympics. It's the 100th anniversary of the modern marathon, and they're going to see the great contributions Ethiopian runners have made. And then they're going to see the misery of Mamo Wolde.' That had an effect. They said they'd try to let him out for a day or 2. I said, 'The Olympics are 16 days.'

"We got 35 minutes with Mamo in prison. What a nice, humble person! Kip was reliving races with Mamo in Europe and Mexico. Everyone there was moved."

Over the next few months, the IOC reaffirmed its invitation to fly Wolde to Atlanta and the reigning Olympic women's 10,000 meter champion, Derartu Tulu, and the rest of the Ethiopian team bravely asked for his release. Wolde began to allow himself to hope. The Olympic offer seemed to resurrect ekecheiria, the mythical Greek Olympic truce under which warriors laid down their arms on battlefields and traveled to the sacred contests of Olympia for 1,200 years.

Unfortunately, that cut no ice with Ethiopia's independent prosecutor, Girma Wakjira. "We know Mamo is a hero of the land," he said. "But how would authorities say, 'OK, Mamo, we shall prosecute the rest of the people but because you are a hero you can go to Atlanta?'" Wakjira said he would prove Wolde was "head of the revolutionary guard in Addis Ababa's Area 16," and involved with the execution of 14 young people in late 1978 or early 1979.

Wolde neared despair. "My lowest point," he would say later, "was when the prosecutor threw all the Olympic appeals in the dump." He was 64, with liver and lung problems, in a country where life expectancy for men was 46. "My days are numbered," he said. "I hope the world will educate my children."

The Atlanta Games took place without him. Ethiopia's Haile Gebrselassie won the 10,000 and Fatuma Roba the women's marathon. And a powerful NBC report showed Wolde racing in Munich and my trek to his home. The last images were of Aberash and the children waiting outside that dismal, decaying prison.

In Atlanta, Billy Mills, the Tokyo Olympic 10,000-meter champion, suggested we sign an Olympic flag for Wolde. He, Toomey, Shorter, Whitfield, Ralph Boston, Willie Davenport, Rafer Johnson, John Naber, Andrea Mead Lawrence, Wyomia Tyus, and I, among many others, covered the white cloth. When Aberash and the U.S. ambassador to Ethiopia, David Shinn, took it to the prison, the wardens were so impressed, they set up a tea party in the yard for the presentation. "It was ecstasy, it was rejoicing," Wolde would recall. "There were 500 other detainees there, many who'd been government dignitaries and university presidents. When Mr. Shinn held up that flag, there was a cheer from them all."

One Sunday after the Olympics, Wolde stretched to take Aberash's hand through the double fence at the prison. He said the only reason he was alive to receive invitations to marathons was her tireless struggle to bring him food and news, and the sight of his kids growing up safe and strong. "I take this oath," he told her. "When I get out of here, and when I get another invitation to go somewhere, I won't accept unless you can come too. You are the marathoner here. You are enduring as much as I."

Aberash wet her fingers with her tears and touched his hand. She had often said that visiting the places Mamo had run was her greatest dream. Now it was their sacred promise.

———————●———————

After 5 years of imprisonment, Wolde was finally indicted in March 1997. He was one of 72 detainees arraigned on charges of "participating in mass killings and torture." Prosecutor Wakjira said, "The trials should take less than 3 years."

Wolde's attorney, Atanafu Bogale, hired by the IOC, objected that the charges didn't include the place and date of the offense, or what weapons were used, as the law required. It took a year for the prosecutor to respond. In 1998, the court let the vague charges stand.

The baton, in our Olympian relay, was seized by an old friend and Oregon track teammate, the indefatigable Jere Van Dyk. A sub-4-minute miler and Sorbonne graduate, Van Dyk went to Addis Ababa in November 1998 to cover Wolde's trial for *The New York Times*. He struck up a relationship with the special prosecutor, and persuaded prison authorities to let him not only interview Wolde, but also photograph him.

"He was small and thin," wrote Van Dyk, "his forehead deeply lined and his eyes watery. He had bronchitis and throughout a 90-minute interview exhibited a deep cough."

When the government's first witnesses testified at the trial, it was front page news in Addis Ababa. "Complete with a picture of Wolde receiving an award many years ago from Emperor Haile Selassie," Van Dyk wrote to me, "a figure despised by many, most importantly Prime Minister Meles Zenawi and his fellow Tigrayans who are running the government."

Under Bogale's cross-examinations, it became clear that no accuser had actually seen Wolde commit any of the alleged acts. "It was hearsay, hearsay, hearsay," Wolde would later say. "The government case was futile. No one came to testify who had witnessed me do anything wrong."

Before a western judge, that would mean case dismissed. But the prosecutor begged the Ethiopian court for more time to dig up the eyewitnesses he'd promised. Multiple delays were granted. Wolde, then 68, kept wasting away.

Hope drained. It seemed Ethiopia was too unreachable, too destitute, too tribal, too proud, too callous to ever let Mamo Wolde walk free. I said as much to a friend, an Oregon circuit court judge. "Let them save face," he said. "Go for a lesser plea. Go for time served." That became my mantra. Time served.

———————●———————

The secret of endurance isn't so much a lesson as an imperative. You obey the dictates of the marathon. You cut your losses and keep on. You go numb, bleed out, and keep on. You fall, get up, and keep on. You go from rock to rock, from tree to tree, and keep on. You take strength in knowing others care about your effort, and keep on.

Wolde kept on. The great, uncrackable marathoner physically outlasted Ethiopia. In January 2002 a judge convicted him of a lesser charge, sentenced him to 6 years and released him because he'd already served 9. Time served. That evening he was home with Aberash and his children. "Thank God, I am free at last," he said. "I hold no malice toward anyone."

The news reached me at home in Hawaii on Martin Luther King Day. "Free at last!" I echoed, and celebrated with a dizzy, whooping run. But even as I imagined Mamo finally reunited with Aberash and his family, a fear knifed me. He must be really sick. Maybe they just didn't want him dying in their prison cell.

Not long afterward, a man called and introduced himself as Mengesha Beyene of the Ethiopian Sports Federation. He wanted to make sure I knew Wolde was free. I told him I desperately wanted to talk with Mamo, and asked if he could help. Beyene not only could, he did, translating during a three-way call with Wolde.

Wolde's first words were, "I feel like we are embracing!"

I said he was a true marathoner.

"Thanks, thanks. Except for the separation from family and the isolation of prison, I haven't felt abandoned. Thanks to the Olympic community."

I asked the big one. "How's your health?"

"Hey," he said, "give me a couple of months to recuperate and I'll race you anywhere you want, any distance you want!"

Wolde said he wanted to stay in Addis "and establish an institute to perpetuate the legacy of Abebe Bikila" (who'd died in 1973). Generations of champions had welcomed him home. Haile Gebrselassie had raised money to help pay off his "prison debts."

"It's reincarnation for me to join my family," Wolde said. "People visit every day and say, 'We recognize you as a great Ethiopian hero.'"

But things were hardly idyllic. "Prices are staggering, and my son is losing his eyesight," he said. "But for now, it's bliss. The children hug me all the time. If I go around the corner to the store, we all have to go together, kids and Aberash and me, all tangled in a group. In the capable hands of my wife, we have made it safely through."

When he hung up, I was weightless. Beyene filled the silence with a few lines from Alfred Lord Tennyson's *Ulysses*, which he learned in Emperor Haile Selassie's secondary school.

> "And though
> We are not now that strength which in old days
> Moved earth and heaven; that which we are, we are;
> One equal temper of heroic hearts,
> Made weak by time and fate, but strong in will
> To strive, to seek, to find, and not to yield."

I couldn't get Wolde's fire out of my mind. So I called Dr. Jon Cross of the Honolulu Marathon Association, and asked whether the old invitation to Mamo still stood. He called back and said, "Get training, buddy! We're not only inviting Mamo and Aberash, but also you, Shorter, and Lismont, the top four from Munich 30 years ago, to run here in December."

We all accepted, none of us sure we could actually make the distance. I had a sore tendon. Frank had just had shoulder surgery. He said, "This isn't fair. Mamo has been safe in prison. We free citizens have crippled ourselves."

I imagined how the story might end, with the four of us old Olympians, perhaps in our Munich uniforms, striding barefoot down my Kailua beach, the turquoise sea breaking upon the level white sand. On the dunes, watching, would be Aberash Wolde and Beyene and our choked-up families. Beyene would declaim more Tennyson into the wind:

> ". . . Some work of noble note, may yet be done,
> Not unbecoming men that strove with gods;
> It may be we shall touch the Happy Isles.
> And see the great Achilles, whom we knew . . ."

And every palm tree, every face, every drop splashed up by our feet would glow with perfect clarity as we ran, in the Happy Isles, with the great Achilles, whom we knew.

So it was that I refused to absorb it, in May, when Beyene called to tell me Wolde had died. Jon Cross was equally shocked. "We just talked to him," he said. "When he accepted our invitation, he said his liver condition was flaring up. I said to fax me his prescription, and I'd shoot him what he needed. But he never did." Ten days later he was dead.

Thousands wept as an honor guard of Ethiopian Olympic champions escorted his casket 3 miles from his home through Addis Ababa to St. Joseph's Cemetery. He now lies beside his inspiration and friend, Abebe Bikila, the man who ordered him to win the Olympic gold medal in Mexico City.

I spoke to Aberash Wolde on her 12th day of mourning, the day in Ethiopian custom when friends call and bring potluck, to assure the bereaved that they're not forgotten. She recalled Mamo's vow not to travel without her. "When Dr. Cross called and invited Mamo to Honolulu in December, he asked if I might come," Aberash said. "And Dr. Cross said I must come. Mamo jubilantly accepted. He was so happy. This was the culmination of our dream. Mamo's liver hurt, but that was completely wiped away by the joy that at last we would keep his promise. And we would do it in Hawaii. It was unimaginable."

Aberash's tears had flowed, she said finally, because she knew he was dying.

The liver pains had intensified a month before. Mamo had looked a little jaundiced, but he played it down. "My husband lived and died a strong man," she said. She got him to a clinic for a checkup, and the doctor told her it was cancer and Mamo had only weeks left. The clinic did what it could to make him comfortable, then sent him home to be with friends and family. He died peacefully, as befits a marathoner, knowing the rightness of all things physical has an end.

So now it would be Aberash coming in Mamo's place to Honolulu in December. "From here on out," she said. "I duly represent the legend."

———————●———————

Aberash arrived in Honolulu the Friday before the race, escorted by two Olympic marathon champions, Fatuma Roba (Atlanta in 1996) and Gezahegne Abera (Sydney in 2000). We draped her with leis of tuberose and ilima, the latter a flower reserved for royalty in ancient Hawaii. She in turn presented Cross and me each an airily soft, white, embroidered dashiki, Ethiopian dress for special occasions. "Christmas," she whispered, "or the coffee ceremony."

Aberash brought out photos showing how fragile Mamo had been—paper and sticks, glue and grit—during the 4 months before he died.

Thinking we'd be good hosts, we unfolded a map of Oahu. Had she and Mamo had something they especially wanted to do? Aberash began to cry, while we writhed at our ignorant presumption. Recovering, she made it clear that her mission had little to do with mooning over waterfalls.

"Life in Ethiopia," she began, "is very difficult." Neither she nor Mamo has any remaining family, so she is the sole support for Adiss Alem, now 13, and Tabor, 11. Mamo's oldest son, Samuel, 26, can't work because of his vision problems. Their only income is a small stipend from the IOC. The public schools are dead ends, and she couldn't afford to put the children in private education. Famine is once again present in parts of the country. Abera and Roba confirmed all this, and said the assistance other Ethiopian athletes can offer is more emotional than financial.

We adjourned to let Aberash rest. I sought out the other two Munich Olympians. Karel Lismont, who'd claimed "my" bronze, was only 53. He'd finished second in 1972 at 22, and run in four Olympics in all, taking the bronze in Montreal in 1976, 3 seconds ahead of Don Kardong of the United States. As Shorter put it, "He's kept more Americans from medals than any other runner." Lismont turned out to be a man of strict pronouncements. He said running 30 minutes three times a week was all men of our age should do, and so didn't enter the Honolulu marathon.

I had developed a sore hip in training ("See. See!" said Lismont), so didn't run the marathon either. But Shorter did, and beautifully, covering each mile in exactly 7 1/2 minutes to finish in 3:23. It was his first marathon in 7 years. Afterward, the old Olympians were of one equal temper. We wanted to help Aberash.

Things came together over lunch in Kailua the day before she had to leave. Cross reported that the Honolulu Marathon Association was contributing a grant. Shorter and I had taken up collections at runners' gatherings. All told, we presented Aberash with enough for a year of schooling and support for the children.

Beyene translated Aberash's response, not that he needed to, given the relief on her face. "Thank you from my children," she said. "Thank you from my husband, your friend."

Serious matters concluded, the sentimental Cross, who'd never been able to shake the image of us all striding together on my beach, proposed that we actually do it.

Kailua's sands were windswept and gray as Shorter arranged us in the order we'd finished 30 years before. He was on the high side, then Lismont, then Aberash—a yard ahead, as she was representing our Achilles here—then me, with my toes in the Pacific foam. We walked along tentatively for a while, feeling odd, with Aberash looking back occasionally to see if she was doing what was wished. At last we just clumped together and walked on in each other's arms.

Cross, backpedaling with his camera, shouted and pointed. A rainbow arched down, pouring upon us all the colors of the Olympic rings. Aberash turned and saw it. Her flinch was as electric as Wolde's embrace had been in prison. I looked down. She too has a faint widow's peak.

Her jolt passed through us all, and the circle of 30 years was at last closed. It was so perfect that we hesitated to speak of it. As we drew apart, all the talk was of the future, of safe travel, of hopes for the children, even as we stared up at Mamo's rainbow, strengthening in the sky, signifying that it was all right to go on, that the bond is as strong as ever.

The Brotherhood

Rich Elliott, 2007

Jeff Bailey was one of the top high school distance runners in suburban Chicago, and life was good. He was entering his senior year, and he had great expectations—training hard with his running buddies, setting PRs, racing in the state meet. But things don't always go according to plan.

Jeff Bailey is in the middle of a hard run, but he's thinking about next week. That's when he leaves for the distance camp in Michigan, the highlight of his summer running. Camping out, training twice a day, beach runs on the dunes, speedwork on the trails—what could be more fun? And best of all, hanging out with your teammates, your running buddies.

Jeff has run with most of the guys for years, since junior high. It's a close-knit group. Something happens when you put in so many miles together on the roads. The shared pain creates bonds. You've seen each other at your best and your worst. You do crazy stuff like jump fences and sprint across private property, or run in the hottest part of the hottest day, just for toughness. To stir things up, you race without shirts in a big pack through the center of town, flying past startled pedestrians. You crack each other up; you talk in shorthand. The group has a favorite line, "Don't waste a heartbeat." Outsiders don't get it. Doesn't matter—they don't get runners anyway.

Jeff is the captain and best runner on his high school team. He stands 6'2", has an easy smile and hair that comes down to his collar. He's just come off a successful track season, run his personal best in the two mile, and despite missing the qualifying time for the state track meet by one second, he knows that next year, his senior year, will be his best season ever.

Before he leaves for camp, Jeff has a few last errands. One is the annual pre-season physical required by his school. The drill for guys is always the same. The doctor says—Pull down your pants, let me feel you, turn your head, cough. Except this time the doctor tells Jeff—You know, one testicle looks swollen. We better have a urologist take a look. Right away.

So Jeff and his mother Jo go to the urologist, who takes one look at him and says—You have testicular cancer. We have to operate right away. The walls close in, Jeff's thoughts are swirling. What about the running camp? What about my summer of running with my buddies? How soon can I run again?

Two days later a testicle is removed. The tumor is examined to see what kind of cancer cells it contains. He is told there is a 50-50 chance the cancer will return.

It's not long before Jeff is running again, and soon he's feeling like his old self except for the cloud of anxiety that rolls in each time he has a blood test.

In the fall cross country season Jeff's times get faster and faster, but again he narrowly misses qualifying for the state meet. By now he has some perspective on life's frustrations, though the failure doesn't hurt any less, and he's not sure he wants it to.

To his running buddies, Jeff's not a cancer victim, he's just Jeff. He's just one of the guys they hang out with and talk about girls and movies and running. They normalize his life when it's anything but normal.

In December there's a temporary scare when he has one bad blood test, but then the tests return to normal. The roller coaster ride, living from test to test, drains his energy, but his spring track season is impressive, and by mid-April he runs 9:42 for the two mile, virtually all alone. Qualifying for the state track meet now seems like a lock.

Jeff gets his next blood test the following week, and the tumor marker has doubled. "You need to start treatment," the doctor says, meaning chemo, meaning his season is through.

Jeff runs his final high school race the following weekend, anchoring a four-mile relay. As he races, his teammates line the track, cheering wildly for him. The word passes, and now runners from other teams are lining the track too, jumping up and down, just going nuts. The memories of that race will help him handle what he faces next.

Jeff starts treatment—three 3-week cycles. In the first part of the cycle he sits each day for five days, six hours a day, while bags of chemicals drip into his body. Six hours is a long time to sit and think. He prays a lot, and some of his prayers are pretty angry.

During the first week in the cycle, the doctors let Jeff run a little because they know it will help his morale. His high school coach asks him to continue to lead the team in stretching. "You're still the captain," he tells Jeff. "They need your leadership." In the second week of the cycle the full effect of the chemo hits. Jeff is sick to his stomach all the time and wrung out with exhaustion. He watches his running buddies, experiencing the end of the season vicariously through them.

But now Jeff has a new worry, and it is consuming. His hair is falling out. He is 18 and prom is in one week and he wants to look great and there'll be photos. Every morning he looks at his pillow, and he sees more hair. He's afraid to wash his hair for fear of more of it falling out. He cuts it shorter to make it look presentable. It's a race to the finish line, but by God, his hair hangs in there through prom night. The following day it comes out in huge clumps.

Jeff decides it's time for all of his hair to go. Jo grabs an electric shaver, and they go to the bathroom to cut it off. Jeff turns on a rock song that he listens to before races. When Jo finishes cutting his hair, he looks at himself in the mirror. Taken aback, he quickly puts on a bandana.

Now the doorbell is ringing, which is weird because it's 10 PM, and what could someone want? Jeff opens the door, and there they are, the guys. His running mates are standing there on the front porch laughing sheepishly and shoving each other through the door, all twelve of them, pointing at each other and laughing at their very shaved heads.

Their noise fills the Bailey home. "Check it out, Jeff," one guy is rubbing his bald head. "Smooth as a baby's bottom!" They take a group photo. They tell about the reluctant teammate they had to tackle before he'd cut his hair. And how their graduation caps no longer fit. They tell stories about their crazy runs that season, stories that Jeff and his buddies still tell each other years later. They talk about their last summer together before college. And tomorrow's workout.

And as they leave that night, they tell each other their line, their valediction, "Don't waste a heartbeat."

Someone to Run With

Sara Corbett, 2009

We relish distance running's many tangible benefits—fitness, medals, personal records. But ultimately, the best, most lasting reward comes from the friendships we make. Writer Sara Corbett charts the course of one friendship forged over many miles.

1

Really, this is a sad story. It's about a once-together woman who manages to lose her independence over many, many miles of running and eventually turns into a jealous and out-of-shape shrew who feels like she ought to run a lot more miles just to beat some of the loneliness out of her bones. But she doesn't. She just goes for a short run and then calls up her friend Clare.

Clare and I used to have a friendship that was all about running, but now it is mostly about talking. Clare lives in New Mexico, and I live in Maine. The good news is we talk a lot about running. There are days I will go out for a 40-minute run and then call up Clare to tell her, over the course of a 60-minute conversation, that I went running. This is how it works with us. I don't run without calling Clare afterward, and she doesn't run without calling me. Sometimes we call each other to report that we actually won't be running—that we have conferences with our kids' teachers or a deadline at work or our backs are aching or one of us has just accidentally eaten a gigantic bag of M&M's and couldn't possibly think about moving. At which point the other person says, pretty reliably, in a sing-songy voice, "I think you should sneak out for a run anyway. Remember how it makes you fe-el!"

Every so often I bring my cell phone and talk to Clare *while* I am running. I know this makes me sound lonely and pathetic, but keep in mind this is supposed to be a sad story. I wear an earpiece headset and narrate the important parts—*Hey, my knee isn't hurting!* Or *Boy, that was a pretty fast mile!*—as we keep up our usual patter about our jobs and kids and husbands, who are awfully sweet but nonetheless require ongoing scrutiny.

Out on a trail around the bay near my house, I pass women pushing baby joggers in the other direction. I pass a couple of older men chugging along. The high school girls cross-country team blows by me just as Clare, in her office in Santa Fe, says something funny about her dog and I burst out laughing. The girls look back at me over their shoulders, startled. "Time to hang up," I say through the headset. "I'm making people nervous."

From *Runner's World,* January 2009. Reprinted by permission of Rodale, Inc.

2

When I first met Clare, I didn't like her so much. This was mostly because she was from California. A lifelong New Englander who just recently had moved west to Santa Fe, I treated Californians with the same sort of suspicion I treated, well, everybody. It was 1995, and Santa Fe was full of transplanted Los Angelinos walking around in sequin-studded cowboy hats and hugging everybody they met. Back east, we were not huggers. Californians, I'd figured out in my six months in Santa Fe, loved both new people and new things—spirulina drinks, past-life rebirthing, high colonics, and so forth. On weekends, I called my mother in Massachusetts and described my new life out west with a mix of horror and intrigue, like a frontierswoman sending dispatches back to the Puritans at home. "They burn sage *why?*" my mother would say. "Your neighbor is a vegan shaman and he did *what?*"

Anyway, here was Clare, hugging my friend Andrew, whom she knew from California. Clare worked for a vitamin company and looked the part: She was a narrow-shouldered woman, 30ish, with a golden-girl tan and supermuscular legs. She wore an enormous pair of mirrored wraparound sunglasses. The first thing I remember thinking about Clare is that she looked like the Terminator, if only the Terminator had a perky little ponytail and a freckled nose.

"Clare just did an Ironman," Andrew announced, casually. And then he said something I didn't appreciate.

"Sara's a runner," he told her.

"Recreational runner," I added, but it was too late.

Maybe she was desperate for company, or maybe she found some sort of sick pleasure at the thought of overpowering lesser humans, but behind her Terminator sunglasses, Clare lit up. She gave me a big hungry smile. "Oh, goody," she said. "I really want to do a marathon soon. We should run!"

3

A first run is not unlike a first date. Early one fall morning, I met Clare at a trailside parking lot, where she continued to intimidate me. She wore shiny technical fiber clothes. She stretched her Ironwoman quads and took long pulls on a bottle of energy drink that the vitamin company sent her for free. Next to her, in my cotton college T-shirt, with my plain-Jane water bottle and underdeveloped pasty white legs, I appeared purely amateur. And that was fine, I kept telling myself. Because I'm only doing this once.

We trotted out of the parking lot and along a sandy, sage-dotted trail that built slowly into a mountainside. As a teenager and right through college, I'd run with only one friend—my old best buddy, Sue—and since then, nobody had quite lived up. I'd run with people who were too fast or too slow or too silent for me. But Clare was none of these things—especially silent. Over the course of an hour, we rambled through stories about her move from San Francisco, about our respective pets and our respective boyfriends and underwhelming jobs and how someday we were each going to do something spectacular and also have enough money to take beach vacations at least twice a year. I missed the Atlantic and she missed the Pacific, but it was the Caribbean we agreed to pine for. Hammocks and waving palms and rum drinks, and so on. We were, as they say, off and running. We ran up the mountain without a single thought toward slowing down. We ran across switchbacks and up a few steep pitches, with my dog racing alongside through the scrubby pine. Pace never entered the conversation, but I calculated that I was running just faster than I normally ran by myself. This was better, in other words, than being by myself.

Back down at the bottom, Clare gave me a big fat Californian hug. Releasing me, she said, "We should do a marathon."

"Nope, not me, no marathon," I said. I'd run exactly one marathon and I would not be running a second with any hardcore triathlete. "You frighten me," I said, just to make things clear.

"What about just a run then? Up the hill again?" said Clare, climbing in her car to go home to her dogs and horses and her sandy little ranch south of town. "Tomorrow, same time?"

4

The marathon went pretty well, thanks for asking. After leisurely chatting her way up and down that mountain in Santa Fe with me nearly every day for four months, Clare had lost some of her triathlete steel and I'd grown a smidge more fit. We were, it turned out, a good athletic match. We'd also taken to getting giant full-fat lattes after our runs, sometimes with pastries, sometimes with waffles. This helped my cause. My mediocrity, we might say, was prevailing over her superhumanity. In the midst of all the talking and all the eating, I had let Clare sign us up for a marathon in Utah. She advertised it as a "downhill marathon," something we could dispense with quickly and painlessly—qualifying for the Boston Marathon while we were at it—and then we could go spend the night at a spa built next to some hot springs.

Clare has a credo. It goes like this, and I am quoting her: "Pamper, pamper, pamper!" Which is to say she doesn't believe in running a marathon if there is not a spa involved on the other side. In Clare's universe, the body performs; the body gets its payback. Over the years, she has marched my conservative New England bones in and out of all manner of bodyworkers' offices. Postrunning, we've had acupuncture, Thai massage, shiatsu, mud baths, IV vitamin drips, and once she took me to have what she called "internal acupuncture," involving wires and electrodes and something called the Quantum Xrroid machine. ("The Quantum *what?*" my mother practically shouted into the phone from back east. "Really, isn't it time to move home?") In preparation for the Utah marathon,

Clare found us a massage therapist named Big Jim. Big Jim was about 6'5" and his particular genius was how he could drive an elbow expertly and with the full force of his body weight into our glutes. We took our glutes to him weekly. We had earned it, after all.

I have learned so much from Clare over the years. I have learned a lot about vitamins and also that it is not so bad to talk to strangers or to spend money on fresh flowers and keep them for yourself. She is a look-on-the-bright-side kind of girl, a devotee of small indulgences, a believer that a gift should be exquisitely wrapped, that a houseguest should be served coffee in bed. She is a horse-loving ranch dweller who walks around caked in manure but not without her toes painted. She lights candles on the dinner table every night of the year.

But still: There is no such thing, really, as a downhill marathon. I learned this halfway up what amounted to a four-mile megahill beginning at mile seven of the Utah marathon. My mind was trying desperately to float away from my body. Next to me was Clare, doing the same agonized shuffle but saying in her chirrupy way, "This isn't so bad. Really, this is not so bad!" To get ourselves over the top, we started fantasizing about waving palm trees and beachy rum drinks, and right to the moment we flopped over the finish line, Clare was still talking about how not bad and not hard it all was.

I do love her for this.

Within hours, we lay starfished on our respective beds in our room at what turned out to be not so much a spa but rather a rustic wilderness retreat that had already basically closed down for the season. We were the only guests. We'd been dreaming about cold postmarathon beers only to have the idea crushed by the discovery that we were in a dry county and that beer was 25 miles back down the road. Even the hot springs were a 10-minute hike from our room, and now that both of us felt like we'd been beaten with a big stick for three hours and thirty minutes (and three seconds, if you care to know), there would be no hiking. Not even to the other side of the room where we had left the Advil marooned on a dresser.

"I'll pay you five dollars to bring me three Advil," Clare said.

"Ha," I said from my spot on the bed.

"Ten dollars," she said. "And I'll give you an extra 200 if you drive back to town and get us a six-pack."

"Ha, ha," I said. But then, feeling suddenly like I owed her a whole lot more than this, I stood up and hobbled across the room to fetch the ibuprofen, free of charge.

5

"How many miles do you think we've run together?" I ask Clare one day on the phone.

"Hundreds," she says. "Definitely. Over a thousand? Two thousand? I don't know."

We mull this over for a minute and then decide it's not worth calculating.

6

After a couple of years in Santa Fe, I moved back east, to a small town in rural Maine, far away from Clare and Big Jim and the Quantum Xrroid machine. Suddenly, I was running alone again, on the empty country roads near where we lived. The silence was daunting. It rained a lot. My seven-mile runs became six-mile runs and then four-mile runs. Back in New Mexico, Clare had taken up yoga.

One fall day, she and her boyfriend arrived for a visit. Clare and I immediately put on our running shoes and headed out the door. It was deer season. I made her wear a blaze-orange cap so she wouldn't be confused for a deer, since in western Maine deer were a lot more common than runners. We started down the long, narrow road that ran ribbonlike through the dense forest near my house. The trees seemed to lean in on us, idly dropping red and golden leaves as we passed under—a scene that might have felt sylvan and magical were it not for the bursts of rifle fire coming from the woods all around us. It took less than a mile for me to understand that Clare and I were both miserable. I was lonely living out in the country, and her relationship was ending, in excruciating slow motion. We talked a little but not a lot. We just ran hard.

A few months later, the boyfriend was gone. Clare and I were on the phone. She was lying on the floor in New Mexico. I had been promising her that someday soon life would be so good that this would all seem trivial, that she'd be thankful it happened even. I tried to make her bet me money on it, but she wouldn't do it.

"Okay, you have to get up now," I said to her.

"I don't think I can."

"Get up and go outside and go for a run. It will help," I said. "I promise, I promise."

7

Any friendship that is based on running is, in essence, about accrual—of time, of miles, of intimacy built over a lot of small steps forward. It sneaks up on you that way, I think. It can seem merely enjoyable until you need it for more. One winter day, just after my 30th birthday, my mother was killed in an accident. For weeks Clare, who had lost her own mother to cancer years earlier, called on the phone and tried to talk me off the floor. Then she flew to New England and sat on the couch with me and let me weep for a good long time. Afterward, she stuffed my feet into my running shoes and pulled me out the door, not needing to say a word about why it was necessary now to go out and breathe.

It would be easy to be sentimental here. Having told you some of the sad parts of my running days with Clare, I could balance them with the joyful ones. I moved out of the boondocks to a small city near the ocean that I cherish and married my steadfast Santa Fe sweetheart. We've gone on to grasp some version of the fat domestic enchilada my mother had wished for me—having three children; buying the house, the minivan, the power mower. All good and fulfilling, but my running, over time, has become less regular, less liberating. Every year Clare and I pick out a race or two we're interested in—the New York City Marathon, a trail run in Colorado, the all-women's marathon in San Francisco, or something on Maui, maybe—but in truth we almost never get past checking out Web sites for spas in those places. Life has grown too full, too frenzied, too loaded with little competitors for our time.

As for Clare, she met her true love. On the day she married him, she and I rose early at her house in Santa Fe and went for a long, meandering run in the sage and scrub, during which I took the opportunity to gloat about how I had been right when I told her things would get better.

I credit Clare with teaching me, over so many miles, to cling to my optimism. Because if you want to see it this way, life is something like a downhill marathon. You have to believe it's easier than it is. Or at least it helps to have a friend who views it that way.

8

Then last year we pulled it off. Clare rented a house on the beach north of San Francisco and found a massage therapist who made house calls. We signed up to run the half-course version of the Nike Women's Marathon, in San Francisco. I invited my old running friend Sue, with whom I'd run practically every day for four years during college. Sue was my old Clare. Or Clare was my new Sue. In any event, the women's marathon went right through the heart of San Francisco, but according to Clare, who claims to have carefully inspected the elevation map on the race Web site months earlier, it was "really pretty flat," and therefore none of us bothered much with hill training.

You'd think I would've learned by now.

Before the race, Clare and Sue and I gathered at dawn in Union Square where someone announced on a loudspeaker that about 10,000 women would be running the race that day. We huddled in close to one another, joking, telling meaningless stories, waiting for the starting gun. I was happy to see Sue and Clare, who'd never met, gabbing like old friends. It hit me that I have been running since I was 15 years old and that truly all of my dearest female friendships have been built around running. I was thinking how lucky I am, how unique this was, how sustaining. But the sun was coming up and all around us there was a sound starting to mount, a murmuring that seemed to reach across every corner of the city square, ballooning through the open spaces and growing slowly louder. I recognized it then and knew it was something to marvel at—a familiar force that would carry us all once the gun went off and we started to run.

I looked at my friends. "Do you hear that?" I said, a little bit incredulously. "That's the sound of 10,000 women chatting."

9

Here now is the bitter part of my tale. Clare has a new running friend in Santa Fe. Her name is Laura. Laura is very fast, I'm told, and she runs races all the time without a whole lot of effort. Her son goes to school with Clare's daughter, and so it's all very cozy. I am trying to feel good about Laura. But Laura has helped Clare get faster, which is to say that she is suddenly out—way out—ahead of me. She calls me to tell me she just ran 12 miles. I call her and tell her I ran 3.6 miles, maybe 3.7.

"That's so great!" says Clare.

"Oh, come on."

"No, really."

I am silent, sullen.

"I need someone to run with," I say. "I need a Laura."

Clare and Laura recently went back to California to run a half-marathon. I was feeling spiteful and jealous about this right up until the minute Clare called me up to tell me all about her race, and I found myself whooping congratulations. I can't help it. I've known her too long. It's not that I'm jealous of Laura, exactly; it's that I miss being 28 years old with no dependents and bountiful time for friends and running followed by waffles and massage.

And, by the way, I did get myself a Laura, in the form of a friend who'd just moved back to Maine from Italy. Lily. Lily and I meet on a trail by the ocean regularly and crank out a bunch of miles without pausing one single second in our talking. It's fall again. The trees throw their leaves at our feet. Lily is my Laura. She makes me faster and stronger and happier about life. Or maybe Lily is my Clare, as much as Clare can never be replaced and I still call Clare every time I finish a run. But Clare was once my new Sue, who will always be my first old running pal. And maybe Laura is Clare's Sara. And Clare is Laura's somebody else. Maybe there's really only one thing to say about all of us women who run in tandem or in groups, who configure and reconfigure like kindred constellations moving across the sky. Maybe it's that we're all wrapped up in the same cosmic downhill-but-not-really marathon and more than anything, we just don't feel like doing it alone.

Team Hoyt Starts Again

John Brant, 2006

Dick and Rick Hoyt make up "Team Hoyt," a father-son running phenomenon from Massachusetts. Over the last 30 years, the two have completed over a 1,000 events, including over 200 triathlons and 27 Boston Marathons. In these races, Rick, who has cerebral palsy and is confined to a wheelchair, is pushed by his father. John Brant, writing about the Hoyts for *Runner's World*, tells their story of extraordinary endurance and devotion.

Rick Hoyt lies awake but unmoving, watching clear winter sunlight spill into his bedroom. He often spends whole days watching light move across a room, or along the course of a road race—the pale April sunshine filtering through the bare trees along Route 135 in the early miles of the Boston Marathon, for instance, or the tropical sun lancing the clouds that shroud Mauna Loa volcano at the Hawaii Ironman.

He lies on his belly, his head turned to the right, alone in the apartment, in exactly the position that Naomi, his personal care attendant, left him at ten o'clock the night before. You would think that Rick's nights would seem endless, but the medication he takes to relax his chronically clenched muscles allows him to sleep soundly for twelve hours at a stretch. Unable to voluntarily move any part of his body but his head, and that just barely, Rick lies calmly, studying the morning light. By its slant and texture he reckons the time to be around ten.

The sunlight keeps filling the bedroom, like April in January. It must be warm out on the streets. The women would have shed their heavy coats. From the vantage point of his wheelchair, Rick regards women from an arresting, navel-level angle. His two brothers give him a hard time about that. They call it a perk of cerebral palsy.

He hears the key in the lock, and then a step in the hallway. Then, "Good morning, Rick."

———————•———————

At 8:00 A.M. on this Saturday morning, Dick Hoyt swings his van onto the Mass. Pike, heading east toward Boston, seventy-five miles away. He lowers the visor against the rising sun and turns the car radio to an all-news station. "I've driven this route so often all I gotta do is sort of point the van and it finds the apartment on its own," Dick jokes.

He yawns behind the wheel. It's been a crazy week. On Tuesday, he was in Florida to give a motivational speech to business executives. On Wednesday,

From *Runner's World*, May 2006. Reprinted by permission of Rodale, Inc.

he was in Texas giving another one. Thursday night he and Rick were honored at a dinner in Hopkinton, where the Boston Marathon starts every April. Now, on to Boston. He makes this ninety-minute drive to Rick's apartment, in the Brighton section, almost every Saturday morning. He'll pick up Rick, bathe and shave and feed him, and then they'll drive back together to Dick's house in Holland, a village on the Connecticut border. Most Sundays they'll rise at 5:00 A.M. to prepare for whatever 5-K, 10-K., marathon, or triathlon is coming up. They race forty times a year, in a manner that, over the past quarter-century, has become no less miraculous as it has become familiar: a short-legged, barrel-chested, sixty-five-year-old man with a rocklike jaw, running at an 8:30-per-mile pace pushing a slight, forty-four-year-old quadriplegic in a twenty-seven-pound wheelchair.

Seven miles into his drive Dick pulls off the Pike to make his ritual Starbucks stop. "I shoulda bought stock in this place ten years ago;" he says with a grin. The barista starts Dick's drink the moment he steps in the door—a vente chai tea, extra hot. He has been careful with his diet ever since his heart attack three years ago. The scare caught the extremely fit Dick by total surprise, as have several other setbacks the Hoyts have faced of late. Last December, a gale raked New England, sending a tree through Dick's roof and into his living room. Days later the lift on Rick's specially designed van broke down, necessitating the purchase of a new rig. Then, just before Christmas, Dick needed arthroscopic surgery on his left knee to repair cartilage damage, the first serious injury of his twenty-nine-year running career. The knee is still healing, and has kept Dick from running for a month, his longest inactive stretch ever. The Boston Marathon is only three months away.

Dick's tea is ready, but just before he turns to head to the door, he spots the Starbucks manager and asks him if the store might contribute to the Easter Seals fund-raising drive he has launched in conjunction with the Boston Marathon. "We want to raise a million dollars," Dick tells him. The manager pledges his support. Smiling, Dick heads out the door, back to his van, and back on the Pike.

He's drinking his tea and talking about races and running while changing lanes frequently and making great time getting to Boston. By 10:00 A.M. he's steering off the expressway and threading through the streets near Boston University. He parks near Rick's building, takes an elevator up five floors, and moves down a long corridor to Rick's apartment. He puts a key in the lock and turns. He opens the door and steps into the hallway.

"Good morning, Rick!"

———————•———————

The athletic phenomenon that is known as Team Hoyt began one spring day in 1977. Rick was fifteen at the time and came home from school asking his dad if they could run a five-mile road race together in their town of Westfield, Massachusetts, to benefit a local college athlete who'd been paralyzed in an auto accident. It was a strange request considering Rick's situation.

Cerebral palsy is a debilitating condition often caused by complications during pregnancy or at birth. In Rick's case, the umbilical cord got tangled around his neck, cutting off the oxygen supply to his brain and causing irreparable damage. Aside from his head, the only other parts of his body he can voluntarily move even slightly are his knees. His muscles chronically contract, hence the need for muscle relaxants. He can't control his arms, which jerk and wave spasmodically. He has a "reverse tongue," meaning he drools and reflexively expels food and drink, so he can't eat on his own. His head is usually tilted, his smile lopsided, but genuine, accompanied by a mischievous glint. He can't speak at all, but because he can move his head, he can communicate with the help of a specially designed computer. As a cursor moves across a screen filled with rows of letters, Rick highlights which letter he wants by pressing his head against a narrow metal bar attached to the right side of the wheelchair. When he completes a word and then a thought—a tediously slow process—a voice synthesizer verbally produces it.

At the time Rick asked to run that race, Dick was a forty-year-old nonrunner. When he and Rick got to the event, organizers saw the wheelchair, the disabled son, and the middle-aged dad and gave them a look that said, "You two won't make it past the first corner." They didn't know Dick. It wasn't in his nature to quit a job he'd started. And besides, by that first corner, Rick was having too much fun. They ran the entire five miles, and didn't finish last. Afterward, a wild grin lit up Rick's face. Later he tapped out: "Dad, when I'm running, it feels like I'm not handicapped."

Dick had a slightly different reaction. "After that race I felt disabled—I was pissing blood for a week," he says. "But we knew we were on to something. Making Rick happy was the greatest feeling in the world."

Running made Dick happy too. A career Army guy, he felt like he was back in basic training again, breezing through a forced march while the other guys struggled and bitched. And, like the military, running was structured. If you followed the program, you got faster. Dick bought a pair of running shoes and researched a training schedule. Judy, Rick's mother, located an engineer in New Hampshire to build a wheelchair modified for running, with three bicycle wheels and a foam seat molded to Rick's body. The Hoyts' first running chair was produced for $35, and its basic design forms the template for all the racing chairs the men have subsequently used.

Since 1977, Rick and Dick Hoyt have completed more than nine hundred endurance events around the world, including sixty-four marathons and eight Ironman triathlons. They've run their hometown Boston Marathon twenty-four times, and plan to do their twenty-fifth on April 17. With a marathon PR of 2:40:47, and a 13:30 personal best for the Hawaii Ironman World Championship, they are the furthest things from charity cases. Just consider how they managed the 1999 Hawaii Ironman. After completing the 2.4 mile swim (for triathlons, Rick lies in an eight-foot Zodiac raft, Dick pulling him with a strap fastened around his waist), their brakes froze with 30 miles left in the 112-mile bike leg, and lacking a replacement part they had to wait more than an hour for the mechanic's truck. When the repair was finally completed, Dick asked the wind-blasted and sunburnt Rick if he wanted to continue. (Rick rides on a specially constructed seat that fits on the bike's handlebars.) Rick instantly nodded yes. So they soldiered through the bike phase in last place, and then transitioned into the marathon, their strongest event. There seemed little hope of completing the run by midnight, the deadline for official finishers. But feeling stronger as the night wore on, Rick and Dick passed dozens of runners and powered across the finish line with forty-five minutes to spare. They had run the notoriously difficult marathon leg in a remarkable 3:30.

Over the course of their quarter-century-long career, the Hoyts' incredible athletic achievements have made them, arguably, the most famous distance runners in America. They've met Ronald Reagan and Rudolph Giuliani, appeared on *Oprah,* and been the subject of a full-length documentary. In 1996, during the Boston Marathon's centennial celebration, the Hoyts ranked tenth in a poll of the most influential runners in marathon history—a list that included such legends as Bill Rodgers and Joan Samuelson. Dick has become a sought-after motivational speaker, making fifty appearances a year before corporate groups. Inevitably, after such speeches, Dick will hear the same well-meaning questions: *How do you and Rick communicate during a race? What happens if Rick has to go to the bathroom?* And, of course, *How much longer can you do this?* When the questions come up, he replies readily and cheerfully. "We feel real good. . . we love what we're doing. . . we've got no plans for quitting." But the questions, and the implication that Team Hoyt's run has to end at some point, still rankle.

The fact is, Dick Hoyt can expect to keep hearing the questions, especially after the heart attack, the knee surgery, the missed training. All that, and Dick turns sixty-six in June. Twenty-four Bostons have passed. How many more are really likely?

People can keep asking that question, Dick insists, but if they do, it means they don't know what drives the distance runner.

———————————•———————————

A few minutes after arriving at Rick's apartment, Dick lifts his naked, 110-pound son off his bed as if he weighed no more than a case of beer and sits him on the toilet. Dick is built like a catcher, his position as a star high school baseball player (he had a tryout with the Yankees, who rejected him, ironically, because he was too slow a runner), with a stocky frame and heavy legs featuring such exceptional muscular definition that his physical therapist jokes that he ought to model for an anatomy class.

Rick has trained himself to use the bathroom just twice a day, upon rising and retiring, a boon to his father and personal care attendants. (Similarly, Rick doesn't ingest fluids during marathons or shorter road races; during triathlons, he drinks only at the transition areas.) Lifting Rick again, Dick places him in the steaming water of the bathtub, where he bathes and shaves him. The water feels good. Rick gives a crooked smile of pleasure. Although he looks childlike sitting in the tub, his shoulders are surprisingly broad. Dick explains that the chronic contraction caused by Rick's spastic condition, along with the stress and stimulation of his athletic career, have given him excellent muscle tone. Paradoxically, Rick emanates an air of health and well-being.

"The human performance lab at Boston Children's Hospital wants to study Rick," Dick says. "His life expectancy is the same as any other man his age."

As he works, Dick talks quietly about the weather, last night's Celtics game, and his recent visit to the physical therapist for a checkup on his knee. "Jackie says I'm ahead of schedule," he says, toweling Rick's close-cropped, gray-flecked hair.

Dick originally injured his left knee in San Diego last November. The two were running with students from an elementary school through a bumpy field when Dick twisted the knee, tearing cartilage. Then, a few weeks later, when the Hoyts were in Florida for a race, their hotel's fire alarm sounded in the middle of the night. It was almost certainly a false alarm and another man—even another father—might have turned over in bed and gone back to sleep. But Dick didn't have that luxury. He got Rick into his wheelchair and humped down a narrow fire escape. While making one of the tight turns, Dick again twisted his knee. There was no denying this injury, and three days before Christmas he underwent surgery. Thus the doctors' orders not to run for a month.

Dick lifts Rick into his wheelchair and guides him to the kitchen table. The walls are covered with running memorabilia, including a quilt stitched out of T-shirts from 1980s-vintage road races, and a photo of Rick and Dick being greeted by then-President Reagan. Dick pours orange juice into a tumbler and, for the next twenty minutes, feeds it sip by sip to Rick, palpitating his jaw and neck with a milking-like motion to assure the juice stays down. Each moment ministering to Rick requires exacting effort, but his father never seems to lose patience.

"I was never angry or resentful about the hand we were dealt," Dick says. "People assume that I work out my rage through running, but that's not the case."

———————●———————

Rick Hoyt is one of an estimated 760,000 Americans who suffer from cerebral palsy. Unlike such crippling conditions as spinal cord injuries or Parkinson's disease, cerebral palsy research currently offers little hope of a cure. Through technology, physical therapy, counseling, and prodigious work, however, the condition can be managed. Perhaps the best indicator that Rick has successfully dealt with his condition is that in 1993 he completed a special education degree from Boston University, though it was an arduous process. A PCA had to sit with him through every class, taking notes, and then reading assignments aloud to him. He had to communicate with professors through the voice synthesizer. With such impediments, he could only take two classes a semester and he needed nine years to complete the degree.

Still, a college degree was hardly what Judy and Dick Hoyt expected from their firstborn when he arrived in January 1962. One pediatrician told the couple that their new son, his condition classified as nonverbal spastic quadriplegia, would be a vegetable for the rest of his short and miserable life; place him in an institution, the doctor recommended, and, in effect, forget him. Judy and Dick adamantly refused, though the first weeks and months with their severely disabled boy were unquestionably hard ones.

Judy and Dick had met in high school in North Reading, a community fifteen miles north of downtown Boston. She was a cheerleader and he was captain of the football team. The sixth of ten children, Dick was always a demon for work. At the age of eight he was earning money by odd jobs, and at sixteen he was running a crop farm. He taught himself masonry and other construction skills. After high school he joined the National Guard. He loved basic training—the order, the challenge, the physical rigor—and decided to make the military his career. The army placed him in the Nike missile program, assigning him to posts around New England.

When Rick was on his way, two years after they had been married, the couple looked forward to having a boy who would grow up to play catcher like his old man and go fishing with his grandfather. Instead, when he arrived, he couldn't manage a newborn's cry. Judy was crushed, and fell into a deep depression. "I hated Dick, and I hated all the mothers in the hospital and all my friends who were mothers of babies that were not handicapped," Judy says in the Hoyts' biography, *It's Only a Mountain*. "My feelings kept seesawing from hate to denial for months. . . . Rick couldn't suck, he couldn't even open his little clenched fists. He was tight, tight, tight. We had to force him to eat every two hours just to keep him alive. We would wake him up by pinching the bottom of his feet."

Judy soon recovered from the depressive bout, and insisted, along with Dick, on raising Rick at home. She started to fight for her son's rights and those of other disabled individuals. After earning a degree in special education, she helped establish a summer camp for children with disabilities, and she battled endlessly to enroll and keep Rick in Westfield's public schools. While an estimated two-thirds of people with cerebral palsy suffer some degree of mental retardation, Judy says she could tell just by looking at Rick's eyes as a baby that he had an active mind. "His eyes would follow me around the room. My son was intelligent. He was alive inside."

As Judy worked this front, Dick was busy with his military career, rising through the enlisted ranks to attend Officer Candidate School and eventually attain a rank of lieutenant colonel. Nights and weekends, to pay for Rick's wheelchairs and other necessities, he moonlighted on masonry jobs. But for all their varied activities, Judy and Dick tried to maintain a typical family life. Rick's two younger brothers, Rob and Russ, both healthy, were taught to treat their older brother as normal as possible. Rick played goalie in neighborhood hockey games. Dick or the brothers would tie the goalie stick to the boy, then steer him in his wheelchair as he tried to block shots in the crease. Rick would go wild with each blocked shot. There would also be family hiking trips. Dick would drape Rick over his shoulders and carry him up mountains.

Then came that race in Westfield in 1977, and the family's life changed forever. The epiphany of that first race fed a desire to do other races around New England. But just because the Hoyts wanted to run more didn't mean they were necessarily welcomed by the running community. At a 10-K in Springfield, Massachusetts, Dick remembers getting snubbed by the other athletes. "They shied away from us as if they thought they were going to catch a disease," Dick recalls. The race officials were even less hospitable. "The officials said they didn't fit because Dick was pushing him," Judy remembers in the Hoyts' biography. "Dick did it 'differently' than all the other runners. The wheelchair athletes didn't want them because Rick wasn't powering his own chair, and the able-bodied runners said, 'You're just going to get in the way. Why do you want to push this kid of yours who doesn't talk and just sits in the wheelchair?'"

Judy was there to watch the two at all their races, strongly supporting them through the early stages of their running career, when even some people questioned Dick's motives. "I got maybe twenty or twenty-five letters," Dick says. "Parents with disabled kids saw the stories about us, and they assumed that running was my idea, not Rick's. They thought I was using him to get publicity for myself."

Four years after their first race, Dick and Rick sought to run the 1981 Boston Marathon, but again met resistance. They were told that they needed to meet a qualifying time, just like any other runner officially entered in the race. There would be no exceptions, even for a guy pushing his kid in a wheelchair. "The Hoyts were proposing a nontraditional form of participation and, at the time, any change at Boston was a big deal," says Jack Fleming, spokesman for the Boston Athletic Association, organizers of the marathon. Fleming, who was not with the BAA at the time, adds, "It wasn't just Rick and Dick; the same thing had happened with women running for the first time, and then professionals."

Team Hoyt decided to run the 1981 race unofficially, as bandits, and clocked a remarkable debut marathon time of 3:18. They ran unofficially again in 1982, going under three hours for the first time (2:59), and then shaved another minute off in 1983. Still, no waiver came from the BAA. Finally, in October 1983, they went to Washington, D.C., to run the Marine Corps Marathon, looking to clock a 2:50, the time Boston required for runners in Rick's twenty-to-twenty-nine age group (even though Dick, who was doing all the running, was forty-three and would have qualified with a 3:10). On a cold, rainy morning, they ran 2:45:30. They officially raced the Boston Marathon the following spring and have run all but one since, becoming two of the event's most popular participants. "They personify the race as much as the elite athletes do," says Fleming. "Besides being inspirational role models, they are also quintessential New England guys. The crowds love them."

In those early years, Judy proudly watched as Rick and Dick's celebrity grew with each Boston or with their first Hawaii Ironman in 1989. Her pride, though, faded as Dick began assuming more responsibilities for their son and, over time, supplanted Judy as Rick's primary caregiver. Rob, the Hoyts' middle son, says he can understand how Judy must have hurt. "I think my mother had a hard time with all the attention that my father got through running," says Rob, forty-two, who lives in Holyoke, Massachusetts. "The accolades seemed to come much thicker and faster for him than they had with her. She had been everything for Rick. My mother got a nonspeaking spastic quadriplegic through high school and then through college, and now that role was taken by my father, and in a much more public manner."

Judy's frustration and alienation culminated in 1992, when Dick and Rick completed a 45-day, 3,753-mile, bike-and-run trek across the United States. Her men's interest in running had morphed into a time-consuming obsession. After thirty-four years of marriage, she and Dick divorced in 1994.

After so many years, Dick tries not to dwell on what happened to the couple's marriage. "I know that Rick's and my involvement in running and racing was hard on Judy," he says. "First, because of all the attention that got put on me, and second, because, for all the time she spent around the sport, she never understood distance running—why Rick would want to spend all that time on the road, and why I would insist on going to bed at nine o'clock on a Saturday evening so I would be fresh to race the next morning."

Today, Judy lives in Union, Connecticut, just a few miles from Dick's house, but she avoids contact with him. She visits Rick once every three months or so, but no longer attends Dick and Rick's races. Her animosity toward Dick is still fresh. "I fear that Dick is going to drop dead some day in the middle of a marathon, and I just pray that Rick doesn't go down with him," she says one recent afternoon while sitting in her kitchen. "Why should Rick suffer more, and put himself at risk, just to please his father?"

———————●———————

It's just about noon as Dick pushes Rick through the parking garage of his apartment building and over to Rick's new van. Dick had shopped carefully and found the slightly used vehicle, with a working lift, at a dealer near his house. Dick lowers the lift, eases Rick on to it, and then works the lever. Staring into a private middle distance, Rick rises into the van. Dick snaps the chair's wheels into the locks on the van floor and fastens the shoulder belts so that Rick will ride securely.

Still not totally familiar with how the van maneuvers, Dick spends the next several minutes hassling it out of the garage; the customized raised roof clears the garage ceiling only by a few inches. He must back up and pull forward repeatedly to get past a car that is parked illegally in the exit lane. Once out of the garage, he retraces his route to the Mass. Pike and points the van west, back toward Holland. In the back Rick listens to NBA scores on the radio.

As they get close to home, Dick stops at a Greek pizza joint to pick up a couple of oven-baked grinders. The shop owner is a friend of Dick's, and with the sandwiches he sends along a flagon of homemade ouzo.

Once inside the house and settled in the kitchen, Dick sets the ouzo aside. He purees Rick's grinder in a food processor and then spoons it into his mouth. In between spoonfuls, Dick takes bites out of his own sandwich, and talks about what's planned for the year ahead. After the Boston Marathon, he explains, he'll begin serious training for the Hawaii Ironman in October. He and Rick are both eager to vindicate themselves after what happened in the 2003 race, when they wiped out at the eighty-five-mile mark of the bike leg.

"The last thing I remember, we were gliding into a water stop," Dick says. "I still don't know what happened. Most likely we skidded on an empty water bottle. Anyway, when I came to, we were both on the road, and blood was gushing from Rick's forehead. An ambulance took him to the emergency room. The doctors there were concerned because of all the blood and the fact that Rick was a quadriplegic. I kept telling them he was okay, but they insisted on taking fifty-two X-rays. Later, I got a bill from the hospital for $6,000. I refused to pay it, of course."

Hawaii, though, is still nine months away. As always at this time of year, the two are focusing on Boston. Rick and Dick prepare for the marathon by running several half-marathons from January through March. Because Dick trains solo during the week, typically running about eight miles a day, he relies on the half-marathons for building upper-body strength, and adjusting to pushing Rick and the wheelchair. He frets over the missed training.

"I've put on seven pounds since my knee operation," Dick says. "I'm heavier now than I've been in years, although the weight should come off pretty quickly once I start running again." He frowns at his grinder. Watching what he eats isn't always easy, as much as he has tried since the heart attack.

Midway through a half-marathon in the winter of 2003, as he and Rick prepared for that year's Boston, Dick felt an unfamiliar tickling sensation in his throat, along with an unusual build-up of saliva. The sensation passed, and they finished the race without difficulty. But the phenomenon recurred at races over the next few weeks. Dick consulted his doctor, who administered an EKG.

"A day later I'm driving to my gym when my cell phone rings," Dick recalls. "It's my doctor. She asks me, 'Where you going?' I tell her, 'I'm going to work out.' She says, 'No you're not. You're coming straight to the hospital for a stress test. The EKG showed that you had a heart attack.' My problem is strictly hereditary—high cholesterol. She said that if I wasn't in such good shape, I'd probably be dead by now." The stress test indicated he needed an angioplasty. That procedure was done just days before the Boston Marathon, and meant Team Hoyt would miss the race for the first time in twenty-two years.

While Dick tells the story, Rick listens intently. His eyes flicker and his right arm jerks in a slow, almost graceful fashion.

Word got out about Dick's heart attack, and then he began getting calls from around the country from people offering to push Rick in his place. One running club offered to bring in twenty-six people, and each would push the chair for a mile. "They said they would consider it an honor," Dick says. "I left the decision up to Rick. He said no. Team Hoyt was exactly that, a team. We would run, or not run, together."

Rick's decision echoed one his father had made many times before. Shortly after the pair began running—as soon as Dick's vast latent talent for the sport manifested—people suggested that he should launch a concurrent solo career. If Dick ran so fast pushing a 140-pound load, the reasoning went, imagine what he could do unencumbered. But Dick declined to compete without his son. "The only reason I race is Rick," he says. "I've got no desire to do this on my own."

Dave McGillivray, the race director of the Boston Marathon and a close friend of the Hoyts, thought that if Dick had competed solo, he could have become a world-class age-group runner. In fact, it was McGillivray who first suggested that Dick try triathlons. "Maybe Dick has been fooling us all these years," McGillivray says. "Maybe Rick has been his big advantage, and not his handicap. Look at Dick's stride when he's pushing the chair—it's amazingly clean, he's doing a minimum of pounding, and with both hands on the chair he's always well balanced. He's always leaning forward, even when he's climbing a hill. Of course, he's also pushing 140 pounds. If there were a real competitive advantage, you'd see hundreds of guys in marathons pushing baby joggers. But you don't see that. In fact, after twenty-five years, and all the publicity, only a few have ever tried."

And that's okay, because watching the Hoyts roil down Commonwealth Avenue in the final mile of the Boston Marathon can be a near mystical experience. The roars of the spectators reverberate off the brick buildings and swell behind the two men like a following wind. Dick bears down and begins to sprint. Rick writhes and jerks ecstatically, the screams of his fans shooting through him.

The event in Hopkinton in early January demonstrated the intense emotional bond that the Hoyts have forged with their fans. A local newspaper had gotten wind of their recent difficulties—Dick's knee surgery, the tree coming through the roof, Rick's van breaking down—and ran a story that seemed to suggest that the two had fallen on hard times. The Hopkinton Athletic Association started a funding drive and hundreds of people from around the country sent in checks—a poor old lady didn't buy a Christmas tree so she could send a few dollars, and an anonymous wealthy donor contributed $50,000.

When Dick learned about the size of the gift, his first impulse was to refuse it or funnel it into his Easter Seals drive. But ultimately, given the need for a new van and other things for Rick, he accepted the association's check for $90,000 and the accolades that came with it. He and Rick had sat quietly on the stage of the school auditorium and patiently listened to a series of speakers. There were tears and testimonials. The Hoyts were made honorary citizens of Hopkinton. A state senator read a proclamation. Bob Lobel, a popular Boston sportscaster, called Dick and Rick the greatest athletes in Boston over the last thirty years, greater than any of the Red Sox, Celtics, Patriots, or Bruins. "Rick and Dick are originals," Lobel told the crowd. "We will never see their likes again."

Twenty-four Bostons have passed. How many more are really likely?

"I can understand why people always wonder when I'm going to quit," Dick says, finally willing to offer more on this subject. "It's a natural question to ask a man my age. But I can honestly say that stopping never crossed my mind. And I know Rick feels the same way. What keeps us going is that we see how much good we're doing, and not just for disabled people. We have inspired a lot of able-bodied people to start running or try some other kind of exercise."

Like the Austin insurance executive who heard Dick speak at a company sales meeting. His talk on overcoming obstacles, whether physical or mental, so inspired her that she used not just his message but Dick himself to fight through a long marathon training run. "I've been sitting here brainstorming the past week and trying to come up with a way to show how much your presentation meant to all of us, not only in our professional lives, but personally," she later wrote Dick, "When I was running my longest prerace run, twenty-two miles, Saturday after the meeting, I kept picturing your face, and it truly helped keep me going." There are other stories like this, too many to count.

After finishing lunch, Dick wheels Rick into the living room and places him in his favorite spot by the bay window, where he can look out over the sloping lawn to the edge of Hamilton Reservoir. His father hooks him up to the computer and headpiece equipped with a mouse that rests just behind his right temple. Now it's Rick's turn to answer questions.

Letters appear on a small screen at Rick's eye level. He twitches his head to move the cursor through the letters, double-twitching when he wants to select one. Each twitch requires a concentrated effort. As he works, his arm waves spasmodically, occasionally getting caught in the computer wires.

He is asked, "Do you ever have a bad race?"

Rick considers for several moments, then sets to work. He scans down the letters, each twitch of his head accompanied by a small electronic beep, like a bird chirping. *Y*, he types. Then, three minutes later, *E*, and, after a similar interval, *S*.

The next question comes, but Rick isn't finished with the first one. *W* . . . three minutes . . . *H* . . . three minutes . . . *E* . . . three minutes, and so on for a half-hour. Rick communicates no sense of frustration or impatience. "*Yes, when the weather is too cold . . .*" finally appears on the screen. The reply is read aloud, but Rick still isn't finished. The twitches and chirps continue. And then the full reply sounds through the voice synthesizer. "Yes," the disembodied electronic voice says after several more long minutes, "when the weather is too cold and the women are too covered up."

Rick laughs, his face twisting into a grin, his shoulders shaking. Forty-five minutes after the first question, the next one comes.

"Do you ever regard running as an unhealthy obsession? Do you ever think you should stop or cut back?"

"*No. By running we are actually educating the public.*"

"Do you think that not being able to speak gives you a special insight into people?"

"*Yes. I understand them not in terms of running, but as far as general life.*"

"What do you do when you feel down or depressed?"

"*I just think about the poor people in the world.*"

The final, two-part question comes as dusk falls and Rick's father quietly enters the room to turn on a lamp. Three hours have passed since the Q&A started, roughly how long it takes Team Hoyt to run a marathon.

"Was fate at work at the time of your birth, and on that day nearly thirty years ago when you told your parents that you wanted to run? And do you think fate chose you to live such a confined life, but also one so free?"

Rick doesn't need the computer to answer this one. His face lights up. His whole body says yes.

heart

The human body can do so much.
Then the heart and spirit must take over.

~Sohn Kee-Chung, winner of the
1936 Olympic Marathon

The Battle of a Lifetime

Norman Harris, 1963

New Zealand's Murray Halberg is one of running's most unlikely champions. He had a distinctly awkward running style due to his paralyzed left arm, the result of an old rugby injury. But he also had a severe determination. After finishing a well-beaten 11th place in the 1956 Olympics 1,500 meters, Halberg vowed that his next trip to the Olympics would be different. He planned a race that would leave no regrets, leave nothing to chance, and prove who was the strongest man. Norman Harris, the noted British sportswriter, gives a memorable description of Halberg's race in the book *Lap of Honour*.

He went to the Rome Olympics with his young contemporary Snell. He was the complete opposite of Snell in build and nature; he was totally unlike Lovelock who had run with perfect poise twenty-four years before. He was an athlete without comparison in the history of New Zealand athletics, a man built like barbed-wire, who ran with ferocious determination.

His determination was his particular way of proving himself. With Murray Halberg it had been like this ever since the school football injury which had shattered and paralysed his left arm. In his early running days he had had to ask teammates to help him on with his blazer and to cut his meat for him. Always the arm was to cling uselessly to his body because his shoulder would carry it no longer. So this struggle began at the age of 17—a fight against Fate for which the only victory would be an Olympic title.

In 1956 he had stood watching the opening of the Melbourne Olympic Games moved to tears. He said: "If the final of the 1,500 metres was run right now, I could beat anyone in the world." When it was run, days later, he was well beaten. But he stood afterwards on the red cinder track, alone in the giant stadium, and vowed that when he returned to the Olympic track he would be victorious. When he returned it was to Rome in 1960. He had been beaten by the great at Melbourne, he had raced a dozen times in the wake of the magnificent Elliott. After running for so long in the shadow of the great, he sought his consecration in Rome.

All the thousands of miles in training, the long runs around the Waitakere Ranges near Auckland, and the sharp, successive sprint work on the track, so perfectly blended by his coach Arthur Lydiard, would culminate on Friday, September 2nd, the day of the 5,000 metres. The day had been fixed many years in advance, and on that day he would know that he was right.

From Norman Harris, 1963, *Lap of Honour: The Great Moments of New Zealand Athletics* (Wellington, New Zealand: Reed). Reprinted by permission of Penguin Group (NZ).

Training in the intense Roman heat he achieved the best training trials of his career. With him at every session was Lydiard, sent from Auckland by public subscription. Lydiard was able to tell Halberg exactly how hard to run each trial. When Halberg suggested, "About 13 mins 50 secs" for a three miles, Lydiard told him: "No, no. You'll have to break 13 mins 30 secs." This was world-class time for a race, yet in a solo training run Halberg recorded 13 mins 26 secs. Each lap was run exactly to plan. The day after, he ran three quarters of a mile in 3 mins 3 secs, the best of his career. Lydiard, the psychologist and friend as well as trainer, would tell him to "shoot off down to the Tiber and run along beside it for an hour" or to "come and have lunch with me in town." As the race approached Halberg was being mentally as well as physically freshened.

Yet all the time he retained his determination and his dedication. He kept his training times to himself and answered questions guardedly. Observers respected this. They regarded with awe the man who gave an overwhelming sense of inner toughness, who looked physically indestructible even with his withered arm.

Once his restraint was broken by an interviewer who asked, "Which men do you consider to be your most serious rivals?" The taciturn Halberg launched forth.

"Look," he said, "I'm not even considering any of those others. I think it's the worst thing in the world to go to the start being conscious of the record of this one or that one, because you're almost sure to pick the wrong man. I'm not going in there with any illusions—they must all be pretty good, otherwise they wouldn't be in the Games. I'm not going to build up some runner in my mind and then miss the really dangerous one. Remember at Berne in 1954 how Chataway followed Zatopek instead of Kuts?

"I don't care what the pace is or who tries to break records. I'm in there just to win. I don't care about world records anyway. You break one and the next week some Russian or other comes along and goes a bit faster, and that's that. But you win an Olympic title and no one can ever take that away from you. On a certain day after four years' preparation you're the best in the whole world. That takes some beating, I reckon. They remember you then."

Yet Halberg was not without a plan. In the days before the race he and Lydiard devised a strategy that was frightening in its very conception. At the last Olympics Vladimir Kuts had won the 10,000 metres with a series of persistent and savage sprints. Halberg's plan was going to be even more cruel. Towards the end of the race he would launch himself into a breakneck speed for a whole lap. He would hold this speed for as long as possible. It would gradually and inevitably fade until he and the whole field were drained of all their speed.

They would then have to run the last lap in a state of utter exhaustion, on rubber legs, gasping for breath. In 1930 Savidan was forced to run another lap after he had thought he had finished the six miles. Halberg would do the same thing—deliberately. In this great trial he was convinced that he could weather the punishment better than the others.

He realised that he would probably have a fair chance of winning with a straight-out last lap sprint of about fifty-four seconds. But the plan left nothing to chance. He would not be surprised by anyone, and after the race he would have no regrets. If he was the strongest man in the field his plan would prove it and ensure victory. It didn't really matter if his plan was known; the opposition would still have to be stronger than him to beat it. The Australians, Thomas and Power, would probably expect it. He had beaten them with similar tactics at the Cardiff Empire Games—except that then he had run steadily away to the finish, and this time it would be a slow and grim finish. All that was necessary for the plan to work was to have the early pace sufficiently strong. The opposition had to be tired enough for his move to hurt.

Where would he make the move? Probably with about three laps to go, Lydiard told him. Lydiard classed the opposition in two groups—the miler types and the distance men. The miler types had a fast finishing burst. The distance men could run steadily from start to finish. The types of abilities were seldom coordinated perfectly. Lydiard thought he had a man who had coordinated the endurance and speed by his training during ten years. He would take advantage of this late in the race. Somewhere between two and two and a quarter miles there would come a stage where the one-miler speed-men would be running out of steam and the distance men would be debating. The pace would drop as the field rested in preparation for the big effort of the last lap. And here Halberg would make his move.

Halberg knew his job when, in the middle of a hot afternoon on that Friday, he left the dressing-room and moved out on to the training track, one hour before the start of the 5,000 metres. He was one of twelve men who jogged or strode strongly around the training track to the accompaniment of surging cheering coming from the main stadium alongside. Of the twelve he knew two men well, the Australians Thomas and Power, but he had avoided the rest of his opposition—he hadn't wanted to end up respecting a man so much that he became worried by him. For this was a superb field.

There were three men from "Down Under," and the Kenyan runner Nyandika. The other eight were men from the Continental countries, countries that had produced the winner of every Olympic 5,000 and 10,000 metres, from the Finns in the first years through to the Russian Kuts. Of these eight men, three were from Germany. Grodotski had won the first of the four heats, Flosbach the second, and Janke the third. Each victory had been acclaimed by the 10,000 German students, assembled in a block on the first bend to chant for their men. The Germans could be expected to run as a team. Individually any of them could take the title—tall Grodotski with his long, blond hair, the slight Flosbach, and the big, dark man with the fast finish, Janke. So much for the Germans. Then there were one Russian, Artinyuk; the young Frenchman, Bernard; the old Hungarian campaigner, Iharos; the Pole with the great reputation, Zimny; and the local hero, Conti.

They were all moving around the track now. Each man warmed up by himself. As Halberg moved past, he saw only blank faces, drawn and pale. Already the tension was taking its toll. Halberg was not nervous, only restless. He did not want to speak to anyone. He had a job to be done and he wanted to be left alone to get on with it. In the dressing room he hadn't been able to sit still. Now he moved around the track like a caged lion.

Finally they were called across to wait in the shadow of the tunnel leading into the main stadium. They stood grouped there like gladiators awaiting the call into the arena. No one could look at anyone else. At last the rumbling from inside the stadium erupted into a huge, reverberating roar, then sustained applause. Officials and athletes came bursting back through the tunnel, shouting the news that Snell had won the 800 metres. Halberg, inspired, knew that what his friend Peter could do, he also could do in the next event. The gate was opened and they were led through the tunnel, into the blinding brilliance of the Stadio Olimpico, before the eyes of 60,000 people. With relief they strode up and down the finishing straight, separated once again and not having to avoid each others' eyes. By the time they were called to the mark they were ready for the 5,000 metres and Halberg was ready for the battle of a lifetime.

When, at the sound of the gun, they pounced forward, Halberg delayed and settled in last. He was not going to worry about disputing the lead until the time of his move. At the Melbourne Olympics he had finished the 1,500 metres battered by pumping elbows and disappointed after being hemmed in. He had never complained; to every probing question he had replied brusquely, "Experience. Just experience." So now he ran last. Up front he could see the troubles, the blocking and the checks. The first lap was very fast 62.3 secs in a race where a fast pace averages 66 or 67 seconds a lap. They ran the first half-mile in the cracking pace of 2 mins 8 secs.

Lap times are not announced at Olympic Games but Halberg could gauge the pace exactly. At the head of the straight, light bulbs showed the time for each kilometre. After the first kilometre Halberg looked up and he knew that the pace was fast enough for his plan to work. He did not need to look again.

After the sudden rush at the start, with everyone looking at everyone else to see who would lead, it was the tall, ascetic-looking Pole, Zimny, who made the decision to go to the front and set a strong pace. At the first mile the little Australian, Albert Thomas, took over without increasing the pace. Zimny soon took it back again and moved with increasing tempo through the second mile. The three Germans were not yet moving as a team. Perhaps it was because Flosbach was a West German while Janke and Grodotski were from the East. Anyway, Flosbach seemed to be tiring slightly. The French were looking to Michel Bernard, and his early running seemed to justify it. And as they all went round in Indian file, Halberg shared last place with the Italian, Conti, who, paying the price of his crowd-stirring win in his heat, was struggling now.

In the eighth lap Conti dropped back. Still the skeletal figure of Halberg trailed the bunch. While the men up front strode strongly on, Halberg circled the track easily behind them all. He ran with a choppy stride and an insistent rhythm, like a rail-car on an endless bend.

He ran at the rear, until, on the seventh circuit, he saw the fair-haired Grodotski move quickly up. Halberg pulled out from the rear and headed up towards the leaders, settling down alongside the Hungarian, Iharos. Ahead were Zimny, still leading, the Australian, Power, and Grodotski. Halberg was in position for his big move, only one lap away. Then suddenly Power dashed to the front. For a moment he seemed to be going away, but he couldn't keep going. The field lengthened their stride with this burst, the pack began to stretch—Thomas, Artinyuk, Flosbach and Iharos were lost forever off the back. The contenders were reduced to seven. Two of them were Germans, Grodotski and Janke. The chanters in the German sector became strident: "*Ja, Ja, Ja, Ja,*" they insisted. Just as Armin Hary's 100 metres victory the day before had been greeted with roars of "*Ha-ray! Ha-ray!*" they waited now for Grodotski to take the lead so that they could call his name.

The field turned out of the back straight, around the bend towards the home straight. After Power's move they were resting, just as Lydiard had predicted, in preparation for the final drive two laps away. Ahead was the straight, and then there were three laps. The straight would be Halberg's killing ground. As they entered it he slipped out and moved quietly past Grodotski, then Zimny, then Power. One second he was easing past Power's shoulder. The next second he was away, a black eagle taken flight. He sprinted for fully 220 yards, down the straight, around the bend, past the German chorus. It was not frantic, violent—he seemed to be drifting away. Ten yards had been gained with shocking speed just in the length of the straight.

His move brought startled gasps from the crowd, then roars of applause. Up in the Press-box Americans were saying, "The guy's gone mad. Doesn't he know how many laps there are left?" Halberg knew how many laps—this one, really fast, then another one as fast as possible, and then the grim last lap. Now, with the last lap in mind, he was desperately accumulating a lead to hold against that time. The ten yards widened to fifteen by the back straight. The field, dazed by the move, had made no real chase. At last Grodotski started off in pursuit. He pulled away from the others but he could not hold Halberg. Halberg completed his violent lap in the time of 61 seconds. By now he had stacked up twenty yards with which to hold off Grodotski.

This time as he came past the German sector it was silent. Halberg prepared himself for another lap as hard as he could, a lap which would use up all the speed he had left in him and bring him down to the sheer pith of his strength. His pace slackened only slightly. Grodotski seemed still dazed from the initial shock, unable to make the desperate decision to move up. The two ran the whole lap at exactly the same speed—64 seconds. Halberg was still twenty yards ahead, but as he came up to get the bell he was rolling his head in distress and baring his teeth. Grodotski began to hack down the precious twenty yards, but slowly and tensely. The excitement had gone; now it was sheer drama, and 60,000 people, gripped with anxiety, could only stare open-mouthed from now to the finish.

Now Halberg was throwing glances continually over his shoulder. Perhaps they were encouraging Grodotski. Down the back straight the German, with his prancing stride, his long blond hair bouncing in the air, had reduced the twenty yards to fifteen. Halberg, looking back again, seemed to falter slightly. Yet he did not stumble. The lead was twelve yards.

Around the bend they came—the little figure in black carrying a twisted arm, and Grodotski, coming at him. Two-thirds of the crowd were convinced that the little figure would never make it. He was throwing his head around with every few strides to look for Grodotski.

They were desperate glances. Halberg was watching for the German to come up to his shoulder. He was ready to turn for a final tooth and claw battle of utter ferocity. If he was physically incapable, then it would come from the subconscious . . .

Then he was out of the corner, the tape was in sight, and he still had ten yards over Grodotski. They could not take ten yards away from him in the final home stretch. His face was masked with strain, but he mustered a final drive down the straight, still running with that insistent, quick-rocking rhythm, like some clockwork toy that would never quite run down. The only thing that would stop it would be the tape. He reached his haven, clutched the tape in his hands, and fell on his back inside the track. Eight yards later Grodotski followed him, and collapsed beside him. Then the others, shattered by the sledge-hammer blow of that violent lap, were coming in and sprawling everywhere.

Snell came running over and clasped Halberg's hand between both of his, but Halberg made no response. His body was shaking quickly with his breathing, like a fish just taken from water. Some thought that he had gone beyond the limits of his endurance. But then, as he lay stretched out there with the tape entwined in his fingers, there could be seen on his face the faintest trace of a smile. The battle that had lasted for ten years had been won. He had done it by taking a day fixed years in advance, and on that day being invincible.

" . . . On a certain day after four years' preparation you're the best in the whole world. That takes some beating, I reckon. They remember you then."

Through the Tunnel

Joan Benoit Samuelson with Sally Baker, 1987

The details of Joan Benoit's story are the stuff of legend: Her knee injury in 1984, followed by surgery just days before the Olympic Trials marathon; her miraculous recovery to win that race; and then, in the Los Angeles Olympics marathon, her courageous decision to break out alone and early in an attempt to steal the race. But in the following excerpt from her autobiography *Running Tide*, we hear Joan Benoit's own story of the race and see the unique personality behind her achievement.

I had every reason to think that the sentiments my parents inscribed in the *New Yorker Diary* they gave me for Christmas would be affirmed in 1984. My mother wrote: "May this year be as good to you as the year before. Take care of yourself and enjoy each day. Love, Dad and Mother." In spite of the hubbub at home, I was living as quietly as I could and putting in over a hundred miles of training every week. I knew I was approaching the best shape of my life.

In February I ran the 3,000m at the Olympic Invitational track meet at the Meadowlands in New Jersey. Suzanne Girard won; I was second by a very close margin, an adequate performance. My training was not yet in high gear and I didn't feel as fast as I had in 1983, when I lost the same race to Patti-Sue Plummer by an even closer margin.

I was careful to tell my friends (and myself) that I was putting in a lot of solitary training miles, aiming for the marathon trials. I wanted only to make the Olympic team—anything more would be gravy. My deepest wishes stayed buried; it wouldn't do to get all worked up about an Olympic race I might never run. Friends playfully slugged me on the shoulder and as much as said, "But we all know you'll be in L.A." The fact was, I didn't know. I wanted to get to Olympia, Washington, for the trials. L.A. could take care of itself.

On March 17 I drove to Cape Elizabeth so I could run the twenty-mile loop that was the best indicator of my fitness. I'd been running that loop since the first time I tried the distance; it was completely familiar. When I ran it well, I knew I was in excellent condition. This day I expected to do better than ever: my training was paying off by then and I felt glorious.

At Meetinghouse Hill in South Portland, about seventeen miles into the run, I had a sensation in my knee. It was as if a spring were unraveling in the joint. The knee became sore immediately and I veered off my normal course and altered my stride. I hobbled along for two miles, but I finally had to start walking a quarter mile from home. The farther I went, the tighter the knee got—something seemed to be obstructing its movement.

When I reached my parents' house I was a wreck. By some act of Providence Mom wasn't there to see my condition; every time I suffer an injury she feels the pain. I don't think she could have stood seeing me panic. This was the most frightening moment of my life, and the first time I ever panicked as an athlete. I knew the problem wasn't muscular: it happened too quickly. One moment I was fine, the next I was limping. Muscle injuries give you the luxury of adequate warning, unless the muscle is turned or pulled abruptly. Nothing in my fluid running that day would have led to a muscle strain. This was something alarmingly, paralyzingly different. I wasn't thinking clearly, but I remember the fear vividly. I was like an artist who crafts a masterpiece over the course of ten years and then sees it consumed in a sudden fire. She wonders what the ashes will reveal and is afraid she won't be able to replace the work of art.

Bob Sevene was visiting his mother in Massachusetts and planned to be in Freeport that afternoon. (He was still living and coaching in Eugene and would stay at Athletics West until the fall of 1986.) I couldn't wait that long. I called him from the heap I was in and told him what had happened. He kept his voice steady and suggested I take it easy. Sev was once quoted as saying, "My problem has always been holding runners back, getting them to cut down on mileage or take a day off. All runners seem to push themselves too hard."

Sev calmed me down and convinced me to call Dr. Leach. It was Friday afternoon, though, so I decided to stay off the knee for a day and see how it felt on Sunday. If it didn't improve, I'd call Dr. Leach on Monday.

I walked around all day Saturday and the knee didn't bother me, so on Sunday I tried an eleven-mile run. The knee tightened up and became sore in the last mile, but I was optimistic enough to think it was getting better. On Monday morning I ran a very familiar six-mile loop in Freeport and felt okay. But that afternoon I set out on the same loop and hadn't gone a half mile before the pain stopped me. I arranged to see Dr. Leach the next day.

I wanted to say to him, "I think there's something floating around in there, obstructing the joint," but I'm not an orthopedic surgeon and it wasn't my place to tell him what to look for. He injected the knee with cortisone and told me to back off for a few days. He said, "I'm going to be in charge of the [Olympic] team physicians and I want to see you with a medal around your neck." That made two of us.

I felt fine for the next couple of weeks. I ran fifteen to twenty miles daily and did track and Nautilus workouts besides. Naturally, I thought the problem was solved. The knee was still a bit tender, but I could run with it, and that was the only thing that mattered.

Everything came tumbling down on April 10. I took a long run in the morning and, always hopeful, recorded in my diary, "No knee pain." At seven that evening I had a track workout at Harvard, where I ran three sub-five-minute miles and felt terrific. I stopped to talk to John Babington before doing my cool-down laps, and when I began running again, there was the lock. It got tighter with each lap. The next morning I went out for a ten-mile run with a friend. I got to the subway station on Commonwealth Avenue near Boston College and had to stop; I wanted to gut it out, but something in the knee just wasn't right. I apologized to my friend and told him to go ahead because I'd have to walk from there. Later I called Dr. Leach and said I hated to be a pain in the neck, but I thought he'd better take another look at the pain in my knee. He gave me an appointment for the next day.

Always wanting to test myself, I ran twelve miles Thursday morning before seeing Dr. Leach. My diary entry says it all: "Last 3+ miles were completely miserable. Would have walked if I had had the time but was probably going through the motions of running slower than I would have walked. A real effort to lift my right leg over a twig." And that was no exaggeration—I remember stopping at every curb to step off with my left foot and drag the right down behind it.

Dr. Leach gave me another shot of cortisone. We both knew time was running out: the trials were slated for May 12 and it was now April 12. He told me to take three or four days off. As always, I treated his words as gospel; I could only hope that the rest and medication would solve the problem.

I swam and lifted weights to stay in shape; the stationary bicycle bothered the knee. I knew I wasn't getting the kind of cardiovascular workout I needed to keep my edge, but anything was better than sitting around brooding. Lots of times I thought, "Why bother to go on? This isn't going to work"; then I'd go exercise to lift the depression. I couldn't give in to the fear that was just waiting for a weak moment to break through and take over.

On April 14 I flew to Tucson for meetings with the Dole sales force. I had just signed on as a spokesperson and fitness consultant for Dole pineapple juice. In Arizona I really began to fret; the knee was tightening up even while I walked, especially if I walked downhill. I spoke to the group on Monday and tried to run with them on Tuesday, but my mind was focused on my problem. I don't know how I got through those two days. After running on Tuesday I wrote, "Right knee not right. Tight, catching feeling seemed to subside a little into the run but certainly not to the extent that I could have opened stride enough to run smoothly. Flew to Eugene."

There are no further entries in my running log until the day of the Olympic trials. I couldn't bear to write about my problems. I tried to adjust to things as they arose, but all along something in my brain was muttering, "If we don't think about this, it might go away." Writing it would have put the lie to that hope.

Escaping to Oregon seemed like a good idea—maybe a few massage sessions and some physical therapy would work things out. Bob Sevene was at the airport to meet me, and we drove straight to Dr. Stan James's office, hoping he would be the miracle man I needed. Again, I wanted to come right out and say, "Listen, I know this is mechanical," but, again, how do you tell a highly respected orthopedic surgeon what to do? After he examined the knee he told me any number of things could be wrong and he didn't want to do anything rash, like operate, until I rested it for five more days.

Bob took me to the Athletics West office building and I had to fight back the tears all the way. When we got there I went to the ladies' room and broke down. Mary Angelico, with whom I would stay in Oregon, found me there and held me. I kept telling her I knew something was wrong and this wasn't the time for resting, not with the trials so close. "This is ridiculous," I sobbed. "I shouldn't be this upset. This is only running. I could be dying of cancer."

That was Wednesday. On Saturday I was so antsy I had to test things. Every day I didn't run robbed me of fitness, even though I was exercising however I could. I ran two or three miles on the Amazon Trails in Eugene with Bob Sevene before the knee shut down. I thought my heart would break.

On Easter Sunday I went to mass in the morning and asked God why He had sent this injury to me at this time. Why me? Why now? After praying those questions I looked across the church and saw Alberto Salazar. At first I was jealous of his health; Alberto had been prone to injuries in the past, but he was ready for the trials. Then, when my envy passed, I reconfirmed what I'd always believed: that God has a reason for everything He does. The whole situation was in His hands, not mine. I prayed, then, that if I couldn't run in the trials and Olympics, God would grant Alberto the two best races of his life.

The next day Stan James called Dr. Leach and consulted with him. I don't think he was comfortable with the ethical ramifications of taking over my case, but I was desperate and Leach was in Boston. After my history was carefully described to him, Stan decided to get an arthroscope into my knee and see what was wrong. That made me happier than I'd been in two months. Finally, there would be action—no more passive therapy. I think we were all worried that Stan might not find anything in there, which would mean I'd have the original problem plus a surgical wound, but I was sure the problem could be solved with surgery.

I think everyone figured there was no way I'd be able to run the marathon on May 12 but supposed I might be in shape for the 3,000 at the track trials in Los Angeles in June. I didn't have a great chance of making the team at that distance—I wasn't world class in the 3,000—but there was always hope.

That afternoon I ran with a brace made of wetsuit material on my knee, but the joint locked anyway. I called [my brother] Andy that night and said I was going ahead with surgery; he thought I should try more rest, and his doubts gave me a few seconds of pause, but then I said, "I have to be the one to decide what the risks are and whether they are worth taking."

The next day I was set up for surgery in a pre-op room and told I would wake up there or in Recovery. I was supposed to leave the hospital that day. But I regained consciousness in a regular hospital room. I was scared, thinking something major had been found in my knee and further surgery would be necessary. I lifted my head to take a look at my leg—it was wrapped in elastic bandages. That was a relief. In my doped-up condition, I'd almost believed they had lopped the leg off. There was no feeling in it, but as long as it was there I figured I could use it: I called Mary Angelico and asked her to pick me up on her way home from work so I could go running. She said, "Uh-huh, yeah, sure, Joanie," and hung up.

When my head was clear Stan James told me I was being held in the hospital overnight to keep the swelling to a minimum (he knew too well what I might do to his handiwork if he let me out of his sight). The procedure had turned up a fibrous mass, called a plica, which had become inflamed and interfered with the joint. Stan had to look carefully, scoping up and down each tendon, before he found it; the correction was prompt and uncomplicated.

He told me not to run until he saw me a week later, on the thirtieth. I could swim at the Eugene YMCA and pedal a stationary bicycle slowly, but that was the only exercise I was allowed.

I avoided reporters; I was afraid they might talk me out of trying to run. I knew my chances were slim, but as long as the possibility existed I needed all of my confidence to make the effort.

Which is where my fellow athletes came in. Many runner friends called me over the next few days, and there was a mountain of mail. Other athletes wrote to say they hoped an exception would be made for me if I couldn't run in the trials; one woman said: "If I could run as fast as you and qualify, I'd give you my berth."

In Beaverton on the twenty-ninth, the day before I had my appointment with Dr. James, I couldn't stand the suspense anymore; I ran a little and everything was fine. I worked out in the Nike weight room that afternoon, then drove to Eugene. The next day Dr. James gave me a green light to run if I promised to start slowly, which I did. The next day I roamed Eugene at a leisurely pace.

On May 2, however, I woke up saying, "I'm back to normal. I'm going to start running." The knee was fixed. I had to get on with it if I wanted to be on the starting line in Olympia on May 12. My daily schedule from then on was grueling. Mary would wake me at six a.m. and take me to the weight room, then she would do aerobics while I rode a bike or sat in the whirlpool. After that she dropped me off at the Y for a swim and one of my Athletics West teammates, Dan Dillon or Larry Mangan, picked me up from there and took me to a physical therapy session. I spent several hours a day in therapy and also ran as much as I could. Most days I didn't get back to the apartment until eleven at night. I was so eager to make up for lost time that I forgot my promise to Stan James and pushed myself harder than I had since the knee problem first cropped up. But I was still nervous about the knee and favored my right leg. The result was a pulled hamstring in the left leg. Instantly, the knee was downgraded from a major problem to something that wasn't even relevant anymore: if anything was going to keep me out of the trials now, it would be the hamstring.

My mood stayed upbeat; I tried to cope with the new emergency. I added hamstring treatment to my knee rehab therapy. Part of the therapy I could do at home with Tens, a form of electrical stimulation. Larry Standifer, a physical therapist, gave me a little black box with electrodes sticking out of it and told me how to attach them to the knee and hamstring. I was supposed to use the device when I had some free time, so I would clamp it on while Mary and I were eating dinner late at night. Once in a while I turned the juice up too high and my leg would start flopping all over the place as I yelled and fumbled for the knobs. For a person who didn't like quirky remedies, I was putting myself through a lot to regain my fitness.

Even with ice therapy as part of my routine, the leg was still sore. On May 4 I ran with Sev and Doug Brown, who at the time was Athletics West's team administrator, and though they maintained an easy pace, I could only stay with them for two miles. The next day I attended a track meet at Hayward Field at the University of Oregon. It was frustrating to watch people run smoothly when I couldn't think of competing. I was so desperate for a solution by then that Dick Brown, Mary Decker's coach at that time, introduced me to Jack Scott, who was attending the meet to tryout his Myopulse and Electron Acuscope. These were new treatments Mary had used with some success for pulls and tendonitis. Once again my attitude was "What have I got to lose?" I had a four-hour treatment that night and went for five days more of six to ten hours of treatment per day. In order to accommodate these long treatment sessions I had to cut out all activity except for early-morning swims.

I still didn't feel right, but I slowly started to run. On May 9, three days before the trials, I gave myself a short speech: "This is it. You have to go out and run at least fifteen miles. If you can't, there's no way you're going to run in the trials." I ran two repeat loops that day for a total of sixteen miles. I was so unsure of my footing that I had to concentrate to put one foot in front of the other—it was like working a marionette. My stride was way off; there was nothing fluid in my motion. Running was a huge effort, and I knew if I overdid it I could rip the hamstring. The one consolation—besides making my goal—was my strong cardiovascular condition.

I'd been on the phone daily [my fiancé] to Scott since the whole business began, of course, but that night he came to Eugene and I thought, "Now I'll be okay." Having him there to hold on to would make things turn out fine. The next morning we ran together and I felt wonderful.

Peter [my other brother] and Andy and Andy's wife, Stevie, came to watch me run in Olympia. Earlier in the week, before Scott had arrived, I had told them not to come because things didn't look promising. They arrived anyway, under the guise of a vacation in the Pacific Northwest.

Even as I was jogging to the starting line, I honestly didn't know whether I could manage the race. I don't think the other competitors gave me a chance of finishing. But when I spotted Scott and my brothers and sister-in-law climbing into the van that would take them to the first checkpoint, I vowed to pull it off somehow.

I began to run as conservatively as possible, because I felt immediate pain and weakness in the hamstring. I tried to ignore it by taking in the scenery on the quiet course as it wound through the state capital. It was easy to imagine that this was Maine—there was plenty of water to look at, crisp spring breezes blew, and I could pretend I was on a loop in Freeport. Only the spectators and my worries about the knee and the hamstring broke the pleasant reverie, because I wasn't aiming to win the race. Third place would be fine; the first three finishers would qualify.

For the first three or four miles I ran with the leaders and let them set the pace. Then Betty Jo Springs, who I thought would win, and I broke away from the pack. I passed her, she passed me, and we continued on that way until mile fourteen, never more than a couple of steps apart. At this point I took the lead for good. I knew I had to get well in front and hope my momentum would carry me to the finish line, since I could tell my legs wouldn't have anything left for a surge at the end. I still expected Betty Jo or maybe Julie Brown to pass me, but they never appeared.

In the last six miles I ran slower and slower, showing the disjointedness of my training. There were lots of turns in the course and I had to be especially careful about the way I planted my feet on them to avoid excess torque on the knee and hamstring. Miraculously, my legs held up and I finished first in 2:31:04. Julie Brown was second at 2:31:41, and Julie Isphording third.

When I crossed the finish line I broke into sobs in Sev's arms. The television people were right there, so I pulled myself together and told them what was in my heart: that without the support of family and friends, I wouldn't have made the race. They had crashed through my self-imposed isolation in the days preceding the race to tell me they were there with me. Theirs were the voices that spoke simple facts—that I would be valuable to them with or without Olympic dreams; that Maine was there waiting for me, as always; and that they would be taking every step with me at Olympia. Because I was buoyed by these people, I ran what I still consider to be the race of my life that day. They helped me find a miracle.

I've often been asked whether I think an exception should have been made for me if I hadn't been able to qualify in the trials. It is true that, given the time between the arthroscopic surgery and the Olympic Marathon, I would have had a chance to get healthy at a reasonable pace. I knew I'd be fine in another month. Fred Lebow, the director of the New York Marathon, told the press he thought both Alberto Salazar and I should get automatic marathon berths because we had world bests; Jacqueline Hansen, Doris Heritage Brown (the coach of the female Olympic qualifiers in Washington), and others who were highly respected in the sport put in their pleas, but the U.S. Olympic Committee held fast. Thank goodness. Even at my lowest ebb, I knew I should not ask for special treatment. Other athletes had experienced similar problems in previous years and the rules should not be changed. The trials are a tough school, but to choose Olympic teams on the basis of past records is to invite favoritism and politics.

———————•———————

Over the next several weeks in Maine my training was sluggish; the summer was unusually hot. But with the Olympic Marathon in early August it was easy to persuade myself to work hard. I traveled as infrequently as possible, preferring to put in my hundred-mile weeks on thoroughly familiar loops.

I did go to New York to appear with Grete Waitz on "Good Morning America." She was there for the L'eggs Mini, and even though I wasn't in the race, GMA thought it would be interesting to interview us together. Much was being made of the fact that the Olympics would be our first meeting as marathoners. We had breakfast after the show and talked about our training and the race in Los Angeles. By then Grete was very comfortable in the United States and her English was perfect, so she was more relaxed than I'd ever seen her. But we were both excited at the prospect of competing.

On June 17 I ran in the Olympic Trials Exhibition 10,000 meter race, which was held in the L.A. Coliseum. I won the event in 32:07, which convinced me that I was fully recovered. The race itself was symbolic, because it had not yet been approved as an Olympic event, but it will be included at Seoul in 1988. Symbolic or not, I won by a considerable margin and was eager to come back to Los Angeles the following month.

When I returned there on July 23 for the Olympics I was told that my quarters were at the University of Southern California Olympic Village. I should have stayed in the Village and absorbed the entire ambience of the Games, but the athletes were allowed to make alternate arrangements as long as the officials knew our whereabouts. Since my dorm was next to the swimming pool, where the first events would take place, I was afraid the excitement would get my adrenaline flowing too early. So Jacqueline Hansen found a place for me with Sherrill Kushner and Ed Klein in Santa Monica. They had a small guesthouse, and I could come and go without disturbing them.

Everything was perfect until I went out to run—it seemed as if all the Olympic athletes were training in Santa Monica. The cyclists zoomed along San Vicente Boulevard overtaking the runners, who then turned to training on the gorgeous beaches. It was an ideal setting, but my face and reputation had preceded me and every time I went out for a run somebody challenged me to race. I felt like Gregory Peck in *The Gunfighter*. I should have ignored the challenges, but my competitiveness rose to every occasion. Before long I was tired and knew I had to get away. I decided to stay until the opening ceremonies, then fly back to Oregon for some peace.

On the day of the opening ceremonies, I got to USC in time to throw my stuff in my room, change, and head out to the track for a few strides. My way was blocked, however, by several security people. I couldn't get to the track because President Reagan's helicopter was scheduled to land in the infield in an hour or so; he was going to address the assembled athletes before we went on to the Coliseum. I got lost, finding that I couldn't take familiar paths because they were too close to the President's chosen route, and thereby missed the team picture. But I was back in time to hear Mr. Reagan speak. When he finished we were loaded onto buses and driven to the Coliseum.

What I said to the policeman in Brookline was equally true of this trip across Los Angeles: I could have run faster than we were driving. The city was filled with people trying to reach the Olympic stadium. We finally made it and were marched into a building near the Coliseum to watch the opening ceremonies on a huge TV screen. There would be a long wait in the program before the parade of nations was to begin.

As soon as they turned on the screen it malfunctioned and nobody could repair it. The athletes missed the Gershwin number and everything else that came before our entrance. We became bored and restless. Already worked up with emotion, the last thing we needed was a bad omen. But everyone made the best of it; the noise in the hall grew deafening as we circulated, trading team pins with athletes from different countries. It was a scene.

As the hall cleared for the parade the Americans got together in small groups and vented our complaints about the ugly uniforms we were wearing. Various team managers, coaches, and officials from the USOC told us to wait until we saw all the uniforms together. And when we lined up, forming a field of red, white, and blue, I understood what they meant. It really was magnificent.

To get to the Coliseum we had to walk through the same tunnel the marathoners would enter to run their final lap on the track. I thought how terrific it would be if I came through here into a full stadium in first place. I didn't dwell on the possibility, though, not because I wasn't ready to run, but because the events of the evening made everything else fade. Marathon day might have been a year away. Like everything else, it was on hold during producer David Wolper's show.

We marched in and took our places on the infield. I had the shakes as I realized where I was; it is a moment I find difficult to describe. Gina Hemphill, Jesse Owens's granddaughter, bore the Olympic flame onto the track and hundreds of prohibited cameras were whipped out of our pockets as we surged toward her. The security people hissed at us to get back as poor Gina broke her stride time and again to outmaneuver the crowd. Finally she passed the torch to Rafer Johnson, who ran up the long staircase at the head of the stadium and touched off the flame that would burn throughout the Games. To call these minutes electric would be to understate the case; my whole body was tingling with awe and pride. Balloons and doves were released into the air. The crowd in the stands stomped and cheered. We held hands and sang "Reach Out and Touch"—Dr. Leach found me during the song and took my hand. I wish I had told him what I was thinking: "If it hadn't been for you and Dr. James, I wouldn't be here." But I was on the brink of tears; one word and the flood would start. I sang, hoping he'd hear the thanks in my voice.

When the ceremonies were over some of us raced out of the Coliseum, too pumped up to ride the slow buses back to USC. We jogged on air all the way to our rooms. I decided to sleep in the Village that night, and the next day I went to Eugene.

I was feeling so good and so fast that it was all I could do to hold myself back in my training. When I'm in that condition I want to run until I drop. Bob Sevene was there to remind me that the Olympic race would suffer if I pushed myself too hard. It was difficult to find alternatives to running. Mary Angelico and I tried playing Scrabble, but I couldn't keep my mind on it and drove her crazy by jumping up and down to get the phone or do my laundry in the middle of a game.

The biggest drawback in preparing for the Olympics was that it had kept me out of the berry fields in Maine, so I picked lots of raspberries in Oregon to make jam for Christmas gifts. One morning Mary left the house just as I started boiling jam, and when she got home the whole kitchen was covered with it and I was out for a run. One of her roommates answered the telephone and his ear stuck to the receiver. As he wiped the jam off his head he turned to Mary and said, "*When* is she going to L.A.?"

On August 3 Sev and Rich Phaigh (the Athletics West masseur) and Mary and I headed for the airport for the flight to Los Angeles. I spotted some wooden toys in the airport gift shop and Mary and I stopped to examine them while the men boarded the plane. I found the perfect ornament for the top of our wedding cake: a wooden boat with two people sitting in it. Scott had built a boat for me as a birthday gift; if we painted the toy boat green it would be an ideal miniature. I took it to the counter, and as I was paying Mary tugged on my sleeve and said, "Hey, do you know our plane is leaving?" We just made it.

Then my carefully arranged facade began to collapse. I was relaxed until the plane took off. When the captain told us over the intercom about the weather in L.A. my stomach began to hurt. An upset stomach is my perennial marathon companion (I have that in common with Grete Waitz); this one was bad enough to erase everything else from my mind. When the plane landed I had one goal—to find a bathroom. So much for Oregon and my composure.

I half sprinted to the restroom, head down, holding my stomach. All of a sudden I was stopped by a punk with purple and green hair; he grabbed my arm and held me. There were three others dressed in L.A.-punker garb with weird hairdos and metal things hanging off their ears. I was furious. I reared back to yell at them and the tall one who'd grabbed me said, "Oh, Joan," and I finally recognized Scott. The other "punks" were my brother John, his wife, Holly, and Martha Agan, who would soon be my matron of honor. (Martha was there because she'd written "When you get to the Olympics, I'll be your coach. Ha ha" in my high school yearbook. She added the "Ha ha" because when we were youngsters she always beat me in races up the hill to her house.) I laughed, but I also made Scott release me so I could run to the bathroom. The idea of the costumes was to break the tension, and it worked. My stomach problems didn't go away, but my song changed from the monotonous "I just can't deal" to "Let's get this show on the road."

I joined my family and relatives for a relaxing dinner before heading back to Sherrill and Ed's house to stay until the marathon. August 4 passed slowly; it was one of the few days in my life in which there were too many hours. That night I used the bathroom every half hour or so; I couldn't sleep. I lay in bed and listened to the theme from *Chariots of Fire* over and over again on a Walkman. I slept for about an hour and dreamed I was trapped in a department store.

Sunday, August 5, fifty of us gathered at Santa Monica College to start the race. The stands weren't filled, as I'd imagined they would be, and the day was gray, without distinct features. At first it all seemed like an anticlimax. My stomach was still bothering me, so I waited for the other athletes to vacate the stadium bathroom and cleared my system. When I emerged from the bathroom, officials were lining up the athletes for the march onto the track. The competitors were in alphabetical order according to the countries they represented. The U.S. marched last, as the host country. The athletes of each nation were lined up according to height. I took my position at—needless to say—the tail end of the group. It was at this time that I thought of something my mother had been saying for as long as I could remember: "First shall come last and last shall come first." There was a little music and some flag-waving; then we all milled around for a while. I couldn't focus; I heard popping sounds in my head, as if my brain were breaking free of its moorings before floating away. I worried that I'd have to make another pit stop before the race began. Jitters galore. There was some medication in a plastic bag attached to the inside of my shorts for me to take in the event of stomach problems, but once the gun went off I was darned if I was going to reach into my shorts on ABC television.

At last, we lined up and were sent on our way. I was wearing a white cap to keep the sun off my head, but it wasn't shining strongly yet. We were grateful to be running in the morning, before the city heated up and the smog reached choking levels. I actually wasn't bothered by the heat at all.

My memories are fragmentary. For the first three miles I ran with the pack, but then I decided to break away because I felt hemmed in. I couldn't stride properly surrounded by all the other runners. If I had to be the pacesetter in order to run my own race, that was fine. Right after I broke free the first water station came up, and I was darned if I was going to get into a crowd again just for a drink, so I skipped it. Most of the others took water and I pulled farther away. I had prepared properly as far as drinking water in the days leading up to the marathon—as evidenced by my frequent bathroom trips the night before. Once we got past that station the lead was mine for good.

I couldn't believe the other runners weren't coming after me. I glanced over my shoulder a few times in the next two miles, expecting to see Grete Waitz or Ingrid Kristiansen or Rosa Mota within range, but no one appeared. It was like a dream: here I was, running comfortably and in control of the Olympic Marathon with no visible opposition. The gap widened as each mile ticked off.

Ingrid was quoted in *Sports Illustrated* as saying that she was waiting for Grete Waitz to make her move. "If I'd followed Joanie, maybe three or four other girls would have come too. It might have been a different race. But I waited for Grete."

I dreaded the stretch on the freeway. In Maine there is nothing that even approximates the highway system around Los Angeles. All my life I'd heard about the L.A. freeway in comedy monologues and from friends who lived in California. It was a great surprise to discover that the freeway stretch was the only part of the course that reminded me of Maine. There were no spectators allowed, so except for the pace car, I was alone. If I'd closed my eyes I could have pretended I was in Freeport. Next to the finish line, the freeway was my favorite part of the race.

Normally I am concentrating so intensely on my running that I register the details of a course only in retrospect, if at all. But when I looked over at the sidewalk in Marina del Rey and saw a black and white Bowdoin banner I had to grin. There's usually one Bowdoin banner somewhere in the crowd when I run a marathon and it always gives me a lift.

Not that I needed much inspiration. I've seen the videotapes and I know the ABC commentators thought I had taken the lead rashly, too early. I admit I had one or two brief flashes of doubt and imagined the pack thundering by me in the last few miles. But when sixteen miles passed, then twenty, and I still felt completely in control, I knew I wasn't going to be caught. Unlike in the late stages of the trials, I was sure I could pick up my pace if need be.

The sun was beginning to show its face during the last miles and the temperature was rising, but nothing seemed to bother me. Runners often talk about their best races being their easiest races. The Olympic Marathon was that way for me.

Just before entering the ramp leading down into the Coliseum tunnel I took a quick look at a bigger-than-life mural of me finishing the 1983 Boston Marathon. Nike had commissioned an artist to paint the mural on a windowless side of a tall brick building. The building stood by itself outside the Coliseum, and here I was about to enter the stadium by myself. I had seen the wall painting the previous fall; I was a bit uncomfortable with it, but I think it played a positive role in my preparation for the Olympics.

Shortly after I looked away from the mural the tunnel was in sight. When I got close I could hear the crowd rumbling inside—they had been watching the race on a pair of giant screens and knew who and where I was. As I ran into the tunnel the noise was muffled and I heard my own footfalls. I thought, "Once you leave this tunnel your life will be changed forever." I fastened my eyes on my shoes and kept running.

My mother later said that I looked like a little gray mouse skittering out of a hole. The crowd bellowed as soon as I emerged into the sunlight to run the final lap. My legs were wobbly with emotion; I put my head down even further and said aloud, "You're not finished yet. Get around the track and nail this thing down." With about two hundred meters to go, I took off my cap and waved to the crowd. I was so charged up that when I broke the tape I could have turned around and run another twenty-six miles, though maybe not in a time of 2:24:52, a minute and a half ahead of Grete Waitz. Somebody from Nike handed me a big American flag that Bob Sevene's teenaged son Trent had brought to the Olympics and I took my victory lap trying to get it to unfurl in the strong breeze. My father vaulted out of the stands to join me on the track. I didn't see him, and the second he hit the ground a swarm of security people were there to stuff him back into his seat. The security force couldn't worry about who he was; it was their job to keep the athletes safe. Later he said he was glad he hadn't made it to the track.

When I finished jogging I was grabbed by ABC for a quick interview, and then I searched the stands for my parents. There was no hope of finding Scott—he was sitting with my brother John and Holly and Martha and Sev in the nosebleed section—but Mom and Dad had places down front, if I could just figure out where. I had a rough idea, but it was difficult to find them because everyone I looked at was smiling and waving. The first person to embrace me was Dr. Leach, who was close to the finish line. Several months earlier he had said he wanted to see me at the tape, and there we were.

After a few moments I located my parents and got the big hugs I wanted. From there I went to the medical compound to have my urine tested for drugs, and then Grete Waitz (second) and Rosa Mota (third) and I met the press. They all wanted to know how we felt about the collapse of Gabriela Andersen-Schiess, but none of us had seen her or heard what happened.

I met my parents at the USC sorority house Nike had rented, and I put my white hat on a table in the front room, but later it was gone. Somebody may have thrown it away, thinking it was a discard. Because Olympic tradition doesn't permit medals to be awarded until the afternoon, I had time for a massage and fun with family and friends before returning to the Coliseum for the presentation.

When the U.S. flag was raised over my head and the national anthem was played, I was beyond feeling. I had to take several long breaths to make it through the ceremony.

But Only on Sunday: Ron Clarke

Kenny Moore, 1973

Although Ron Clarke was the premier long distance runner of the 1960s, breaking 17 world records, he never won at the Olympics, and for that, some judge him harshly. A proud man, Clarke adhered to a code of racing that defied conventional wisdom and cost him Olympic fame. Three years after Clarke retired from racing, *Sports Illustrated* writer Kenny Moore visited him in his home in Australia and gave this memorable profile of a remarkable man.

———————●———————

In 1970, Frank Shorter and I ran in an international 10,000-meter in Oslo. Frank won. I was fifth, and a gentleman named Ron Clarke was sixth, the pair of us laboring silently together for the last mile.

At the award ceremony we pushed the bone-tired Clarke onto the top level. The crowd stood in tearful ovation as the Norwegian officials presented him with a pair of cross-country skis to symbolically ensure his return. This had been Ron Clarke's last race.

Later, I visited him in Australia, to review a career as important for its philosophical integrity as for its world records.

———————●———————

Sunday mornings Ron Clarke drives out from Melbourne past Puffing Billy and up Ferntree Gully into the Dandenong Hills. He parks near a roadside general store and waits. Other automobiles arrive filled with men wearing running shoes and shorts. T-shirts bear the names of nations, universities, beers. When their number reaches two dozen the men set off, trotting comfortably along the road's grass verges. Suddenly a runner veers into the bush and sprints away madly. The rest, Clarke among them, give howling chase. The trail, rich with loose rocks and tree roots, is overhung with brittle eucalyptus and huge wet ferns that Clarke, taller than his hurtling companions, catches squarely in the face. In half a mile the leaders regain the road and jog, listening to the stragglers, the thump of bodies against the trees. The pack re-forms, gathers its strength, and begins another wrenching charge through the forest. "I've been doing this since 1961," pants Clarke. "I don't care if I never set foot on a track again but I can't leave this."

The run is seventeen miles. The road, with Australian bluntness, goes right at its hills, two- and three-mile stretches of rough gravel without a curve or dip or chance to rest. On the summits everyone wheezes and looks vaguely ill. "This is the best," says Clarke at the base of mile of thirty-degree pitch. "You know

From *Sports Illustrated*, February 26, 1973. Reprinted by permission of Kenny Moore.

Dave Power, the bronze medal in Rome? He had to walk here." When Clarke has willed himself up and some color has returned, his voice is touched with reverence: "Such a hill. A brutal, magnificent hill."

Between 1963 and his retirement in 1970, Ron Clarke took part in 313 races over distances of half a mile to a marathon and won 202 of them. Along the way he broke 17 world records. Yet Ron Clarke did not win an Olympic or British Commonwealth Games gold medal and upon that omission he has been sternly judged.

Derek Clayton, once the world's best marathoner, trained with him. "I know Clarke better than he does himself. No emotions. The man couldn't lift himself in the important competitions. A machine. The Olympics or a club race, it was all the same to him."

"He was gifted physically, his records prove that," said Coach Percy Cerutty, who attempted to advise Clarke early in his career, "but he had no real mental drive. When he came up against men with spirit, he let them beat him."

In Australia, Clarke has in fact become a symbol of promises unfulfilled, of excellence somehow gone to waste. "Ron Clarke?" asks the cabbie or the girl who brings your bitter. "Isn't he the bloke who never won anything?"

———————————●———————————

The kids are in bed. Ron and Helen Clarke, the latter a composed, capable woman with a soothing, mellifluous voice, invite friends over for an evening swim. After a few laps in the frigid little pool, Ron climbs onto one of the rocky ledges that make up the backyard. His Afghan hound, Shendi, attacks him with love. Since his retirement from racing Clarke has reversed the aging process. The graying crew cut has given way to thick, black curls that frame a face less drawn, less lined than the one that agonized through all those miles.

"I apologize for the mess this place is in," he says. Barbells and pulleys and sit-up boards that once had dominated the family room are being moved outside, displaced by a billiard table and a bar. "I've been too busy to see to things properly." He is general manager of Australia's largest sport-shoe company, has three corporations (to receive royalties from endorsements and development of health and fitness products), a position on Australia's Film Censorship Board of Review, and a newspaper column.

Despite the assertions of his countrymen that his racing character was flawed, Clarke, relaxing in the warm December night wind, is clearly not freighted with remorse. "That's over," he says. "The races blur. My God, most of the time it seems as if the competitive runner was another person." Reminded of the 10,000 meters he won in the 1969 U.S.-U.S.S.R.-British Commonwealth meet in Los Angeles, Clarke had to consult a log of his travels to satisfy himself that he had run in the Coliseum at all that year.

"I did not win the Olympic gold medal," he says, "and that has given rise to the idiotic idea that I was no good in *real* competition. My only contention, and I'm leaning over backward to be fair, is that because of the altitude at Mexico

City I had no chance against the Africans, and therefore the critics' point that I was incapable of winning remains unproved. Personally, I have no doubt at all that I was the best 10,000-meter runner in the world in 1968. At sea level I would have won easily." With some finality he dives back into the pool.

Clarke seems justified. In Europe before the Mexico Games he defeated 10,000-meter champion Naftali Temu of Kenya and 5,000-meter gold and silver medalists Mohamed Gammoudi of Tunisia and Kip Keino of Kenya by margins that were comparable to those by which they beat him in the Games.

But there were other chances for gold. In the 1964 Olympic 10,000, Clarke led for most of the race and was outkicked by Billy Mills of the United States and Gammoudi. In the 1966 Commonwealth six-mile in Kingston, Jamaica, Clarke led most of the race and was beaten by Temu. At the 1970 Commonwealth Games in Edinburgh, Clarke was still in front down the last backstretch, but was out-kicked by Scotland's Lachie Stewart. These races gave him his reputation for crumbling under pressure. And even though they came following injuries or in tropical heat or during Clarke's decline toward retirement, in each he was probably the equal of any other entrant. Except for the peculiar nature of his running, he might have won them all.

Ron Clarke defied the one edict that, in contests among equals, approaches law: *The pacesetter never wins*. Front running has an element about it of keeping one's nerve, familiar to those who move in high, unprotected places. The leader competes against footsteps, specters. He struggles to escape the clinging pack at the same time he fights to down his own cowardice. "There is fear," says Clarke. "I usually didn't think I'd be able to finish until I got into the last lap."

The follower has only to match the leader's pace. He enjoys a compara-tive calm in which he can relax and conserve his emotional energy for a final, unanswerable assault. Given these realities, few men running at the head of a pack can avoid a feeling of sacrifice. Steve Prefontaine, explaining the savagery of his bursts to break contact with his followers, said, "I hate to have people back there sucking on me."

Ron Clarke was a front runner, yet not in the classic mold of an athlete who has no finishing kick and therefore must set a hard pace out of desperation. On those rare occasions when Clarke followed instead of led, he outsprinted such fast finishers as Keino and West Germany's Harald Norpoth. Shunning expediency, Ron Clarke was a front runner out of principle. He accepted each of his races as a complete test, an obligation to run himself blind.

Over a late dinner of salad, a lean steak, and five glasses of chartreuse Vigo-rade, he makes his case.

"The single most horrible thing that can happen to a runner is to be beaten in the stretch when he's still fresh. No matter who I was racing or what the circumstances, I tried to force myself to the limit over the whole distance. It makes me sick to see a superior runner wait behind the field until 200 meters to go and then sprint away. That is immoral. It's both an insult to the other runners and a denigration of his own ability."

So Clarke took the lead in Tokyo and Kingston and even in Mexico with the understanding that doing so was likely his ruin. "If you're the world-record holder, as I was, and nobody else will set the pace and make a real race of it, and it's your style to have a demanding pace, then you have to do it yourself. If that is going to diminish your chances of winning, well, you still have to do it. I was very conscious of that pressure. Perhaps one should resist it. I couldn't."

Although he calls it his "style" or "impatience," Clarke's flaw was a driving moral imperative to go flat out, to impose an order on each race, to make sure the winner was the fastest, toughest competitor. "I loved testing myself more than I feared being beaten," he says, "and front running is the ultimate test. You need a total, irrevocable commitment to see the race through to the end or it cannot justify your effort."

Clarke takes a text from his bookcase. "Any athlete who thinks he suffers ought to read this." The book is Heinrich Harrer's *The White Spider*, an account of the climbing of the north face of the Eiger in Switzerland, of the men who died attempting it, and of those who finally succeeded. In it, one finds a passage Clarke has underlined: "There is nothing new to be said about the behavior of man in exceptional circumstances of danger or crisis. . . . I would not find better words than those used by the Athenian, Menander: 'A man's nature and way of life are his fate, and that which he calls his fate is but his disposition.'"

Ron Clarke's fatal disposition took shape early. His older brother Jack was long an outstanding professional Australian Rules football player. "My only consolation," says Ron, "the only one I could have, since he beat me at everything, was the satisfaction of trying my hardest."

When he began running competitively Clarke was moved by the examples of two men, Emil Zatopek and John Landy, both inexhaustible trainers, front runners, and gentlemen. Zatopek, the only man ever to win the 5,000, 10,000, and marathon in one Olympics, was the more distant idol. The Czech ran as if tortured by internal demons. He seemed a sign, a proof that if athletes chose to force themselves through the pain and doubt, there could be no limit to human performance.

Landy, the second four-minute miler, helped plan Clarke's early training. His races, as did Clarke's later, often demonstrated a kind of noble perversity. Though he recognized that his best chance to win the 1954 Mile of the Century against Roger Bannister lay in upsetting the Briton's wait-and-kick strategy by sitting back himself, Landy led from the gun. The race had been the object of so much attention he felt obliged to ensure a fast time, "otherwise the sport might have suffered." Bannister outkicked him.

In the 1956 Australian National Championship mile, Clarke, then nineteen, fell during the third lap. Landy bounded over him and, thinking he had spiked him in the head, stopped, came back, and helped him up. Once assured of Clarke's safety, Landy went after the field, now 60 yards ahead. He drove into the lead with 10 yards to go and won in 4:04.2.

In that same year Clarke set a world junior mile record of 4:06.8. Thereafter, because of a chronic sinus infection and the demands of business and family, he fell away from running. In 1961 through the urging of a neighbor, former Olympian Les Perry, he began again. This five-year hiatus, which has no parallel in the career of any other world-class runner, seems a key to Clarke's determination to run on his own terms. "It was a hobby when I came back to it, and although I was totally involved in each of my races, my whole life did not hang on the results. I could afford to take a few chances." Clarke had then and has today strong views on the relative importance of amateur sport and earning a living. "I just read something of Jim Ryun's financial sacrifices for his running. Jim was wrong. If you have that conflict there is only one way to resolve it. You shouldn't run."

Clarke's confirmation in his ethic came when he began to break records. "I've never felt more depressed or disappointed than in the days following my first world record. I was down, completely adrift. I realized that the excitement had been in the challenge of the training and in the race itself. The competition was what drew me on, the actual testing, not the hope of good results, because the best of all possible results, a world record, made me miserable."

He understands the strangeness of this remark and turns to Helen, across whose lap he is sprawled, for corroboration. "Do you remember how bad it was?"

"Yes," she says softly. "And everyone else so happy."

For years Clarke scoured the world for tough races. "I had a need, almost like a gambler's compulsion, to test myself against the best." It didn't matter that he had raced hard the day before or that the local champion was lying in wait or that the distance was not his best. In 1965, to have a 10,000 put on the program, Clarke had to promise an Oslo meet promoter not only that he would break the world record in the event but would come back the next day in a featured 3,000 against fresh Olympic champion Mills. He set his world record, one that stood for seven years, and won the short race as well. But neither was in the Olympics.

Clarke changed his basic tactic in the last years of his career. He devised one that added to suffering: a full-bore sprint away from the field with a mile or more to run. "It increased the challenge. But in a way it was refreshing. I knew I could make it through. So instead of dreading those footsteps behind I wanted them to stay there because whoever was making them was killing himself." If the footsteps were not there and Clarke had broken contact in this way, he was never beaten. He tried to sprint away in Mexico during the 10,000-meter race with a kilometer to go, but he could not escape the altitude natives who swarmed past on the last lap. Clarke finished sixth. Three steps past the line, for the only time in his career, he lost consciousness. When he awoke a few minutes later, an oxygen mask was pressed over his face. The Australian physician attending him was cursing the IOC for having permitted the Games at that altitude. "Oh, God," he railed. "Look what the bastards have done."

"I wanted to tell him it was all right," recalls Clarke, "but I couldn't. My tongue was so swollen it filled my mouth. I couldn't speak for two hours."

The Melbourne newspapers shouted CLARKE FAILS AGAIN.

———————————●———————————

Ron and Helen Clarke are dining at a friend's Melbourne beef house. The friend is not much in evidence but a hostess keeps fluttering by, demanding to be told how she can serve.

"Well, I want a very simple salad," says Clarke. "Just lettuce and tomatoes, no dressing, no croutons, no frills."

Derek Clayton has been invited. "He claimed he had another engagement," says Clarke. "Then I told him I was paying. But it was too late."

The salad is placed before him, with parsley and sculptured radishes. Clarke sighs and picks out the offending vegetables. Only very gently does he try to make the nature of his running understood to the others with him, perhaps reasoning that a world that cannot hold the parsley is not ripe for a philosophy of sport any more complicated than winner take all.

"It's been upsetting that people have seen my attitude not as recklessness but weakness," he says. "The Australian behavior toward losers is far from healthy. If youngsters are taught that losing is a disgrace, and they're not sure they can win, they will be reluctant to even try. And not trying is the real disgrace."

———————————●———————————

The chorus, whenever Ron Clarke is consigned to insignificance, is "Who ever remembers second place?" But that is the gulf between spectators, who seem to believe that runners are drawn to compete only in order to make themselves immortal, and amateur athletes, who are private men doing what they do for myriad private reasons. Among distance runners, who understand something of what Clarke attempted, will be found his most thoughtful judges.

In 1966 Clarke spent a week in Prague with Zatopek, who at the time was not yet cast into official disgrace for having supported the liberal Dubcek government. Clarke retains the whole of that visit in softly gilded memory. He speaks of his boyhood hero's grace, his standing in the eyes of his countrymen, his unabated fitness and energy. As Clarke departed, Zatopek accompanied him through customs and, in violation of regulations, onto the plane itself.

"He stood by me and then slipped a little box into my pocket. He seemed embarrassed and clearly didn't want anyone to see what he'd done. For a moment I wondered what I was smuggling out for him. Later, when the plane was in the air, I unwrapped it."

The memento that dropped into his palm, inscribed "To Ron Clarke, July 19, 1966," was Zatopek's Olympic gold medal from the 10,000 meters in Helsinki.

"Not out of friendship," Zatopek had whispered to Clarke as he turned to go, "but because you deserve it."

One One-Hundredth of a Second

Marla Runyan with Sally Jenkins, 2001

Marla Runyan had a brilliant running career: She was a two-time Olympian, a former American record holder in the 5,000 meters, and a world-class marathoner. What makes her even more remarkable is that she is legally blind. The following excerpt from her autobiography *No Finish Line: My Life As I See It* is her account of her breakout year in running. Before 1999, Runyan had battled injuries for two years as she transformed herself from a heptathlete to a distance runner.

Perhaps only runners and watchmakers truly understand the power and delicacy of time. A subtle regulation of movement makes and marks each second. Running fast is a far more complicated business than most people realize: open the back of a clock and you will see that, in the dozens of tiny dials and cogs and coils that comprise a timepiece. Running is about the body as clock: arms as pendulums, legs as escapement. A runner organizes a million tiny motions, separate and precise, from toe flexes to arm positions, into a natural rhythm. Yet the end result should not be technical. When a runner runs, it doesn't necessarily look fast. It simply looks like a weightless, out-of-body, absence of slowness.

Running is about training the body to imitate physical laws in order to move through space as efficiently as possible. It is the most primary building block of athleticism—there isn't much besides golf that you can do without it—and it has a scientific language all its own. We runners discuss our sport in terms of pace: we spout streams of numbers that are unintelligible and insignificant to anyone but us, we mull over records and time differentials—separated not by minutes, but by seconds, and tenths and even hundredths of seconds—as if they were the Dead Sea Scrolls. You might hear me say, "My workout today was three times one-K cut-downs in 2:56 and four times 200 accelerations in 28 to 30." Or you might hear me talk about negative splits, positive splits, pickups, surges, and tempos.

Every runner knows that the clock is not the only opponent. There are actually three races taking place: against the clock, against the other competitors, and against your biggest opponent, the self. There comes a point in almost every contest when you come face-to-face with yourself. The lactic acid fills your body, and the pain consumes you, and you ask the inevitable question, "What kind of person am I?"

The best runners answer the question not with thought, but with instinct. They react. There is no pondering, or questioning, or doubt. They keep moving forward, despite the excruciating pain, and against all common sense. This response is not something that can be coached; an athlete must inherently possess it.

The race against self is the most important, and the most decisive, of the three races being run. The race for medals, money, or status is only the most externally important one. At the finish, the medalists will take the podium and be interviewed on television, and the order of finish will be printed in the newspapers. Everyone but the winner is considered a loser. But runners understand that there is a whole set of different criteria by which to judge a race. Even if I don't win the race against my opponents, I might win the internal race against myself by not giving in to pain or self-doubt, or win the race against the clock by setting a personal record. Despite what the spectators see, or what place I finish, I might very well walk away feeling victorious.

But by the spring of 1998, I barely remembered what any of these things felt like, because I had not been in a major race in over two years.

One Saturday afternoon in April, [my coach] Dick Brown asked me if I'd like to go to a collegiate meet at the University of Oregon. I accepted the invitation, even though it was difficult for me to see from the grandstand. I knew Dick wanted me to study races even if I couldn't run them. I took along my monocular, and we sat in the bleachers above the back straightaway. It was raining, as usual, but the bleachers were almost full, typically. Rain never kept the die-hard Eugene track audience away from a meet.

The last race was the men's 5000 meters. "There's supposed to be a pretty good kid in this one," Dick told me.

I'm ashamed to admit this now, but I didn't even know how many laps a 5000-meter race was, or what was a respectable time. All I knew was that the conversion was 3.1 miles. The gun sounded, and I raised my monocular to my right eye and moved the telescope back and forth until the runners came into view. The runner who Dick wanted me to see was named Adam Goucher, and he was easy to spot, even for me. He went straight to the front of the pack, and he never looked back. He ran like a madman: he completed the first lap in 64 seconds, and each lap after that fell somewhere between 66 and 67 seconds. He ran alone and in the rain, and he seemed to move effortlessly.

I couldn't make out the details of his face, but I could see his movement, which was dramatically different from the pack of runners who trailed him. He was linear, and slightly forward leaning, with no wasted energy, while the others seemed to bob up and down as if they were hopping in place. When he was leading by nearly half the track, the knowledgeable Eugene crowd rose to its feet and began clapping in sync to his cadence. He continued to knock off each lap at exactly the same pace.

For the first time, I understood the principles Dick Brown had been preaching, because I could actually see them at work. The runner's pace and rhythm were contagious, and I found myself rising and clapping with the crowd. I put my monocular over my right eye and studied him more closely each time he came down the straightaway beneath us. On the final two laps of the race, he actually *picked up* his pace. He charged home with a final 64-second lap.

"How'd he do that?" I wondered.

He had increased his pace at the finish—the very concept that Dick had stressed most, and that I had struggled most to grasp. Now, I had a perfect picture of what he meant.

Goucher's time turned out to be the fastest collegiate performance of the year.

A couple of days later, I told [my boyfriend] Matt all about the race. But it wasn't news to Matt, who had an encyclopedia of running in his head and who followed every happening in the sport. He could recite every Boston Marathon champion over the last twenty years. He knew who won which medal at which Olympic Games, and by how much, and he knew the personal-best times of international elite runners today, and what they ran when they were in college. Matt didn't just watch the sport; he studied it. And he was becoming as much of a running teacher to me as Dick Brown was.

He read deeply and avidly on the subject: he spent his Saturday mornings in my kitchen sipping coffee and buried in *Track & Field News*, or buried in a book, whether *A Cold Clear Day* or *Once A Runner* or *The Purple Runner*.

What he didn't know from reading, he knew from experience. He had competed in distances from 1500 to 10,000 meters as a collegiate runner at the University of New Hampshire, where he had captained the team and led them to a conference title in his senior year, and he still ran 85 miles a week and competed at distances up to the marathon, in between working at the medical lab and as a massage therapist. Although he stood 5'11", he weighed just 140 pounds in a black T-shirt and a pair of baggy shorts, which he had to pin at the waist so they wouldn't fall down. In comparison, I stood 5'8", and weighed 136 pounds, because I had been working out my frustrations in the weight room, doing pyramid sets of squats and dumbbell bench-presses.

"I want to learn to run like that. I have to get my foot better. I just have to," I told Matt.

"I know," Matt said. "So let's get started."

But by the summer of 1998, I was still trying to find a cure for my foot. Dr. Leahy called it "the worst case I've ever seen." It continued to nag at me, preventing me from working with Dick Brown on anything close to a full-time basis. Instead, I was working full-time at the Y as an aerobics coordinator, teaching senior fitness classes in the mornings and preschool movement classes in the afternoons.

In the mornings, Matt would read aloud from the sports pages for me, narrating the results of the Grand Prix meets in Europe. I needed to know what was going on at the world-class level, but at the same time, it hurt.

"Suzy broke four minutes in the 1500 in Monaco," he said.

"No way," I said.

"Masterkova won, barely, outkicking Szabo. The top eight times were all under four minutes."

Matt was always impressed with other runners, and it began to gnaw at me. I wanted more than anything for him to be impressed with me, too. Instead, I might as well have quit the sport, for all the running I'd done in the last two years. Maybe someday, just maybe, Matt would pick up a newspaper or open *Track & Field News* and it would be me he was reading about.

What if I did quit? I wondered. I brooded on that. Could I sit in the stands as a spectator, as I had with Dick at the collegiate meet, trying to squint at the track through a monocular? Could I sit there and wonder, *What if I hadn't given up?* No, I decided; I couldn't quit. Not and be a happy person. And especially not now that I had met Matt, whose passion for the sport I lived with, too.

But something had to change. I wasn't getting anywhere. I would walk with Summer along the Amazon Trail, the meandering wood-chip path that passed near my apartment, and brood as joggers passed me. To me, walking was a grueling and boring activity. *I could have run five miles by now*, I'd say to myself.

One day, while I was walking at the Y, Matt called to report that he'd met a chiropractor who had some experience with Active Release, the same technique that Dr. Leahy had used successfully on my foot in Colorado Springs. I couldn't afford to travel to see Dr. Leahy regularly, so the idea that someone in Eugene might be able to treat me meant that I might finally have some prospect of recovery. I made an appointment to see Dr. John LeGat.

He turned out to be a young man in khaki Dockers and a white polo shirt. As he took my foot in his hands, he explained that he would try to duplicate the treatment that I'd had. He could feel the lumps of scar tissue along my arch and heel. From then on, Dr. LeGat treated me every other day for three weeks. The condition got worse before it got better; at work, I had to put my foot in a tub of ice water under my desk while I signed time sheets and did other paperwork. I even bought a rolling pin that I used to roll under my arch. Before long, I was running between seven and ten miles a day, although slowly.

It was too late, however, for my relationship with Dick Brown. He spent most of the late spring and summer traveling with his other athletes, and I didn't mind his absence. Actually, I was relieved not to have to report to him each day the status of my foot—he usually asked me to give him a number between one and ten. I felt a responsibility to paint a pretty picture of what was going on, because I didn't want to disappoint him. But it was a welcome respite when I could just deal with the injury, instead of trying to convince Dick that I was getting better.

The American record in the 800 fell that year—and not to a practiced distance runner, but to a sprinter. Jearl Miles-Clark, an Olympian at 400 meters, had moved up to the 800 and stunned everyone with her performance of 1:56.78. (In the next two years she would lower it twice more, to 1:56.40.) I was more frustrated than ever, and I began to question some of Dick's theories on endurance and what I felt was a lack of intensity in his regimen. I wanted some faster stuff, form-drills, and "strides"—quick bursts of speed at a relaxed effort-level.

Finally, I confronted him. Sitting in the cafe at the Y, we got into an uncomfortable discussion that left me in tears. I challenged his program. "It's monotonous," I said. And then I accused him of making me vulnerable to injury; the six to seven months of steady mileage had been a significant factor in my foot pain. This was unfair of me: my string of injuries was not Dick's fault. It was no one's fault but my own. But I'd simply had enough. The lack of variety was driving me crazy.

"What about drills, and strides?" I asked. "Maybe even a time trial once in a while?" Dick said he was agreeable to that. But then I said, "What about breaking apart some of the long runs into two runs in a day?"

"They need to be continuous," Dick insisted.

I couldn't face it. I needed a change. Dick was an intelligent coach and a kind man, and he had taught me everything about how to run. But his program required patience and trust, and by this point, I had neither. We weren't working well together. By the end of the discussion, we agreed to part ways.

After our meeting, I sat in an office and cried. *What the hell was I doing with my life?* I wondered. I was almost 30, and to leave Dick was difficult. I had moved to Eugene for him. I had all but convinced myself that if it didn't work out with him, my career was over.

Running at an elite level now seemed totally out of the question.

———————————●———————————

But I still had Matt. He became an even more integral part of my life, and gradually, as my spirits improved and my foot felt a little better, we began some light trail running together. "Just a few easy miles, to see how your foot is," Matt coaxed. It felt so good to just run again. I told myself that I was running strictly to enjoy Matt's company and Eugene's beautiful summer mornings. I didn't ask for much more.

Then one day, Matt said, "There's a 5K road race at Alton Baker Park in September. Do you want to run it?"

It was a low-key, 3.1-mile race along the bike path that I was quite familiar with.

"Okay," I said hesitantly.

I won the 5K race with a pedestrian time of 17:57, but, frankly, I was just elated to break 18 minutes. More important, my foot held up throughout.

Soon, I was back running mileage again. I still felt aches and pains—bursitis in my hip socket was injury number four in two years—but gradually they ebbed away, and I wondered if I might resume my career. My mood improved, too, when I left my unchallenging job at the Y and began teaching children again. Initially, I was hired by the local school district to help part-time with an Easter Seals swim program for multiply disabled students, but soon I branched out into home-schooling kids who were too ill to go to class. The income was more than my full-time job at the Y paid, so I quit. Teaching brought back my confidence; I was good at it. And it gave me more free time—which meant more time to run.

I needed a coach, I decided. There were other first-rate coaches in Eugene, I'd learned. One of them was Mike Manley, a 1972 U.S. Olympian in the 3000-meter steeplechase, who had known and trained with the late Steve Prefontaine, possibly the greatest male American distance runner in history. I knew Mike by reputation only—he coached a large group of runners of widely varying abilities—while he didn't know me at all. I called him up cold, one night in December.

"Hi, my name is Marla Runyan, and uh, I run the 800 meters . . . uh . . . I ran 2:04 at the Trials in '96."

"Uh-huh," he said, unimpressed.

"Well, I wondered if maybe you might work with me."

"I've got several runners right now, and I've got my hands full," he said. "I don't think I can take anyone new right now. Call me back at the end of January."

"Okay," I said, disappointed.

I continued to train on my own. One rainy Saturday morning, I suited up and stretched on the living room floor.

"My hip is tight," I told Matt.

"You know, there will always be something," he said. "Sometimes you just have to run through it, a little each day, and it actually gets better."

"Should I go out there?" I asked, pointing to the living room window, which was dripping with condensation. The temperature was about 35 degrees.

"I can't tell you what to do. It's your hip. You can always try, and if it hurts, stop."

It sounded simple enough. Either you can run, or you can't. No more walk-jogging. No more babying my body. Just get out there and get on with it.

I headed out. I'd heard through word of mouth what kind of tough workouts Mike Manley gave his runners, among them a horrendous hill run up in Hendrix Park, over a series of rarely traveled paved roads, rough and full of potholes. The trail wound through a beautiful series of pine- and fern-covered undulations, where some of the wealthier homes in town were. It made for a perfect continuous hill circuit.

I decided to try it. I came to a climb of a quarter mile or so to the top of Hendrix Park. I changed gears and charged upward. Near the top, I did a U-turn and headed back down. I decided to repeat it six times before moving on. Up again, this time faster, trying to maintain my pace from beginning to end. And again, and again.

On the sixth hill, I didn't stop. I kept going, up toward Skyline Drive, where I passed a memorial to Prefontaine. To the right of the narrow road was a wall of rock—the place where Prefontaine had crashed his car and died in 1975. I knew the memorial consisted of a picture and an engraving, from what Matt had told me, although I wasn't able to make it out clearly. Scattered about were old ribbons and medals that local runners had placed there in his honor. As I ran past the plaque, breathing hard from the hill, I managed to say out loud, "Hey, Pre, how's it going?"

I reached the top of Mount Hendrix, and paused for a moment to decide what to do next. A steeper and longer hill to the west looked good, so I headed upward again, and tried to keep my pace steady. I repeated this hill four times. Each time, I talked myself to the top. *This is how it's going to feel, just like this, it's going to hurt. This is the race right here, this is where you have to pick it up.* In my mind I wasn't on a desolate hill in the rain, my breath a cloud of fog. Instead, I was on a track, nearing the final turn, as the burn entered my legs.

I headed back down the mountain, on a winding road through tall trees and ferns, and even though the rain still fell, I wasn't cold. It had been a good day. I arrived back at the apartment and threw open the door, exultant.

"I did it," I said to Matt, "and my hip was okay."

————————————●————————————

In January, I was dying to call Mike Manley. I knew his group met every Tuesday evening at a certain trail, and I wondered if he would let me join in. I called him one evening and asked if I could just tag along.

"As long as you know I'm not officially coaching you."

"I know," I said.

I suited up in my old Moving Comfort gear and a few Nike remnants: long tights, a long-sleeved Lycra shirt, a second layer on top, a jacket, a pair of Matt's running gloves, and a hat. I laced up a pair of trainers I'd bought on sale. Then I stood in the middle of our tiny apartment waiting for 4 P.M. to arrive.

It was cold and raining hard, and very dark, but I didn't care. I didn't worry about the weather, or if I would be able to see the trail in the dark. I would run no matter what, because this could be my future coach. I grabbed the doorknob and turned to Matt and said, "If this doesn't work, I don't know what I'm going to do." I went out into the dark.

The workouts I'd done on my own paid off: I handled Mike's regimen and stayed with the group easily on that first day. From then on, I continued to run with his group every Tuesday and Saturday, on an informal basis. Each week, I watched enviously as Mike gave his athletes sheets of paper with their week's workouts written out.

One Tuesday evening, after we had finished a trail run, Mike handed me a piece of paper, too.

"I guess I'm coaching you now," he said.

I rushed home and burst through the door. "Matt, come look at this!" I yelled. "I got a piece of paper, too!" I threw it under my CCTV and began to study Mike's writing. I got so much happiness and relief from that single sheet of paper. It meant I had a coach. I had no idea where I would go from here, but I was an athlete again.

Mike and I sat down and discussed my training and my goals for the upcoming season. "I would really like to qualify for the Nationals in the 800," I said. The U.S. Nationals that year would be held right at home in Eugene, and I longed to run in front of that crowd.

I had another, more far-fetched goal. In national and international competition, there are three rounds, or heats. Only the top eight qualify for the final. "Maybe . . . maybe I could even make it to the final," I added.

"That seems reasonable," Mike said.

We got down to work. Mike's emphasis was on strength and stamina, similar to Dick Brown's, but he also introduced me to the "tempo run"—a three-to-five-mile run at an even pace, maximizing breathing, but just shy of oxygen debt. At first, I couldn't maintain the 5:20-per-mile pace like his other runners. But, gradually, I improved. I was getting stronger, and I didn't even know it.

My first test would be an early-season race called the Mount SAC Relays, a popular annual meet in southern California in April, a four-day affair during which high school, college, open, and elite athletes would all compete. The 800 was an invitational event, and in order to get an invite, I needed a fast time. I didn't have a fast time—I had no time at all. My last race had been three years earlier.

I lied on the application. I wrote down a personal record (track people call it a "PR") of 2:03.8, and stated that I had run it in Canada the year before. The truth was, I'd spent the entire season sitting on a stationary bike at the YMCA. I wasn't anywhere near Canada. But I tossed it in the mail and hoped for the best.

I got in. I would be competing in a field of eight elite international athletes, among them Michelle Ave, Dick Brown's former 800 runner. Matt and I packed our bags and headed for California.

There was a lot riding on this race: it would tell all. It would tell me if I was training in the right way, or if my move to Eugene had been one big mistake. What's more, it was my first trip back to California since I had left in 1996, and my parents would be in the grandstand. There was an added element of pressure: I would be running in front of my former college coach, Rahn Sheffield.

The day of the meet was hot and smoggy, with temperatures approaching 105 degrees on the track. I warmed up with a twenty-minute jog in a field behind the stadium, where it was quiet and less crowded and where there was some shade. I checked in at the last minute to avoid that relentless sunshine. The runners crowded together under a small patch of shade provided by an official's umbrella.

Finally, they called our race. I stepped onto the synthetic surface, and my spikes dug in, and I ran down the straightaway. To those in the stands who knew me, I was scarcely recognizable, at 124 pounds and with a completely different build. I wore a red and-orange Moving Comfort running top and a pair of old black briefs, not exactly cut to modern-day standards. They looked like control-top underwear. I also wore an old pair of Killer Loop sunglasses from 1995, with no idea that they were completely out of style.

I heard a voice say, "All right, Marla!"

It was Rahn. After three years, that voice still meant speed to me. "You got this, girl, you can do it," he said. I could hear a laugh in his voice, and it relieved me. In the back of my mind, I'd wondered if he would hope for me to fail. Instead, he was *cheering for me*. But it made me nervous, too. I wanted to show him what I'd learned.

To calm myself down, I reminded myself to be grateful that I was not on a stationary bike at the YMCA, nor was I aqua-jogging in the pool or running up a lonely hill in the rain. I was about to run a race. Just a race.

The gun sounded. Tina Paulina from Mozambique took off next to me. I immediately fell to the back, holding on at the end of the string of runners. Coming around on the first lap, I was still in last. I thought, *Maybe I'm not ready for this.*

The leaders came across the 400-meter mark in 56 seconds. I crossed the mark in 60-flat—still in last place.

"Catch 'em on the backstretch!" It was Rahn again.

Off the third turn, I started passing people. They began to tire, and I moved up. Now I could see the shapes of the leaders—which meant they weren't too far off. I gritted my teeth. It was starting to hurt.

Everyone began screaming, typical of the audience at Mount SAC, coaches screaming at the top of their lungs at young kids and Olympians alike. As we headed into the final turn, the screams intensified, and so did the pain. But I was still gaining ground, still moving up. I kept my pace even, and finally I passed one more runner. Then I locked up. I held on, somehow—and crossed the line in fourth.

That had better be a PR, was the first thought that entered my mind. For that much pain, there had better be some kind of reward. And there was.

In the infield, I asked an official my time, in between pants and moans with my hands clasped over my knees.

"Runyan? Let's see here . . . Runyan . . . 2:03.81," he said.

"2:03!" I screeched.

It wasn't a lie anymore. The time qualified me for the U.S. Nationals.

———————●———————

Life was good: I was able to train and race again, and I had renewed faith in what I was learning about running. I was able to feel and experience it without pain.

One day at the track as we practiced technique and form, Mike said to me, "You see that line right there . . . the white one?" He pointed to the white lanes painted on the red surface.

"Yeah," I said. I was standing right on it.

"You only need to pick your feet up high enough to step over that line."

His point was that I didn't need to waste time and energy lifting my knees and feet up high. That motion had no bearing on forward motion.

"Run from the inside," Mike would say. He would lean his body up and forward on the track, and insist, "Feel like a rope is pulling you up and out." My form was changing: I could feel my legs underneath me, not breaking my momentum but propelling me forward.

When we ran long intervals or tempos on the track, Mike would stand on the infield and yell, "Rhythm, rhythm, rhythm!" He wanted us to feel the pace, to memorize it and ingrain it into our systems, so that we could find it again in a race without ever thinking about it.

I was good at pace, I discovered. I could find a 66-second pace per 400, on every lap, almost to within a tenth of a second. And I could maintain that pace, 33 seconds flat for every 200 meters, for a full 800. I was experiencing something new, and I liked it. I was beginning to wonder if I was meant for longer distances.

At the end of May, the best runners in the nation flocked to Eugene for the Prefontaine Classic. The "Pre" meet, as it's fondly known, is a Grand Prix event broadcast on CBS and is perhaps the most prestigious annual track event in the country.

For the last two years, I'd watched it from the stands, but this year would be different. Mike went to the race organizer, Tom Jordan, and told him about my 2:03, and asked him to enter me in the 800 meters. Jordan refused; only runners who were sub-2:00 would be in the field, he said. But Jordan did offer me $500 to rabbit the 1500, meaning to run the race as a pacesetter for the real contenders. Or, he said, I could just run the 1500 as a competitor.

Mike reported all this one afternoon about ten days before the meet, after a long trail workout. I looked down at my mud-caked legs—it had been a hard day. I glanced back up at Mike and said, "I'm running."

He smiled. "I was hoping you would say that."

Ten days later I stood on the starting line for the first 1500-meter race of my career. I had no idea whether or not I was ready for this distance, especially not in this company. Some of the best runners in the world were there, including Regina Jacobs, the three-time Olympian, and Leah Pells, the Canadian national champion. I stood way out, in position No. 17. There were seventeen runners in the field, and I was the least of them, just a local girl with no qualifying time.

The gun sounded, and we were off. The early pace was tolerable, I decided, and I found myself near the front of the pack. I didn't know how to feel. This distance was a total unknown to me. *When will I start to hurt?* I wondered.

I remained steady as we approached the end of the third lap. The bell clanged. Now everyone started to move. Time to run. Around me, I sensed the shifting of gears. I started to pick it up, too. With 300 meters to go, I moved into fourth place. I was running just outside the leaders.

Regina Jacobs showed why she was among the best in the world: she moved to the front and took off for home, unchallenged. Still in fourth, I headed off the final turn for home, too, with every bit of remaining energy I could muster. But just before the line I tied up, barely able to lift my legs off the ground. I was passed—and finished fifth.

But for me, this was a victory. I bent over, gasping.

My time of 4:11.81 qualified me for the National Championships. It was a total surprise, and caused a stir in the knowledgeable Eugene crowd.

It also caused a quandary for Mike and me. Not long afterward, we stood on the track at Hayward Field and discussed our options. We had to choose which event I would run at the Nationals, the 800 or the 1500. My performance in the Pre had baffled everyone, including us.

"I still think you can run a good eight," Mike said, shrugging.

But I was tempted to run the 1500—perhaps because it was new, and I felt untapped in my potential at the distance; or perhaps because I suddenly felt there was little room to improve in the 800, while the 1500 had brand-new possibilities.

"Let's flip a coin," Mike said.

He pulled a quarter out of his pocket.

"Heads, you run the 1500; tails, you run the 800, okay?"

"Okay," I agreed.

Mike flipped the coin, caught it, and slapped it on his forearm.

"What do you *want* it to be?" he asked, teasing me.

"Heads," I replied.

Heads it was.

That's how I became a 1500-meter runner.

———————●———————

The 1999 Nationals came to Eugene. I was about to race against some of the biggest names in track and field; people I had only heard about, or read about, or seen on television. I was a total novice, and, to compound my inexperience, the semifinal heats were cancelled. That meant there would be just one heat, the final, and this made me extremely nervous. The race would be my second attempt ever at the 1500.

I stood on that line, in my marmalade-colored uniform, old granny briefs, and store-bought spikes, and as I waited for the gun, I knew that I had no business being in the race.

Regina Jacobs bolted off the starting line. As usual, Regina was the class of the field, a smooth and distinctive runner, all legs, with a pixie haircut. There was talk that she was chasing the stadium record of 4:00, or maybe even going after Mary Decker Slaney's American record of 3:57. Regina was always chasing some kind of record; for some years now she had been America's strongest distance runner, the lone U.S. medalist in the company of Romania's Gabriela Szabo and Russia's Svetlana Masterkova.

When she bolted, the entire field went with her—and I went straight to the back. I was wary of running at such a pace so early. It seemed ridiculous to go out so hard when there were still two and three-quarters laps to go.

At 400 meters I was still in last place, with a lap time of 64 seconds. I began to doubt myself. *Maybe I can't do this. Maybe this isn't my event.* The leaders were not within my view. Instead, I relied on the commentator calling the meet over the loudspeaker to tell me what was going on. *There's nothing like being a spectator at your own race.*

Gradually, I passed a couple of people. . . and then a couple more. I couldn't count how many, but it seemed as though on every turn and every straightaway, I moved up in position. I still doubted myself, however. I ran hesitantly; the leaders were still somewhere beyond my vision. They might as well have been a mile away, as far as I was concerned.

Finally, the bell sounded. The field was thinning in front of me. Things grew clearer. I heard the announcer call off the order of position by last name, like roll call. To my surprise, I was in sixth. And I hadn't yet extended myself.

What the hell are you doing? Go! I went into an all-out kick. It was as if I had finally started running the race. I moved up, and up. Off the final turn, I could see the second- and third-place runners, Stephanie Best and Shayne Culpepper, and I knew I was gaining ground on them.

But the finish line was too close by this time, and I ran out of room to catch them. I crossed the line in fourth.

I just stood there in disbelief. I wasn't even tired. Two competitors were half-carried off the track, completely exhausted. Others were down on their knees. And I just stood there. *I wasn't even tired.*

And that's when it began to hurt.

There is a pain worse than what you feel in a race: the pain of knowing you didn't run your best. That pain, I suddenly understood, I would have to live with for days, months, and perhaps even the rest of my life. It was worse than losing. *There's something worse than losing*, I realized.

Had I finished fourth with an honest effort, after giving it my all, I could have lived with it. Had I been half-dragged off the track in utter exhaustion, I could have lived with that, too. But to walk off the track feeling that there was more inside me that I could have given—that was the greatest pain I've ever experienced. I felt something close to sickness; it was as though my heart had turned black inside my body.

I didn't sleep. It was such a missed opportunity: here were the U.S. National Championships in Eugene—my home—and here I was in a new physique, with a new coach, running well, *and I'd blown it.* Had I run harder, I could have finished in the medals and qualified for the World Championship team. Instead, I had doubted myself.

I lay there in the dark. Matt was fast asleep. I stared at the ceiling, the blot in my eyes flitting across it as usual. Then I noticed something. On the north wall of my bedroom hung the Olympic flag, with the five colored rings intertwined and the giant red letters "USA" just above it. The flag had been there for months. The only light that entered our room came from the parking lot outside, where a floodlight stayed on all night.

A beam of light streamed through the curtains and hit the flag, illuminating it against the wall. It glowed. It was the only thing in the room that was visible to me—everything else was black. I hesitate to tell you this story, because it sounds too stagey, like a cinematic cliché. But the Olympic rings were aglow. I tried to make sense out of what I was seeing. Was it a sign or a message, telling me I was capable of more?

I never did sleep. I stared at the flag, and relived that terrible race over and over in my head until the sun came up. I got out of bed, put on my shoes, and went for a run.

———————●———————

Sometimes a mistake is the best thing that can happen to you. It depends on what you choose to do about it: whether you ignore it, and thus repeat it, or whether you decide to learn from it, so as not to repeat it ever again. I decided that I had to right my wrong.

There was a race in Maine on the Saturday following the Nationals, part of a string of meets in the Northeast and Canada known as the Can-Am series. I had every intention of being there. There was still an outside chance that I could qualify for the World Championships, if I could run a fast enough time in Maine.

I whipped out my Visa card, bought airline tickets to Boston for myself and Matt, and laid down the plastic again for an SUV rental.

Here was the deal: the runners who had beaten me at the Nationals, with the exception of Regina Jacobs, had not run fast enough to qualify for the World Championships. To be named to the national team that would travel to Seville, Spain, for the Worlds, you had to log a time under 4:08 in the 1500. There were five of us who still had a shot at it, and we all headed to Maine, where we had hopes of meeting the qualifying standard and thus making the team.

As we lined up at the start in Maine, each of us had one and the same thing in mind: to nail that time.

The gun sounded, and we took off. No doubts this time, and no regrets; I intended to walk away proud, no matter what happened. For the first lap and a half, I was in third place, running stride for stride next to Stephanie Best, who had finished second at the Nationals. Then I picked it up. I passed Stephanie, and then a girl in red I didn't recognize. As it turned out, she was the rabbit— the designated pacesetter for the field.

Matt stood on the infield and gave me my split-time as I passed the 800-meter mark. "2:12!" he yelled. I was on pace, but barely. I was also in the lead now—and I wasn't looking back. When I had less than a lap to go, Matt tried to shout my 1200 time at me, but it was inaudible because a roar had started to build in the crowd. Bells were clanging, the announcer was screaming over the loudspeaker, and the track was encircled with howling, distance-loving fans.

I bore down, as acid began filling my legs. Just 200 meters to go. 100. I gripped at the track with my spikes as hard as I could and a white paper banner broke across my chest at the finish line. I stumbled onto the grass. There was a large digital clock just in front of me but I couldn't see the time that it displayed. "What was my time?" I demanded, gasping for air.

Matt came bounding over. "4:06!!" he screamed, and vaulted over me as I crumpled to the grass.

When I finally got my breath back, I borrowed a cell phone from an official, and I called Mike Manley.

"Mike, we're going to Spain!"

———————————•———————————

Initially, I cared very little about the Pan-American Games. I was anxious to get to Seville and the World Championships, but first I had to run in the Pan-Am Games. They seemed in the way, an inconvenience.

The Pan-Ams take place every three years and are like a smaller version of the Olympic Games, for countries from North, South, and Central America. On this occasion they would be held in Winnipeg, and the U.S. national team would send two athletes. Regina Jacobs, the national champion, turned down the invitation, and Shayne Culpepper, the third-place finisher, was injured. That left Stephanie Best and me, and I felt obliged to go.

To help me get ready for world-class competition, Matt and I studied tapes of classic races. We watched footage of famous Olympic runners, and studied their strategies, learning from them. Matt got a copy of Steve Prefontaine's famed Munich Olympic 5000 meter race, and I crouched in front of the television and watched him run lap after lap, his hair flying behind him. That race has haunted runners for years, and it began to haunt me.

The race was painfully slow. Early on, the field ran so sluggishly that they seemed to be at a 10,000-meter pace. It was the kind of race that grated the nerves and tested your patience as much as your stamina. Often, races in the Olympic Games or World Championships are slow, tactical ones, because there is no pre-established pacesetter. In races for medals, no one wants to lead. To lead means to jeopardize your stamina. The other runners will "sit" on the leader, who is doing all the work. Physiologically, it takes 10 percent less energy to follow in a race than to lead—much like drafting in cycling. When winners are decided by mere fractions of seconds, this extra expenditure is significant.

Steve Prefontaine found himself in that very situation in 1972. He knew that if he sprinted to the front and took the race out fast, his opponents would use him, only to pass him on the final lap. So, he sat. He ran within the pack, waiting . . . waiting. He was waiting for the *real* race to begin. The result? With a mile to go, fearing that he lacked the sprint-finish speed of his opponents, he began a long drive, hoping to wear the kick out of their legs. With a lap to go, he was in third place. He could have stayed there, and sat, and perhaps taken the bronze medal. But he wanted the gold, because that was Pre, and he went after it on the backstretch of the final lap. He surged to the front, but he didn't have enough left. He had made that last mile the fastest of any 5000 that had ever been run—close to four minutes—but he faltered just five meters from the finish and placed fourth. Even so, Pre's brave tactic became both legendary and widely debated, because every runner eventually confronts the basic dilemma of a tactical race, and fears that sickening sensation of finishing a race with something still left.

The Pan-Ams would be another crucial piece of my runner's education. I arrived in Winnipeg to find that Leah Pells, the Canadian national champion, was entered. Leah had finished fourth at the 1996 Olympics, and she had just run 4:04 for 1500 in Europe that summer. And she would be running in front of a home crowd.

The night before the race, I called Mike Manley from the hallway of the dorm where I was staying.

"Mike, Leah Pells is in the race," I said.

"Well, she's tough," Mike said.

He didn't always say the right thing.

"How do I beat her?" I asked.

"It will be a tactical race," he said. "If you ever take the lead, you had better be prepared to finish with it."

It sounded more like a threat than a piece of advice. I took it to bed with me that night, and I thought about it all through the next day as I prepared for the race.

The following evening, we gathered in the starting area as the sun was setting. The stadium was full, and the air was warm, and as I shook out my nerves, I reminded myself once again to see the race as a blessing and an opportunity.

As Mike had predicted, the race started slowly—so slowly, in fact, that I had never experienced anything like it. We practically walked around the track. We clocked 76 seconds on the first lap. I sat, and I sat, lurking somewhere in fifth or sixth place. *Let someone else lead . . . the race hasn't even started yet.* But always, I kept the red of Leah's uniform within view.

I tried to stay as smooth and efficient as possible. The pace picked up slightly, to a 65-second third lap, but I barely noticed. It felt comfortable. Finally, the bell clanged.

Leah bolted.

She passed Stephanie Best.

I hesitated for a moment. But with 300 meters to go, I told myself, *Now. Go now.* I hoped that I had an edge; that I had conserved that anaerobic fuel tank Dick Brown had taught me so much about. I moved quickly into second place, watching the red of Leah's uniform from the corner of my eye.

She was in front of me by four strides. But gradually, I could feel her coming closer to me. I was gaining.

We flew into the final turn. I didn't dare try to change gears, I just maintained my stride, and I ran wide, out in Lane Two. I came up on her shoulder. The crowd was deafening, pulling for their own runner. But I turned it around. *They're cheering for me.* I knew it was a lie, but I needed their energy.

We ran in unison down the straightaway, arms and legs moving side by side, as if we were attached at the hip. I couldn't move any faster—and neither, it appeared, could she. If I bore down any harder, I knew I would tie up and falter. *Just get to the finish, and get your torso across that line first.* I could feel we were almost there, even though the finish line was invisible to me. I could see shapes of the timers on the infield just to the left of the line.

Moments before we hit the finish, I lunged. I planted my right foot into the ground and thrust myself, like a takeoff for the long jump. We crossed the line.

It was too close to call. A photo finish.

My first thought was *That was awesome!* I didn't care whether or not I had won. I had run the best race I could ask of myself, and the reward was in knowing that.

Leah took my hand and we jogged a victory lap together, still not sure of the order of finish. As we came past the final turn, Leah looked up at the large Magnavision screen, which was displaying a continuous slow-motion instant replay of our race.

Suddenly the crowd moaned. A black-and-white Acutrack photograph of the finish had appeared on the screen, but I couldn't see it.

"Who won?" I asked.

"You did," she said.

I had won—by one one-hundredth of a second.

I threw my arms in the air. As much as I had told myself to run for the sake of running, and not for medals, I did want the gold medal, after all. Leah remained standing as I continued the victory lap down the straightaway. After the lap, the medalists were escorted to a fenced-in holding area where the media waited. The press came at me like a large, anxious creature. Tape recorders were thrust in my face, and voices yelled questions at me simultaneously. Then one voice separated itself from the others.

"Marla, tell us about your eyes!"

You have got to be kidding me. After I've won a gold medal in only my fourth 1500—you want to know about my eyes?

I wanted to say, "Did you watch the race?" At that moment the subject of my eyesight seemed the most inappropriate and irrelevant topic I could think of. *Weren't they paying attention?* They had overlooked the excitement and the drama of the race itself. Why couldn't they let my accomplishment stand on its own?

I paused. I didn't want to answer the question, especially with my opponents nearby. But I knew if I refused, my answer could be misconstrued, and they would think I was angry or bitter about my disability. I decided to answer the question as quickly as possible, and maybe they'd be satisfied and we could talk about the race.

I took a deep breath and I rattled off, "I have Stargardt's disease, spelled S-T-A-R-G-A-R-D-T-apostrophe-S, which is a juvenile form of macular degeneration, and I've had it since I was nine years old, and it caused me to have 20/400 vision in both eyes and it is not correctable with glasses or contacts. But I don't feel it impairs my ability to run competitively."

It didn't work.

"What do you see right now?"

"Can you see that man over there?"

"How do you run?"

"Have you ever fallen down?"

"Why did you start running?"

Not one question about the race. Finally, the creature put away its pens and microphones and receded. A single figure remained, a man. I couldn't see his face, but I could feel his eyes looking at me. As I began to pull on my sweats, he approached me calmly, as if he had been patiently waiting for the media creature to leave.

"Hello, Marla, I'm Ray Flynn," he said with a touch of an Irish accent.

"Oh, hi!" I said. "I've seen you race."

I had watched Ray Flynn on one of the classic race videos that Matt had shown me. Ray had run in the 1984 Los Angeles Olympics and was Ireland's national record-holder in the mile. Now he was working as an agent, representing track and field athletes.

"You know," he said, "if you can run every race like that, the way you did today, you have a future."

Finally, here was someone who wanted to talk about the race and who didn't seem to care about my eyes. He saw me as an athlete, and that was all that mattered to him.

"I know you need to go," he said. "But let's talk again."

I'd never had an agent before. Was he suggesting he would be willing to represent me? I had a million questions. I knew Ray was not your stereotypical agent. He was no "Jerry Maguire," and I wasn't a football player saying "Show me the money." But a free pair of shoes would be nice.

Later that evening, I stood on the top platform of the awards podium and was presented with a gold medal. The U.S. national anthem played for an almost-empty stadium, but I cried anyway, thinking about how much things had changed. I had not given up, even when my body had told me to. *One year ago today you were on a stationary bike at the YMCA.* I'd cried on that bike, too.

The American Dreamer

Dave Kuehls, 2005

In 2004, Meb Keflezighi won the silver medal in the Athens Olympic marathon, the first American male distance runner to medal at the Olympics in 20 years. He is also the former American record holder for 1,000 meters and the '09 winner of the New York City Marathon. With these achievements, Keflezighi should be hailed as an American hero, but because he is not "home-grown," the public has not embraced him. Sportswriter Dave Kuehls writes this story of a dream deferred.

The mother tells the father to leave. Now. To save the family, the father must abandon it. Go. Find somewhere safe. And when the time is right, call for us. We'll come. If the father stays, the mother knows he will be killed by an Ethiopian bullet or be held captive in an Ethiopian jail. Either will destroy the family forever.

The year is 1981, and Eritrea, a tiny country near the Red Sea, has been at war with neighboring Ethiopia for 20 years, ever since Ethiopian emperor Haile Selassie laid claim to the area and its people. Eritrea in the early 1980s is divided into sections—Eritrean and Ethiopian—depending on which army controls a given piece of land. The family already has moved several miles away from the turmoil, from the city of Asmara to the village of Adi Beyani. But even here, war is catching up. The other day a boy was playing with a toy he found in the road. Then the toy blew him to pieces.

Even with such destruction, the father cannot understand why he must leave his wife and five children. Yet the mother, not known for her assertiveness, insists. Fighter jets scream overhead as she makes her case, walking the dirt floor of their hut barefoot, her belly swelling with the couple's next child. There is no other way, the mother says. If he needs something to take with him, take the name of the unborn child Bemnet or Amina, depending on the sex. Both translate to the same thing: "with trust." That is how he should leave his family. That is how they know that one day they will be reunited.

It is decided, then. And on the day of his departure, the father tells his four sons and daughter that he is leaving for one of his "trips to the city." But Papa is no good at charades, and the oldest son, Fitsum, knows something is up. He sees his father's throat tighten at the door. Then Papa is gone.

Five years pass. A famine caused by the chaos of war claims roughly half a million Eritrean lives in 1984 and 1985 alone. And yet the family, now numbering six children with the arrival of the boy Bemnet, survive by farming their small piece of land. Then, one day in 1986, the father does call. He is in Italy, having arrived by plane after walking 150 miles out of Eritrea and into Sudan.

From *Runner's World*, September 2005. Reprinted by permission of Rodale, Inc.

A friend in Milan helped file the right paperwork, and Papa has worked odd jobs to raise the money needed to get the family out of Eritrea.

The family finally reunites in Italy, but the odyssey is not over. It's decided they'll move to the United States, to San Diego, where friends tell them of an Eritrean community that can help them start their lives anew. So, they travel on to America, to a small apartment in the North Park section of San Diego. One day, the father takes his third son into the local Payless shoe store. There, amid the shelves and boxes of shoes, 12-year-old Mebrahtom Keflezighi picks out a pair of Pro Win sneakers, a size too big so he can grow into them.

They are his first running shoes.

———————●———————

On a sunny morning last May, "Meb" Keflezighi (pronounced "Kef-lez-gee") pulls up in his white Toyota 4-Runner to the entrance of the Miramar Reservoir just north of San Diego. In town for his sister Bahghi's wedding, Meb arrived the day before from his training base in Mammoth Lakes, California. The Toyota has a souvenir USA Olympic bear hanging from the rearview mirror and "I Love Eritrea" and "UCLA Alumni" license-plate frames. As he jumps out of the Toyota, I expect to see the bright smile and hear the joyful laugh that is such a part of his persona. Dan Browne, his Olympic teammate, will sometimes call Meb just to hear him laugh. Instead, Meb, who looks small up close (he's 5'5", 125 pounds) even with his tight musculature, gives me a quick hello and starts prepping for a training run.

While Meb gets ready, I run through his monster 2004 resumé: First in the USA 8-K championships; first in the USA 15-K championships; runner-up at the Olympic Marathon Trials; winner of the Olympic Track Trials 10,000 meters in a trials record time of 27:36 (he also holds the American record at 27:13.98); second place at the New York City Marathon in November in a personal best of 2:09:53; and, of course, the topper—a silver medal in the Olympic Marathon in Athens, the first Olympic medal won by an American male marathoner since Frank Shorter's silver in 1976. Consider just how long ago that was: Gerald Ford was president, ESPN was yet to be born, and Meb Keflezighi was one year old.

Now, after finishing a six-mile tempo run along the reservoir in 29:31, Meb stretches the hip he's been nursing for several months. It's the aftereffect of trying to compensate for an Achilles he injured when, on a training run, he rushed to get away from an attacking dog. The injuries kept him from competing most of the winter and spring. As he continues to stretch, a 60-year-old transplanted Texan named Jack comes over and introduces himself. "Meb, you are a shot in the arm for U.S. running," he says. Meb thanks him and autographs a postcard for him.

It's a nice scene, except for one thing. Not everyone feels the same way as Jack. For all he has accomplished—the Olympic medal, the records set, the six-figure endorsement deal from Nike—Meb has failed to gain total acceptance in his own country. And make no mistake, to Meb, the United States—where he has spent nearly two-thirds of his life, where he's won everything from high school state cross-country championships to Olympic Trials titles, and where he's been a naturalized citizen since 1998—is definitely home.

But log onto running Web forums and you'll find track fans taking swipes at Meb's accomplishments. Go to www.letsrun.com where one track fan wrote, "No matter what Meb does . . . he'll always have that asterisk next to his name because he was not born in America." Or go to his hometown newspaper, *The San Diego Union-Tribune*, where one column, headlined "Winning 26-Mile Races Simply Un-American," said this: "The United States used to be good at home-growing marathoners—Frank Shorter, Bill Rodgers, Alberto Salazar, Joan Benoit—and some say we're making a comeback of sorts with Deena Kastor, Alan Culpepper, and Ryan Shay. Our marathoner of the moment—Athens silver medalist Meb Keflezighi—was born in Eritrea."

Meb is acutely, painfully aware of these slights and disclaimers, and as he finishes today's workout I'm ready to ask him about them. When I try, though, he shoves the topic aside. Right now, he says, he just wants to get back into race shape for a summer season that includes the World Championships in Helsinki (where he'll run the 10,000) and then a return to New York City for the marathon in November, where his second-place finish last year was the best by an American since Bob Kempainen's runner-up finish in 1993. The whites of Meb's eyes, which flash when he's relaxed and in a joking mood, appear muted, as if a switch has been turned down, bright lights to running lights. So, instead of talking about his place in the sport or the asterisk by his name, I ask him for a report on his hip. "Good, but I'm monitoring it day-to-day." And then about his sister's wedding. Does he approve of the groom? "He's a good guy," Meb says, looking up from the ground where he uses a rope to stretch his hip around his trunk, like he's striking a pose for the Heisman Trophy. "Besides," he continues, "my sister made the decision. She is old enough."

And, as if to reemphasize the morning's business-like manner, Meb stops stretching, punches the recall button on his stopwatch and corrects some splits he had given me earlier. The second mile, which he had said was 4:57, was a 4:58. And the third mile, which he said was 4:56, was a 4:55. And the fourth mile, which he said was 4:55, was a 4:57.

That he'd have to set the record straight about split times during an ordinary training run might seem strange. Then again, to Meb Keflezighi, small details say a lot.

———————————•———————————

Russom Keflezighi arrived in San Diego with his wife, Awetash, and their six kids on October 21, 1987, and immediately started looking for work. He found a job at an East African restaurant where he bussed tables and cleaned floors, and often got back to the family's small, three-bedroom apartment well after midnight. The kids had to pad around quietly in the morning, holding down their voices, so Papa could sleep. But those six children (and the four more the couple would have once in the United States) picked up on Russom's work ethic. "Through the years you always knew where to find the Keflezighis at noon—every single one of them would be at a desk in the library," says Pat Anderson, a junior high school history teacher.

Meb pushed himself outside of school, too. By the seventh grade he had run a 5:20 mile, and he was so talented at soccer his teammates called him Pele. But before he started high school, he took a suggestion from his father and picked one sport to concentrate on. Meb chose running for its simplicity and definitiveness. "You run from here to there and see who gets there first," he says. And also because running was something that, if you put in the work, you saw results. That fall Meb finished sixth in the sectional cross-country championships, leading a San Diego High School team that included two of his older brothers, Fitsum and Aklilu, to a spot in the state meet. "Meb was quiet, not one to brag or show off," says head coach Ed Ramos. "Like his brothers, he always said, 'Yes, sir,' and 'Good morning.'"

Meb was fast and strong, yet Ramos says if his young runner had one weakness, it was a tendency to run too safe, to hold back, even when it was clear that he was the best runner in a race. Ramos coached two eventual Olympians, steeplechaser Marc Davis in the mid-1980s and Meb in the early '90s. "Davis was like, 'C'mon, you have to catch me,'" Ramos says. "But with Meb we had to tell him to take the lead, to go for it." At the 1993 Foot Locker National Cross-Country Championships during Meb's senior year, he took an early lead, but instead of trying to break away, he hesitated and let Adam Goucher regain contact and win the race. Meb finished second. "I'm convinced a move earlier could have beaten Goucher," says Ramos.

Still, Meb managed to win three state titles his senior year (cross-country, 1600 and 3200 meters) and was elected San Diego High's "best all-around" student. (He was also prom king, but he arrived late with his date because the state track meet was earlier that day.) Along the way he caught the eye of Bob Larsen, coach of UCLA's highly regarded track and field program. Larsen saw something in the kid from San Diego by way of Eritrea that made him think he could be a good investment even though UCLA usually earmarked scholarships for sprinters and throwers. "I wasn't going to offer Meb a full scholarship, but then I met the family," Larsen remembers. "I saw they were tough people. Life was not easy for them, yet the family had accomplished a lot. I had been raised on a farm. They were from a rural area [in Eritrea]. There was a connection."

UCLA in the mid-1990s one of the most glamorous programs in the country—Ato Bolden and John Godina, who would go on to win Olympic medals, were teammates. Yet in going to UCLA, Meb was entering a conference, the Pac-10, that had a history of prickly feelings about foreign-born athletes. In the late 1970s, Kenyan runners such as Henry Rono and Samson Kimobwa (world record holders who ran at Washington State) were virtually imported just to dominate American underclassmen. At the time, Blaine Newman, a columnist for *The Register-Guard* in Eugene, Oregon, the University of Oregon's hometown newspaper, made it a point to refer to these athletes as "the Kenyans" and not Washington State runners. And yet his UCLA teammates knew that Meb—at the time still not a naturalized citizen—was hardly a hired gun.

"People on the inside knew Meb wasn't an import," says teammate Scott Abbott. "He exemplified what America was all about: Great family. Works hard." He was also supportive, always doubling back after his finish to cheer on teammates. "Meb was everybody's best friend," says roommate Dan Brecht. "He must have had 15 best friends." He was disciplined, too. Study breaks lasted 10 minutes, just long enough to watch the end of a football game. He downed three glasses of water before each meal to avoid overeating at the dining hall. Morning runs were on grass, never concrete, to lessen the chance of injury.

Meb won four NCAA championships at UCLA, but perhaps more critical to his long-term success was that Larsen, who's now retired from the school but continues to coach Meb, finally cured him of his tendency to hold back during races. The tipping point? The NCAA 5000 final in Meb's junior year, raced on a wet track and with a field that included his high school rival, Adam Goucher. In spite of the rainy conditions, Meb pressed the pace over the final two laps and won easily. But perhaps the moment of truth had come minutes before the race as Larsen and Meb stood under cover from the rain. Larsen worried that his runner might use the weather as a reason to run conservatively. "Then Meb looked up with this big smile on his face," the coach recalls, "and I knew everybody was in trouble."

———————————●———————————

A Little League game is in progress across the street from the Normal Heights United Methodist Church in San Diego, and, as I duck inside, the ping of aluminum bats is replaced by a rhythmic reading. The church is nearly filled for the Greek Orthodox wedding ceremony of Bahghi Keflezighi and Layne Tadesse. Eritrean weddings last six days in the native country. Here, it has been pared down to a weekend so family and friends can get back to work in San Diego, Los Angeles, San Francisco, Boston, New York, and elsewhere. Each row in the church is festooned with a white carnation.

I take a seat in the back next to Biniyam Yacob, one of Meb's cousins, who has flown in from Washington, D.C. Last November he stood in Central Park while Meb tried to catch South Africa's Hendrik Ramaala for the New York City Marathon title. Meb was attempting to become the first American to win at New York since Alberto Salazar in 1982. As it turned out, he lost to Ramaala by 25 seconds. "What did you yell when Meb went by?" I ask. "*Ajoka*," Biniyarn says. "It means, 'Go for it.'"

Looking around the church and at everyone who has gathered here, I begin to realize how much the Keflezighis' lives have changed since they arrived in the United States 18 years ago. Russom and Awetash now live in Mira Mesa, a comfortable suburb of San Diego where Meb has a home, too. (He co-owns a second house in Mammoth Lakes with another 2004 Olympic Marathon medalist, Deena Kastor, and her husband, Andrew.) Each Keflezighi child of age has gone on to college or beyond. Fitsum has a degree in electrical engineering; Aklilu and Bemnet have business degrees; Bahghi graduated from medical school; and Merhawi, who has completed his second year at UCLA law school, is Meb's new agent. Yet, for all these changes, the family hasn't forgotten Eritrea or its customs and traditions. For instance, the wedding service is performed in three languages: Eritrea's ancient language, Geez; its modern language, Tigrinya; and English. At one point, the priest asks the bride and groom if they will understand the vows if he says them in Tigrinya. Laughter bubbles from the 50 or so older women wearing the traditional white headdress. They giggle because it is not uncommon for the generation raised in America to forget the native tongue. But in this case, the couple says Tigrinya is fine.

Meb certainly hasn't forgotten his roots, either. In 2000, in the months before Meb competed in the Sydney Olympics (where he placed 12th in the 10,000 meters), Merhawi hawked "Let's Go, Meb!" T-shirts from a booth at Eritrean-American festivals in Los Angeles and Washington, D.C. The shirt was done up in the colors of the American flag and Eritrean flag (yellow, red, green, and blue) and with a map showing Meb's journey from Eritrea to Italy to California to Sydney. At another Eritrean festival, Meb met his future fiancée, Yardanos Asgedom. In 2002, for the first time since leaving the country as a 12-year-old, he visited Eritrea to see his grandfather.

Yet his connections to his native land have also stirred controversy. In July 2004, following his win in the 10,000 at the Olympic Trials, Meb did a victory lap holding both the American and Eritrean flags, which drew criticism from some track fans. Meb, who often wears a pin displaying the American and Eritrean flags on his singlet while racing, chooses his words carefully when he explains. "I could just carry the U.S. flag, but something else is built into me—the war, my dad, the journey," he says. "It's the path that took me here. I can't just delete it."

———————●———————

The night before the Olympic Marathon last August, Meb and Larsen sat on the open-air patio of an Italian restaurant in Athens. During dinner Meb recalled a vow he had made in a letter he sent to the major shoe companies in 1998. He had just completed his UCLA career, which had actually ended on a down note: a fourth-place finish in the 5000 meters at the NCAA championships. To keep his running career going he needed a sponsorship. In the letter, he told potential backers, *If you put faith in me, Meb Keflezighi, I'll bring U.S. distance running back to world prominence.* Six years later, even with his lucrative Nike deal, Meb knew that it was getting close to put-up or shut-up time on that vow.

Meb came to Athens with just the 39th best marathon time in the 101-person field. Most running experts considered him a filler, one of the two or three dozen runners who gave the pack depth but would eventually fall off when the notoriously hilly route and the killer Athens' heat became too much. And there was also history, too. Since 1976 no American man had cracked the top 10 in an Olympic Marathon. In 2000, the United States sent just one runner, Rod DeHaven, who finished 69th.

Still, Meb wasn't thinking of the past. In his day planner for August 29, 2004, Marathon Day, he wrote: "Olympic Marathon goal: top three." Plus, he felt ready even though Athens would only be his fourth marathon. In the months prior to the race he had run the mileage (up to 120 miles a week), done the acclimation workouts (80 minutes in full sweats at 7,000 to 9,000 feet), and completed the 15-mile race-pace workouts that mimicked the course's elevation change. He then arrived at the U.S. training base in Crete three weeks before the event so he could acclimatize fully. "Meb had done everything right," says Larsen. Thing was, most of the others in the field could say the same thing.

At the start Meb wore a white hat and dark sunglasses. He had snipped the bottom of his white USA singlet short so it could hang loose, leaving his midsection open to the air. Larsen had told Meb to ignore world record holder Paul Tergat (this would be hard to do because Meb has a poster of Tergat on his refrigerator at home) and instead keep an eye on Italy's Stefano Baldini, a hot-weather runner who won bronze medals in the marathon at the World Championships in 2001 and 2003. Early on Meb disappeared into the pack. Larsen caught sight of him at mile 10—the last time he would see Meb until after the finish—and Meb flashed him a thumbs up.

Meb shadowed Baldini through the middle miles. The Athens course crested at mile 20, and the runners started downhill and into town as the sun began to set. They were going hard—Meb, Baldini, and Tergat together, with Brazil's Vanderlei de Lima ahead by 38 seconds, about 250 meters. Then it happened. A crazed man jumped from the sidewalk to grab de Lima; de Lima broke free, and continued on. At the same time, though, something else occurred: Meb Keflezighi, once known for holding back in races, made a move for an Olympic medal. He increased the already brutal pace for one long, drawn-out surge, about half a mile of pure gut check. (Larsen estimates Meb ran that half mile in 2:14 after having run the previous one in 2:20.) "I knew there were three of us in the chase pack and one in front," says Meb. "This was an opportunity to get it down to the medal contenders—gold, silver, and bronze."

Back in California, Russom and Awetas huddled around a cell phone. On the west coast the marathon was scheduled to be broadcast on tape-delay. So they listened as a friend described the race as he watched it, live, on his TV in New York City: *Meb's surge has dropped Tergat. Meb and Baldini have gone by de Lima. Baldini has pulled ahead, but Meb's hanging tough.*

As he entered 109-year-old Panathinaiko Stadium, a giant marble bowl of white light and noise, for the final 400 meters, Meb silently recited the names of family, friends, teammates, and coaches—anyone who had supported him in his quest. He crossed the finish line 34 seconds behind Baldini but ahead of everyone else, a silver medal all his. Back home, Russom told everyone that his son had run like a lion, which in Eritrean culture means "true man." Later, at a press conference, Meb told the media, "USA running is back. Wonderful, wonderful, wonderful."

———————————●———————————

In November, just three months after his Athens triumph, Meb stood up during a ceremony at the Nike Team Nationals in Oregon. A speaker had just said that Ron Tabb, an elite marathoner who advised Meb during his high school years, was the major influence on Meb's early running.

Meb could have kept quiet and let the comment slide. Instead, in front of the audience, he corrected the speaker and said it was Ramos, his old high school coach, who deserved the credit. When word got back to Ramos about Meb's remark, the coach was touched, recalling that Meb once told him, "Recognition goes where recognition goes."

But when I meet Meb in New York a few months later, on a cold March day, he's the one feeling underappreciated. The recognition due him, it seems, has not fully come his way. It's midday, an hour after he has finished running laps around the Central Park Reservoir on his sore hip. We're in a crowded French restaurant where Meb eats chicken and sips orange juice. I mention a *Sports Illustrated* story that had come out the week before touting Dathan Ritzenhein, the young 10,000-meter runner, as, finally, an American distance runner who can compete with the Africans. It is my attempt to pull Meb out of his doldrums, get his competitive juices flowing, maybe hear him say, "Can't wait to meet Dathan on the track this summer." It never comes. Instead, Meb responds sadly. "How many Kenyans beat me last year?" he says. He raises one finger.

Meb's response is not a knock on Ritzenhein as much as a sign of his frustration with the perception that an athlete must be born in the United States to be claimed as a true American running hero. (Ritzenhein, 22, is originally from Michigan.) Meb is all too familiar with the Web posters who chide his success. For instance, one writer to a www.letsrun.com discussion remarked, "All very fine if one accepts an Eritrean mercenary as a genuine contender [for] the greatest all-time 'American' distance runner."

Such comments could be ignored as just rantings from anonymous, and ignorant, running fans. What hurts more are when the slights come from track officials and the running press. Last July, at the postrace press conference following the Olympic Track Trials 10,000 meters, a reporter began by saying the race had been special because it featured longtime American runner Bob Kennedy and Ritzenhein, "the next great American distance runner." There was no mention of Meb—who had *won* the race. And this winter, Glenn Latimer, an official with USA Track & Field, the sport's governing body, said in an interview: "We could build a whole new running boom for the sport of running around Dathan at the world level." Again, no nod to Meb. Why not? When asked later, Latimer said he was not dismissing Meb but only looking ahead to the Beijing Olympics in 2008 when Ritzenhein would be just 25 and ready to enter his prime. But Meb, who will then be only 33, expects to be at the next Games, too.

If others either knock him or neglect him, Meb, for his part, has no misgivings about representing the United States. He proudly notes what flag was raised during the medal ceremony in Athens. "I didn't see the Eritrean flag go up after 28 years," he says. "It was the American flag. If people can't see that . . ."

Actually, plenty do. Meb's U.S. Olympic teammate, Dan Browne, says, "Meb's as American as they come." And Mary Wittenberg, race director of the New York City Marathon, expects to play up Meb's nationality when he races again this fall. "Meb is an American success story," she says. "In an international field, we want Meb headlining as 'The American.'"

After our lunch I walk Meb back to his hotel. Now, instead of being frustrated or angry, he's philosophical. "At the end of the day, it is more important to be appreciated by the people who know you and see you every day," he says. As I turn to leave, the hotel manager at the front desk walks over to Meb and congratulates him on his Olympic medal.

————————•————————

The mother and the father from Eritrea raise a son who one day trades up from discount-store running shoes to top-of-the-line Nikes. He races on the world's best tracks and in the biggest stadiums, far from the tiny farming village that they once called home. Their story sounds so perfect, so American—and yet it's not totally satisfying. Not only does the son excel in a sport that most Americans seem to notice just once every four years, but many of the fans who do appreciate the sport aren't willing to give him the credit he deserves. They're still waiting for an American running hero, not convinced that he's the one. Yes, even after he's achieved the greatest American distance-running feat in nearly 30 years.

How come? Is it the strange-sounding name in a world of Dans and Alans and Bobs? Is it because they don't know his family's story and how truly American he is? Should he change his ways? Should he not show the colors of his native country as proudly as he shows the colors of his home country? His answer: *No way*. He is an American. He is proud of his heritage. If other people can't see that, it's because they don't want to see that. Some days this is harder to take than the dead, exhausted feeling that comes with running 20-plus hard miles. But in the end, he knows it's up to others to change, not him. So he waits.

In the meantime, the father and the mother and their children gather for a daughter's wedding reception. More than 800 friends and relatives pack the hall. Eritrean music—joyous and up-tempo—pulsates during a dinner of beef, chicken, and rice that some will eat with their hands, others with silverware. The third son, the runner, finishes his meal doing a little bit of both. Afterward, the best man gives a long but touching tribute to the value of friendship. Then Papa gets up to recite a poem he has written in Tigrinyan. He is a short, compact man with a big smile and a forehead forever popping with sweat. The poem calls out to dead relatives and friends, here and in Eritrea, to witness this union.

Then an uncle takes the microphone. In a tribute to the mother, he lists the accomplishments of her children.

". . . your daughter is a doctor," he says. "And one of your sons is an Olympic champion."

The son smiles quietly, blinking back tears.

In Pre's Footsteps

Don Kardong, 1991

For Steve Prefontaine's many fans, their feelings about the former Oregon star are unqualified. For them, he remains the greatest American distance runner, the gutsiest, the most charismatic racer of his era. But for those who had to battle Pre in races, the feelings are more complicated. Don Kardong, a contributing writer for *Runner's World*, wrote this moving remembrance of his longtime rival.

I suppose this could be almost any road race. The morning is overcast but pleasant. Hundreds of runners of all ages, shapes and sizes are warming up, pinning on numbers or nervously shaking out hamstrings and doing half-hearted stretches. Officials scurry back and forth making last-minute system checks.

As the starting time approaches, I finish my own warmup and sit down to lace up my racing flats. I had hoped to be more ready for this, to come here with an appropriate sense of athletic mission, perhaps, even, to win. But a virus has interrupted my training, and its vestiges still rumble vaguely in my lungs. This excuse, though, the very *fact* of excuse in this race, makes me ashamed.

As I get to my feet, I realize how familiar this all feels. Jitters, sweat, self-doubt, adrenaline, impending doom. All of it connects me to my past.

And then I notice a man in the street, dressed in the red polo shirt of a race official. He is short, somewhat round in girth, with dark hair. A mustache gives a sense of wit to his smile. There's something in his brown eyes, too, a certain ironic spark, that I recognize, and it takes me back in years.

This is Ray Prefontaine, father of Steve Prefontaine, whose life and death inspired this event: the Prefontaine Memorial Run. It's named after the man many consider the greatest American distance runner of all time. This could be any road race, but it isn't. It's the 11th edition of Pre's Run, held every September in his hometown of Coos Bay, Oregon.

I'm here on a pilgrimage of sorts. Touring the course yesterday, I was surprised to see signs teasingly lined up in classic Burma-shave style:

"Who was Pre?"

"Come and See."

"September 15."

Who was Pre? Who, I wonder, could possibly wonder?

At the time of his death on May 30, 1975, Steve Prefontaine held every American outdoor track record from 2000 meters through the 10,000. In all, he set 14 American records and broke the 4-minute mile barrier nine times. While at the University of Oregon in Eugene, he won three NCAA cross-country championships and four outdoor track titles.

From *Runner's World*, May 1991. Reprinted by permission of Rodale, Inc.

Good statistics. But there have been other great American distance runners in recent decades—title holders, record breakers, Olympic medalists. Jim Ryun, Gerry Lindgren, Billy Mills, Craig Virgin, Alberto Salazar and more. Still, Prefontaine holds a special place in the minds, the hearts and most importantly, the guts of those who've witnessed his exploits.

Ask the question, "Who was Pre?" and someone will start telling you about one of his races. Maybe of several. The 1970 NCAA 3-mile in Des Moines, Iowa, for example when, despite starting the race with a foot laced in stitches from an accident the day before, he gutted out a 2-minute final half-mile to hold off Garry Bjorklund and Dick Buerkle. Or the '72 Olympic Trials, when Pre led most of the race, shadowed by older, wiser veterans who eventually faded in the wake of the 21-year-old's punishing kick.

Or the '73 NCAA Cross-Country Championships in Spokane, Washington, when Nick Rose pushed to a 50-meter lead at halfway, and observers began to believe that, this time, the Pre magic was smoke. And then Pre proved otherwise, summoning his strength to reel in the Western Kentucky star and capture a third NCAA title.

Ask the question, too, and you may hear of a workout. A time he gobbled quarters, halves and 1320s like mixed nuts. A 10-mile run when the pace spiraled out of control. A track session when a teammate challenged Pre's dominance, and the carefully planned splits suddenly became as irrelevant as last week's weather, with a furious Pre redefining the concept of interval training.

Ask the question and more than anything you'll hear about an attitude, an alloyed personality forged of guts, pride, determination, cockiness and a few other basic elements that were hard to identify. Inevitably, those who ran against Prefontaine were struck by his demeanor, unusually blunt for a distance runner, and by his tactics, which smelled of challenge.

"Pre was the first person I met," noted longtime rival Garry Bjorklund, who ran for the University of Minnesota, "where there was so much to bite off, you couldn't chew."

Steve Prefontaine was a constant source of irritation, confrontation and inspiration to those who knew him. There was a certain look he had, a way of glancing back as he rounded the turn in the lead, that seemed to say, "I've got this thing in hand now, and I'm only mildly interested in seeing where the rest of you are." And then he would surge.

In spite of repeated attempts, I never beat Pre. In the '70 NCAA Cross-Country Championships, I caught him at 4 miles. Then he glanced back and that was it. I was a goner. In our conference meet the next spring, I challenged him twice for the lead. He hung on both times and finally blasted away for the win. The photo in the next day's paper showed Prefontaine grimacing at the finish, painfully wasted.

"I was hurting," he told me. "If you'd gone hard for a couple of laps, you would have had me."

It was the ultimate compliment: to have made Pre hurt. But it was also a sign of my inadequacy. Why hadn't I gone harder, longer? Why couldn't I be more like him?

"His talent was his control of his fatigue and his pain," his Marshfield High School coach Walt McClure once said. "His threshold was different than most of ours, whether it was inborn or he developed it himself."

On the morning of the Prefontaine Memorial Run, there is something I see in his father's eyes that reminds me of all this. And as we begin the run, the suddenness and finality of Pre's death, the tragedy that snuffed a special spirit and the sadness of passing things is inescapable.

———————————●———————————

Coos Bay, Oregon. Home of Steve Prefontaine and a whole lot of people in the logging industry. Much of the Oregon coast seems designed for city people escaping from accounting, law and business for a weekend of sand between the toes. Coos Bay is different. It has an edge of sweaty legitimacy, born of cutting and hauling large trees to market. Signs in the back of pickups announce: "This Family Supported by Timber." In the Coos Bay of the 1990s, downtown is spruced up to lure the tourist dollar, but the railroad runs right down the waterfront. Mountains of wood chips are piled up for export, and the work ethic hangs in the air like drizzle.

Steve Prefontaine seemed a perfect reflection of Coos Bay, tough and independent. He liked to describe his teenage years as, more or less, a decision between running the hills and flashing a switchblade. Running won out, but one always felt he might revert at any time and join the darker elements of Coos Bay.

Those who knew Steve Prefontaine well insist his hard shell covered a warm interior. There were times one got glimpses of a different Pre—friendly, community-minded, struggling with self-doubt. Mostly, he just seemed tough, irascible and anxious to get on with whatever life had in store.

Pre was said to react with disdain when he first noticed runners in Coos Bay, but once he tried the sport, he found himself in a fast-flowing stream. At age 16, he told his mother he would go to the Olympics one day. Senior year, he broke the U.S. high school record for 2 miles by nearly 7 seconds, running 8:41.5.

Pre's next four years at the University of Oregon established a legacy. The already powerful track program prospered, with Steve Prefontaine its most famous member. He trained hard, raced savagely, broke new ground. And when he stepped in front of the Eugene crowd, *his people* . . . magic.

Sport is entertainment. These days, it seems to have something to do with color-coordination and the prancing of prima donnas who carefully orchestrate their competitive spats. With Pre, the entertainment was pure knife-edged, transcendent. "Here I am," he announced without words, warming up on the track. "Wait'll you see what I do this time. Watching him sent chills running down the back, and "Go Pre!" exploded from within.

He never let his people down, taking on any rival in any circumstance, sometimes seeming to be on the brink of disaster and then, just when you thought it was over, dredging and grasping a final something from a place deeper than the pain, deeper than self-doubt, deeper than despair. He would rally, and he would win.

"The characteristic that separated Pre from the rest of the world was his pride," says Coach McClure. "To be the best was his only goal. Man imposes his own limitations. Limitation was not in Steve's frame of reference."

Steve Prefontaine was so at home on the track, so cosmically centered there, that the Prefontaine Memorial Run is something of an anomaly. Pre never competed in a road race, never realized his sport would become the passion of the masses, never heard the term "running boom." He did, though, train on the course over which I am now struggling, one of the hillier, testier routes in the asphalt pantheon.

The first hill on this course is vintage Pre. A straight shot from the town to the hills, a gnarly test of fortitude. Ray Prefontaine remembers his son running repeats here. Others recall seeing their native son run up a lot of hills, but, selective memory being what it is, never down.

As I round the final turn and pass the house where Pre grew up and where his parents still live, I see Marshfield High School perched on the hillside like a Tibetan monastery. A minute later I'm on the school's track finishing 10 kilometers in 34:15, well behind winner Don Clary.

It's a pleasant place, this track, on a pleasant morning. The sun has broken through, a gentle breeze whiffles through the trees and the race finishers are enjoying the atmosphere. Looking around, I can imagine the young Prefontaine training here, alone, on one of those bone-numbing Oregon winter afternoons, with dark clouds crashing across the sky, rain pelting the face and the runner holding on to his dreams. Five more quarters to go.

There is a room dedicated to Steve Prefontaine in the Coos Bay Art Museum, and I visit it later. Ray Prefontaine is there, watching the film of his son in the 1972 Olympic 5000, when the 21-year-old went for broke, leading stronger, more experienced runners. But he stumbled a few meters from the finish and was nipped for third, losing the bronze medal to Ian Stewart of Great Britain. It was a hard Olympic experience for Pre, first the murder of Israeli athletes, then doubts about the meaning of the Games and the attempt to hold on to a vision that turned Kafka-esque. It left him disappointed, disillusioned and emotionally spent.

When he recovered, Pre came back strong, attacking the track with renewed vigor. In the next two seasons he set and reset American records at 2 miles, 3 miles, 6 miles, 2000, 5000 and 10,000 meters. Occasionally he lost, but even beaten he never seemed vanquished. Oddly, he sometimes described himself at the time as just "going through the motions." Some motions. For all of us competing then, Pre was still the standard.

In the wake of the Munich Olympics, too, Pre seemed more accessible, more at ease, more at peace with life. His ferocity on the track remained undiminished, but his relationships with other runners seemed to grow. He fought on their behalf with the archaic Amateur Athletic Union (AAU) and invited foreign runners to Eugene to train and race.

It was during this time, in June of 1974, that I chased him for eight laps of a 3-mile race in front of his Eugene crowd, before he and Frank Shorter surged away in the final mile. A picture of this race hangs in the museum in Coos Bay, a black-and-white photo with a much younger me tagging along in the background. It was another epic battle for Pre, a race where the challenger, Shorter, took the lead with 200 meters to go and that look came over Steve Prefontaine, determination overcoming inertia, pride conquering apathy, anger overpowering pain. On the homestretch, he muscled and squeezed his way past Shorter by a fraction of a second and set an American record of 12:51.4. The crowd stomped the wooden stands and screamed so loudly that I felt disoriented and almost stopped before the finish.

I could *not* beat this guy, but I had slipstreamed in his emotional wake to a personal record of 12:57.6, probably my best performance ever. It gave me confidence and opened doors. The following spring, largely as a result of this race, I was invited to the People's Republic of China as part of a U.S. team. When I returned, still flush from the adventure of my life, Dick Buerkle, one of the few Americans who ever beat Pre, approached me in the airport.

"Did you hear the news?" he asked, ashen-faced. "Prefontaine died. In a car crash."

————————————•————————————

The day after the Prefontaine Memorial Run. I am back in Eugene, taking a run for old time's sake. I jog along "Pre's Trail" and trot down streets filled with memories. I stop at Stevenson Track at Hayward Field, site of so many of his spectacular races.

This is the track where Pre ran his last race, on the evening of his death. It was a 5000 in which he beat Frank Shorter in 13:23.8—not the best effort of Pre's life, but he had a lot on his mind. He had been fighting the AAU over whether he and others would be allowed to race when and where they wanted. Beyond that specific issue, he was frustrated by the general lack of support for American track athletes.

"I'm just like any other American," he told a reporter from the *Oregon Journal*. "If I don't pay my electric bill, they turn off my lights. After college, our athletes are turned out to pasture. We have no Olympic program in this country. It's as simple as that. No sportsmedicine, no camps, no nothing. I'm not talking about subsidizing us. I'm just talking about a national plan. I want to see some interest from somebody. In the past, we've sat back and let our natural talent do it. Well, the rest of the world has caught up."

So Pre was feeling a bit scattered at the time of his final race, not quite at the top of his form. And still he finished just 1.9 seconds off his American record. It was his 25th straight win in Eugene in distances over a mile.

At this same track, friends and fans held a memorial service for Pre a few days after his death. The speeches ended early so thousands of fans could sit in silent appreciation while a clock ticked off the seconds of an imaginary race. And as the clock wound down to what would have been his last lap, they could contain themselves no longer.

"Go Pre!"

The circumstances of his death remain unclear. He had been drinking at a party that evening, but that doesn't totally explain why, at 39 minutes past midnight, his MG convertible veered off a road he'd driven and run hundreds of times. The car flipped over, crushing him to death.

But even though we'll never know what caused the accident, we do know this: Steve Prefontaine lived 24 years, during which time he became one of the most remarkable and memorable distance runners the human race has ever known. And when he ran in front of *his people* . . . .

I think about all of this as I leave Hayward Field and jog up into the hills where Pre spent the last minutes of his life. I stop running, walk to the side of the road and find the cold black rock that marks the spot. After 15 years, I still feel melancholy reading the simple inscription in hand-painted white letters.

"Pre 5/30/75 RIP"

Toughest Miler Ever

Woody Woodburn, 2000

In the 1930s, Louis Zamperini was one of the brightest young stars on the American running scene. He placed 8th in the Berlin Olympics 5,000 meters, set the college mile record, and seemed on the verge of even greater accomplishments. But they were not to come on the track. World War II intervened, and Zamperini's greatest feats would come as an Air Force officer and prisoner of war. Sports columnist Woody Woodburn, writing for the *Daily Breeze* (Torrance, California), uncovered this story of an American hero.

Louis Zamperini is sitting in a cafe in Hollywood, not far from his home in the hills, and orders the day's luncheon special: meatloaf.

Apologetically, the comely waitress informs him they are out of gravy for his meatloaf and mashed potatoes, expecting him to order something else. As though no gravy would matter to a man who once had no water for seven days, and no food—other than two small sharks, a few fish, and a couple of birds he managed to catch while floating nearly two thousand miles in the South Pacific—for forty-seven days.

No gravy? That reminds Zamperini of a story. But then everything reminds "Louie" of a story. This one is about the boat trip to the 1936 Olympic Games in Germany and the recipe for winning a medal that a U.S. Olympic coach gave him:

"No pork, no gravy, and no women."

Louie's smile tells you that he followed two-thirds of the advice.

He didn't win an Olympic medal in Berlin, placing eighth as the top American in the five-thousand-meters, but it wasn't because of pork, gravy, or women. Rather, because of youth. Louie was only nineteen years old, freshly graduated from Torrance High School.

Surely at age twenty-three or twenty-seven he would have won a medal in the 1940 and/or 1944 Olympics had World War II not canceled both Games.

"In '40 and '44, I would have been at my running peak," Zamperini confirms matter-of-factly, not a trace of braggadocio in his voice. "Those would have been my Olympics. I'd have brought home a medal.

"Or two."

And that he didn't?

"It doesn't bother me," Zamperini, now eighty-three, replies. His eyes remain as blue as the summer sky, but oh what darkness they have witnessed. "Not after what I'd gone through."

Hell is what he went through.

From *Daily Breeze* (Torrance, CA), July 1, 2000. Reprinted by permission of *Daily Breeze*.

And lived to tell about it.

Devil at My Heels he titled his autobiography, to give you an idea.

———————•———————

On May 27, 1943, United States Air Force Captain Louis Zamperini was a bombardier on a B-24 Liberator flying a secret experimental mission when it was shot down south of Hawaii. Eight of the eleven men aboard were killed in the crash.

Zamperini and another crewmate—the third crash survivor died in the life raft—drifted nearly two thousand miles in the South Pacific, living in terror twenty-four/seven of enemy attacks while fighting hunger, fighting thirst, even fighting sharks.

"Two big sharks tried to jump in the raft and take us out," Zamperini retells.

That wasn't the worst of it, though.

"We went seven days without water—that was brutal," he adds, ironically taking a sip of ice tea before continuing.

"We managed to catch some fish, a couple of birds, two small sharks—even took their livers out for nourishment."

On the fifth day of the seventh week, the two survivors were picked up by a Japanese patrol boat. The 5'9" Zamperini, who had weighed 160 pounds when *The Green Hornet* crashed, was now down to 67 pounds, and about 37 were his heart.

When the famous Olympian refused to make propaganda broadcasts for the Japanese, he was imprisoned. Ask him about the slave labor camp and Zamperini responds politely, "Those are stories for another time."

This time being lunch time, he merely offers an answer that won't ruin your meal or his; an answer that you can read here over breakfast: "It was daily torture, beatings, starvation. It was hell."

Hell for two and a half years.

Initially listed as "Missing in Action," Louis Zamperini was declared officially dead by the War Department in 1944.

"Lou Zamperini, Olympian and War Hero Killed in Action" read one newspaper headline.

New York's Madison Square Garden held "The Zamperini Memorial Mile."

Zamperini Field at Torrance Airport was christened.

———————•———————

One problem—Louie was not dead. He was living in hell.

Louis Zamperini remembers the hell that was his very first track race—660 yards—as a freshman at Torrance High in 1917.

"It was too much pain. I said, 'Never again,'" he retells. "I thought that was the worst pain I could imagine."

He thought wrong.

He never imagined war, never imagined forty-seven days in a raft adrift at sea, never imagined two and a half years as a prisoner of war in Camp 4-B in Naoetsu.

And, even in his worst nightmares, never imagined "The Bird." That was the nickname the POWs gave Japanese Army Sergeant Matsuhiro Watanabe, the devil incarnate in this hell.

The Bird preyed on Zamperini, using a thick leather belt with a steel buckle to beat him bloody. In one mean streak, he belted Louie into unconsciousness fourteen days in a row.

A devout Catholic, Zamperini's faith was tested supremely. But, like his iron will, it was never broken.

"Faith is more important than courage," he allows.

We often make sports out to be more important than they are. And yet in Louie Zamperini's case, you cannot overestimate the importance.

"Absolutely, my athletic background saved my life," Zamperini opines. "Track and field competition sharpens your skills. I kept thinking about my athletic training when I was competing against the elements, against the enemy, against hunger and thirst.

"In athletics, you learn to find ways to increase your effort. In athletics you don't quit—EVER.

"I'm certain I wouldn't have survived if I hadn't been an athlete."

He survived hell, Louis Zamperini did, but this hero—an authentic hero, mind you, not one created by Nike—was never the same athlete after Camp 4-B.

"My body never recovered," he shares. "My body was beaten."

His body weighed just eighty pounds at war's end, sixty-seven pounds below his running weight. The Olympic Games resumed in 1948 without Louie. He never won the Olympic medal—or two—he thought he would. But he was a mettle winner. He had already proved himself to be the toughest miler who ever lived.

The Toughest Miler Who Ever Lived will be the honorary starter for today's seventh annual Keep L.A. Running 5K and 10K races at Dockweiler Beach in Playa del Rey. The event is expected to raise $100,000 for various charities.

It is not just a one-time good deed. Louie Zamperini has been working with youth since 1952, taking them running and camping and skiing, and most importantly, taking them under his guidance.

To this day he gives a couple of speeches a week at schools, churches, and clubs, reaching out to as many as three thousand youngsters and teens a month.

———————•———————

The sixty-plus-year-old scrapbook, its leather cover cracked and spine long ago broken, shows the wear of passing decades much more than does the man who was the boy featured inside.

Louie Zamperini, who turned eighty-three in January, turns the tattered pages chronicling his athletic life. Here he is in Torrance High where he set a national schoolboy record. There he is in Berlin for the 1936 Olympics where he represented America proudly. Here he is at USC where he was twice the national champion at the distance of one mile.

The scrapbook is about the size of a large couch cushion, and just as thick, with yellowed newspaper clippings from the defunct *Torrance Herald* and *New*

York Times and more. But the amazing thing is that this glorious memorabilia very nearly could have been a police rap sheet instead.

"I was a juvenile delinquent," Zamperini says, confessing to belonging to a gang, to stealing pies and food and, this being the Depression and Prohibition, even breaking into bootleggers' homes to steal their illegal hooch.

"At fifteen years of age, it was touch and go," he continues. "My parents were really worried. My dad, my [older] brother Pete, the principal, and the police chief all got together and decided track was the thing to straighten me out."

This was a strange choice, because other than fleeing from the law, young Louie had shown no aptitude for running.

"At picnic races, the girls beat me," Louie shares, laughing at the distant memory. "I hated running. 'Boy,' I thought, 'this is not for me.'"

His first track meet didn't change his thinking.

"I came in dead last in the 660 behind a sickly guy and a fat guy. The pain and exhaustion. The smoking, the chewing tobacco, the booze—I was a mess.

"Running? 'Never again!' I said."

Never came just a week later. Coerced into competing in a dual meet as the only 660 runner from Torrance High, Louie again found himself in last place.

"I didn't care," he retells, "until I heard the fans cheering, 'Go Lou-EE! Go Lou-EE!' When I heard them cheering my name, I ran my guts out and barely passed one guy."

The moment mattered.

It matters still.

"That's the race I remember most fondly, even more than the Olympic race in Berlin, more than the NCAA titles," Louie says, the memory warming him like the summer sun.

More fondly than the Olympics?

"Yes, truthfully," he rejoins. "You have to understand, that race changed my life. I was shocked to realize people knew my name. That was the start. You never forget your first anything, and that was my first taste of recognition."

Cue the *Rocky* theme music.

"Instantly, I became a running fanatic," Louie points out, proudly. "I wouldn't eat pie or ice cream. I even started eating vegetables."

And he ran. Everywhere. He ran four miles to the beach. And four miles back. He ran in the mountains, sometimes while hunting rabbit (so his mom could cook rabbit cacciatore) and deer, running up the steep slopes with a rifle slung over his shoulder.

His unique training methods worked. Soon he won a race. And another. Once without direction, he now had one forward, fast.

As a sophomore in 1933, Louie set a course record (9:57) in a two-mile cross-country race, winning varsity by *a quarter-mile*. He didn't lose a race (cross-country or track) for the next three years!

En route of the amazing streak, as a junior, Louie broke the national high school record in the mile (4:21). If the time on a cinder track doesn't overly impress you, this will: his mark stood for a full twenty years.

———————————●———————————

Impressive, too, was being invited to the 1936 U.S. Olympic Trials at the tender age of nineteen.

Unfortunately, the trials were across the country in New York.

Fortunately, Louie's father worked for the Southern Pacific Railroad and got one free pass each year good to any destination. Torrance (pop. 2,500) merchants donated a suitcase and new clothes to the local hero and even some money for food and lodging.

Skipping the mile—"Glenn Cunningham and a few others ran around 4:10, so I thought I had no chance"—Louie entered the five-thousand-meters instead. Smart move. "The Iron Man," as one newspaper headline referred to the thickly muscled Zamperini, tied for first to make the Olympic team.

He was not so wise during the long—and luxurious—boat trip across the Pond.

"My big mistake was eating all the good food until I was too heavy to run," explains Zamperini, who roomed with the great Jesse Owens. "I put on about ten to twelve pounds. I ate myself out of a medal."

Still, he might have turned in the greatest eighth-place showing (in a field of forty-one runners) in Olympic history.

"My brother had always told me, 'Isn't one minute of pain worth a lifetime of glory?'" Louie shares.

He got his glory thanks to a final minute of pain.

Actually, only fifty-six seconds of pain, that being how quickly Louie ran the final lap. Running his guts out like he had in that high school race when he finally beat a runner, Louie gained fifty meters on the winner and passed so many runners that Adolf Hitler was so impressed he asked for the Italian kid from America to be brought up to his box to shake his hand.

After the Olympics, Zamperini took his racing spikes to USC.

With no mountains to climb while chasing after rabbit and deer, Louie would scale the fence at the Los Angeles Coliseum and run up and down the stairs "until my legs went numb."

It worked.

He became a two-time NCAA champion in the mile (1938-39), the first mile champ ever from the West Coast. His mile mark of 4:08 stood as the national collegiate record for fifteen years, but it almost was a mark for the ages.

"I didn't even push it," Zamperini allows. "I was so mad at myself afterwards. I could have run four-flat."

Four minutes flat? In 1939? A full fifteen years before Roger Bannister would make history by breaking the four-minute barrier?

"Yes. I know I could have run four-flat that day," Zamperini insists.

Even if he had, that feat wouldn't have been half as remarkable as what he did do: survive forty-seven days adrift at sea in a raft; surviving seven straight days without water; surviving on a couple of birds and little sharks and courage; and then surviving daily torture in a Japanese slave labor camp for two and a half years.

His older brother Pete miscalculated. Louie's lifetime of glory came at a considerably steeper price than one minute of pain.

————————●————————

"Age has a way of catching up to you," says the man who never saw anyone catch up to him from behind on the track.

Actually, he seems to be outrunning Father Time, too.

Sure, the thick, dark, curly hair on the dashing young man seen on page after page in the oversized scrapbook has thinned and turned white. But watch Louie Zamperini, princely in posture still, nimbly climb up a flight of stairs to his second-floor office at the First Presbyterian Church of Hollywood and you can almost picture him, even in his eighty-third summer, chasing deer up a coastal mountainside with a rifle slung over his back.

Louie closes the book of memories and then shares a memory from the pages of his mind: "Gregory Peck once sent over a bottle of champagne to my table with a note: 'Race you around the block.'

"We didn't, of course."

In his day, Louie Zamperini was the fastest around the block, but the most amazing thing is not the national prep mile record he set that stood for two decades or his collegiate mile mark that stood for fifteen years, nor the glory of competing in the Olympics or even surviving forty-seven days lost at sea and two and a half years more in hell.

No, the most amazing thing of all is this: "I forgave The Bird," Louie Zamperini, sitting in a Hollywood cafe, tells you, and he means it.

In fact, he tried to set up a meeting with Watanabe—who had avoided prosecution as a war criminal by hiding out in the remote mountains near Nagano until the statute of limitations ran out—during the 1998 Nagano Winter Olympics. Alas, the extended olive branch was crushed under the heels of Watanabe's family members.

The hell of Camp 4-B was a lifetime ago.

Lunch on a heavenly July afternoon is now.

No gravy?

No matter.

The Toughest Miler Who Ever Lived smiles at the young waitress and orders the meatloaf anyway.

about the editor

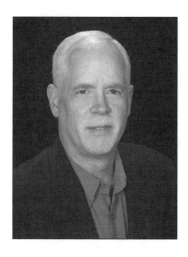

Rich Elliott competed at Kansas University from 1968 to 1972, qualifying for the NCAA Division I national meets in both track and cross country. In 1971, he was the Big Eight Conference three-mile champion.

In 1976, Elliott was named Illinois Distance Coach of the Year while working at Willowbrook High School. He moved to Deerfield High School in 1977 and was an assistant coach with the state cross country championship team before becoming the program's head coach for both cross country and track. Elliott coached at the high-school level for 12 years, producing a pair of All-Americans and several all-state athletes. During this time he also wrote *The Competitive Edge: Mental Preparation for Distance Running*, a book that Track and Field News magazine called "the best work on the subject" and "a modern classic."

Elliott then worked for many years in educational publishing as a textbook editor and technology producer. He returned to coaching from 2008 to 2010 to head the men's and women's cross country teams at Dominican University in River Forest, Illinois. He is now a freelance writer and editor.

Elliott lives in Winnetka, Illinois, with his wife and three children.

biographical notes

Sally Baker is a writer and editor as well as the coauthor of *Running Tide* (1987), the autobiography of Olympic champion Joan Benoit Samuelson. Baker has worked as director of communications for several universities; she is now the vice president and secretary of Colby College in Waterville, Maine.

On May 6, 1954, **Roger Bannister** became the first person to run a mile in under four minutes, breaking the most famous "barrier" in sports. Three months later, he outkicked John Landy at the Empire Games in a thrilling battle dubbed the "Miracle Mile." Bannister then retired from racing to pursue a career in medicine. He trained at Britain's National Hospital for Nervous Diseases and became a distinguished neurologist. Over the years Bannister has spoken out against the commercialization of sports and the use of performance-enhancing drugs.

In 1984, **Joan Benoit Samuelson** won the gold medal in the first-ever Olympic marathon for women, one year after she had run the world's fastest time ever for the distance. In 1985, she was presented with the Sullivan Award as the top amateur athlete in the United States. She has gone on to become a book author, coach, motivational speaker, and sports commentator. Benoit Samuelson continues to run and occasionally races, setting a masters indoor record for 3,000 meters in 2009.

Marc Bloom is one of the leading authorities on running in the United States. He is a contributing editor for *Runner's World*, features writer for the *New York Times*, and publisher of *The Harrier*, a magazine devoted to cross country. He is a past winner of the Journalistic Excellence Award, given by the Road Runners Club of America. Bloom is the author of seven running books, including *God on the Starting Line: The Triumph of a Catholic School Running Team and Its Jewish Coach* (2004), which chronicles one of his seasons coaching the St. Rose (Belmar, New Jersey) boys' cross country team.

John Brant is a senior writer for *Runner's World* and a contributing editor for *Outside* magazine. He has also written for several other major publications, including *New York Times Magazine*, *Rolling Stone*, and *National Geographic*. Brant's stories have twice been chosen for *The Best American Sports Writing* annual collections; in 2006, Rodale Books published a book version of his story "Duel in the Sun."

Amby Burfoot is the longtime editor (currently editor at large) for *Runner's World* magazine. He is the author of four books on running, including the *Runner's World Complete Book of Beginning Running* (2005). Burfoot was also a notable American distance runner in the late 1960s and early '70s, winning the Boston Marathon in 1968, though he claims his proudest accomplishment is competing in the Manchester (Connecticut) 5-Mile Road Race for 46 consecutive years.

Sara Corbett is a contributing writer for the *New York Times Magazine* and writer at large for *Runner's World*. She has also written for other top publications, including *National Geographic*, *Elle*, *Outside*, and *Self*. Her work has been featured in *The Best American Sports Writing* collections. Corbett is the author of *Venus to the Hoop: A Gold Medal Year in Women's Basketball* (1998), an account of the 1996 women's Olympic basketball team.

Rich Elliott is the author of *The Competitive Edge: Mental Preparation for Distance Running* (1984). He is also the former head cross country coach of Dominican University in River Forest, Illinois. Elliott was a national-class high school and collegiate distance runner and later an English teacher and editor for *Illinois Runner* magazine before working in educational publishing as a textbook editor and technology producer.

Norman Harris, as a young journalist in New Zealand, was so inspired by the victories of his countrymen Murray Halberg and Peter Snell at the 1960 Olympics that he became a runner himself and an eminent writer on running. He wrote *Lap of Honour: The Great Moments of New Zealand Athletics* (1963) and followed with several other running books. For years Harris has been a sportswriter for the *Sunday Times* of London. Harris the runner won the 1985 British title in orienteering, where runners navigate a course with a map and compass.

Roger Hart is a creative writing instructor at Ohio University in Athens. He is the author of a collection of short stories titled *Erratics* (2001), for which he won the George Garrett Fiction Prize. His writing has appeared in several publications, including *Runner's World*, *Ohio Writer*, and *Texas Review*. Hart is also a longtime runner with a personal record of 2:27:48 in the marathon.

Bernd Heinrich is professor emeritus in biology at Vermont University in Burlington. He has written numerous books in the field of nature, including the award-winning *Mind of the Raven* (1999). In his book *Why We Run: A Natural History* (2001), he combined his research on animal motion and body chemistry with his own story of winning the 100K national championship race at the age of 41. In the mid-1980s, Heinrich set American records for 100K, 100 miles, and the 12-hour run; in 2007, he was inducted into the American Ultrarunning Association's Hall of Fame.

Leslie Heywood is a former Arizona high school track and cross country star. She is the author of several books, including her memoir *Pretty Good for a Girl: An Athlete's Story* (1998). Heywood is a professor of English, general literature, and rhetoric at the State University of New York in Binghamton. Still an athlete, she competes in the sport of bodybuilding.

Hal Higdon, one of America's best-known runner-writers, is the author of 34 books, including the best-selling *Marathon: The Ultimate Training Guide* (1999), and numerous magazine articles. He is a contributing editor for *Runner's World*, having worked with the magazine since its inception in 1966. In 2003, the American Society of Journalists and Authors gave Higdon the Career Achievement Award, its highest honor. Higdon was also a noted distance runner, competing in the U.S. Olympic Trials eight times and winning the World Masters Championships steeplechase four times.

Sally Jenkins is a sports columnist and features writer for the *Washington Post* and was a senior writer at *Sports Illustrated*. Jenkins is the author and coauthor of several books, most notably the bestseller *It's Not About the Bike: My Journey Back to Life* (2000), about the cyclist Lance Armstrong. She has also worked as a correspondent for CNBC and National Public Radio. In 2002, Jenkins was recognized by the Associated Press as Columnist of the Year.

Don Kardong is the author of running books and magazine articles as well as a speaker and online coach. He is a contributing editor for *Runner's World* magazine and a past winner of the Journalistic Excellence Award, given by the Road Runners Club of America. A former world-class marathoner, Kardong placed fourth in the 1976 Olympics in Montreal. He is also the founder of the Lilac Bloomsday Run in Spokane, Washington, one of the largest road races in the United States.

Dave Kuehls is a contributing editor for *Runner's World* magazine and the author of several books on running, including the training guide *How to Run a Personal Record* (2009). He has also written for *Sports Illustrated, Men's Health, GQ,* and *ESPN the Magazine*. His feature story "The American Dreamer" was recognized as a notable work in *The Best American Sports Writing 2006*.

Marty Liquori is a former world-class distance runner and Olympian. Liquori once held the American track records for the 2,000 meters, 5,000 meters, and 2 mile, but he is best known as a miler, ranking first in the world in 1969 and 1971. He was the cofounder of the Athletic Attic Footwear chain and has served on the President's Council on Physical Fitness. Liquori is also a television commentator, author, and jazz guitarist.

Kenny Moore was a two-time Olympic distance runner, placing fourth in the 1972 marathon. He is best known for his 25-year career with *Sports Illustrated* as the magazine's writer on running. *USA Today* summed up Moore's work this way: "Kenny Moore was the definitive voice of the sport. . . . He brought alive the European circuit as well as the major distance and middle-distance runners in the 1970s, 1980s, and 1990s." Moore also wrote the screenplay for the film *Without Limits* (about distance legend Steve Prefontaine) as well as a book about his former coach and teammates, *Bowerman and the Men of Oregon* (2006). For more on his writings, visit his personal Web site, Kennymoore.us.

Frank Murphy is the author of three highly regarded books about runners: *A Cold Clear Day: The Athletic Biography of Buddy Edelen* (1992), *The Silence of Great Distance: Women Running Long* (2000), and *The Last Protest: Lee Evans in Mexico City* (2006). Each of these biographies captures an era; *Track and Field News* stated that Murphy "has no peer as a socio-historian of the sport."

Murphy is a practicing lawyer, and in the past he has coached collegiate cross country and taught in the sociology department at the University of Missouri at Kansas City.

Skip Myslenski is a nationally recognized sportswriter. He was a longtime columnist at the *Chicago Tribune* and the author and coauthor of sports books, including *On the Run: In Search of the Perfect Race* (1979), the autobiography of Marty Liquori. Over his career Myslenski has covered Olympic Games, boxing title fights, NBA Finals, and Super Bowls. Currently, Myslenski is a special contributor to NUsports.com, the Northwestern University athletics Web site.

Pam Reed is a prominent American ultramarathoner. She holds the women's age 40-44 world records in four ultradistance events (100 miles, 200K, 24 hours, and 48 hours), and she is the current female American record holder in the six-day marathon. She was twice the overall winner of the Badwater Ultramarathon, a 135-mile race that is billed as "the world's toughest foot race." Since 1995, Reed has been the race director of the Tucson Marathon.

Marla Runyan is a two-time Olympian and the former American record holder for the indoor 5,000 meters. Her rise to the top ranks of the running world is particularly inspiring because Runyan is legally blind. When she was nine, she was diagnosed with an incurable eye disorder known as Stargardt's disease. She tells her story in her autobiography *Finish Line: My Life As I See It* (2001). Retired from running, Runyan is now a motivational speaker and communicative disorders specialist.

Steve Scott is considered one of the greatest milers, setting an American mile record (3:47.69) that stood for over 25 years. From the 1970s to the 1990s, he raced throughout the world and year-round, running 136 sub-4:00 minute miles, more than any other runner. He was a two-time Olympian and the silver medalist at 1,500 meters in the 1983 World Championships. Scott currently resides in Carlsbad, California, and is head coach of the track and cross-country teams at California State University at San Marcos.

Dr. George Sheehan is best known as running's foremost philosopher. His book *Running and Being: The Total Experience* (1978) was a bestseller and helped fuel the running boom. Sheehan had been a collegiate track star before pursuing a career as a cardiologist. At 45, he resumed running and became an accomplished masters runner. As the author of nine books, the medical editor at *Runner's World* magazine, and a popular lecturer on the racing circuit, Sheehan influenced runners worldwide.

Lori Shontz is senior editor for *The Penn Stater* magazine. Formerly, she worked as a journalist for the *Pittsburgh Post-Gazette, Miami Herald,* and *St. Louis Post-Dispatch.* One of her specialties has been women's sports, and in 2001, while at the *Post-Gazette*, she traveled to Kenya to work on a story about the rise of female distance runners there; she produced a series of articles titled "Fast Forward," which was later cited in *The Best American Sports Writing.*

Gary Smith, a senior writer for *Sports Illustrated*, is one of the most highly regarded American sportswriters. His work has also appeared in *Esquire, Time*, and *Rolling Stone*, and he has won the National Magazine Award for Feature Writing four times. Smith describes his approach to storytelling in *Beyond the Game* (2001), a collection of his stories: "I've always had the feeling that the most compelling and significant story was the one occurring beyond the game—before it, after it, above it, or under it, deep in the furnace of the psyche."

Kathrine Switzer is one of the pioneers of women's running. In the 1967 Boston Marathon, a race official attempted to stop her from running; the ensuing controversy helped to change people's perceptions of women in sports. After winning the 1974 New York City Marathon, Switzer went on to create the Avon Running Program, a series of women's road races in cities around the world. Switzer is an Emmy-winning TV commentator and has covered major marathons, as well as the Olympic Games. She is also the author of several books, including *Running and Walking for Women Over 40* (1998).

Rachel Toor is a senior writer for *Running Times* magazine. Her writing has also appeared in *L.A. Times, Glamour, Reader's Digest*, and *Marathon & Beyond*. She is the author of three books, including *Personal Record: A Love Affair with Running* (2008). Additionally, she is a columnist for the *Chronicle of Higher Education*. Toor lives in Spokane and teaches writing at Eastern Washington University.

Woody Woodburn is an award-winning sports columnist for the *Daily Breeze* in Torrance, California. He is the author of *The Pirate Collection* (1995), a compilation of some of his best columns. Woodburn's story "Toughest Miler Ever," about the 1936 Olympian and World War II veteran Louis Zamperini, was selected for the 2001 collection *The Best American Sports Writing*.

Mark Wukas is an English teacher at New Trier High School in Winnetka, Illinois. In the past he has worked as a college writing instructor and as a reporter for City News Bureau and United Press International. He has also enjoyed stints as a track and cross country coach. His story "Running with Ghosts" first appeared in *Sport Literate* magazine and was recognized as a notable essay in *The Best American Sports Writing 1998*.

You'll find other outstanding running resources at

www.HumanKinetics.com/running

In the U.S. call 1-800-747-4457

Australia 08 8372 0999 • Canada 1-800-465-7301
Europe +44 (0) 113 255 5665 • New Zealand 0800 222 062

HUMAN KINETICS
The Premier Publisher for Sports & Fitness
P.O. Box 5076 • Champaign, IL 61825-5076 USA